In memory of Cassandra Versteeg Mitchell
Our sister, friend, student, and teacher,
who loved us and the world with the spirit
of God.

PREFACE

If you want to feed your own hunger, write.

Renita Weems, Just a Sister Away: A Womanist
Vision of Women's Relationships in the Bible

This work grew out of a gnawing hunger that failed to be satisfied until we responded to it. We listened to our inner voices and wrote from within. Although this work is now published, we ask our elders, in the tradition of many of the world's people, for permission to speak. They have been our pathshowers and waymakers. And we are grateful.

We envisioned a book that attended to the convergence (joining, meeting, merging, intersections) of race, ethnicity, gender, and other identities in people's lives and within the context of counseling. Each of these primary identity constructs is crucial to a person's emotional and psychological development. Each intersects with other human dimensions. These intersecting variables have received limited attention in the multicultural counseling literature. Much of the multicultural counseling literature has focused on individual aspects of identity (most often race or ethnicity or both) and their subsequent influences on psychosocial development. A consideration of how multiple identities converge and affect human development was missing. And without a deliberation of class, physical ability, age, religion, and sexual orientation within the counseling context, the typically observable and thus primary identity constructs of race and gender are treated as monoliths. This type of narrow seeing contributes to a gross misunderstanding of the client and his or her unique situation.

Multicultural counseling emphasizes dimensions such as person-environment interaction, importance of identity, culture, ethnicity, family, collective society, and spirituality as fundamental to the understanding of the individual client in the therapeutic environment. Multicultural counseling also recognizes the way dominant cultural beliefs and values perpetuate feelings of inadequacy, shame, confusion, and distrust for clients both in the counseling process and in the larger society.

The overall goal of this work is to engage in a dialectical "both/and" discussion about how identity constructs operate conjointly in people's lives to affect personal development and problem presentation in counseling. Given this focus, implications for counselors are primary throughout the text.

We desire to avoid a bipolar or bifurcated presentation of diversity and to offer instead a new paradigm for imaging differences. In doing so, we seek to assist our readers in the unrelenting process of increasing self-awareness as gendered, racial, ethnic, sexual, and cultural beings. That differences exist is not refuted or regarded as problematic. The extent to which inequity is promoted and perpetuated within a society where human characteristics hold rank is critiqued and criticized.

We have listened to the voices of hooks and West when they said a Black woman could not become an intellectual without first decolonizing her mind.* As African American women in academia, we hold fast to this liberating, albeit daunting, process of unknowing internalized oppression. Suboptimal messages taught us in primarily subtle ways to disown and thus discredit our subjective and constructed knowledge bases. Writ-

* *b. hooks and C. West,* Insurgent Black intellectual life. *(Boston: South End Press, 1991).*

The Convergence of Race, Ethnicity, and Gender

Multiple Identities in Counseling

TRACY L. ROBINSON
North Carolina State University

MARY F. HOWARD-HAMILTON
University of Florida at Gainesville

Merrill
an imprint of Prentice Hall
Upper Saddle River, New Jersey   *Columbus, Ohio*

Library of Congress Cataloging-in-Publication Data

Robinson, Tracy L.
  The convergence of race, ethnicity, and gender : multiple identities in counseling / Tracy L. Robinson, Mary F. Howard-Hamilton
    p. cm.
  Includes bibliographical references.
  ISBN 0-02-402481-3
  1. Cross-cultural counseling. 2. Psychotherapy. I. Howard-Hamilton, Mary F. II. Title.
BF637.C6R583 2000
158'.3—dc21

99-26332
CIP

Editor: Kevin M. Davis
Editorial Assistant: Holly Jennings
Production Editor: Linda Hillis Bayma
Copyeditor: Linda Poderski
Design Coordinator: Diane C. Lorenzo
Text Designer: Ed Horcharik/Pagination
Cover Designer: Ceri Fitzgerald
Production Manager: Laura Messerly
Electronic Text Management: Marilyn Wilson Phelps, Karen L. Bretz, Melanie N. King
Illustrations: Pagination
Director of Marketing: Kevin Flanagan
Marketing Manager: Meghan Shepherd
Marketing Coordinator: Krista Groshong

This book was set in Korinna by Prentice Hall and was printed and bound by R.R. Donnelley & Sons Company. The cover was printed by Phoenix Color Corp.

© 2000 by Prentice-Hall, Inc.
Pearson Education
Upper Saddle River, New Jersey 07458

Printed in the United States of America

10 9 8 7 6 5 4 3 2 1

ISBN: 0-02-402481-3

Prentice-Hall International (UK) Limited, *London*
Prentice-Hall of Australia Pty. Limited, *Sydney*
Prentice-Hall of Canada, Inc., *Toronto*
Prentice-Hall Hispanoamericana, S. A., *Mexico*
Prentice-Hall of India Private Limited, *New Delhi*
Prentice-Hall of Japan, Inc., *Tokyo*
Prentice-Hall (Singapore) Pte. Ltd., *Singapore*
Editora Prentice-Hall do Brasil, Ltda., *Rio de Janeiro*

ing this book has been transforming and liberating. It has required us to renew our minds and to exile the forceful yet often subconscious tendencies to move away from our inner voices that guide our lives and always help us.

We received Peggy Dulany's words: "In order to speak, we must know what we want to say; in order to be heard, we must dare to speak. Coming to know and coming to dare, being empowered, are all part of a complicated process."* By honoring our subjective truths, we lift our voices. This text is a humbling attempt at merging the multiple and layered dimensions of each of our textured lives. In a spirit of unity and respect, we acknowledge and celebrate the good work our elders and colleagues have done and are doing in multicultural counseling. We stand proudly and humbly on the shoulders of our mentors, friends, and teachers. Arredondo, Berry, Cass, Cross, D'Andrea, Daniels, Gunn Allen, Helms, Herring, Ivey, LaFramboise, Lee, Locke, McFadden, Myers, Pack-Brown, Parham, Parker, Pedersen, Pinderhughes, Ponterotto, Pope-Davis, Ossana, Ottavi, the Sue brothers, Takaki, Vontress, Wrenn—we thank you for your boundless blessings. With excitement and anticipation, we invite all of you into the consciousness of our hearts.

OUTLINE OF CHAPTERS

The text is divided into four parts: (a) "Imaging Identities," (b) "Converging Identities," (c) "Contextualized Identities," and (d) "Reimaging Counseling." Every chapter has at least one "Storytelling" feature to honor the powerful tradition of storytelling. This practice is an attempt to honor and celebrate the oral tradition alive in many cultures. Either author has told the story. We anticipate that many students will be reading our book, so to allow readers to integrate and apply the material presented more effectively, we provide a case study in each chapter.

PART ONE: IMAGING IDENTITIES Chapter 1, "Imaging Diversity," provides an overview of culture, race, ethnicity, gender, sexuality, physical disability, socioeconomic class, and religion/faith. Counselors' unawareness of their attitudes about differences contributes to conflict in counseling. For many counselors, the dominant value structure within the United States has been not only emphasized to the exclusion of all others but also touted as normal and often superior. American values are presented as a backdrop for understanding core values within American culture. The development of multicultural counseling is also discussed, as is acculturation and its effect on the values that many people of color have. Its role in influencing the values within one's own cultural group is also addressed.

Chapter 2, "Valued Cultures," acknowledges that differences exist within groups as well as between groups. A succinct overview of common cultural values among African Americans, Native American Indians/Alaskan Natives (referred to as Indians/Natives), Asian Americans, and Latinos is provided. To illuminate these characteristics, communication styles and differences are explored. Conceptions of the self based on value orientations are emphasized as well. With respect to the use of *African American* and *Latino,* Arredondo indicated that whereas the term *Hispanics* is a politically assigned term, *Latino* is a self-defined term.[†] The Office of Management and Budget (OMB) in 1978

---

* *P. Dulany, On becoming empowered. In J. Spurlock and C. Robinowitz (Eds.), Women's progress: Promises and problems (New York: Plenum Press, 1990), p. 133.*

[†] *P. Arredondo, Latino value orientations. (Empowerment Workshops. 1994).*

developed the term *Hispanic* to describe people who were perceived to have a similar ethnic background. Instead of *Hispanic, Latino* is used throughout this text. *African American* is used, according to Fairchild (as cited in Dana), because it "is preferable to 'Black' or 'Negro' . . . and it formalizes the African connection, avoids the ambiguity inherent in the capitalization/non-capitalization issue, adds a consciousness-raising dimension of self-respect and dignity, and may even attenuate hostile Anglo-American attitudes".* At times, however, *Black* and *African American* are used interchangeably.

"Statused Identities" is the title of Chapter 3. Explored are gender, race, sexual orientation, religion, physical ability, and class as sources of differences and status characteristics. Race and gender are presented, however, as primary-status traits. An explanation is given for this perspective. The Robinson model on discourses conceptualizes the discourses of racism, sexism, ageism, class elitism, able-body-ism, and homophobia as intersecting.

PART TWO: CONVERGING IDENTITIES   Chapter 4, "Converging Race," examines race from biological and sociopolitical perspectives. Primary stage models of racial identity development and implications for counseling are presented, as is relevant research. Via the case study, race, gender, racial identity development, acculturation, and assimilation are explored.

Chapter 5, "Converging Gender," is a discussion of gender roles and gender identity and includes a brief discussion of gender development from a biological perspective. Confronted are myths about biological differences between males and females. The extensive literature concerning how children, according to their gender, are treated differently as soon as they are born is included. Sex, sex role typing, and gender identity are explored, and distinctions are made among terms. Strategies are given to counselors for changing gender bias in the schools and in community settings.

Chapter 6 is "Converging Sexual Orientation." Often, counselors do not receive adequate training in this area, yet it is essential that they do. The goal is to expose counselors to the heterosexual bias that exists in this culture and to increase sensitivity about the inherent danger to lesbian, gay, and bisexual clients in a climate and context of heterosexism. When counselors are unaware of their biases, service delivery is seriously hampered. Behavioral/fantasy exercises are provided as a means to help readers identify and confront their fears, attitudes, and biases concerning sexual orientation.

Chapter 7, "Converging Physical Attractiveness, Ability, and Disability," addresses the need for counselors to be aware of how women and men are conditioned to define beauty narrowly. A cultural value of thinness contributes to constant dieting behavior among women, internalized sense of low self-esteem, anorexia, bulimia, and high dependence on others to validate the self. Women particularly are victims because self-worth gets confused with dress size. Attention is also devoted to the silent phenomenon of colorism, self-satisfaction, and physical attractiveness. Steroids and the athletic culture in the lives of men are examined. The culture's preference for the able-bodied, damaging stereotypes regarding persons with disabilities, and counseling men and women with disabilities are emphasized.

In Chapter 8, "Converging Socioeconomic Class," the focus is on class as a status variable that holds considerable rank within society and in the counseling event. Income is inextricably linked to self-worth. The training that counselors receive in traditional counselor education programs emanates from a middle-class bias and is critiqued.

---

* *R. H. Dana, Multicultural assessment perspectives for professional psychology. (Boston: Allyn & Bacon, 1993), pp. 31–32.*

Although unintentional, such a bias may alienate counselors from their clients who are not perceived as economically and financially successful. Furthermore, a myth prevails about the poor—that they are lazy, untrustworthy, and lack ambition. Power and power-lessness are examined with respect to class, gender, and race.

PART THREE: IMAGES OF DIVERSITY IN SOCIETY   Chapter 9, "Images of Diversity in Schools," focuses on the educational system's tendency to track children into specific occupations on the basis of stereotypical beliefs about race, gender, class, and ability. Early tracking has future implications for career development, income, self-determination, and job satisfaction. The subtle and blatant ways in which school curriculum reinforces traditional yet inequitable treatment among students is explored. Strategies for counselors to transform at-risk educational practices are highlighted.

Chapter 10, "Images of Diversity in Family Relationships," examines the relationship between parents and children specifically, not only motherhood and fatherhood but also the varied experiences of being daughters and sons. Unresolved emotional and psychological issues concerning how people were and were not parented affect counseling and the issues that are presented. The goal is to sensitize counselors to the power of these original relationships and the role of unfinished business on subsequent relationships with self and others. Nonacceptance of the past and the inability to forgive are primary issues that transcend gender and race. Family structure, marital status, and diverse family patterns, such as father-headed households and the extended family, are noted.

Chapter 11, "Images of Diversity in Career Counseling," considers how occupational choice is influenced by sources of differences and societal attitudes about them. It is not coincidental that 95% of secretaries are women and 97% of pilots are men, that all U.S. presidents have been White males, and that a disproportionate share of domestics are women of color. This chapter seeks to educate counselors about what they can do to challenge and change some stereotypical notions about gender, race, and class in the vocational and occupational process that affect males and females.

Violence is a major public health problem in society. Chapter 12, "Images of Cultural Violence and Empowerment," examines the cultural and social origins of abuse. Empowerment through counseling and therapy is an important part of this chapter as well. Literature on hormones, aggression, and violence is briefly presented. Statistics on incest, rape, and domestic violence are also provided. Women and men as survivors and perpetrators are depicted. Violence affecting young males of color is discussed. Powerlessness and power are integrated into the discussion. The goal of this chapter is to assist counselors in their nonjudgmental understanding of the client.

PART FOUR: REIMAGING COUNSELING   "Multicultural Competencies and Skills," Chapter 13, presents the knowledge, attitudes, and skills, both verbal and nonverbal, that are essential for the effective counselor to possess. Because nonverbal communication greatly affects the counseling event, the effective counselor attends to what the client says apart from the spoken word. Differences in communication across cultures are highlighted. This chapter discusses these competencies in depth and provides helpful information on how to integrate these competencies in various counseling settings. The importance of the counselor engaging in self-inquiry to be effective with clients is emphasized, as is the ability to refer clients when the counselor perceives that the client's issues exceed the scope of professional training and skills. Finally, ethical considerations are discussed from a multicultural perspective.

The therapeutic process can foster greater self-understanding toward enhanced functioning intrapersonally and interpersonally. This is the message of Chapter 14, "Empowering Clients." Empowerment is viewed as one goal of psychotherapy. Those forces that leave people bereft of power are discussed. The conflict among the traditional male role, empowerment, and seeking therapeutic assistance is a focal point of discussion, as is the challenge of certain counselor and client dyads, because of gender and race.

The final chapter, "Different Counseling Approaches to Understanding Diversity," explores new models for counseling in a diverse society. Empathy, advocacy, and flexibility are identified as essential skills. A psychological resistance model is featured, and several case studies are offered as a way of integrating this concept into various counseling scenarios. Other models that laypeople can initiate are highlighted. Alternative therapeutic approaches are viewed, such as expressive arts, prayer/meditation, and mind/body integration.

An epilogue concludes this work.

ACKNOWLEDGMENTS

We thank our friends, family, students, graduate assistants, and colleagues for inspiration, encouragement, distraction, help, prayers, and love. Dad, Mom, James, Jean, Sue, "the kids" (Mary's cats), Dad, Lo-Lo, C-C, Robin, Jerlissimo, Cousin Dot, Rah, Ole-san, Gerald, and Ms. Fay—you have gifted us with your presence. We also thank Kevin Davis, our editor, for holding this vision with us. Your quiet strength has lifted us higher. Holly, thank you for your kindness, sweet spirit, and professional assistance. Linda Sullivan, thank you for having coffee with us at ACA in Maryland. We shared our ideas with you and, as editor at the time, you moved us forward to a signed contract.

We also thank the following reviewers of this edition: J. Manuel Casas, University of California, Santa Barbara; Ajit K. Das, University of Minnesota; Patricia Hudson, George Washington University, Washington, DC; Kathleen Marie Kirby, University of Louisville; Steven Lopez, University of California, Los Angeles; Christopher Maglio, Truman State University; Brian McNeill, Washington State University, Pullman; Helen Neville, University of Missouri, Columbia; Twinet Parmer, Central Michigan University, Mount Pleasant; John J. Peregoy, University of Utah, Salt Lake City; Stephen Quintana, University of Wisconsin—Madison; Arthur R. Sanchez, California State University, Chico; Clemmie Solomon, Bowie State University, Bowie, MD; Naomi Smith, Vision Counseling Center; Jamie Victoria Ward, Simmons College, Boston, MA.

We also thank our excellent, thorough, and dedicated copy editor, Linda Poderski, for paying attention to critical details of this work.

Tracy L. Robinson
Mary F. Howard-Hamilton

DISCOVER COMPANION WEBSITES: A VIRTUAL LEARNING ENVIRONMENT

Technology is a constantly growing and changing aspect of our field that is creating a need for content and resources. To address this emerging need, we have developed an online learning environment for students and professors alike—Companion Websites—to support our textbooks.

In creating a Companion Website, our goal is to build on and enhance what the text-book already offers. For this reason, the content for each user-friendly website is organized by topic and provides the professor and student with a variety of meaningful resources. Common features of a Companion Website include:

FOR THE PROFESSOR—

Every Companion Website integrates **Syllabus Manager**™, an online syllabus creation and management utility.

- **Syllabus Manager**™ provides you, the instructor, with an easy, step-by-step process to create and revise syllabi, with direct links into Companion Website and other online content without having to learn HTML.
- Students may logon to your syllabus during any study session. All they need to know is the web address for the Companion Website and the password you've assigned to your syllabus.
- After you have created a syllabus using **Syllabus Manager**™, students may enter the syllabus for their course section from any point in the Companion Website.
- Class dates are highlighted in white and assignment due dates appear in blue. Clicking on a date, the student is shown the list of activities for the assignment. The activities for each assignment are linked directly to actual content, saving time for students.
- Adding assignments consists of clicking on the desired due date, then filling in the details of the assignment—name of the assignment, instructions, and whether or not it is a one-time or repeating assignment.
- In addition, links to other activities can be created easily. If the activity is online, a URL can be entered in the space provided, and it will be linked automatically in the final syllabus.
- Your completed syllabus is hosted on our servers, allowing convenient updates from any computer on the Internet. Changes you make to your syllabus are immediately available to your students at their next logon.

FOR THE STUDENT—

- **Topic Overviews**—outline key concepts in topic areas
- **Electronic Blue Book**—send homework or essays directly to your instructor's email with this paperless form
- **Message Board**—serves as a virtual bulletin board to post—or respond to—questions or comments to/from a national audience
- **Web Destinations**—links to www sites that relate to each topic area
- **Professional Organizations**—links to organizations that relate to topic areas
- **Additional Resources**—access to topic specific content that enhances material found in the text

To take advantage of these resources, please visit the Companion Website for *The Convergence of Race, Ethnicity, and Gender* at www.prenhall.com/robinson.

CONTENTS

Part One
Imaging Identities

Part Two
Converging Identities

Chapter 7
Converging Physical Attractiveness, Ability, and Disability   146

Chapter 8
Converging Socioeconomic Class   168

Part Three
Images of Diversity in Society

Chapter 9
Images of Diversity in Schools   188

Chapter 10
Images of Diversity in Family Relationships

208

Chapter 11
Images of Diversity in Career Counseling

230

Chapter 12
Images of Cultural Violence and Empowerment

248

Part Four
Reimaging Counseling

Chapter 13
Multicultural Competencies and Skills   270

Chapter 14
Empowering Clients   288

Chapter 15
Different Counseling Approaches to Understanding Diversity   306

Chapter 1

Imaging Diversity

When we were
created, we were given our ground to live
on, and from this time these were our
rights. This is all true. We were put here
by the Creator—I was not brought from a
foreign country and did not come here. I
was put here by the Creator.

Chief Weninock, The Native Americans: An
Illustrative History

One primary tenet of this text is that effective counselors acknowledge, understand, and appreciate sources of differences among people. The distinction between sources of difference among people and the attitudes people hold about differences is amplified throughout this work.

Diversity across age, ethnicity, gender, race, religion, sexual orientation, and socioeconomic class attest to the strengths of a heterogeneous culture. Yet, our nation continues to wrestle with equity for all. Numerous movements and laws, such as the Asian rights movement, the Chicano moratorium, the civil rights movement, the women's movement, the gay rights movement, Section 504 of the 1973 Rehabilitation Act, and the more recent Americans with Disabilities Act (ADA) inform us of the ongoing struggle for justice, access, and opportunity.

This chapter explores diverse identities within the United States. Race, ethnicity, gender, sexual orientation, physical ability, socioeconomic class, age, and religion are identity constructs and sources of difference crucial to self-concept. Each of these identity markers, in conjunction with one another, influences the process of meaning making in life. Identities are multiple, simultaneous, and ever-shifting. And depending on the contexts, certain identities have more power than others and take on different meanings. Within the counseling event, identity affects a client's problem orientation and the counselor-client relationship.

Implications for counselors within a culturally diverse nation that is challenged by the concept of *equality for all* is explored. Case studies are provided to allow readers an opportunity to integrate the material discussed throughout this chapter.

Admittedly, race and gender are given more attention throughout this text. The rationale for this position is substantiated by two observations. First, gender and race are genetically linked characteristics into which people are born. Second, in this society, race and gender are socially constructed to function as primary status traits (Hughes, 1945; Leggon, 1980; Robinson, 1993). As visible markers, meanings regarding the status of race and gender prevail (see the Storytelling "Five Star Hotel"). Discourses or uses of language and verbal exchanges of ideas operate as forms of social practice to communicate and perpetuate these meanings (Winslade, Monk, & Drewery, 1997).

Despite Mary's perfect Standard English, professional dress, and demeanor, the combination of female gender and Black race became associated with the occupation of housekeeping in the mind of the clerk. The clerk demonstrated that she was a product of her cultural environment and its associated dominant discourses. By asking Mary whether she was applying for the maid's position, the clerk's dominant discourse was unveiled, as was her proximity to it: Black women are maids, but they are not professionals (Robinson, 1999a). In this scenario, socioeconomic class, which may or may not be visible, took on meaning because of the assumptions made about ethnicity and gender (Robinson, 1999a). Cose (1993) said that "for most Blacks in America, regardless of status, political persuasion, or accomplishments, the moment never arrives when race can be treated as a total irrelevancy. Instead, too often, it is the only relevant factor defining our existence" (p. 28).

Within a color-conscious society, people are often judged initially by the color of their skin and by their gender than by the content of their character. Often, stereotypes associated with race, gender, and other sources of difference have far-reaching

STORYTELLING
Five Star Hotel

What a perfect convention thus far. I was attending a 1-day preconvention workshop on gender issues in counseling sponsored by the American Counseling Association. Participants were given a 1-hour lunch break, so I decided to go back to my "five star hotel room" to freshen up and catch my breath. When I entered the room, I noticed that the housekeeper had moved some of my personal food purchases and placed them in the hotel food bar and on the counter. At check-in, I had emphatically stated that I did not want a key to the bar in the room because I remembered previous stays in which I had been charged for items I did not purchase. This encounter, unfortunately, was no exception. I noted what had been moved and proceeded to the hotel registration desk. The woman at the front desk said, "May I help you?" and I said, "Yes, please. I have a question regarding housekeeping." Her immediate response was, "Are you applying for the maid's position?" Needless to say, I was floored. I simply said, "No, I am a guest at your hotel." The clerk became a bit red-faced and then said, "What can I do for you?" Remembering that the pen is mightier than the sword, I wrote a lengthy note to the manager, stating that the clerk should attend some type of racial sensitivity workshop. The manager sent me a personal note, and my roommate (Tracy) and I received a key to the concierge floor and hospitality room for the duration of our stay.

Mary

implications for one's livelihood, place of residence, employment opportunity, educational quality, and access. This process of judging by appearances may be largely unconscious, yet it occurs both within and outside the counseling event.

DEVELOPMENT OF MULTICULTURALISM IN COUNSELING: AN OVERVIEW

Multiculturalism is not a new force in counseling. Dramatic demographic changes within the United States alert the profession to the urgency of reconceiving basic Western assumptions of counseling that have been shaped and framed by culture. Embedded so deeply into the fabric of daily life, culture is sometimes rendered invisible, largely because of its pervasiveness.

Although multiculturalism is the fourth fource in psychology (Locke, 1992), the first emerging force in psychology was Freudian, the second was behaviorism, and the third was humanistic psychology. Understanding the development of multiculturalism in counseling warrants an examination of the ways people of color were often viewed in the mental health literature.

The traditional counseling paradigm, as it is known in Western society, was framed by cultural nuances. Sue and Sue (1990) identified three models concerning cultural differences. The first is the **genetic deficiency model,** which supports the belief that people of color are intellectually inferior to White people. Scientists such as physicist William Shockley, a recipient of the 1956 Nobel Prize in physics for co-inventing the transistor, have argued that research demonstrates that people of African descent are lower on the evolutionary scale. Arthur Jensen, a psychology professor, also has stated that because Black children are genetically inferior and missing innate talents, preschool programs such as Head Start will not have much impact on them.

Parham (1994) exposed early race and intelligence research. For example, because scientists could pour more peppercorns into the cranium of a European, compared with that of an African, they concluded that Europeans were intellectually superior. Clearly, the research methodology was problematic to begin with; however, the conclusion implied that racial purity was real. Given that Africa and Europe are so close in physical proximity and that the world's people have been reproducing lovely children across races, ethnicities, and regions, this conclusion appears ludicrous.

A second model is the **cultural deficiency model.** Although its tenets do not reflect the same animosity evident in the genetic deficiency model, it has been destructive. Emphasis is placed on the cultural deprivation and disadvantaged state of people of color. Norms derived from dominant cultural values of patriarchy, the nuclear family, individualism, competition, and materialism contribute to the view that sociocultural and language differences between Whites and groups of color reflect deficiencies among the latter. For example, the extended family is valued among many groups of color (and Whites too). Multiple generations residing in the same home and sharing child-rearing and household responsibilities is different from the nuclear family of a husband, wife, and biological children. However, this different cultural value is often perceived to be impaired.

The underlying foundation of the cultural deficiency model is monoculturalism or ethnocentrism. Racial and cultural **monoculturalism** represents single-system seeing. It assumes that all people come from the same cultural plane and desire the values of the dominant culture, which have been dictated by those with the most racial and ethnic power (McIntosh, 1990). Given the dynamic demographic shifts taking place in society, monoculturalism is inconsistent with multiculturalism.

A third model is the **culturally diverse or different model.** It maintains that differences do not refer to deficiency but are simply different and that such differences need to be valued. This last model supports the concept of **multicultural counseling.** According to McFadden (1993), "multicultural counseling is an approach to facilitating client insight, growth, and change through understanding and perpetuating multiple cultures within a psychosocial and scientific-ideological context" (p. 6). Multicultural counselors value and appreciate racial and cultural differences. Multiculturalism is respectful of multiple epistemological and philosophical perspectives. As an ongoing process that includes comfort with, support, and nurturance of people from various cultures (Hoopes, 1979), multiculturalism views differences as indispensable to a healthy society. Although used interchangeably, **multiculturalism** is not synonymous with **cultural diversity.** Cultural diversity may more aptly describe the phenomenon of culturally different people coexisting (Robinson, 1992). The nature of the coexistence, whether harmonious or conflictual, is unknown when one is merely observing that people who are different share similar space.

A taxonomy of worldviews on counseling, from monoculturalism to multicultural-ism to transculturalism, has been developed by McFadden (1993). According to this taxonomy, monocultural counseling represents a base on which cross-cultural, mul-ticultural, and eventually transcultural counseling have emerged. Monoculturalism again represents single-system seeing or, within the context of counseling, assessing the client from only one cultural lens.

From within the context of racial identity development, people appear to be cultur-ally socialized toward developing an ethnocentric ideology. For instance, equality for all is taught by clergy, family, and educators, yet many students, regardless of race, admit that they are largely ignorant of the contributions that people of color have made to this nation and to the world. As racial and cultural awareness increase, students might query, "How is it that I could have earned a bachelor's degree from a reputable institu-tion and have such limited and inaccurate knowledge about myself, society, and the people in it?" Just as school curriculum materials are a reflection of what is valued throughout society, history, too, is a phonograph of voices. Although most of us mem-orized "Columbus sailed the ocean blue in fourteen hundred ninety-two," most of us did not hear "America . . . derived its wealth, its values, its food, much of its medicine, and a large part of its 'dream' from Native America" (Gunn Allen, 1994, p. 193). Often, students are unaware that Frederick "Casey" Jones, an African American, invented a method for preserving perishables (Burt, 1989) or that during the 1920s two thirds of the nation's school superintendents in the West and Midwest were women. Awareness and appreciation of this cultural diversity is discussed next.

DIVERSE IDENTITIES: AN OVERVIEW

Appreciating diversity is an alleged position of democracy. Popular sayings within the American culture, such as "Different strokes for different folks" and "People make the world go around," suggest not only an awareness but an acceptance of differ-ence. Although certain differences may be valued, a multicultural society is an ideal and not yet a reality.

Since its inception more than two centuries and two decades ago, the United States has been an extremely diverse country. Some sources of diversity among peo-ple that existed then and continue now are race, ethnicity, gender, sexual orientation, nationality, physical ability, socioeconomic status (SES), and religion (Pinderhughes, 1989; see Figure 1.1). Of all Americans, about one quarter, or approximately 25%, are persons of color. The designation "people of color" refers to individuals who are African American, Native American Indian/Alaskan Native (Indian/Native), Asian American, and Latino. According to the 1990 U.S. Census, European Americans were 75.6% of the population; African Americans, the largest group of color, 12%; and Latinos, 8.5%. Latinos are expected to surpass African Americans as the largest group of color during the early part of the 21st century. Much of the racial and ethnic diversity in U.S. society has been influenced by persons from Latin America and Asia, the areas from which the majority of current immigrants originate (Kromkowski, 1995). Asians, 2.9% of the population, are one of the fastest growing groups. Indians/Natives, approximately 0.8% of the total U.S. population, "are proportionately the fastest growing ethnic group in the U.S." (Peregoy, 1993, p. 164).

Between 1980 and 1990, the European American population grew 6% and the African American population grew 13.2%. During this same period, the growth rate was nearly 38% for Indians/Natives, 108% for Asians and Pacific Islanders, 53% for Latinos, and 45% for persons of "other races" (Kromkowski, 1992). It is projected that, between 1992 and 2005, the labor force growth of people of color will outpace White non-Latinos (U.S. Bureau of Labor Statistics, 1994). Change in the total labor force during this time will be 19%: 11% for White non-Latinos; 25% for Blacks; 64% for Latinos; and 81% for Asians and other groups. Despite the dramatic increases among people of color, White non-Latinos will represent two thirds of labor force entrants because this group composes the largest share of the population. With respect to gender, female and male labor force entrants will be nearly equal: 26 million, compared with 25 million, respectively.

In addition to changes in the workplace, schools will undergo demographic shifts. Nearly 33% of all children under age 18 are children of color. By 2010, however, this

FIGURE 1.1
Sources of differences among people
Source: Adapted with the permission of The Free Press, a Division of Simon & Schuster, from UNDERSTANDING RACE, ETHNICITY AND POWER: The Key to Efficacy in Clinical Practice by Elaine Pinderhughes. Copyright © 1989 by The Free Press.

Race
Ethnicity
Skin Color
Gender
Sexual Orientation
Socioeconomic Class
Age
Ideology
Nationality
Behavior Style
Family Constellation
Occupation
Appearance
Physical Ability
Weight
Height
Religion
Size

is expected to grow to 38% (Kromkowski, 1992). Two other components of the diversity in the United States are gender and sexual orientation. Roughly 50% of the population is female, and human sexuality exists on a continuum including hetero-sexuality, bisexuality, and homosexuality (Morrow, 1993). The incidence of exclusive homosexuality is estimated to range from 5% to 10% for men and 3% to 5% for women (Strong & Devault, 1992).

Ours is also an aging population. According to the 1990 Census, nearly 31.2 million Americans are age 65 or older. Of these, 13.1 million are age 75 or over, and 3 million are age 85 or older (Atkinson & Hackett, 1995). By the 21st century, the population of elders will increase to 35 million, and by 2025, to almost 59 million.

Across all age-groups, religion plays a part in many people's lives. Although the United States was founded on Christian principles, there is much religious and faith diversity within and between groups of Christians and people of other religions. Religion, spirituality, and its various expressions are all affected by the identity dimensions of race, ethnicity, gender, sexual orientation, class, and culture.

A, B, AND C DIMENSIONS

As a means of conceptualizing human differences, Arredondo (1992) referred to the characteristics into which people are born as **"A" dimensions** of personal identity. These include age, culture, sex, sexual orientation, language, social class, and physical disability. **"B" dimensions** are characteristics not necessarily visible to others but influenced by individual achievement; these include educational background, geographic location, income, marital status, religion, work experience, citizenship status, and hobbies. **"C" dimensions** are historical events that have occurred over time.

Understanding the convergence of multiple identity constructs (A, B, and C dimensions) in people's lives is crucial to viewing clients holistically. Although the convergence of race and gender (A dimensions) is given primary focus throughout this text, all dimensions are essential to promoting client development and empowerment in the counseling process. The case study "Work and Family" allows for an integration of Arredondo's A, B, and C dimensions.

CASE STUDY
Work and Family

John Mendoza, a college-educated Mexican American client, presents to counseling with marriage difficulties. Silvia, John's wife, has a job as a pharmaceutical representative, which requires extensive travel and time away from John and their two school-age children. John would like Silvia to change jobs so that she can be at home more. Doing so will result in a demotion and reduced salary for Silvia. John's counselor is Mike Warren, an African American master's-level counselor-trainee.

QUESTIONS

1. What are John's A dimensions that Mike might focus on?
2. How might Mike's focus on visible statuses interfere with his therapeutic judgment?

DISCUSSION AND INTEGRATION
The Client, John

John's psychosocial identity and orientation to his problem have been shaped by a constellation of factors. These include his ethnicity, gender, culture, family, geographic region, education, religion, and personality, as well as other dimensions, such as his ethnic identity development level. To see John holistically, it is imperative that Mike not define John by a visible identity construct, such as being Latino. B dimensions profoundly shape John's presenting issues and self-concept, although they are invisible, such as being a father, a husband, a Catholic, a professional, a college graduate, and a fifth-generation Latino living in Arizona. The length of time that John has resided in the United States need not preclude the presence of culture-bound syndromes that could be associated with the stress of acculturation (Gonzalez et al., 1997). All of these dimensions of John's personhood are vital to understanding him. None should be neglected or minimized regardless of whether these identity components are readily visible or not.

The Counselor, Mike

John's total existence is greater than the sum of any or all of his primary identity constructs (Robinson, 1993). Thus, Mike needs to attend to John's ethnicity and culture while transcending it as well. Although Mike is a person of color, he could be at a low level in his racial identity development. If so, he may be unable to acknowledge ethnicity as a salient facet of John's overall identity. Such a clinical miss may lead Mike to focus primarily on John's male gender issues or on any number of individual statuses.

According to McFadden (1993), **transcultural counseling** is "having the ability and expertise to transcend cultural differences so that active interfacing with other cultures and populations considers cultural identity and contextual assimilation" (p. 8). Essentially, McFadden challenged his readers to a dialectical or both/and approach to transcultural counseling wherein complexity is acknowledged and balance is the goal (Pedersen, 1990). Although culture is directly acknowledged and respected, it does not become the dominant component of the counseling event. To be effective, Mike needs to be aware of the various dimensions of John's life and to understand these without being judgmental or engaging in stereotypical thinking. For example, some Latino men, as do some other groups of men, subscribe to a traditional view of family life: that men are the primary breadwinners and providers for their families. John, however, is unlike any other client Mike has seen. Listening to John tell his unique story is essential. John is an embodiment of multiple constructs that exist simultaneously because of the intricate interrelationships among A, B, and C life dimensions.

IMAGES OF DIVERSE IDENTITIES

CULTURE

Culture is enormous, central to each of our lives, and fundamentally shapes the way we see the world. It has been defined as the myriad ways of people to preserve society and meet a range of human needs. Belief systems, behaviors, and traditions make up the essence of culture (Pinderhughes, 1989). As pervasive as culture is, people are often oblivious to its impact on their and others' lives. For this reason, experiencing other cultures allows for an assessment of one's own.

Bronstein and Quina (1988) said,

> Because a culture consists, in part, of unstated assumptions, shared values, and characteristic ways of perceiving the world that are normally taken for granted by its members, people do not ordinarily become aware of the cultural basis for many of their own behaviors. (p. 14)

Kluckhohn and Strodtbeck (1961) maintained that perspectives about time, nature, people, and mode of activity are culturally influenced and vary among, within, and between racial and ethnic groups. These multiple differences in world-view across cultures are discussed in Chapter 2.

Because **cultural encapsulation,** or viewing the world from only one cultural lens (Wrenn, 1962), can greatly impede effective multicultural counseling, counselors need to address their cultural biases. Dana (1993) said that an **emic perspective** is respectful of, and sensitive to, the native culture's meanings for phenomena and allows for a recognition of persons on their own terms. By contrast, an **etic perspective** emphasizes the observer's culturally driven meanings that are referenced as the standard for interpretation. Within an ethnocentric perspective, the belief prevails that one's own culture and belief systems are superior to those of others who are culturally different. Such an attitude is in direct contradiction to the goals and aims of effective counseling.

ACCULTURATION AND ASSIMILATION   Acculturation and assimilation are important to an understanding of cultural adaptation. Berry and Sam (1997) provided a definition of acculturation from Redfield, Linton, and Herskovits's (1936) definition: "Acculturation comprehends those phenomena which result when groups of individuals having different cultures come into continuous first-hand contact with subsequent changes in the original culture patterns of either or both groups" (pp. 293-294). Although Berry and Sam indicated that *acculturation* is a neutral term because changes may happen in both groups, acculturation tends to bring about change in one group, which is referred to as the acculturating group. Two questions clarify the outcome of acculturation strategies: (a) "Is it considered to be of value to maintain relationships with dominant society?" and (b) "Is it considered to be of value to maintain cultural identity characteristics?" (p. 296).

It appears that **acculturation** is a process of socialization into accepting the cultural values of the larger society. Perhaps this takes place at the expense of one's original cultural values as one internalizes values and traditions. The key difference is that acculturation is not so much identification as it is internalization. Because this process is not always conscious (Sue, 1989), the possibility of cultural alienation from one's traditional culture seems high.

Berry and Sam (1997) discussed four acculturation strategies: (a) assimilation, (b) traditionality, (c) integration, and (d) marginality. Although a dimension of acculturation, **assimilation** is different and describes those persons who do not desire to maintain their cultural identities and thus seek sustained interaction with other cultures outside their own. Sue (1989) discussed a similar phenomenon when describing assimilation. He said it refers to a conscious process in which the person desires to identify with the traditional society because its art, language, and culture are perceived to be more valuable than the person's own. Persons who are acculturated are viewed as being low in a knowledge of, and appreciation for, their own cultures while holding the dominant culture in high regard. The original cultures have been lost or relinquished, and persons have given up most cultural traits of their cultures of origin and assumed the traits of the dominant culture (Berry & Kim, 1988).

According to Steinberg (1989), *assimilation* "meant something less than a total obliteration of ethnic difference. Rather the term referred to a 'superficial uniformity' between the minority and dominant groups that could conceal differences in 'opinion, sentiments, and beliefs'" (p. 47).

Traditionality describes persons who choose to hold on to their cultural connections and avoid interaction with others. Here, people have knowledge of, and appreciation for, their own cultures while holding the dominant culture in lower regard. Berry and Sam (1997) pointed out that when the dominant culture engages in these practices, the term is *segregation.*

Integration describes an interest in maintaining one's original culture while simultaneously seeking interactions with the other culture. According to Berry and Kim (1988), these persons are characterized as being *bicultural.* They are high in knowledge of, and appreciation for, their own cultures while esteeming the dominant culture as well. An integration of both an original culture and the dominant culture has transpired. Mental health and acculturation modality are related. Berry and Kim (as cited in Dana, 1993) stated that "mental health problems will be least intense with biculturality and progressively increase in severity with assimilation, traditionality, and marginality outcomes of acculturation" (p. 112).

Little interest in cultural maintenance and limited desire to interact with others from different cultures is defined as **marginality.** According to Dana (1993), "marginality will often occur when the traditional culture is not retained and the dominant society culture is not accepted" (p. 112). Emotional and psychological stress is associated with seeking to become acculturated within a given culture. Gloria and Peregoy (1995) discussed how alcohol and other drug abuse may be by-products of acculturation stress among some Latino populations. This connection between substance abuse and acculturation stress also seems to apply to Native American Indians and other ethnic and racial groups in their attempts to cope amid cultural devastation (Herring, 1992).

RACE

Every human being is a member of the human race, of the species of *Homo sapiens.* And although typical conceptions of race seem to refer to people of color only (Christian, 1989), *race* refers to European Americans as well. Although race is unchosen at birth, it is an extremely volatile and divisive force in this nation despite heroic efforts of various movements (e.g., the Asian, Latino, and civil rights movements) that coalesced to create greater racial equity. Race accounts for huge varia-tions in income, occupational distribution, educational levels, quality of and assess to health care, and longevity (Jaynes & Williams, 1989; Renzetti & Curran, 1992). Some scientists and academics have advanced that ethnicity accounts for marked differences in intelligence (Herrnstein & Murray, 1994).

Just what is race? According to biologists, **race** or subspecies "is an inbreeding, geographically isolated population that differs in distinguishable physical traits from other members of the species" (Zuckerman, 1990, p. 1297). Healey (1997) said that race was "an isolated inbreeding population with a distinctive genetic heritage. Socially, the term is used loosely and reflects patterns of inequality and power" (p. 309).

Race as a biological phenomenon has been criticized as nebulous (Cornell & Hartmann, 1997; Healey, 1997). Yet, biological properties are represented, such as hair texture and the presence and extent of melanin in the skin. Melanin is responsi-ble for darker skin color hue and represents "an adaptation to a particular ecology" (Healey, 1997, p. 11). Although race is often based on phenotypic variables, they do not accurately reflect one's race, but rather represent a basis for assigning people to a particular racial group. This issue is explored in greater depth in Chapter 4. In this work, it is not the intention to locate people into mutually exclusive racial and gender categories in an effort to conceptualize race and other identities in binary terms. Moreover, from the perspective of biracial or mixed-race persons, having to choose a fixed identity negates their other identities that, though perhaps less visible, are sub-stantial parts of their self-definition (Robinson, 1999b).

ETHNICITY

Typical discussions of ethnicity in the United States tend to include the "melting pot." This pot has been brewing and bubbling for generations. Originating in 1910 at the University of Chicago (Steinberg, 1989), the term described the assimilating tendencies of the more than 1 million European immigrants who were entering the United States each year. Sociologists were interested in knowing how the more than 20 nationalities managed conflict. By outward appearances, they seemed to be adapting very rapidly to the dominant culture.

The melting pot theory differed from the theory of "ethnic pluralists," who main-tained that ethnicity was an enduring factor throughout American life. Yet, the loss of native tongues, the decline of ethnic cultures, the dispersion of ethnic communities, the increase in ethnic and religious intermarriage, and the transformation of ethnic-sounding names to American-sounding names were and continue to be examples of Americanization (Steinberg, 1989). In addition, the melting pot assailed the preser-vation of individual differences in that the pot was dominated by a particular ingredi-ent. This image differs from that of a tossed salad, which is symbolic of multicultur-alism: Each ingredient is visible and not overcome or subsumed (Locke, 1992).

The process of assimilation among White ethnic microcultures differs greatly from that among people of color. Race often makes people of color easy targets for discriminatory treatment. Historical differences exist between race and ethnicity as a function of U.S. policy. The 1790 Naturalization Law, which was in effect for 162 years, stated that only free "White" immigrants would be eligible for naturalized citizenship. This meant that general citizenship was denied Asians until 1952, with the Walter-McCarran Act, and even Native American Indians until 1924 (Takaki, 1994).

Without an understanding of history, current realities become confused and diffused. Alba (1990) referred to persons from Latin America as "new immigrant groups" (p. 1). Such a classification might be based on the fact that during the late 19th and early 20th centuries Europeans represented the largest group of immigrants to this nation. Yet, in the Treaty of Guadalupe, Hidalgo, Mexico, lost half of its national territory, which included Texas, New Mexico, California, Arizona, Nevada, Utah, and half of Colorado (Novas, 1994). Thus, it is somewhat misleading to reference persons who occupy their native homelands as new immigrants.

Often, *race* and *ethnicity* are used interchangeably by some authors and researchers; however, these two terms are not synonymous. According to Pinderhughes (1989), **ethnicity** refers to a connectedness based on commonalities (e.g., religion, nationality, regions) where specific aspects of cultural patterns are shared and where transmission over time creates a common history and ancestry. Smith (1991) defined an **ethnic group** as

> a reference group called upon by people who share a common history and culture, who may be identifiable because they share similar physical features and values and who, through the process of interacting with each other and establishing boundaries with others, identify themselves as being a member of the group. (p. 181)*

Both preceding definitions identify commonality where unique cultural aspects are shared and transmitted. Among some racial groups, *ethnicity* refers more to nationality and country of origin. For others, religion is more readily referenced. Despite the differences regarding how ethnicity is defined, persons can be of the same ethnicity (e.g., Latino) but represent different racial backgrounds (e.g., Caucasoid, Negroid, biracial). Persons can also be of the same racial group (Mongoloid or Asian) but of differing ethnicities (e.g., Chinese, Japanese, Filipino). When transmitted intergenerationally within the culture, language, dancing, dressing, singing, storytelling, quilt making, weaving, and cooking, for example, are ethnic behavior (Alba, 1990).

GENDER

Traditional notions of gender reference nonmales (Christian, 1989), yet *gender* refers to both males and females. Gender has socially constructed categories in terms of roles and behaviors based on a biological given of sex (Renzetti & Curran, 1992). **Biological sex** refers to the possession of an XY chromosome pair for a genetically healthy male and an XX chromosome pair for a genetically healthy female, along with the corresponding anatomical, hormonal, and physiological parts (Atkinson & Hackett, 1995). **Gender** refers to the roles, behaviors, and attitudes that come to be expected of persons on the basis of their biological sex.

In U.S. society, "men are socialized to be emotionally inhibited, assertive, powerful, independent, and to equate sexuality with intimacy, manliness, and self-esteem. Women are socialized to be emotional, nurturing, and to direct their achievement through affiliation with others, particularly men" (Mintz & O'Neil, 1990, p. 382). Despite their socialization, men are emotional beings who need to rely on others, do not always feel strong, and desire to express a full range of emotions. Women, too, are leaders, strong, providers, and caretakers of self and others. Although lactation is a sex role that men tend to be biologically incapable of and penile ejaculation is a sex role genetically normal women are biologically incapable of, changing diapers and taking out the garbage are not sex roles. They are both socially constructed gender roles. There is no gene for changing a diaper or flying an airplane, yet the arbitrary divisions of labor that society has constructed based on biological sex are stringent and far too often attributed to biology.

Rury (1989) stated that, in the 19th century, a prominent member of the faculty at Harvard Medical School argued, "the strain of serious study posed a threat to the reproductive systems of adolescent girls, who were believed to be quite frail" (p. 49). This "uniformity myth," or the assumption that biological sex is synonymous with societal gender roles, has often existed in the literature (Mintz & O'Neil, 1990). More specifically, masculinity is not a biological phenomenon, although it is often equated with characteristics of the U.S. culture, such as self-reliance and individualism. Even the characteristics often attributed to femininity, such as yielding and nurturing, are not specific to the female sex.

Androcentrism is a traditional systematic construct in which the worldview of men is used as the central premise of development for all individuals, including women (Worell & Remer, 1992). The central image underlying this concept is "males at the center of the universe looking out at reality from behind their own eyes and describing what they see from an egocentric or androcentric point of view" (Bem, 1993, p. 42). Until society-ascribed gender roles are transformed, men and women alike will suffer from the constricting consequences of inequities based on biological sex and socially constructed roles.

SEXUALITY

Sexuality exists on a continuum and encompasses homosexuality, bisexuality, and heterosexuality. Arredondo (1992) conceptualized sexual orientation as an A dimension—the ones into which people are born. Other researchers say sexual orientation begins in childhood (Coleman & Remafedi, 1989).

Although there are different expressions of sexuality, the United States is a heterosexist society. **Heterosexism** is the belief that everyone is heterosexual and that heterosexual relationships are preferred and necessary for the preservation of the family, particularly the nuclear family. Heterosexism is institutionalized through religion, education, and the media and leads to homophobia (Pharr, 1988). Related to heterosexism, **homophobia** is the irrational and unreasonable fear of same-sex attractions and "persons whose affectional and erotic orientations are toward the same sex" (King, 1988, p. 168). It also applies to persons perceived to be gay or lesbian and emanates from the perception of homosexuality as an aberration of the correct social order. The term **homosexual** defines attraction to the same sex for physical and emotional nurturance and is one orientation on the sexual orientation continuum. It has become associated with the historical belief that homosexuality is unnatural, a sin, and a sickness. For this reason, the terms *gay* and *lesbian* are preferred. *Homophobia* comes from the Latin *Homo,* meaning "same" (in this case, referring to same-gender attraction), and *phobia,* meaning "fear of."

Heterosexism has implications for the counseling event. It could limit the type of advocacy a heterosexual counselor might engage in for gay or bisexual youths. This is particularly true if the client is extremely self-conscious about being labeled as gay or lesbian because of affiliation with, or advocacy for, gay men and lesbians.

As a reflection of changing times and sentiments regarding sexuality, some corporations are providing benefits for domestic partners who may be of the same or different sex, are not married, and are cohabiting. And at least one state, Hawaii, recognizes same-sex partnerships as legal.

DISABILITY

Section 504 of the Rehabilitation Act of 1973 and the Americans with Disabilities Act of 1990 (ADA) prohibit discrimination against individuals with disabilities. According to these laws, no otherwise qualified individual with a disability shall, solely by reason of his disability, be excluded from the participation in, be denied the benefits of, or be subjected to discrimination under any program or activity of a public entity.

According to the *Americans with Disabilities Act Handbook* (1991), an individual with a disability is a person who has a physical or mental impairment that substantially limits one or more "major life activities" or has a record of such an impairment or is regarded as having such an impairment. Examples of physical or mental impairments include, but are not limited to, such contagious and noncontagious diseases and conditions as orthopedic, visual, speech, and hearing impairments; cerebral palsy; epilepsy; muscular dystrophy; multiple sclerosis; cancer; heart disease; diabetes; mental retardation; emotional illness; specific learning disabilities; HIV disease (whether symptomatic or asymptomatic); tuberculosis; drug addiction; and alcoholism. According to the U.S. Bureau of the Census, almost 13.4 million people who are not institutionalized, ages 16 to 64, had a work disability in 1988.

The nature of disabilities among people varies, and the term itself is resistant to precise definition and measurement (Atkinson & Hackett, 1995). Numerous categories exist in describing persons with disabilities, from mild to moderate to severe.

People need not be born into a disability, but whether it exists at birth or occurs at some juncture in life, it is a biological reality nonetheless. According to Weeber (1993), persons with disabilities are the only minority with an open membership. Anyone can become a member at virtually any time, and most people will become disabled during their old age. Although disability is a reality for millions of Americans, persons with physical disabilities continue to face discriminatory attitudes. How many of us have gone to a restaurant with a friend who had a visible disability to find that the waiter or waitress ignored this friend and asked the person who did not appear to have a disability what the friend with the disability would like to order? Such attitudes are fueled by a societal perception that persons with disabilities are dependent, helpless, and incomplete (Weeber, 1993).

Disability intersects with gender and has class implications. Resource allocation for women with physical disabilities is different from that for men with disabilities and women who are able-bodied. According to Fulton and Sabornie (1994), "nearly twice as likely to be employed, men with disabilities earn more than 44% than women with disabilities" (p. 150). Weeber (1993) reported that the average income of full-time employed women with work disabilities is $11,979, compared with $13,071 for women who are able-bodied and $21,070 for men with work disabilities.

Despite the reality that disability is simply one component of a person's overall identity, Fowler, O'Rourke, Wadsworth, and Harper (1992) noted that the term *disabled* "conveys a message of inability which overshadows other identity descriptors of the person and becomes the exclusive role for persons who are disabled" (p. 102). Thus, disability can function as a primary-status trait when it is visible and regarded as the most salient component of a person's existence. For instance, a counselor who associates the experience of being able-bodied and middle-class with feelings of power may perceive an unemployed client with a disability as helpless and marginal. Actually, the client may be psychologically empowered and have numerous emotional and spiritual resources that enable him to feel powerful about his life.

SOCIOECONOMIC CLASS

Socioeconomic class refers to a person's or group's relative social position within a hierarchical ranking (Jaynes & Williams, 1989). Factors that affect one's socioeconomic ranking include educational level, employment stability, wages, marital status, income of spouse and/or other persons in the home, size of household, citizenship, and access to medical benefits. Exceptions exist, but increased education tends to be associated with higher incomes (Hacker, 1992).

Within the counseling arena, an inordinate emphasis has been placed on career development and assessment without concerted attention to socioeconomic class. Richardson (1993) lamented this neglect:

> The absence in the career development literature of racial and ethnic
> minorities and of the poor and lower classes, all of whom can be character-
> ized as oppressed groups, is a clear sign that these groups have been mar-
> ginalized, that professional efforts to understand and facilitate career devel-
> opment have been focused on White, middle-class, populations. (p. 426)

The intersections of class with gender and race are clear. For instance, in 1996, the poverty rate for all Whites was 11.2%; 8.6% for non-Latino Whites; 28.4% for Blacks; and 14.5% for Asians and Pacific Islanders. For Latinos, who can be of any race, it was 29.4% (Lamison-White, 1997). When the data were disaggregated, differences across race and gender manifested. Among Whites, the poverty rate was less than 11%. The rate was roughly 32% among Blacks and 28% among Latinos. Among women in general, the poverty rate in 1990 was 15% but 10% among men (Women for Racial and Economic Equality, 1991). Napholz (1994) cited in her research on Black women that the poverty rate among women of color is double that of White women. Thus, women of color, as a consequence of poverty, are more likely to suffer from inadequate access to medical and mental health services. Children suffer because of the economic situation of their mothers, particularly when the poor mothers of these children are single parents. In 1996, the largest group in poverty was children under the age of 18 (Lamison-White, 1997). In that same year, nearly 33% of female households were in poverty: 27% were White, 40.7% were Black, and 50.9% were Latino. Reglin (1994) reported that, in comparison with children living in two-parent families, poverty rates are six times more likely for children living in single-parent families.

Socioeconomic class affects other dimensions of one's life, including sense of worth and social status. Schliebner and Peregoy (1994) said,

> The family unit . . . derives its routine and ordering of time, place in a
> social network, status, and economic well-being from the labor force par-
> ticipation of its parental members . . . When productivity is halted, pro-
> found feelings of loss, inadequacy, guilt, and lowered self-esteem can
> result. (p. 368)

Self-construct and feelings of self-worth are affected by employment and socioeconomic class. It is not surprising that child-rearing practices would also be affected. In their study of working parents, McLoyd and Wilson (1992) found that

> working-class parents and lower class parents, compared to middle-class
> parents, put less emphasis on happiness in the child as a child-rearing goal
> . . . working-class and lower class parents are thought to be less imbued
> than middle-class parents with the notions that childhood should be a time
> of boundless happiness and carefree existence and that parental responsibil-
> ity includes the self-conscious provision of "happiness" to the child. (p. 421)

Data presented by McLoyd and Wilson suggest that although socioeconomic class is a construct that can be isolated for the purpose of measurement, it is not independent of other dimensions of one's personhood, such as psychological well-being and attention to happiness.

Regardless of one's race, the last few decades have not been favorable for Americans. Between 1980 and 1990, the median income rose from $34,481 to $36,915, or 8.7%, for European American families. Among African American families, incomes barely changed, from $21,151 to $21,423. Rises in family income among Whites were attributed to wives who worked outside the home (Hacker, 1992). Wilson (1994) argued that to understand the economic plight of people in society, race needs to be examined in conjunction with structural issues such as technology, unemployment, underemployment, and migrant labor:

> Because fewer Black and White workers are willing to accept an economic arrangement that consigns them to dead-end menial, and poorly paid jobs, low-wage service and manufacturing industries have increasingly used immigrant labor, including illegal aliens or undocumented workers from Mexico and other Latin American countries, to control labor problems and keep wages depressed. (p. 250)

Class converges with race and gender. These intersections have implications for the client's problem presentation and the effectiveness of the counseling relationship.

SPIRITUALITY

The United States is based on Christian principles as communicated through Christianity's sacred text, the Bible. The teachings of Jesus as reflected in the New Testament were based on love for everyone in a spirit of justice. The Bible's other teachings include the writings of the apostles and of various church fathers. Other religions throughout the world and within the United States are widely practiced and provide people with a sense of connection with the universe and of harmony, peace, and joy. These religions include Buddhism, Judaism, Islam, Hinduism, Confucianism, Taoism, Shintoism, and tribal beliefs (Wehrly, 1995). Spirituality gives life direction and meaning (McDonald, 1990). Although this book does not devote a separate chapter to religion and spirituality, they are recognized as representing the essence of who people are (Fowler & Keen, 1978). In this work, religion and spirituality are conceptualized differently. Whereas **religion** may be measured by denominational affiliations (e.g., Baptist, Methodist), as well as by empirical indices of righteousness, such as churchgoing, avoidance of denounced (sinful) behaviors (e.g., alcohol consumption, cigarette smoking, foul language, the wearing of short skirts, sexual intercourse outside marriage), **spirituality** is internally defined, transcends the tangible, and serves to connect one to the whole (other living organisms and the universe). Fowler and Keen (1978) said,

> Faith may be, but is not necessarily "religious" in the sense of being informed by the creeds, liturgy, ethics, and esthetics of a religious tradition. Faith, rather, is a person's or a community's way-of-being-in-relation to other persons and groups, and to the values, causes, and institutions that give form and pattern to life. (pp. 23–24)

Faith helps people cope with stress and make meaning in life (Watt, 1996). Many clients find some degree of comfort in their faith when seeking to answer the question "Who am I?" or "What will become of me?"

Parker (1985) saw that faith and development were integrated. He said, "the idea that active participation and struggle is necessary, is common not only to discussions of religious development but to discussion of other forms of cognitive growth and change" (p. 45). Undeniably, adults find comfort in their faith, particularly during crises or intensely conflictual times in life.

As a crucial cultural attribute, the effective counselor should not overlook the power of faith in both shaping and restricting clients' lives. Bishop (1992) said that "counselors who fail to directly assess the client's religious values run the risk of overlooking potentially important aspects of the client's cultural background and current cultural experience" (p. 181). Dissimilarity in religious values between client and counselor, however, may account for a hesitance to explore religion, as well as to a counselor's unwillingness to self-disclose his values. If the counselor lacks knowledge about a client's culture or religion or both, it is crucial that the professional close this knowledge gap. Counselors also need to be aware that, for many clients, religion represents a definite form of oppression and bondage and serves to hinder, not help, the client. Because effective counselors are self-knowing, counselors should assess their own cultural and spiritual belief systems as well.

IMPLICATIONS FOR COUNSELORS

The ultimate aim of multicultural counseling is to recognize and appreciate that differences exist among people. Although people are at various places in their overall development, it is important to acknowledge the need for common ground. Multiculturalism is an ideal and an ongoing process that takes place over time. Once people acknowledge and respect where they are developmentally, however, they can assess their motivation for moving forward. Counselors are encouraged to make this decision, first for themselves, then for their clients, and then for the profession as well. Yet, attitudes about differences can undermine the creation of a mutually respectful counseling climate. Thus, a counselor must understand the strengths of a client's culture and see such strengths as instrumental to healthy development. Counselors also need to develop a way to communicate effectively with clients about the full range of the clients' values in order to see connections among such values, problem orientation, as well as problem resolve. It is important for counselors to be aware of their attitudes regarding differences so as not to be biased against their clients in the counseling event (see the case study "Cultural Encapsulation?").

CASE STUDY
Cultural Encapsulation?

Kelly is working on her master's degree in counselor education in North Carolina. She is 28 years old and European American. Her first practicum student is Amalia, a Puerto Rican second-semester college student studying engineering. Amalia presents with feelings of homesickness. She misses her family greatly and is considering a transfer to a university closer to home. Kelly is surprised to learn that Amalia is a third-generation college student and that her father is a bank president and her mother a pediatrician. Kelly comments to Amalia that her English is good and that she is surprised Amalia is studying engineering and is on the dean's list. Kelly was reared in a White neighborhood. She took one course in cross-cultural counseling last year and made an A grade. All of her close friends are college-educated, White, Christian, heterosexual, able-bodied, and middle-class.

QUESTIONS

1. Why would Kelly be surprised at Amalia's background?
2. How might Kelly's socialization experiences affect her counseling relationship with Amalia?
3. How might Kelly's faculty or supervisor help her become more culturally aware and sensitive?
4. On which set of Amalia's characteristics might Kelly be most likely to focus, given her limited experience with racial and cultural diversity? Least likely? How would this affect her ability to focus on what Amalia has said?

DISCUSSION AND INTEGRATION
The Client, Amalia

Vasquez (1994) identified that "generally Latinas are affected by the triply oppressive experiences associated with being female, ethnic, and often poor" (p. 121). And even though both authors of this text do not agree that being female, ethnic, and poor automatically results in being oppressed, Amalia's gender, ethnicity, and culture largely frame the problem with which she presents in counseling. Amalia may not be experiencing class discrimination, but Kelly's attitudes are most likely reflective of other Americans who may hold stereotypical notions about Puerto-Ricans. Perhaps, Kelly was responding to the fact that the majority of Puerto Ricans in the United States have been occupationally isolated to tertiary labor markets as unskilled labor, service, and clerical workers and seasonal workers (Dana, 1993). Vasquez (1994), however, stated that "the stereotypes most frequently ascribed to Latinos tend to be negative (lazy, dumb, dirty, overemotional)" (p. 115). This is not to say that Kelly perceived Amalia in this way; however, she was surprised at her academic rigor, excellent English, and impressive class and educational background.

Because of the devaluation of women's traditional roles; ethnic, class, and gender discrimination; and feelings of powerlessness over their lives, Vasquez (1994) said, "Latina women are at high risk of experiencing mental health problems" (p. 124). Given the loneliness and cultural isolation that Amalia is experiencing, she may be vulnerable to depression or other mental health concerns if appropriate interventions are not implemented.

It is clear that Amalia has high expectations for herself and appears to be interested in continuing with her education and career. Garcia-Preto (1982) maintained that, among middle-class Puerto-Rican children, they "are not expected to do things for themselves. They are expected to finish high school, to attend college, and to qualify for occupations that will maintain their middle-class status" (p. 168).

The Counselor Trainee, Kelly

Kelly was most likely surprised by Amalia's background because of her own limited exposure to differences. Her circumscribed racial and cultural socialization experiences may create some internal discomfort when interacting with Amalia. Kelly may identify with Amalia's SES or her educational aspirations, given that these characteristics are most similar to her own background. She may focus less on ethnicity and race because of her limited experience with this type of diversity.

Culture-free service delivery does not exist; therefore, it is impossible to help clients examine cultural identity and self-esteem issues if counselors have not done this important work for themselves (Pinderhughes, 1989). Yet, a combination of feminist approaches with multicultural ones might provide the most effective therapy for Amalia and other Latinas (Vasquez, 1994). Currently, Kelly will be ineffective with Amalia if she is unable to combine them.

To increase Kelly's cultural awareness, Kelly's practicum supervisor could expose her to relevant materials regarding sources of differences in society and multicultural counseling competencies. Kelly would also benefit from assessing her own racial and cultural development.

SUMMARY

The various faces of diversity were discussed in this chapter. Included were culture, race, ethnicity, gender, sexuality, disability, socioeconomic class, and spirituality. The inappropriateness of attributing behaviors and attitudes to people on the basis of their visible identity constructs was discussed, as were the intersections of multiple identity components in shaping psychosocial development. Two case studies were presented to illuminate the textured lives of clients. Potential biases of the counselor were pinpointed, and recommendations for improvement were offered.

REFERENCES

Alba, R. D. (1990). *Ethnic identity: The transformation of White America.* New Haven, CT: Yale University Press.

Americans with Disabilities Act handbook. (1991). Washington, DC: Government Printing Office.

Arredondo, P. (1992). *Latina/Latino counseling and psychotherapy: Tape 1. Cultural consideration for working more effectively with Latin Americans.* Amherst, MA: Microtraining and Multicultural Development.

Atkinson, D. R., & Hackett, G. (1995). *Counseling diverse populations.* Madison, WI: Brown and Benchmark.

Bem, S. (1993). *The lens of gender: Transforming the debate on sexual inequality.* New Haven, CT: Yale University Press.

Berry, J. W., & Kim, U. (1988). Acculturation and mental health. In P. R. Dasen, J. W. Berry, & N. Sartorius (Eds.), *Health and cross-cultural psychology: Toward applications* (pp. 207–236). Newbury Park, CA: Sage.

Berry, J. W., & Sam, D. L. (1997). Acculturation and adaptation. In J. Berry, M. Segall, & C. Kagitcibasi (Eds.), *Cross-cultural psychology* (Vol. 3, pp. 291–326). Boston: Allyn & Bacon.

Bishop, D. R. (1992). Religious values as cross-cultural issues in counseling. *Counseling and Values, 36,* 179–189.

Bronstein, P., & Quina, K. (1988). *Teaching a psychology of people.* Washington, DC: American Psychological Association.

Burt, M. (1989). *Black inventors of America.* Portland, OR: National Book.

Christian, B. (1989). But who do you really belong to—Black studies or women's studies? *Women's Studies, 17,* 17–23.

Coleman, E., & Remafedi, G. (1989). Gay, lesbian, and bisexual adolescents: A critical challenge to counselors. *Journal of Counseling & Development, 68,* 36–40.

Cornell, S., & Hartman, D. (1997). *Ethnicity and race: Making identities in a changing world.* Thousand Oaks, CA: Pine Forge Press.

Cose, E. (1993). *The rage of a privileged class.* New York: HarperCollins.

Dana, R. H. (1993). *Multicultural assessment perspectives for professional psychology.* Boston: Allyn & Bacon.

Fowler, C., O'Rourke, B. O., Wadsworth, J., & Harper, D. (1992). Disability and feminism: Models for counselor exploration of personal values and beliefs. *Journal of Applied Rehabilitation Counseling, 23,* 14–19.

Fowler, J., & Keen, S. (1978). *Life maps: Conversations on the journey of faith.* Waco: Word Books.

Fulton, S. A., & Sabornie, E. J. (1994). Evidence of employment inequality among females with disabilities. *Journal of Special Education, 2,* 149–165.

Garcia-Preto, N. (1982). Puerto Rican families. In M. McGoldrick, J. K. Pearce, & J. Giordano (Eds.), *Ethnicity and family therapy* (pp. 164–186). New York: Guilford Press.

Gloria, A. M., & Peregoy, J. J. (1995). Counseling Latino alcohol and other substance users/abusers: Cultural considerations for counselors. *Journal of Substance Abuse Treatment, 13,* 1–8.

Gonzalez, M., Castillo-Canez, I., Tarke, H., Soriano, F., Garcia, P., & Velasquez, R. J. (1997). Promoting the culturally sensitive diagnosis of Mexican Americans: Some personal insights. *Journal of Multicultural Counseling & Development, 25,* 156–161.

Gunn Allen, P. (1994). Who is your mother? Red roots of White feminism. In R. Takaki (Ed.), *From different shores: Perspectives on race and ethnicity in America* (2nd ed., pp. 192–198). New York: Oxford University Press.

Hacker, A. (1992). *Two nations: Black and white, separate, hostile, unequal.* New York: Ballantine Books.

Healey, J. F. (1997). *Race, ethnicity, and gender in the United States: Inequality, group conflict, and power.* Thousand Oaks, CA: Pine Forge Press.

Herring, R. D. (1992). Understanding Native American values: Process and content concerns for counselors. *Counseling and Values, 34,* 134–137.

Herrnstein, R. J., & Murray, C. (1994). *The bell curve: Intelligence and class structure in American life.* New York: Free Press.

Hoopes, D. S. (1979). Intercultural communication concepts: Psychology of intercultural experience. In M. D. Psych (Ed.), *Multicultural education: A cross-cultural training approach.* LaGrange Park, IL: Intercultural Network.

Hughes, E. C. (1945). Dilemmas and contradictions of status. *American Journal of Sociology, 50,* 353–357.

Jaynes, G. D., & Williams, R. M., Jr. (1989). *A common destiny: Blacks and American society.* Washington, DC: National Academy Press.

King, N. (1988). Teaching about lesbians and gays in the psychology curriculum. In P. Bronstein & K. Quina (Eds.), *Teaching a psychology of people* (pp. 168–174). Washington, DC: American Psychological Association.

Kluckhohn, F. R., & Strodtbeck, F. L. (1961). *Variations in value orientations.* Evanston, IL: Row, Peterson.

Kromkowski, J. A. (1992). *Race and ethnic relations, 92-93.* Guilford, CT: Dushkin.

Kromkowski, J. A. (1995). *Race and ethnic relations, 95-96.* Guilford, CT: Dushkin.

Lamison-White, L. (1997). Poverty in the United States: 1996. *Current Population Reports, P. 60-198.*

Leggon, C. B. (1980). Black female professionals: Dilemmas and contradictions of status. In L. Rodgers-Rose (Ed.), *The Black woman* (pp. 189–202). Beverly Hills, CA: Sage.

Locke, D. C. (1992). *Increasing multicultural understanding: A comprehensive model.* Newbury Park, CA: Sage.

McDonald, A. L. (1990). Living with our deepest differences. *Journal of Law and Religion, 8,* 237–239.

McFadden, J. (1993). *Transcultural counseling: Bilateral and international perspectives.* Alexandria, VA: American Counseling Association.

McIntosh, P. (1990). *Interactive phases of curricular and personal revision with regard to race* (Working Paper No. 219). Wellesley, MA: Wellesley College Center for Research on Women.

McLoyd, V. C., & Wilson, L. (1992). Telling them like it is: The role of economic and environmental factors in single mothers' discussions with their children. *American Journal of Community Psychology, 20*, 419–444.

Mintz, L. B., & O'Neil, J. M. (1990). Gender roles, sex, and the process of psychotherapy: Many questions and few answers. *Journal of Counseling & Development, 68*, 381–387.

Morrow, D. (1993). *Lesbian identity development through group process: An exploration of coming out issues.* Unpublished doctoral dissertation, North Carolina State University at Raleigh.

Napholz, L. (1994). Sex role orientation and psychological well-being among working Black women. *Journal of Black Psychology, 20*, 469–482.

Novas, H. (1994). *Everything you need to know about Latino history.* New York: Penguin.

Parham, T. (1994). *African American therapy and counseling.* Amherst, MA: Microtraining and Multicultural Development.

Parker, M. S. (1985) Identity and the development of religious thinking. In A. S. Waterman (Ed.), *Identity in adolescence* (pp. 43–60). San Francisco: Jossey-Bass.

Pedersen, P. (1990). The constructs of complexity and balance in multicultural counseling theory and practice. *Journal of Counseling & Development, 15*, 16–24.

Peregoy, J. J. (1993). Transcultural counseling with American Indians and Alaskan Natives: Contemporary issues for consideration. In J. McFadden (Ed.), *Transcultural counseling: Bilateral and international perspectives* (pp. 163–191). Alexandria, VA: American Counseling Association.

Pharr, S. (1988). *Homophobia: A weapon of sexism.* Little Rock, AR: Chardon.

Pinderhughes, E. (1989). *Understanding race, ethnicity, and power: The key to efficacy in clinical practice.* New York: Free Press.

Reglin, G. (1994, January). Promoting success for the African American male student: A blueprint for action. *A Series of Solutions and Strategies, 8*, 1–8.

Renzetti, C. M., & Curran, D. J. (1992). *Women, men, and society.* Boston: Allyn & Bacon.

Richardson, M. S. (1993). Work in people's lives: A location for counseling psychologists. *Journal of Counseling Psychology, 40*, 425–433.

Robinson, T. L. (1992). Transforming at-risk educational practices by understanding and appreciating differences. *Elementary School Guidance & Counseling, 27*, 84–95.

Robinson, T. L. (1993). The intersections of gender, class, race, and culture: On seeing clients whole. *Journal of Multicultural Counseling & Development, 21*, 50–58.

Robinson, T. L. (1999a). The intersections of dominant discourses across race, gender, and other identities. *Journal of Counseling & Development, 77*, 73–79.

Robinson, T. L. (1999b). The intersections of identity. In A. Garrod, J. V. Ward, T. L. Robinson, & B. Kilkenney (Eds.), *Souls looking back: Portraits of growing up Black.* New York: Routledge.

Rury, J. L. (1989). We teach the girl repression, the boy expression: Sexuality, sex equity, and education in historical perspective. *Peabody Journal of Education, 64*, 44–58.

Schliebner, C. T., & Peregoy, J. J. (1994). Unemployment effects on the family and the child: Interventions for counselors. *Journal of Counseling & Development, 72*, 368–372.

Smith, E. J. (1991). Ethnic identity development: Toward the development of a theory within the context of majority/minority status. *Journal of Counseling & Development, 70*, 181–188.

Steinberg, S. (1989). *The ethnic myth: Race, ethnicity, and class in America.* Boston: Beacon Press.

Strong, B., & Devault, C. (1992). *Understanding our sexuality.* St. Paul, MN: West.

Sue, D. W. (1989). *Cultural identity development* [Video]. Amherst, MA: Microtraining and Multicultural Development.

Sue, D. W., & Sue, D. (1990). *Counseling the culturally different: Theory and practice.* New York: John Wiley.

Takaki, R. (1994). Reflections on racial patterns in America. In R. Takaki (Ed.), *From different shores: Perspectives on race and ethnicity in America* (2nd ed., pp. 24–35). New York: Oxford University Press.

U.S. Bureau of Labor Statistics. (1994). *The American work force: 1992–2005.* Washington, DC: Author.

Vasquez, M. J. T. (1994). Latinas. In L. Comas-Dias & B. Greene (Eds.), *Women of color* (pp. 114–138). New York: Guilford Press.

Watt, S. (1996). *Identity and the making of meaning: Psychosocial identity, racial identity, womanist identity, and faith development of African American college women.* Unpublished doctoral dissertation, North Carolina State University at Raleigh.

Weeber, J. (1993). *"We are who you are": The issue of self-definition with disabled women and a reframed feminist response.* Unpublished manuscript, North Carolina State University at Raleigh.

Wehrly, B. (1995). *Pathways to multicultural counseling competence: A developmental journey.* Pacific Grove, CA: Brooks/Cole.

White, E. C. (1994). *The Black women's health book: Speaking for ourselves.* Seattle, WA: Seal Press.

Wilson, W. J. (1994). The Black community: Race and class. In R. Takaki (Ed.), *From different shores: Perspectives on race and ethnicity in America* (2nd ed., pp. 243–250). New York: Oxford University Press.

Winslade, J., Monk, G., & Drewery, W. (1997). Sharpening the critical edge: A social constructionist approach in counselor education. In T. Sexton & B. Griffin (Eds.), *Constructivist thinking in counseling practice, research, and training* (pp. 228–245). New York: Columbia University Teacher's College.

Women for Racial and Economic Equality. (1991). *191 facts about women.* New York: Author.

Worell, J., & Remer, P. (1992). *Feminist perspectives in therapy: An empowerment model for women.* New York: John Wiley.

Wrenn, C. G. (1962). The culturally encapsulated counselor. *Harvard Educational Review, 32,* 444–449.

Zuckerman, M. (1990). Some dubious premises in research and theory on racial differences. *American Psychologist, 45,* 1297–1303.

Chapter 2

Valued Cultures

You were born God's
original. Try not to become someone's copy.

Marian Wright Edelman, The Black Woman's
Gumbo Ya-Ya

Among baby boomers, much has been written about the hunger many of these 30-to 50-year-old "somethings" have for meaning, purpose, and simplicity in their lives during this information age of dazzling technological advancements (see the Story-telling "Sacramento Memories"). Handheld cellular phones simultaneously function as fax machines, computers, and pagers. In seconds, people have the capacity to fax and electronically dispatch information around the globe. Although these devices enhance efficiency, personal charges are levied for living in a society that is willing to sacrifice human interaction for enhanced productivity.

This work of comparing value orientations is not intended to elevate one worldview over another but simply to illustrate that differences exist in ideology and philosophy. Nor is a discussion of values common to various racial and cultural groups intended to arrange people into discrete, limiting, and binary categories. Although memorizing a laundry list of values may be reassuring to the counselor trainee who is uncomfortable in the presence of culturally different persons, it offers a false sense of security and is offensive to the unique client in the counselor's presence. Culture interacts with individual nuances, group affiliations, and environmental factors. Because people's notions of morality and normalcy are culturally driven, it is crucial to acknowledge ideological differences and similarities, both within and across cultures. Yes, personality differences are greater among racially similar people than between groups of people (Bronstein & Quina, 1988; Zuckerman, 1990). This chapter discusses these themes and considers the impact of culture on counseling theory, practice, and the goals of counseling from the perspectives of both counselor and client.

Finally, even though historical perspectives of each group are discussed in brief throughout this work, the reader is referred to many good sources for more information (see Cao & Novas, 1996; Christian, 1995; Hoxie, 1996; Novas, 1994; Padilla, 1984; Stewart, 1996; Takaki, 1994a; Uba, 1994).

DIMENSIONS OF CULTURE

As a primary socializing tool, culture shapes the most fundamental attitudes that people have regarding themselves, others, and the world. Camilleri and Malewska-Peyre (1997) stated that **culture** is the "most durable, shared, and valued" of all "the various models that circulate in the social domain" (p. 44). Given the saliency of culture in the lives of people, attitudes held about the efficacy of counseling or beliefs about a counselor's ability to help are filtered through a cultural lens. Among some Asian Americans, for example, the road to mental health involves exercising willpower and refusing to participate in morbid thoughts (Sue, 1989). Organic variables may be associated with psychological and emotional difficulties that can be expressed through somatization (Lin, 1994). Clearly, somatization is not peculiar to Asian Americans but is common among other groups as well. The perceived body-mind connection among many Asians, however, in contrast with the body-mind dichotomization evident among many Americans, translates into a different interpretation and articulation of psychological dilemmas (Chang, 1996).

STORYTELLING
Sacramento Memories

"If you want your dreams to be, take your time, go slowly. Do few things but do them well, simple things are holy." I sang this song as a child, and I remember a simple time during the 1960s in my hometown of Sacramento, California. In my community, families knew one another. In fact, the adults collectively raised the children in a spirit of unity and cooperation. I remember being fed, very well, by Mrs. Watson, or being reprimanded by Mrs. Evans for raiding the neighborhood pomegranate and cherry trees. We had a sense of duty and responsibility to one another. My mother was a Block Parent. A tiny but visible insignia was placed in our window. For example, if on the way to or from school a child became ill or was being chased by a dog or harassed by the school bully, the child could run to one of these "Block Parent" homes for help. As a child, it was a tremendous sense of comfort to me, knowing this support was available. The culture informed me that we were a village looking out for each other. We were predominantly Black, but we were also Mexican and White. How grateful I am to have been a part of that sacred community that sustained and helped me along my way. Transmitted to me were values of cooperation, accountability, giving and receiving support, and respect for my elders. I also learned values embodied within the dominant culture of the United States. What were they, and what were the cultural values often embraced by Latinos? Asians? African Americans? Native American Indians/Alaskan Natives?

Tracy

Understanding people's cultural values requires information about their group, exposure to a variety of individuals within the group, and an understanding of the sociopolitical dynamics of justice, oppression, history, and self-awareness. In addition, age, geographic location, ethnicity, and physical ability mediate both the influences of culture and the extent to which an individual personally adopts cultural values. Not all individuals within a given culture will subscribe to the dominant and core values of that culture. The dominant culture in America is characterized by individualistic social relations, yet some European Americans subscribe to collateral relations. Within a collateral worldview, a belief exists that one should consult with family and friends when problems or challenges arise, rather than rely solely on the self for answers.

Kluckhohn and Strodtbeck (1961) proposed five value orientations: (a) human nature, (b) man-nature, (c) time, (d) activity, and (e) relational. Within the *human nature* orientation, four variations were postulated: evil, neutral, mixture of good and evil, and good. These authors contended that Americans were inclined toward viewing human nature as a mixture of good and evil. This orientation describes the importance of discipline and control, evident in the Protestant work ethic value. Yet, within this orientation, allowances are made when such rigor is not dutifully applied.

The *man-nature* orientation includes subjugation to nature, harmony with nature, and mastery over nature. Having mastery and control over nature is descriptive of the U.S. culture. Land takeovers from Native American Indians and Latinos are manifestations of this worldview. Reflective of the diversity within U.S. society, some cultures, such as traditional Indians/Alaskans, subjugate to or coexist harmoniously with nature and do not seek to be controlling.

The *time* orientation pertains to the past, present, and future. Kluckhohn and Strodtbeck (1961) said of the United States, "Americans, more strongly than most people of the world, place an emphasis upon the Future—a future which is antici-pated to be 'bigger and better'" (p. 15). The idiom "Tie your wagon to a star and keep climbing up and up" embodies this perspective. The future-oriented descriptor for Americans is controversial, however. The burgeoning deficit and the massive vio-lation of natural resources appear to emanate more from impulsivity, faulty planning, and a preoccupation with the present, rather than out of a desire to delay gratifica-tion and expand. As a future-oriented society, the United States puts great emphasis on looking ahead, planning, and rigidly watching time. The past is most likely not highly regarded because of the perception that it is a nonreplenishable commodity.

Being, being-in-becoming, and doing describe the *activity* orientation. Being is likened to spontaneity and perhaps allowing the natural unfolding of the person. Being-in-becoming also focuses on that which is more so than on that which is done. More emphasis is placed on development "of all aspects of self as an integrated whole" (Kluckhohn & Strodtbeck, 1961, p. 17). Doing truly characterizes the United States. Underlying doing is the belief that productivity and activity are paramount to success and self-worth. Because this worldview places a premium on incessant doing, some Americans find it difficult to be in the moment without preoccupation with the next day or even the next hour. Even children are socialized to believe that individual effort is fused with self-worth. The competitive nature of schools primes children that to be the smartest, they have to beat their opponents. This perspective ultimately reinforces capi-talistic messages. Supply is limited, demand is great, and to get one's share, one must scramble before one's good is snatched away. Needless to say, mindfulness, a Buddhist practice of being present in the very moment (Kabat-Zinn, 1994), is somewhat remote to many Westerners. True knowledge of one's self requires rendezvous with the quiet and is by its very nature spiritual. Such knowledge is not externally gained or derived and constitutes the basis of wholeness (Ibrahim, Ohnishi, & Sandhu, 1997; Myers, 1991).

Finally, the *relational* orientation includes lineality, collaterality, and individualism. Kluckhohn and Strodtbeck (1961) indicated that each of these dimensions is found in all societies. Even in extreme traditional, folk, and rural communities, individual-ism is manifested. **Collaterality** designates the process through which people become human beings by coexisting within a social order with its cultural overlays and mores. **Lineality** speaks of people's biological and cultural relationship with one another over time. **Individualism** describes the relational orientation in the United States with its emphasis on the person as the primary unit.

CULTURE AND VALUES

The previous section discussed dimensions of culture that give rise to the values among groups of people. Common values in the United States are identified in Figure 2.1. They include individualism, meritocracy, masculinity, autonomy, affluence, competition, and Standard English (written tradition) (Kagitcibasi, 1997; Sue & Sue, 1990). All Americans are exposed to these and other values through school, print and visual media, church, and family. Meanings, interpretations, and subsequent expressions of identities—race, ethnicity, gender, class, political ideology, sexual orientation, religion and spirituality, philosophy, and physical ability—are culturally derived, mediated, and influenced by one another. Thus, a qualifier is in order. Given the patriarchal nature of Western society, these values emanate largely from a White, middle-class, male lens and contrast with the gynarchical traditions in some Native Ameriocan Indian cultures that Gunn Allen (1994) chronicled. Some women across various racial and class groups may find these values to be inconsistent with their worldviews. According to researchers, women's development and the identity development of many groups of color are characterized by forming and maintaining relationships based on cooperation and mutuality (Belenky, Clinchy, Goldberger, & Tarule, 1986; Brown & Gilligan, 1992; Brookins & Robinson, 1995). It is fallacious, however, to generalize these values to all Americans or to a particular group of Americans on the basis of a single group identifier such as race or ethnicity (see the Storytelling "My Country").

CONCEPTUALIZATIONS OF THE SELF

According to Page and Berkow (1991), "the self is, perhaps, an indispensable concept for explaining how persons organize perception, encounter the world of experience, and maintain a cohesive image of identity" (p. 83). In the United States and other Western societies, the self is constructed within the context of individualism. Because of its import, individualism and parallel themes are discussed below.

STORYTELLING
My Country

On a few occasions, students have accused me of being pessimistic about American culture. In times like these, I question my pedagogy for any unexamined biases. Seeing the world through only one set of lenses without questioning my biases interferes with taking a culturally different viewpoint. Yet, I suspect that many students are oblivious to aspects of daily American culture that are inconsistent with other people's own cultural orientations, such as the expectation that everyone is a Christian and lives with a nuclear family. It is important that I ask my students to think about what they believe in order that they may examine these beliefs, become aware of where they learned them, and decide whether they wish to keep them.

Tracy

FIGURE 2.1
Common cultural values and
beliefs in the United States

Individualism

Empiricism

Materialism

Masculinity

Rigid Time Orientation

Competition

Control

Standard English (Written Tradition)

Autonomy

Meritocracy

Nuclear Family

Affluence

Patriarchy

Ethnocentrism

Women's Beauty Based on Being Thin and Able-bodied

Men's Attractiveness Based on Power, Wealth, Physical Ability

THE DISCRETE SELF

Individualism has its roots in philosophy. According to Castenada (1984), Rousseau more than any other modern person shaped the concept of the monolith. Kagitcibasi (1997) argued that individualism and collectivism have roots in a variety of domains, including political and economic history, religion, and philosophy. Thomas Hobbes, a 17th-century British philosopher, believed that free expression of an individual's will was the essence of balance and efficacy. In **individualism,** the person is regarded as discrete from other beings. The human being is considered the essential cornerstone of society (Kagitcibasi, 1997). Myers (1991) maintained that because Western society is philosophically oriented to individualism, individuals are the primary referent point and separate from others. Fragmentation between spirit and matter (or bifurcation of the self) is thus an outcome of an individualistic frame of reference. Yet, Parham (1992) observed that bifurcation of self is apparent in major theoretical approaches to counseling. For example, Freud identified three aspects of the psychic apparatus: id, ego, and superego. Transactional analysis distinguishes between parent, adult, and child ego states. The dimensions of self are often categorized within three distinct domains: cognitive, affective, and behavioral.

Individuality, particularly as it relates to personal responsibility for knowing the self, is not being minimized; however, excessive forms of individualism interfere with the ability to ask for and receive help from others. This is especially true regarding psychological help, particularly for men whose socialization processes often discourage asking for help from others. In educating people about the benefits of obtaining psychological resources, an examination of how individualism contributes to help-avoiding attitudes is warranted.

Ironically, individualism may work to suppress personal delineation of the individual (Pedersen, 1994). For example, external conformity and individualism appear to be in contradiction, yet these are two cultural themes in the United States (Locke, 1992). On the one hand, Americans are encouraged to be their own persons and to do their own thing, given the cultural emphasis on autonomy. On the other hand, conformity, the status quo, and "not rocking the boat" are valued as well. There is almost an unwritten edict against extreme levels of individuality as they tend to be indicative of nonconventionality. U.S. society often espouses the sentiment "Be all you can be," but another confusing message is transmitted: Do not cross the border of what is acceptable thinking and behavior. Color within the lines and stay within the box!

Gender intersects with this largely unwritten doctrine of external conformity. Across racial and ethnic groups, and even after more than two decades of the women's movement, teenage girls and their mothers often find themselves estranged from the empowering process of self-definition. Tolman (1991), in discussing the missing discourse around adolescent girls' sexual desire, which is silencing and contributes to disassociation from the self, said,

> Because adolescent girls live in a culture which obscures, denigrates, silences and is silent about their desire, I think that most girls can and will speak in the voice of the culture. If no one around them speaks about girls' desire, then girls may have trouble speaking directly themselves. (p. 61)*

Men, too, operate within a very narrow box. The dictates of masculinity mandate being heterosexual and being an economic provider. By not knowing the self or being able to ask and answer the questions "Who am I?" "What do I want to be?" and "What and whom do I want?" one is excessively vulnerable to adopting others' answers to these questions. Although some external messages are helpful, they do not originate from within and thus are disempowering when they create dependence on others for self-definition and acceptance. Whereas dependent people often feel powerless and are not likely to oppose the status quo or existing power structures (Pinderhughes, 1989), self-determined and autonomous persons tend to define themselves according to a subjective or intuitive knowledge base. They are freer from the pressing need to have others approve of them (McBride, 1990).

One consequence of individualism and assimilation for some people of color is "racelessness." According to Fordham (1990), it is the desire to minimize cultural connections. Self-alienation and psychological separation from the larger community result. Fordham defined the raceless individual as lacking a racial identity, which can lead to self-denigration and confusion (Pinderhughes, 1989).

---

* From "Adolescent Girls, Women, and Sexuality: Discerning Dilemmas of Desire," by D. L. Tolman, 1991, Women & Therapy, 11, p. 61. Copyright 1991 by The Haworth Press. Reprinted by permission.

In addition to socialization factors, structural issues mediate individualism. When the United States was more agrarian and people had less money and were less mobile, interdependence was greater than it is in today's technological and highly mobile society. Individualism and empiricism are interrelated in that they both focus on categorization into discrete, separate units. The scientific tradition in academia emerged from a positivistic-empirical model that emphasizes quantification, statistical measurement, and validation of reality by using the five senses. The visible is essential, and the invisible becomes suspect because it cannot be proved, counted, and thus controlled. Yet, Albert Einstein knew that "Everything that counts cannot be counted, and everything that can be counted does not necessarily count."

In Western ideology, competition and domination are not only cultural values and orientations but powerful players in shaping the policies, programs, and politics of the United States, past and present. Were the early explorers simply eager to discover new territories "and go where no one had gone before," or did they have an insatiable need to conquer and master even if it meant taking people from their land and taking the land from its people? Competition has some advantages. It can serve as a motivator and provide people with a sense of purpose. Moreover, individual effort and achievement are important to establishing personal boundaries and forging an identity. In the extreme, the constant demand to strive and rival can create enormous psychological stress.

THE EXTENDED SELF

Figure 2.2 presents common values among groups of color. Again, this discussion is not meant to stereotype any group but to discuss characteristics common among African Americans, Asian Americans, Latinos, and Indians/Alaskans. The primary focus on the individual is not standard in all the world's cultures. Among many people throughout the world, the self is conceptualized within the context of the collective or the community, not as a separate entity. Acculturation, migration status, income, education, and racial/ethnic identity development affect internalization of certain values.

NATIVE AMERICAN INDIANS/ALASKAN NATIVES   "American Indian is an ethnic description that refers to all North American Native people, including Indians, Alaskan Natives, Aleuts, Eskimos, and Metis, or mixed bloods" (LaFromboise & Graff Low as cited in Peregoy, 1993).

The origins of Indians/Alaskans have been linked to the *Bering Strait theory.* Held by many European scholars despite the various migratory patterns of Natives, this theory maintains that migration occurred from Asia to North America. Although dental and genetic tracing suggests Asian origins for Indians/Alaskans, if Indians/Alaskans controlled universities, there might be different explanations of "the peopling of the New World" (Deloria as cited in Ballentine & Ballentine, 1993).

Because of the decimation of Native American Indians, they are less than 1% of the U.S. population and number just over 2.3 million (Garrett & Garrett, 1994). Between the 1980 and 1990 Census, however, their 38% growth rate exceeded the growth rate for African Americans and non-Latino Whites (Fost, 1998). A small

FIGURE 2.2
Common cultural values and
beliefs among many people of
color

Spirituality (Great Spirit)

Nature (Mother Earth)

Noninterference/Self-Determination

Unity, Cooperation, and Sharing

Extended Time Orientation

Oral Traditions

The Extended Family (the Tribe)

Personalismo (Intimacy)

Dignidad (Personal Honor)

Familism (Faith in Friends and Family)

Respeto (Respect)

Selflessness

Deference to Elders

Enryo (Reserve, Constraint)

Jen (Benevolence, Humanity)

group, Indians/Alaskans have been described as representing "fifty percent of the diversity" that exists in this country (Garrett & Garrett, 1994, p. 135). The majority of Indians/Alaskans have mixed backgrounds as a result of reproduction with African Americans, Asian Americans, European Americans, and Latinos (Locke, 1992; Peregoy, 1993). Thus, a variety of phenotypic characteristics are found among Native American Indians. Over half of Indians/Alaskans are concentrated in the Southwestern states of Oklahoma, California, Arizona, New Mexico, and Texas (American Association of Retired Persons [AARP], 1994).

Indians/Alaskans are a young group, with a median age of 22.9 years (Peregoy, 1993). The proportion of elderly among the Indians/Alaskans population has grown faster than in other groups; between 1980 and 1990, their numbers increased by 35% (AARP, 1994).

Indians/Alaskans form a heterogeneous group with 252 tribal languages and 365 state-recognized tribes (Garrett & Garrett, 1994). Approximately 517 tribes are recognized by the federal government (Peregoy, 1993). Among these tribes is tremendous diversity across custom, language, and family structure (Hoxie, 1996). Apache, Arikara, Blackfoot, Catawba, Cherokee, Cheyenne, Choctaw, Comanche, Cree, Creek, Erie, Eskimo, Haida, Hopi, Hupa, Iroquois, Lumbee, Mi'kmaq, Mohave, Navajo, Seminole, Shawnee, Sioux, Tlingit, and the Zuni are just a partial roll call of Indian/Alaskan people.

Because the tribe is a source of belonging and security for Indians/Alaskans, personal accomplishments are honored and supported if they serve to benefit the entire tribe or collective. Although their values vary from tribe to tribe, Indians/Alaskans believe in a Supreme Creator that is considered both male and female and is in command of all the elements of existence. Indians/Alaskans also believe that all things are connected and that all things have purpose (Garrett & Garrett, 1996). According to Garrett and Garrett (1994),

> Spirituality focuses on the harmony that comes from our connection with all parts of the universe in which everything has the purpose and value exemplary of "personhood" including plants (e.g., "tree people"), animals ("our four-legged brothers and sisters"), rocks and minerals ("rock people"), the land ("Mother Earth"), the winds ("the Four Powers"), "Father Sky," "Grandfather Sun," "Grandmother Moon," "The Red Thunder Boys." (p. 138)

Respect for the sacredness of the Creator is central to Indians'/Alaskans' harmonious relationship with nature and all things. Garrett (1998) said that "the wellness of the mind, body, spirit, and natural environment is an extension of the proper balance in the relationship of all things" (p. 78). Thus, sharing is valued over materialism as all belongs to Earth.

Elders are valued among Indians/Alaskans "because of the lifetime's worth of wisdom they have acquired" (Garrett & Garrett, 1994, p. 137). About one quarter of Indian/Alaskan elderly live on Native American Indian reservations or in Alaskan Native villages. More than half of the total Native American Indian population resides in urban areas. Because of high unemployment on the reservations, many have moved to urban areas.

Native American cultural values emanate from a spiritual center that emphasizes coexisting in harmony with nature. This entails a respect for Earth as natural medicine (Peregoy, 1993). Native people have always depended on the land, for it was life and medicine. For instance, the Paiute boiled sagebrush to relieve headaches and rheumatism. Even dandruff was cured by rubbing boiled willow leaves into the hair and scalp (Ballentine & Ballentine, 1993). Implicit in this value system is an attitude of acceptance of life as it is, as well as of that which cannot be changed (Sue & Sue, 1990). Nature, in its natural, undisturbed state, is respected, and coexisting with nature rather than seeking to control it is central. Looking back to proven traditional ways reveals a respect for the past and the contributions of the ancestral spirits. According to Peregoy (1993), "the traditional Indian/Native's system of life is intertwined with the tribe and extends further into a metaphysical belief system" (p. 172). Because Indians/Alaskans see the extended family and the tribe as taking precedence over the self (Garrett & Garrett, 1994; Gunn Allen, 1994; Locke, 1992; Peregoy, 1993), competition with others is contradictory to the primacy of sharing resources, which belong to everyone. The universe, or Mother Earth, belongs to all people. About this female energy, Paula Gunn Allen (1994) said, "There are many female gods recognized and honored by the tribes and Nations. Females were highly valued, both respected and feared and all social institutions reflected this attitude" (p. 193).

As stated earlier, acculturation influences value structures. Although Herring (1992) stated that Indian/Alaskan people are "more unalterably resistant to assimilation and integration into mainstream society than are other minority groups" (p. 135), this phenomenon does exist among some Indians/Alaskans. Persons who do not perceive their Native American Indian heritage to be salient may be more likely to deny and lack sense of pride in being Indian/Native. These persons may feel pressure to embrace majority cultural values, experience guilt feelings over not knowing about or participating in cultural activities, possess negative and stereotypical views of Indians/Alaskans, and lack a support and belief system (Zitzow & Estes as cited in Sue & Sue, 1990).

Indians/Alaskans who possess a strong sense of heritage and honor tradition, or heritage-consistent Native Americans (HCNAs), are more likely to feel secure on the reservation and to focus more on nonverbal rather than verbal communication. For example, in the Indian/Alaskan culture, a bowed head is a sign of respect, whereas in the Western culture, a bowed head may suggest a person is shy, guilty, or lying (Taylor, 1993). They may also socialize with other Indians/Alaskans as a means of honoring their culture and people. A preference may be expressed for a more fluid time orientation over a rigid one that is dictated by the future. Also, reciprocal relationships that emphasize cooperation with others and respect for tribal values based on ritual are characteristic (Gunn Allen, 1994).

The experiences of Indians/Alaskans in the United States have been fraught with problems of wide-scale genocide, cultural decimation, and Western domination. Some demographers estimate that by the 17th century, more than 50 million Native Americans of North and South America had died as a result of war, disease, imprisonment, and the inhumane behavior of Europeans (Ballentine & Ballentine, 1993). Many Indians/Alaskans experience difficulty with expectations of the U.S. culture or have distrust of the dominant culture or both (Heinrich, Corbine, & Thomas, 1990).

Partly as a result of this difficulty, alcoholism causes social problems for many Native Americans, affecting their family life, employment, and other social areas. In addition, alcohol abuse is a leading cause of health problems, including accidents, cirrhosis of the liver, suicide, and homicide (AARP, 1994). Despite these problems, commitment to peoplehood and a strong sense of identity are characteristic. Survival amid a backdrop of inhumanity has been painful and a testament to a commitment to balance and harmony.

Although they have been ignored for their inimitable contributions to the Western world, Gunn Allen (1994) reminds us of the glorious presence and irrefutable influence of Indian/Alaskan people (see the Storytelling "The Genius of the Native People"):

> During the ages when tribal societies existed in the Americas largely untouched by patriarchal oppression, they developed elaborate systems of thought that included science, philosophy, and government based on a belief in the central importance of female energies, autonomy of individuals, cooperation, human dignity, human freedom, and egalitarian distribution of status, goods, and services. Respect for others, reverence of life, and as a by-product, pacifism as a way of life. (p. 193)

LATINOS   Much can be said about the term *Hispanic*. According to Novas (1994), "'Hispanic' comes from España, Spain, the country that led conquest (as in

STORYTELLING
The Genius of the Native People

In a cave in northwestern Nevada, back in 1924, a 2,000-year-old blanket made from the skins of 600 meadow mice was found and in perfect condition to ward off the severe cold of the desert. To make this blanket, each mouse had to be carefully skinned and the fur cut into tiny strips. Then each piece of skin had to be joined and the strips sewn together (Ballentine & Ballentine, 1993).

This story is a testament to a spirit of creativity and conservation of Earth's treasures and a celebration of mindfulness, of being present in the moment. Gratitude for the Creator's provisions by not wasting any precious resources is evident.

Tracy

conquistadors) of the New world" (p. 2). This included the various Native people (Arawak, Maya, Aztecs, and Incas) whom the Spanish encountered, as well as the African people who were brought to the Caribbean and the Americas as slaves and intermarried and intermixed with the European conquistadors.

Although the *Monitor Stylebook* (cited in Kromkowski, 1994) stated that "Hispanic is an umbrella term for anyone of Spanish or Portuguese descent, in or outside the United States," Novas (1994) clarified that Brazilian Americans speak Portuguese and are of Portuguese, not Spanish, descent. Novas reiterated that, for many Latinos, "'Hispanic' is merely a bureaucratic government census term" (p. 3), with many persons preferring to be called "Latino" or "Latina," depending on gender. The term *Latino* is widely used to refer to persons with Spanish ancestry: Puerto Ricans (*Puertorriquenos*), Cubans (*Cubanos*), Central Americans and South Americans, Latin Americans (which include Dominicans [*Dominicanos*]), and Mexican Americans (*Mejicanos*). Central America is composed of Belize, Costa Rica, El Salvador, Guatemala, Honduras, Nicaragua, and Panama. South America is composed of Argentina, Bolivia, Brazil, Chile, Paraguay, Peru, and Uruguay. Columbia and Venezuela constitute northern South America. It should be noted that millions of Latinos from countries such as Argentina and Costa Rica are not of Spanish or Indian descent, but rather descend from European or Antillean nations (Beals & Beals, 1993).

The Western world's Latinos are *La Raza,* which means, "the race" or "the people." Representing nearly 10% of the U.S. population, Latinos are expected to exceed soon the number of African Americans. Although Latinos in the United States are united by the Spanish mother tongue, they do have language differences. Beals and Beals (1993) stated that the majority of Spain's citizens speak Castellano, whereas the majority of Chicanos (Mexicans) speak Pocho. According to Carballo-Dieguez (1989), many Latinos are fluent in both Spanish and English, others know very little English, others have limited knowledge of Spanish, and others speak "Spanglish," a mixture of both languages. Countries of origin among Latinos are diverse and varied. Mexican Americans make up 63% of Latinos, and their high rate of immigration has given rise to rapid population growth. *Puertorriquenos* represent 12%; Central and South Americans, 11%; other countries, 8%; and Cubans, 5% of

Latinos (Nicolau & Santiestevan, 1990). Of the 22 million Latinos living in the United States, two thirds live in California, New York, and Texas; 55% of Latinos reside in California and Texas alone (Stavans, 1995).

In addition to geographic diversity, income varies as well among Latinos. Puerto Ricans have the highest poverty rate, and Cubans have the lowest (Comas-Diaz, 1993). Yet, despite the attention often given to the high poverty rates among Latinos, substantial income gains have been made. As of 1992, nearly 50% of Latinos had incomes of $25,000 or above. This represents nearly a 200% change since 1982 (Arana-Ward, 1997).

As for educational attainment differences among Latinos, whereas the average number of years of schooling is 12.7 for non-Latinos, it is 10.8 for Mexican Americans, 12 for Puerto Ricans, and 12.4 for Cuban Americans (Stavans, 1995). Whereas the average age of non-Latinos in the United States is 33, the average age among Cuban Americans is 39; among Puerto Ricans, 27; and among Mexican Americans, 24 (Stavans, 1995).

Among the diverse group of Latinos, differences exist across geography, country of origin, race, class, traditions, acculturation, and the time and sociopolitical circumstances in which persons entered the United States (Beals & Beals, 1993; Nicolau & Santiestevan, 1990). About this diversity, Stavans (1995) said, "We Latinos have an abundance of histories, linked to a common root but with decisively different traditions. At each and every moment, these ancestral histories determine who we are and what we think" (p. 20).

Cultural heritage commonalities are strong. For instance, among most Latinos, cooperation rather than competition is stressed. The extended family and friendship networks are held in high esteem and are the basis of Latino culture (Gloria & Peregoy, 1995). Family members feel a sense of obligation to provide for, and to receive support from one another both emotionally and materially (Vasquez, 1994). In many Mexican American families, the extended family is strong and includes *compradazgo,* or godparents, and among Puerto Ricans, *compadres,* or special friends, who often act as coparents and receive a high place of honor, affection, and respect in the family (Locke, 1992). Gloria and Peregoy (1995) stated that more status is given to a person who honors family than to someone with material possessions.

Although family structure would appear to influence the decisions an individual would make, it need not negate the power and possibility of individual choice or personal honor. For instance, among Puerto Ricans, *dignidad* refers to a strong sense of self-worth and personal dignity that has enabled Puerto Ricans to withstand various forms of oppression (Locke, 1992). A focus is also placed on being in the moment, with emphasis on the present.

Family structures are often formal and hierarchical, in that deference to elders and males is practiced. Although often misunderstood as related to men's sexual prowess and women's objectification, *machismo* is a part of Latino culture. It describes stoicism, the need for *dignidad,* or dignity, *respeto*, or respect, and in some instances dominance within the family (Vasquez, 1994). Adherence to family roles, such as males outside the home and females inside, represents another value orientation practiced by some Latino families (Arredondo, 1992).

In Latino culture, a premium is placed on personal relationships (Banks, 1979). *Personalismo*, or a desire to be close, to know one another intimately, and to communicate personally rather than impersonally, represents a value orientation common to many Latinos (Arrendondo, 1992; Gloria & Peregoy, 1995). *Simpatia* is a value of smooth and harmonious interpersonal interactions (Gloria & Peregoy, 1995).

Demonstrated through loyalty for one's family, cultural pride is significant (Rendon & Robinson, 1994; see also the Storytelling "The Spirit of the Aztecs"). According to Comas-Diaz (1993), the concept of *respeto* "governs all positive reciprocal interpersonal relationships, dictating the appropriate deferential behavior toward others on the basis of age, socioeconomic position, sex, and authority status" (p. 250).

For most Latinos, the bond to Catholicism is strong. In fact, the concept of *Marianismo* "is based on the Catholic cult of the Virgin Mary, which dictates that when women become mothers they attain the status of Madonnas and, accordingly, are expected to deny themselves in favor of their children and husbands" (Vasquez, 1994, p. 202). Clearly, conflicts can emerge within this cultural value system, particularly for Latinas who may be more acculturated. Overall, the church and faith play a crucial role and shape core beliefs, such as (a) the importance of sacrifice, (b) charitability and service to others, and (c) long suffering, even in the face of adversity (Sue & Sue, 1990). As is consistent with other groups who are more oriented toward collectivism than individualism, there is a holistic connection between the mind and body. *Curanderos,* or spiritual and herbal "folk" healers, who are primarily women, practice an ancient Native American art (Novas, 1994). They hold special status in many Mexican and Mexican American communities and often work in consultation on psychiatric cases with priests and other religious authorities (Arredondo, 1992). Given the rich history of the Aztecs as herbalists, healers, botanists, and medical doctors (Padilla, 1984), it is not surprising that their descendants would have the gift of healing.

Communication styles represent a significant part of the way meanings are expressed and interpreted. Many Latinos tend to speak softly, avoid eye contact when listening to or speaking with persons perceived as having high status, and interject less. Often, the manner of expression is low-key and indirect (Sue & Sue, 1990). For many Latino youths and adults, being linguistic minorities represents a real barrier to education and employment.

Colorism refers to differential and often inequitable treatment because of skin color hue (Robinson & Ward, 1995). As with African American communities, colorism affects Latino communities. Sue and Sue (1990) indicated that "the more a person resembles an Indian, the more prejudice and discrimination he or she will encounter" (p. 298). A variety of hues—white, black, brown, and red—compose the Latino population. This attests to roots from Africa, Spain, other parts of Europe, and with Native Americans.

ASIAN AMERICANS   Approximately 7 million Asian Americans live in the United States. Highly concentrated in the West, 56% of the Asian population resides in this part of the country. California has 36% of the Asian population alone. Hawaii and New York rank second and third in terms of states with the largest Asian populations.

STORYTELLING
The Spirit of the Aztecs

Angelina was born in Mexico. Her mom had 16 children, but only 10 survived. Her father worked in the United States for 10 years until he was able to bring his wife and all his children to be with him. Angie was the only Latina in her school. She graduated from elementary, junior high, and high school without being able to read or write. She would make tortillas for the family from 4 to 6 A.M. She said, "You become a woman by learning to cook and clean house." At 18, she married. For her, "marriage was a way out." Five months after she married, she became pregnant with her first son. She said, "My kids were the best thing that happened to me." When she would talk with her mother about her feelings of marital dissatisfaction, her mother would say, "Tears are a part of the marriage." Angie became involved in a home-building program in which she helped build her own home. She said, "While digging the foundation . . . at each step, while I was doing that, I felt that Angie, in a way, herself, was being built." Her brother encouraged her to go to college. Although she said she was terrified that first year, she said she was happy. Through her studies, she identified with her Aztec ancestors and started to feel their power inside her. Her dream is to open her own agency to help Latinas get into higher education.

Angie's story, told in the video *Stories of Change: Angelina,* by Thereasa Tollini (1992), details the struggle of many migrant families. It is also a celebration of hard work, communion with ancestors, and forging an identity.

Tracy

Tremendous diversity is found within the Asian community, which represents one of the fastest growing groups in the country. Uba (1994) said, "The term 'Asian culture' is technically a misnomer. Although Confucianism, Taoism, and Buddhism, underlie many Asian cultural values—and although the tenets of these belief systems are shared by many cultures—there are also significant differences among Asian cultures" (p. 12). Ethnicity, migration or generational status, assimilation, acculturation, facility with the English language, political climate in country of origin, religion, socioeconomic status, occupation, transferability of skills, foreign credentials to the United States, and educational level are the sources of differences within the group (Sue & Sue, 1990; Tsai & Uemura, 1988).

Chinese Americans had been the largest ethnic group among Asians. As of 1990, however, Filipinos surpassed them. The other ethnic groups represented within the United States are Japanese, Asian Indians, and Koreans. Within a 13-year period, nearly 1 million Southeast Asian refugees entered the United States. Southeast Asia represents the Asian subcontinent south of China and east of India. Although persons from Vietnam, Laos, and Cambodia are neighbors, the countries of Indonesia, Malaysia, Thailand, Burma, Bhutan, and Bangladesh are also included (Tien, 1994). These groups are less researched and perhaps less well known than other groups who have lived in the United States for several generations. Asian Indians, Guamanians, Samoans, and the Maori (indigenous people of New Zealand) are also Asian.

According to Sandhu (1997), more than 40 cultural groups compose Asian and Pacific Islander Americans. Pacific Islanders encompass dispersed areas, including Australia, New Zealand, Tasmania, Polynesia, Fiji Islands, and the islets of Micronesia, Melanesia, and extending through New Guinea. Uba (1994) indicated they have been rarely studied by psychologists.

Values common to many Asian ethnic groups include emphasis on harmony in relationships, emotional restraint because emotional expression may be interpreted as a sign of immaturity, precedence of group interests over individual interests, extended family, deference to authority, obedience to and respect for parents, emphasis on hard work, fulfilling obligations, and high value associated with education (Sandhu, 1997; Uba, 1994). Despite diversity among Asians, certain ethnic groups share some similarities, such as the Chinese and the Japanese. Sue and Sue (1995) said,

> In both cultures, the families are patriarchal. Parent to child communications are formal and flow downward. Relationships among family members are well defined and members' position are highly interdependent. . . . An individual's behavior reflects upon the entire family. Control of the children is maintained by fostering feelings of shame and guilt. (p. 74)

Restraint of emotions represents a value for many Asian Americans. This is not to be confused with the absence of a sense of humor; however, *enryo,* or reserve and constraint, is an important value and represents a primary mode of communication. Uba (1994) said,

> This syndrome may be manifested in a number of ways, as in a hesitancy to speak up in class or to openly contradict a person in a position of authority . . . Another part of the *enryo* syndrome is a modest devaluation of oneself and one's possessions. (p. 18)

Family is given respect and honor. Among the Vietnamese, for example, it is not uncommon for multiple generations to reside collectively in one home. Elders are honored, respected, and cared for because of the importance of family. According to McFadden (1993), Asians tend to believe that marriage is the most important event that can occur in a person's life and is perceived to be long-lasting, until the end of one's life, with divorce being considered the greatest possible tragedy that could occur.

Among the Chinese, selflessness, obedience to authority, or deference to the collective unit is a primary value and is manifested in relations with elders or those in authority. The concept of *jen,* or personhood, is emphasized (Pedersen, 1994). Humility is regarded as a cultural value, as is the notion of loss of face. Leong, Wagner, and Kim (1995) stated that communication styles among Asians allow participants to maintain face. Therefore, direct communication styles, reflective of a Western style and involving confrontation and challenges, tend to be less desirable.

Of all ethnic groups, the Chinese have been in the United States the longest, as they were the first Asian ethnic group to be recruited to the West Coast during the

1840s. At that time, there was a need for cheap labor to work on the transcontinental railroads (Tsai & Uemura, 1988). U.S. policymaker Aaron H. Palmer predicted that with a connection to the East Coast, San Francisco would become the "great emporium of our commerce on the Pacific" (Takaki, 1993, p. 192). Chinese were perceived to be more suited for "cleaning wild lands and raising every species of agricultural product" (Takaki, 1993, p. 192). Many Chinese were motivated to go to America, given the floods that were making it difficult to harvest their crops, as well as political situations, such as taxation and ethnic conflict. Finding gold in California was also a dream of many Chinese (Cao & Novas, 1995).

Understandably, there are differences in the values expressed in Asian cultures and in the United States. Hsu (1953) accurately observed that "the most important thing to Americans is what parents should do for the children: to Chinese, what children should do for their parents" (p. 72). Locke (1992) said that "in the traditional Japanese ethical system, the central value is duty—social obligation and social responsibility" (p. 74). *Jen,* a Confucian virtue, refers to responsibility for kin as expressed through respect, loyalty, and love (Dana, 1993).

Asian newcomers speak hundreds of languages and dialects and practice a broad array of religions. Many ethnic Asian newcomers are more likely to identify with specific national or regional ties (e.g., Vietnamese, Korean, Hmong, Punjabi Sikh, Cantonese, Taiwanese).

Despite any initial language barriers, the successes and creativity of many newly migrated groups from Asia are inspiring. These have been attributed to the informal network system of valuing the group, being a member of the group, and attending to the needs of others through sharing financial and human resources, from employment information to housing, for the betterment of all (Chang, 1996; Sue & Sue, 1990). Among some Asian groups, even among newly arrived immigrants, a substantial number have higher education and substantial career experience. Yet, Sue and Sue (1990) cautioned against acceptance of the myth and stereotypes that Asians in America are "model minorities" who have no difficulties (see the Storytelling "Hope and Justice"). About this myth, Takaki (1994b) stated,

> Asian-American "success" has emerged as the new stereotype for this ethnic minority. While this image has led many teachers and employers to view Asians as intelligent and hardworking and has opened some opportunities, it has also been harmful. Asian Americans find their diversity as individuals denied. (p. 57)

This myth often interferes with Asian American communities receiving the necessary emotional and financial resources and creates division among groups of color as one group is pitted against another. Some suffer because of unemployment, and some newly immigrated groups have very high poverty rates and difficulties with social adjustment. Moreover, Asians also suffer discrimination on the job, and career choices are skewed because of racial inequities. Educationally, some Asians have problems with the English language on standardized tests, and conflicts exist between American and Asian values. For some youths, the pressure to succeed academically can cause enormous stress. Chang's (1996) research on coping styles of Asian students is a welcome contribution to the literature, given the stress experienced by many Asian youths. He found in his study of 111 Asian college students and 111 White college students that the Asian students used more problem avoidance and social withdrawal than the White students. Also, the Asian students, though more pessimistic in their orientations than the White students, were not less optimistic. Amid the expectation of negative events, the Asian students employed active coping styles.

AFRICAN AMERICANS   As the largest group of color in the United States, the 32 million African Americans come from diverse cultures, including Africa, the Caribbean, central Europe, and South America. The majority of African Americans reside in the southern part of the United States despite their diverse origins and the great migration North during two periods. First, World War I created a huge demand for unskilled labor in the urban North; recruiters went to the South to bring Black workers to northern cities such as Pittsburgh, Chicago, Detroit, and Indianapolis. Between 1916 and 1919, 500,000 African Americans migrated North (Stewart, 1996). After World War II, nearly 5 million Blacks went North between 1940 and 1960.

The term *Black* is too narrow to describe adequately the "rich history of the peoples who came to the United States from the continent of Africa" (Locke, 1992, p. 15). Although history books focus on slavery, the exalted west African empires of Ghana, Mali, and Songhai were in existence between A.D. 500 and 1600 (Christian, 1995). Each had a pwerful king and was very wealthy, with an abundance of gold, thriving agriculture, and successful trading efforts. The year 1619 is designated as the date when the first African settlers reached North America; however, this small group of 20 were not the first Africans to arrive in North America. Estevanico was one of America's Black Spanish explorers. A member of the expedition of Pánfilo de Narváez, in 1538 he explored the area that became Arizona and New Mexico (Christian, 1995).

The median age of African Americans is 24.9, with half of the population under the age of 25. Over three quarters (75%) of the population have a high school

STORYTELLING
Hope and Justice

Lau v. Nichols, a 1974 landmark court case, involved non-English-speaking Chinese students. These students filed a successful lawsuit against the San Francisco Board of Education for failing to provide equal educational opportunity for all students. This lawsuit mandated bilingual-bicultural education in the United States; yet, Asian Americans are rarely acknowledged as playing a pivotal role in defending the rights of limited-English-speaking students and for "recognizing the pluralistic nature of our society" (Wei, 1993, p. 3).

The cultural styles of humility, *jen,* nonconfrontation, and interdependence within the group are evident from the persevering and groundbreaking work of Asians in the bilingual-bicultural language movement.

Tracy

diploma (U.S. Bureau of the Census, 1997). Over 12% have completed community college or a bachelor's degree or both (U.S. Bureau of the Census, 1997). In 1997, 54.2% of African Americans ages 25 to 34 had never been married, compared with 34.5% of all people (Lugaila, 1998). Over one third (34%) of African Americans were married, with their spouses still present.

To understand the value system of African Americans, one needs to examine a variety of sociopolitical factors. For instance, in 1996 the poverty rate for African Americans was 28.4% (Lamison-White, 1997), compared with approximately 11% for the nation at large. Although 3% of African American men are in jail, they represent 46% of the prison population (Hacker, 1992). Health outcomes are related to lifestyle choices, such as smoking and nutrition. For instance, of the entire U.S. population, African Americans have the highest overall rates of cancer (Belgrave, 1992). Despite a backdrop of struggle and hardship, strengths of persistence, forgiveness, and resilience are evident (Exum & Moore, 1993).

According to Nobles (1972), African Americans' sense of self and cultural traditions have been derived from several cultural and philosophical premises shared with West African tribes. Myers (1991) states:

> Afrocentricity refers to a worldview that believes reality is both spiritual and material at once . . . with highest value on positive interpersonal relationships between men/women; self knowledge is assumed to be the basis of all knowledge, and one knows through symbolic imagery and rhythm. (p. 19)

Within Africentric thought, the self is extended in unity with others and emphasis is on the collective. An African proverb, "I am because we are and since we are, therefore I am," summarizes the saliency of the collective. Among some African Americans, *consubstantiation,* or the sense that everything within the universe is connected as a part of a whole, is a way of seeing the world (Parham, 1992). Myers (1991) stated that, in the Africentric paradigm, spirit and matter are one and is a representation of one spirit manifesting good.

Common values that many African Americans share include valuing family, which encompasses the extended family and outside blood relatives; education as a means of self-help; a strong work ethic; and maintaining a strong connection with the church. Historically, the Black church has been a focal point in the African American community and an advocate of social and political change. Although a variety of religions and spiritual expressions exist among African Americans, the majority of African Americans are Christians.

Worldview refers to the way people make meaning. African Americans tend to have a nonlinear, or present time, orientation with less emphasis on particulars, a spirit of coexistence, and harmony with nature (Locke, 1992; Sue & Sue, 1990). Relations with people tend to be collateral, as opposed to individualistic (Sue & Sue, 1990; see also the Storytelling "Sweet Africa"). Communication patterns are not limited to verbal dialogue, and these tend not to be strictly linear as in Western society (Exum & Moore, 1993). Body movement, postures, gestures, and facial expressions represent dominant patterns of communication within the African American community. Dialect is a cultural element that has survived (Locke, 1992).

Adapted from Hilliard's work, Exum and Moore (1993) summarized elements of African American worldview. These include emphasis on the whole, as opposed to the parts; preference for approximations over accuracy; focus on people rather than things; and acceptance and integration with the environment. In addition to these values is a respect for nature and emphasis on groupness, and an extended or present time orientation.

The *Nguzo Saba,* or classical African values, also provide insight into African American values (Karenga, 1980). They are discussed in greater detail in Chapter 15. The first and third principles are *Umoja* and *Ujima* and refer to unity and collective work and responsibility. These principles endorse solidarity, harmony, cooperation, and connection with others toward a common destiny. The second principle, *Kujichagalia,* means self-determination and naming for the self who the self will be, despite others' definitions. *Ujaama*, the fourth principle, refers to cooperative economics, in which resources are shared for the good of all. Within an Africentric framework, the I is not separate from the We. *Nia,* the fifth principle, is purpose that benefits not only the self but also the collective, for which one has responsibility. The sixth principle is *Kuumba,* or creativity. Creativity is inextricably linked to imagination, ingenuity, and leaving the world a better place than it was when you first arrived. *Imani,* or faith, is the last principle and encompasses the past, present, and future.

African tradition includes a strong tie between the living and the world of the dead in defining the scope of community. J. A. Opoku (personal communication, April 3, 1994) said about Ghanaian culture, "The dead are still with us."

IMPLICATIONS FOR COUNSELORS

A presentation of some dominant values embodied in the U.S. culture can provoke dissonance. The English language often equates black with bad luck, death, tragedy,

STORYTELLING
Sweet Africa

Cocoa beans are sweet. I realized this while in Ghana, West Africa. Talking with Kofi Opoku on a beautiful, sunny day, we stood under a cocoa tree and enjoyed the sweetness of the beans fresh off the tree. I remembered Kofi saying as he opened the fruit against the ground, "Who would have thought that dark bitter cocoa could come from this white sweet bean. Africa is a wonder."

I watched the sense of wonder, awe, respect, and pride on his face as he affirmed the vast, rich, and irrefutable wonders of Africa.

Tracy

and illegality. Consider *black market, blackball, black comedy, black sheep,* and *black Thursday* (one of the days of the week that the stock market crashed). Even the generic use of *he* or *mankind* to encompass women, particularly in religious contexts, continues to be widespread. The language of *wheelchair-bound* evokes images of being imprisoned by one's natural body. *Minority,* a derivative of *minor,* is synonymous with *ancillary, frivolous,* and *inconsequential.* For this reason, *minority* is not used in this work to describe people.

Values emerge from philosophical tenets, and the presenting issues in counseling originate from cultural beliefs. Unhealthy self-reliance that equates asking for help with weakness needs to be resisted because the ability to seek assistance is a strength, not a defect. This has particular relevance for men, who tend to be socialized to think that needing and seeking help is not masculine (Good & Mintz, 1990). Males often are taught and thus learn to flee from any behavior that can be construed as feminine or "other" (Bem, 1993). Yet, as a primary value, individualism has implications for counseling. Extreme individualism endorses the notion that one is independent of others. Although this may be true to some extent, collective-oriented people recognize their interdependence with others.

Despite people's need for one another, the current value of the nuclear and patriarchal family structure prevails. Less than 15% of Americans have an arrangement wherein the husband works outside the home and the wife remains in the home to care for the children without earning a paycheck (Renzetti & Curran, 1992). Single-parent households, families headed by grandparents, and parents who are gay or lesbian describe an increasingly larger share of families. Simply put, cultural values can be a by-product of an ideal more than reality. Knowledge of cultural dynamics may enable people to see the contradictions between stated values and behavior (see the case study "Women in Counseling"). Thus, counselors can support clients in becoming aware of how self-construction is culturally influenced and largely subconscious.

CASE STUDY
Women in Counseling

Carol Mason is a single, 34-year-old African American community counselor at a mental health agency. She grew up in the Northeast but lives in Virginia. Carol is active in her church and is also involved in professional organizations that seek to empower women and people of color.

Her client, Lin, is an unmarried Vietnamese female in her late 20s. She came to the United States from her homeland when she was 6 years old. Although Lin has a master's degree and a full-time job, she lives at home with her parents. Lin would like to move out but feels conflicted in her decision. This is Carol's first experience with an Asia-born client. Lin presents with frustration about her work and family situation.

She has been overlooked for promotions, and her parents do not know that she has come to see a counselor. Lin would also like to move in with a man she has been dating, but she knows that her parents would disapprove of this decision.

Carol assesses that Lin has low assertiveness skills and autonomy conflicts, which explain her living situation. Carol believes that Lin's quiet demeanor makes her largely invisible on the job and easy to be overlooked. Carol encourages Lin to do some role-play to rehearse how to tell her parents she is planning to move in with her boyfriend. Carol believes that this is important for Lin to live authentically. She also plans to rehearse Lin asking her employer for a raise. Much to Carol's dismay, Lin does not return to counseling after the first session.

QUESTIONS

1. What were Carol's value orientations?
2. What were Lin's value orientations?
3. What might have been a more culturally appropriate assessment for Carol to have made?
4. How did Carol's therapeutic intentions conflict with Lin's culture?

DISCUSSION AND INTEGRATION
The Client, Lin

Lin's living situation need not be reflective of emotional dependence. The belief that it is, is culturally driven. According to Uba (1994), Southeast Asian girls are raised more strictly than boys and are given less freedom in their activities. Moreover, Southeast Asian children are generally taught that relationship to family is crucial and comes with certain obligations. Granted, Lin may be low in emotional autonomy; however, culture plays a powerful role in shaping peoples' lives. Lin's religion affects her view of the world. More specifically, the basic teachings of Buddhism say that there is suffering, the first Noble Truth, but there is also understanding the roots of suffering, the cessation of suffering, and being on the path to refrain from that which causes suffering (Nhat Hanh, 1998). For Lin, close and collateral family ties are valued to the extent that her living arrangement is preferred by her parents, but not by her personally.

Lin is not very verbal. This could be a result of personality and cultural dimensions. Ibrahim (1992) indicated that "most immigrants from Asia are socialized to be stoic and uncomplaining" (p. 49). Bradshaw (1994) discussed the cultural inconsistency of anger among Asian women, given the values of deference and meekness. It is important, then, that Carol not presume that Lin is resistant or an involuntary client. Uba (1994) said,

Many Asian Americans are hesitant to discuss their feelings and problems openly. Some of the same attitudes that discourage Asian Americans from seeking mental health services discourage them, once they are in therapy, from discussing their problems. (p. 222)

Chow (1994) informed us of four cultural dilemmas facing Asian American women: (a) obedience versus independence, (b) collective (or familial) versus individual interest, (c) fatalism versus change, and (d) self-control versus self-expression or spontaneity (p. 186). Each of these forces was operating in Lin's life.

The Counselor, Carol

As a contrast, Carol believed that Lin could not only change her situation but also rise above it (mastery orientation) by altering her belief system. In this situation, Carol was not as sensitive to multicultural concerns. If she had been, she would have understood Lin's cultural orientation and the importance of being interdependent with her family. Carol would have also understood the challenges facing Lin as a professional woman of color. Contending with racism, sexism, family expectations, few role models, and intimacy issues represent some of the real-life events that Lin has in her life (Comas-Diaz & Greene, 1994).

Carol is African American, and her culture is more likely to support a direct type of communication style. For this reason, Carol encouraged Lin to engage in role play that would ready her to be assertive and confrontational. Carol's approach was centered in Gestalt and rational emotive behavioral therapy. She emphasized the role play, wanted to clear Lin of any resentments and unfinished business she may have toward her parents, and sought to replace irrational cognitive structures with those that were more functional. In Lin's culture, however, deference to the family is paramount.

Although Carol, too, comes from a collectivistic orientation, as an American and most likely an acculturated, independent woman she has undoubtedly been influenced by Western thought, which encourages individualism and living one's life as an autonomous adult. It would have been beneficial for Carol to consult with Asian colleagues, to acquire an understanding of how culture influences problem orientation and resolve, and to respect the differences between her value orientations and that of her Vietnamese client.

SUMMARY

This chapter addressed common values in the culture at large and values particular among African Americans, Asian Americans, Indians/Alaskans, and Latinos. A summary of these values can be found in Figure 2.1 and 2.2. The goal of this discussion was not to elevate one system or philosophical paradigm above the other. Yet, it is essential for the reader to discern that values do not emanate from a vacuum, but rather are influenced by worldview, cultural ideology, and personal philosophy. Individualism was discussed at length because of its primacy in American society and its interface with other themes, such as empiricism, competition, and materialism. The importance of counselors knowing their personal value orientations to determine how these may interfere with and/or strengthen counseling was stressed.

REFERENCES

American Association of Retired Persons (AARP). (1994). *A portrait of older minorities.* Washington, DC: Author.

Arana-Ward, M. (1997). Magazines, Latinos find themselves on the same page. In J. A. Kromkowski (Ed.), *Race and ethnic relations 97–98* (pp. 125–127). Guilford, CT: Dushkin.

Arredondo, P. (1992). *Latina/Latino value orientations: Tape 1. Cultural considerations for working more effectively with Latin Americans.* Amherst, MA: Microtraining and Multicultural Development.

Ballentine, B., & Ballentine, I. (1993). *The Native Americans: An illustrated history.* Atlanta, GA: Turner.

Banks, J. A. (1979). *Teaching strategies for ethnic studies.* Boston: Allyn & Bacon.

Beals, M. J., & Beals, K. L. (1993). Transcultural counseling and the Hispanic community. In J. McFadden (Ed.), *Transcultural counseling: Bilateral and international perspectives* (pp. 213–238). Alexandria, VA: American Counseling Association.

Belenky, M. F., Clinchy, B. C., Goldberger, N. R., & Tarule, J. M. (1986). *Women's ways of knowing: The development of self, voice, and mind.* New York: Basic Books.

Belgrave, F. Z. (1992). Improving health outcomes of African Americans: A challenge for African American psychologists. In A. Burlew, W. Banks, H. McAdoo, & D. Azibo (Eds.), *African American psychology: Theory, research, and practice* (pp. 356–358). Newbury Park, CA: Sage.

Bem, S. L. (1993). *The lenses of gender: Transforming the debate on sexuality inequality.* New Haven, CT: Yale University Press.

Bradshaw, C. (1994). Asian and Asian American women: Historical and political considerations in psychotherapy. In L. Comas-Diaz & B. Greene (Eds.), *Women of color: Integrating ethnic and gender identities* (pp. 72–113). New York: Guilford Press.

Bronstein, P., & Quina, K. (1988). *Teaching a psychology of people.* Washington, DC: American Psychological Association.

Brookins, C. B. & Robinson, T. L. (1995). Rites of passage as resistance to oppression. *Western Journal of Black Studies, 19*(3), 172–185.

Brown, L. M., & Gilligan, C. (1992). *Meeting at the crossroads: The landmark book about the turning points in girls' and women's lives.* New York: Ballantine Books.

Camilleri, C.,& Malewska-Peyre, H.(1997). Socialization and identity strategies. In J. Berry, P. Dasen, & T. S. Sarawathi (Eds.), *Cross-cultural psychology* (Vol. 2, pp. 41–68). Boston: Allyn & Bacon.

Cao, L., & Novas, H. (1996). *Everything you need to know about Asian-American history.* New York: Penguin.

Carballo-Dieguez, A. (1989). Hispanic culture, gay male culture, and AIDS: Counseling implications. *Journal of Counseling & Development, 68,* 26–30.

Castenada, A. (1984). Traditionalism, modernism, and ethnicity. In J. Martinez & R. Mendoza (Eds.), *Chicano psychology* (pp. 35–40). Orlando, FL: Academic Press.

Chang, E. C. (1996). Cultural differences in optimism, pessimism, and coping: Predictors of subsequent adjustment in Asian American and Caucasian American college students. *Journal of Counseling Psychology, 43,* 113–123.

Chow, E. N-L. (1994). The feminist movement: Where are all the Asian American women? In R. Takaki (Ed.), *From different shores: Perspectives on race and ethnicity in America* (2nd ed., pp. 184–191). New York: Oxford University Press.

Christian, C. M. (1995). *Black saga: The African American experience (a chronology).* Boston: Houghton Mifflin.

Comas-Diaz, L. (1993). Hispanic Latino communities: Psychological implications. In D. Atkinson, G. Morten, & D. W. Sue (Eds.), *Counseling American minorities: A cross-cultural perspective* (pp. 245–263). Madison, WI: Brown and Benchmark.

Comas-Diaz, L., & Greene, B.(1994). Women of color with professional. In L. Comas-Diaz & B. Greene (Eds.), *Women of color: Integrating ethnic and gender identities* (pp. 347–388). New York: Guilford Press.

Dana, R. H.(1993). *Multicultural assessment perspectives for professional psychology.* Boston: Allyn & Bacon.

Exum, H. A., & Moore, Q. L. (1993). Transcultural counseling from African-American perspectives. In J. McFadden (Ed.), *Transcultural counseling: Bilateral and international perspectives* (pp. 193–212). Alexandria, VA: American Counseling Association.

Fordham, S. (1990). Racelessness as a factor in Black students' school success: Pragmatic strategy or Pyrrhic victory? *Harvard Education Review, 57,* 54–84.

Fost, D. (1998). American Indians in the 1990s. In J. A. Kromkowski (Ed.), *Race and ethnic relations, 98-99* (pp. 63–65). Guilford, CT: Dushkin.

Garrett, J. T., & Garrett, M. W. (1994). The path of good medicine: Understanding and counseling Native American Indians. *Journal of Multicultural Counseling & Development, 22,* 134–144.

Garrett, J. T., & Garrett, M. W. (1996). *Medicine of the Cherokee: The way right relationship.* Sante Fe, NM: Bear.

Garrett, M. (1998). *Walking on the wind: Cherokee teachings for harmony and balance.* Santa Fe, NM: Bar.

Gloria, A. M., & Peregoy, J. J. (1995). Counseling Latino alcohol and other substance users/abusers: Cultural considerations for counselors. *Journal of Substance Abuse Treatment, 13,* 1–8.

Good, G. E., & Mintz, L. B. (1990). Gender role conflict and depression in college men: Evidence for compounded risk. *Journal of Counseling & Development, 69,* 17–21.

Gunn Allen, P. (1994). Who is your mother? Red roots of White feminism. In R. Takaki (Ed.), *From different shores: Perspectives on race and ethnicity in America* (2nd ed., pp. 192–198). New York: Oxford University Press.

Hacker, A. (1992). *Two nations: Black and White, separate, hostile, unequal*. New York: Ballentine Books.

Heinrich, R. K., Corbine, J. L., & Thomas, K. R. (1990). Counseling Native Americans. *Journal of Counseling & Development, 69,* 128–133.

Herring, R. D. (1992). Understanding Native American values: Process and content concerns for counselors. *Counseling and Values, 34,* 134–137.

Hoxie, F. E. (1996). *North American Indians: Native American history, culture, and life from paleo-Indians to the present.* Boston: Houghton Mifflin.

Hsu, F. L. K. (1953). *American and Chinese: Two ways of life.* New York: Abeland-Schuman.

Ibrahim, F. (1992). A course on Asian American women: Identity development issues. *Women's Studies Quarterly, 1&2,* 41–57.

Ibrahim, F., Ohnishi, H., & Sandhu, D. S. (1997). Asian American identity development: A culture-specific model for South Asian Americans. *Journal of Multicultural Counseling & Development, 25(1),* 34–50.

Kabat-Zinn, J. (1994). *Wherever you go, there you are: Mindfulness meditation in everyday life.* New York: Hyperion.

Kagitcibasi, (1997). Individualism and collectivism. In J. Berry, M. Segall, & C. Kagitcibasi (Eds.), *Cross-cultural psychology: Vol. 3. Social and behavioral applications* (pp. 1–49). Boston: Allyn & Bacon.

Karenga, M. (1980). *Kawaida theory.* Los Angeles: Kawaida.

Katz, J. H. (1985) The sociopolitical nature of counseling. *Counseling Psychologist, 13,* 615–624.

Kluckhohn, F. R., & Strodtbeck, F. L. (1961). *Variations in value orientations.* Evanston, IL: Row, Peterson.

Kromkowski, J. A. (1994). *Race and ethnic relations, 94–95.* Guilford, CT: Dushkin.

Lamison-White, L. (1997). Poverty in the United States: 1996. *Current Population Reports, P. 60-198.*

Leong, F. T. L., Wagner, N. S., & Kim, H. H. (1995). Group counseling expectations among Asian American students: The role of culture-specific factors. *Journal of Counseling Psychology, 42,* 217–222.

Lin, J. C. H. (1994). How long do Chinese Americans stay in psychotherapy? *Journal of Counseling Psychology, 41,* 288–291.

Locke, D. C. (1992). *Increasing multicultural understanding: A comprehensive model.* Newbury Park, CA: Sage.

Lugaila, T. A. (1998). *Marital status and living arrangements* (P-20-508). Washington, DC: U.S. Bureau of the Census.

McBride, M. C. (1990). Autonomy and the struggle for female identity: Implications for counseling women. *Journal of Counseling & Development, 69,* 22–26.

McFadden, J. (1993). *Transcultural counseling: Bilateral and international perspectives.* Alexandria, VA: American Counseling Association.

Myers, L. J. (1991). Expanding the psychology of knowledge optimally: The importance of world view revisited. In R. Jones (Ed.), *Black psychology* (2nd ed., pp. 15–28). Berkeley, CA: Cobb & Henry.

Nhat Hanh, T. (1998). *The heart of the Buddha's teaching.* Berkeley, CA: Parallax Press.

Nicolau, S., & Santiestevan, S. (1990). *The Hispanic almanac.* New York: Hispanic Policy Development Project.

Nobles, W. (1972). African philosophy: Foundations for Black psychology. In R. H. Jones (Ed.), *Black psychology*. New York: Harper & Row.

Novas, H. (1994). *Everything you need to know about Latino history*. New York: Penguin.

Padilla, A. M.(1984). Synopsis of the history of Chicano psychology. In J. Martinez & R. Mendoza (Eds.), *Chicano psychology* (pp. 1–19). Orlando, FL: Academic Press.

Page, R. C., & Berkow, D. N. (1991). Concepts of the self: Western and Eastern perspectives. *Journal of Multicultural Counseling & Development, 19,* 83–93.

Parham, T. (1992). *Counseling African Americans* [Video]. Amherst, MA: Microtraining and Multicultural Development.

Pedersen, P. (1994). *A handbook for developing multicultural awareness*. Alexandria, VA: American Counseling Association.

Peregoy, J. J.(1993). Transcultural counseling with American Indians and Alaskan Natives: Contemporary issues for consideration. In J. McFadden (Ed.), *Transcultural counseling: Bilateral and international perspectives* (pp. 163–191). Alexandria, VA: American Counseling Association.

Pinderhughes, E. (1989). *Understanding race, ethnicity, and power: The key to efficacy in clinical practice*. New York: Free Press.

Rendon, L. I., & Robinson, T. L. (1994). A diverse America: Implications for minority seniors. In W. Hartel, S. Schwartz, S. Blue, & J. Gardner (Eds.), *Ready for the real world: Senior year experience series* (pp. 170–188). Belmont, CA: Wadsworth.

Renzetti, C. M., & Curran, D. J. (1992). *Women, men, and society*. Boston: Allyn & Bacon.

Robinson, T. L., & Ward, J. V. (1991). A belief in self far greater than anyone's disbelief: Cultivating resistance among African American adolescents. *Women & Therapy, 11,* 87–103.

Sandhu, D. S. (1997). Psychocultural profiles of Asian and Pacific Islander Americans: Implications for counseling and psychotherapy. *Journal of Multicultural Counseling & Development, 25,* 1, 7–22.

Stavans, I. (1995). *The Hispanic condition: Reflections on culture and identity in America*. New York: Harper Perennial.

Stewart, J. C. (1996). *1001 things everyone should know about African American history*. New York: Doubleday.

Sue, D. W. (1989). *Cultural identity development* [Video]. Amherst, MA: Microtraining and Multicultural Development.

Sue, D. W., & Sue, D. (1990). *Counseling the culturally different: Theory and practice*. New York: John Wiley.

Sue, D. W., & Sue, D. (1995). Asian Americans. In N. Vaac, S. B. Devaney, & J. Witmer (Eds.), *Experiences and counseling multicultural and diverse populations* (3rd ed., pp. 63–90). Bristol, PA: Accelerated Development.

Takaki, R. (1993). *A different mirror: A history of multicultural America*. Boston: Back Bay Books.

Takaki, R. (1994a). *A different mirror: A history of multicultural America*. Boston: Little, Brown.

Takaki, R. (1994b). The myth of the "model minority." In R. C. Monk (Ed.), *Taking sides: Clashing views on controversial issues in race and ethnicity* (pp. 55–61). Guilford, CT: Dushkin.

Taylor, O. C. (1993). Clinical practice as a social occasion. In D. E. Battles, *Communication disorders in multicultural populations*. Boston: Andover Medical.

Tien, L. (1994). Southeast Asian American refugee women. In L. Comas-Diaz & B. Greene (Eds.), *Women of color: Integrating ethnic and gender identities* (pp. 479–503). New York: Guilford Press.

Tollini, T. (1992). *Stories of change: Angelina* [Video]. San Francisco: New Day.

Tolman, D. L. (1991). Adolescent girls, women, and sexuality: Discerning dilemmas of desire. *Women & Therapy, 11,* 55–69.

Tsai, M., & Uemura, A. (1988). Asian Americans: The struggles, the conflicts, and the successes. In P. Bronstein & K. Quina (Eds.), *Teaching a psychology of people* (pp. 125–133). Washington, DC: American Psychological Association.

Uba, L. (1994). *Asian Americans: Personality patterns, identity, and mental health.* New York: Guilford Press.

U.S. Bureau of the Census. (1997). *Selected characteristics of the population by race* (Current Population Survey). Washington, DC: Author.

Vasquez, M. J. T. (1994). Latinas. In L. Comas-Dias & B. Greene (Eds.), *Women of color* (pp. 114–138). New York: Guilford Press.

Wei, W. (1993). *The Asian American movement.* Philadelphia: Temple University Press.

Zuckerman, M. (1990). Some dubious premises in research and theory on racial differences. *American Psychologist, 45,* 1297–1303.

Chapter 3

Statused Identities

When one cannot influence a situation, it is an act of wisdom to withdraw.

From the I Ching

The counseling event is affected by the perceptions that clients and counselors have about identity, particularly those constructs that are visible. For this reason, it is necessary to examine attitudes about sources of difference and to ascertain their subsequent impact on counseling effectiveness. This chapter explores sources of human differences. That these identities have status in U.S. society is conveyed via the Robinson model on discourses. Implications for counselors and their client populations are emphasized throughout.

IDENTITIES AS STATUS: THE ROBINSON MODEL ON DISCOURSES

More than 50 years ago in a classical piece, Hughes (1945) addressed dilemmas of occupational and ascribed status. He stated that occupational or vocational status has a complex set of supplementary characteristics that come to be expected of its incumbents. For example, often, it is expected that a receptionist will be a female. Such expectations are largely unconscious as people do not systematically expect that certain people will occupy given positions. Yet, through a process of cultural socialization from the media, educational systems, clergy, and family, people "carry in their minds" the auxiliary traits associated with many specific positions available in society. Persons who newly occupy prestigious positions contend with ongoing suspicions from those who have maintained these positions and from those who have observed these others occupying such positions. That people are not qualified and that they have their jobs because of affirmative action and not as a result of their own merit underlie this thinking. Although modified to a certain degree, as new groups occupy positions that had been held almost exclusively by one racial and/or gender group, stereotypes do not completely disappear. It is possible to internalize negative stereotypes and to embody the belief that luck or quotas, not merit or skill, were responsible for occupational success.

In the society about which Hughes spoke, race membership was a status-determining trait. This was the case because race tended to overpower any other variable that might run counter to it, such as vocational achievement. Because racism and sexism are interlocking paradigms of oppression, gender membership, for example, is also a status-determining trait. Despite affirmative action and the women's movement, Hughes's observation has contemporary relevance.

According to Reynolds and Pope (1991), a customary norm by which people are evaluated in the United States is based on how close they are to being White, male, middle-class, Christian, heterosexual, English-speaking, young, and mentally, physically, and emotionally able. When an established set of criteria for evaluating people's worth exists, economic exploitation, religious bias, homophobia, and able-body-ism ensue.

Many entrenched and long-standing social problems have plagued the United States since its infancy. Because these practices can be executed institutionally—for example, giving preferential treatment on the job to someone who is able-bodied over a person who has a physical disability—institutional discrimination exceeds the scope of individual prejudicial attitudes.

The **Robinson model on discourses** (see Figure 3.1) proposes that human characteristics operate as status variables in society. The model advances that, in the United States of America, identities are socially constructed, are statused, and have particular meanings. Interlocking dominant discourses maintain in both subtle and blatant ways that persons who hold membership in groups on the top of the line are valued in ways that those who hold membership in groups on the bottom of the line are not. Conveyed are culturally based attitudes regarding differences within a horizontal and hierarchical value system and their social consequences. This stratification of identities is a social construction because, in themselves, visible and invisible identities (e.g., race, gender, sexual orientation, religion, ideology, family constellation) are not oppressive. Racism, sexism, homo prejudice, and able-body-ism are oppressive and discriminatory (Robinson, 1999).

The basis for all of society's "isms," according to Myers et al. (1991), is "an extrinsic orientation and need to be 'better than'" (p. 56). Within such a conceptual system, people struggle with maintaining a positive sense of self. Isms emanate from a rank-and-file orientation regarding sources of differences among humans (Myers et al., 1991). Hughes (1945) contended that human characteristics have status because they denote rank.

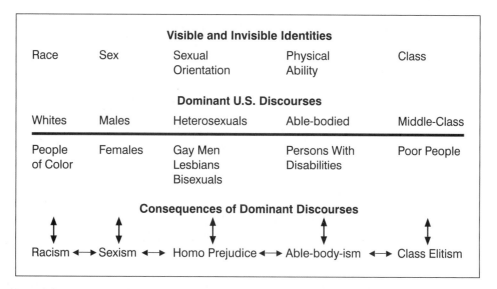

FIGURE 3.1
Robinson model on discourses
Source: From "The Intersections of Dominant Discourses Across Race, Gender, and Other Identities," by T. L. Robinson, 1999, Journal of Counseling & Development, 77, *73–79. Copyright 1999 by the American Counseling Association. Reprinted by permission. No further reproduction authorized without written permission of the American Counseling Association.*

ASSUMPTIONS OF HIERARCHICAL SOCIALIZATION PATTERNS

The Robinson model on discourses portrays a hierarchical approach to sources of differences. Dominant discourses and their consequences are also conveyed. In this section, the underlying assumptions of viewing differences in this manner are considered.

Sources of differences between and among people become primary status-determining traits when they are viewed as possessing rank and having value. Ultimately, preferred characteristics are perceived as normal and, within monoculturalism, thought to be desired by all. Characteristics held in lower esteem tend to be regarded as deviant and substandard. Within this hierarchical framework, the most and/or conceivably least valued aspect of a person may not be an achieved property. Instead of human similarities being the tie that binds people together, differences among people become inflated and artificially elevated above human similarities. This framework sets the stage for stunted human development and fans intense conflict among diverse human beings who, in their diversity, are more similar than different.

Conversely, if differences were not stratified hierarchically, society would be different. For instance, in a framework of cultural pluralism, race, gender, and other differences would not have rank and value. Essentially, each person would be regarded as worthy because people are "unique expressions of spiritual energy" (Myers et al., 1991, p. 56). Within such a framework, immutable characteristics would not be perceived as either normal or deviant. Human similarities would be more important than differences. Imagine a world where a Korean American girl would be just as likely as her European American male classmate to grow up to be president of the United States.

Clearly, this latter model approaches multiculturalism in that cultural diversity would be valued. Human rights would be respected; racial harmony and understanding would be enhanced; social justice and equal opportunity would exist for all; and racial and gender power would be distributed equitably among members of all ethnic groups (Gollnick, 1980, p. 9). Mary and I dream of this world, and we know that many of you do as well.

RACISM

Race is an unchosen characteristic of birth. Racism, however, can be changed because attitudes that are depreciative of racial differences can be unlearned. New cognitions can replace old ones that have been surrendered. Racism involves the total social structure where one group has conferred advantage through institutional policies. **Racism** is a social construction based on sociopolitical attitudes that demean specific racial characteristics.

Pinderhughes (1989) said the following about racism:

> Racism raises to the level of social structure the tendency to use superiority
> as a solution to discomfort about difference. Belief in superiority of Whites

and the inferiority of people-of-color based on racial difference is legit-
imized by societal arrangements that exclude the latter from resources and
power and then blame them for their failures, which are due to lack of
access. (p. 89)

Discussing racism is an unsettling experience. People are often reluctant to
engage in dialogue about racism, yet racism is a major part of this country's origins.
It has been said that America was built by taking land from a people and people from
a land. Racially discriminatory practices were underway when the Africans were taken
from their land centuries ago and brought to the Americas. America was arrogant
and inhumane when Native American Indians, during the 20th century, had their land
stolen and then were placed on reservations. America behaved in a racist manner
when first- and second-generation Japanese Americans were interred in U.S. concentration camps during World War II, whereas German and Italian Americans were not.
A racist ideology existed when the Southwest, which was once Mexico, was ceded to
the United States by the Treaty of Guadalupe Hidalgo. People became "foreigners in
their native land" that they had inhabited for centuries. A racist ideology existed when
laws, such as the 1882 Exclusion Act, restricted Chinese from this country while
white-skinned European immigrants flooded in. Racism was practiced when the 1790
Naturalization Law was in effect for 162 years; this policy reserved naturalized citizenship for Whites only (Takaki, 1994). At various junctures in U.S. history, laws forbade
women across racial groups and men of color from voting, becoming literate,
becoming educated at all-White institutions, owning property, working, and drinking
water from public facilities. Such policies attested to the institutionalization of racism
and sexism as blatant devaluations of race and sex diversity.

Racist attitudes portrayed in sentiments against racial intermixing were not simply
between races but within ethnic groups as well. In the Nazi publication *Neues Volk,* it
was written, "Every German and every German woman has the duty to avoid association with other races, especially Slavs. Each intimacy with a people of inferior race
means sinning against the future of our own people" (Rogers, 1967, p. 19).

Scientific notions about intelligence were developed against a sociopolitical backdrop of racism. Herrnstein and Murray (1994), in their controversial work *The Bell
Curve,* examined ethnic differences on intelligence tests. They concluded that "for
every known test of cognitive ability that meets basic psychometric standards of reliability and validity, Blacks and Whites score differently" (p. 276). These authors indicated that the differences are reduced once the testing is done outside the South,
after age 6, and after 1940. Herrnstein and Murray argued that even once socioeconomic differences are controlled for, the differences do not disappear but class may
reduce the overall differences in intelligence testing by about one third.

People have questioned this line of thinking. In an effort to investigate the claim
that Blacks are genetically inferior to Whites on intelligence testing, Grubb (1992), a
clinical psychologist specializing in the treatment of childhood/adolescent disorders,
examined 6,742 persons with developmental disabilities from three western states.
He surmised that if the argument that Blacks were genetically inferior to Whites were
true, then one could expect to see a higher proportion of Blacks identified as having

mental retardation, in comparison with Whites. Grubb found that, of the total population included in this project, 0.03% had developmental disabilities. This figure was consistent across racial groups. He stated, "The assumptions of the hereditary viewpoint, as regards the Black race, was, however, not upheld in this study but would lead one to reject this line of reasoning" (p. 227).

Nisbett (1995) also challenged Herrnstein and Murray (1994). Nisbett argued that comparing Blacks at high socioeconomic status (SES) with high-SES Whites is inherently flawed, given the higher income levels of these Whites in comparison with Blacks. Nisbett also stated that socialization and social factors affect ability levels. Finally, claims by Jensen and other authors stating that "g-loaded" tests differed between the races, with Whites having faster reaction times on complex maneuvers, was subjectively interpreted. Nisbett explained that, "for skills such as spatial reasoning and form perception, the g-loading was relatively low and B/W gap relatively low" (p. 44).

Psychologists have also levied destructive professional judgments on people as a function of their biased ideology. Bronstein and Quina (1988) reported that, during slavery, two forms of psychopathology were common among slaves. The first, "drapetomania," consisted of a single symptom of slaves running away. The second, "dysathesia aethiopica," consisted of numerous conditions such as destroying plantation property, showing defiance, and attacking the slave masters. This second condition was also known as "rascality," and both were nerve disorders coined by reputable physicians. Although liberty is explicit in this nation's charter, the desire for it among Blacks was appraised as pathological. Although Blacks were caretakers of others, they were perceived as childlike, incapable of providing for themselves, and dependent on their benevolent White masters. Clinicians of the day interpreted 1840 Census data that reported higher rates of psychopathology among Blacks to support the belief that "care, supervision, and control provided by slavery were essential to the mental health of Blacks" (Bronstein & Quina, 1988, p. 39). This paradigm supported a faulty belief that Blacks were not only different but inferior. How could (can) Blacks be diagnosed accurately when the psychological community perceived them to be chattel? Subsequent implications for mental health were and are profound.

CONSEQUENCES OF RACISM FOR EUROPEAN AMERICANS   Just as there are consequences of racism for people of color (e.g., identity diffusion, stress), there are consequences of racism for Whites (Pinderhughes, 1989). How can there not be, given the pernicious nature of racism? Because race often refers to "other," Whites may lack understanding about the effects and consequences of race and racism on their own lives.

One way to facilitate the discussion of racism is through an examination of unearned White skin color privilege. McIntosh (1989) maintained that privilege is an invisible knapsack of assets an entitled group can refer to on a regular basis to negotiate their daily lives more effectively (see the Storytelling "Disadvantaging Privilege"). It is unearned and yet is a fugitive subject, partly because many European Americans are oblivious to it and partly because non-Whites do not share in the privileges Whites take for granted. Unpacking privilege produces dissonance among many Whites because it assails fundamental Western beliefs of meritocracy and creates confusion about the meaning of being White.

STORYTELLING
Disadvantaging Privilege

After discussing McIntosh's (1989) article on privilege in my Gender Issues in Counseling course, a European American male graduate student lamented that although his race and gender provided him with certain unearned privileges, he had subsequently not developed a clear sense of identity as a gendered and racial being. His sadness was obvious, but it was clear that his dissonance served as a precursor to his self-reflection and growth.

Tracy

One consequence of racism for European Americans is that it limits emotional and intellectual development (Pinderhughes, 1989). Inattention to race as a factor in identity formation can contribute to a void in self-conception because the self is constructed apart from a conscious and often accurate understanding of the dynamic of race. Unfortunately, ethnocentric perspectives limit awareness of other legitimate worldviews besides one's own. Ethnocentrism also supports ignorance about oppression, which contributes to domination and exploitation.

Among many European Americans, the consequences of racism in their lives are invisible, as are the skin color privileges. Two conditions seem to intensify obliviousness to unearned privilege. The first is unawareness of the circumstances surrounding group membership, which entitles an individual to privileges. The second is the inability to see how others who do not share group membership also do not share privileges. Among counselors, this non-seeing could translate into reduced empathy. Empathy being the quintessential tool in counseling, counselors are severely limited in their effectiveness when they are unable to empathize. Although one may not have choice about being a member of a group in which unearned privilege is bestowed, one can choose how to respond to earned and unearned privileges. Privilege in its various forms can also be used to empower or equalize systems of injustice.

McIntosh (1989) identified several benefits that enabled her to negotiate her daily existence more effectively. She could choose not to teach her children about race or racism if teaching it would cause them some discomfort. She could shop alone most of the time, being pretty well assured that she would not be followed or harassed. She also knew that her children would be given curricular materials that testified to the existence of their race.

It appears that privilege has a flip side that is a considerable distance from the alleged benefits and bonuses typically associated with it. This subtle point is illuminated in the movie *The Scent of Green Papaya*. The primary character was a Vietnamese girl who, as a child, was a servant to a middle-class family. As she grew, she developed an endearing relationship with the mother of the family, who never had a daughter. Although the servant girl had no literacy skills, her power to love, surrender, and persevere were obvious. McBride (1990) referred to this as "the ability to act upon the world, carry on activities, cope with problems, and take action to meet one's needs" (p. 22). After the mother died, the Vietnamese girl, who was now a young woman, was sent to work for a family friend who was engaged to be married to a sophisticated woman from a rich family. The Vietnamese servant was disadvantaged educationally, occupationally, and fiscally; the bride-to-be, a rich woman, was not. Yet the rich woman, with all her privilege and money, could not match the unassuming and gentle power of the servant that eclipsed the material domain. Although poverty is not being glamorized, the lesson of this story is that privilege can be disadvantaging, particularly when it denies one the glorious opportunity to sculpt an identity.

PATRIARCHY

Patriarchy is a sex/gender system that involves the total social structure (Renzetti & Curran, 1992). Within this system, men have advantage conferred on them because of their prescribed rank or societal status or both. For example, more than two decades of the women's movement has been accused of being class elitist and racist in some of its orientations. This same time frame has seen increases in the college-going rates of women and dramatic rises among women in the workforce. Amid these and other advances, gender inequity continues. In the United States, women earn $.75 to men's $1.00. Women pay more for dry cleaning and automobiles, and women of color pay more for their cars than males and European American women.

Once the layers of class and race are imposed, the extent and effects of gender inequity intensify, but so does the potential for personal empowerment. As patriarchy is intertwined with power and privilege, the ascribed status of sex becomes elevated as a primary-status trait over achievement. This system is inherently unjust because biological sex is not chosen; nonetheless, it represents an extremely potent determinant of how people are treated. Both women and men make up society and are necessary to its maintenance, yet through an elaborate socialization process, expectations and behaviors are disseminated and internalized. These socialization practices, both blatant and subtle, maintain a system not only in the United States but also in other countries throughout the world, where women are not as advantaged because of their less prominent status as females. Haider (1995) said,

> In many cultures, the notion of male dominance—of man as woman's "god," protector and provider—and the notion of women as passive, submissive, and chaste have been the predominant images for centuries. In many cases, customary practices have been based on a pecking order that has not always been conducive to the well-being and personal development of those lower down the status line. (p. 53)

One consequence of patriarchy for men is that it creates a skewed emotional existence. Many men are unable to experience comfortably and thus express a full range of emotions, such as fear, dependency, and uncertainty, because of the narrow parameters of patriarchy. By its very nature, patriarchy is a system of wide-scale inequity wherein differences are viewed hierarchically. In themselves, differences are not problematic. The attitudes about differences lead to either their celebration or their condemnation.

Given the potential disadvantages of patriarchy for men, are there possible benefits of patriarchy for women? Patriarchy has its genesis in injustice. If any presumable benefits of patriarchy result for women, they are temporary and elusive, primarily because the benefits would be dictated by women's adherence to the parameters of patriarchy and their compliance with subscribed gender roles. Does equality for women apply primarily to those women who subscribe to at least some value of a male-oriented society (e.g., self-sufficiency, assertiveness, competition)? According to Bem (1993), if this is true, it is a result of **androcentrism,** or male-centeredness, where the male standard prevails. Counselors need to understand this dynamic as they educate female clients about engaging in self-care, which tends not to be sup-ported by conventional norms of gender behavior. Some clients will encounter oppo-sition, from women and men alike, as they attend to self. About this, Tolman (1991) said, "I realize that when girls know, experience and speak about those fabulous feel-ings in their bodies, trouble follows—for them and for their parents, teachers, and therapists" (p. 67).* Tolman spoke to the reality that girls' sexual desire creates disso-nance because it tests the cultural ideals concerning girls (and women) disconnecting from their bodies and their sexual desires. Counselors can help clients identify what they want while helping them cope with significant others who may not be supportive.

SEXISM

The women's movement challenged many traditional stereotypes about women, their work, and their place in society. That women wanted equal pay for equal work, respect in a society that too often reduced them to sexual objects, and denied them choice about their bodies was the message echoed across numerous platforms. Another part of these platforms encouraged women to consider seriously the social-ization experiences that contributed to their reliance on others for their emotional and financial well-being. **Sexism,** an institutionalized system of inequity based on biological sex, was brought to the nation's attention.

Bem (1993), author of the Bem Sex Role Inventory, maintained that androcen-trism responds to men as human and to women as other. Given this perspective, it is easy to understand that men enjoy certain privileges that women do not. Although ours is a society where men, for the most part, benefit over women, male privileges do not bestow power on all men and ultimately deny all women. In fact, one benefit of the men's movement is that it has brought attention to the myth that women's powerlessness translates into men's power. Swanson (1993) recognized this as the "new sexism." Although individual men may feel powerful, not all men do. Swanson said, "Some men, rather than feeling like patriarchs, often feel like workhorses, har-nessed with the burden of being family provider, trying to pull the family wagon up a muddy hill of financial debt" (p. 12).

Although unearned privilege does not dictate real power, many White men, men of color, or poor, disabled, and/or gay men do not share the same privileges that

---

* *From "Adolescent Girls, Women, and Sexuality: Discerning Dilemmas of Desire, by D. L. Tolman, 1991,* Women & Therapy, *11, p. 61. Copyright 1991 by The Haworth Press. Reprinted by permission.*

some economically privileged, able-bodied, and/or heterosexual men do. Thus, many men may not perceive a sense of personal power because of the absence of crucial markers that society deems normative. The presence of these critical markers, however, does not ensure that individual men will automatically feel powerful. Counselors need to understand this lest they make inappropriate attributions regarding their clients' known and visible identity constructs. Race, class, and physical abilities intersect with male privilege and in some contexts serve to mediate it. Ours is a society where men, for the most part, benefit over women.

Another identity construct that may mitigate the privileges that men share is sexual orientation. Some of the privilege associated with maleness has a qualifier of heterosexuality. Gay men who are "out" experience the attacks from a homophobic society in the form of ostracism, discrimination, and in some instances violence. Gay men of color contend with racism along with homophobia (Loiacano, 1989). Other privileges associated with being male still remain, however, such as not being charged excessive amounts for car repairs by mechanics.

The irony of socialization is that although men are trained to be providers, protectors, and ready for combat, they often experience pressure from women to be nurturing, soft, and intimate (Skovholt, 1993). Undoubtedly, these conflicting messages are confusing. Men's socialization to be protectors leaves them vulnerable to not asking for help, thus stifling healthy development.

CONSEQUENCES OF SEXISM FOR MEN   Racism adversely affects people regardless of their race and ethnicity, in that racism contributes to a dehumanizing stance and limits human development (Pinderhughes, 1989). Sexism adversely affects all people, men included. The male gender role often results in men being restricted in their emotional expressiveness and promotes a limited range of behaviors available to them. "Restrictive emotionality involves the reluctance and/or difficulty men have in expressing their feelings to other people and may be related to their hesitancy to seek help from others" (Good, Dell, & Mintz, 1989, p. 295). Men have gender and are influenced by rigid and sexist discourses whereby they are oriented toward success, competition, and the need to be in control (Robinson, 1999). The danger in the male role is that it has been connected to "Type A" behavior patterns and to depression (Good & Mintz, 1990).

HOMOPHOBIA

Homophobia is "the unreasonable fear of same-sex attractions, attentions, relationships, and persons whose affectional and erotic orientations are toward the same sex" (King, 1988, p. 168). This fear emanates from the perception of homosexuality as an aberration of the correct social order.

CONSEQUENCES OF HOMOPHOBIA FOR HETEROSEXUALS   Many men are often concerned that engaging in any behaviors deemed "feminine" will be misconstrued as a loss of masculinity and thus a threat to heterosexuality. Men are often taught that anything associated with femininity is anathema. Within this restrictive context, heterosexual men may feel real fear over expressing physical affection with another man because of connotations of homosexuality. This concern may explain why many men, on greeting one another, engage in rough-rousing, evidenced by vigorous slaps on the back. Such behavior, however, is culturally dictated. In Ghana, West Africa, or in Cairo, Egypt, for example, it is quite natural to see men holding hands while walking together. Within these cultural contexts, affection and endearment support this behavior. In the United States, similar behavior would be interpreted as a blatant expression of homosexuality.

Homophobia also interferes with the formation of cross-sexual orientation friendships out of fear that such interaction and proximity would be misinterpreted by others. In this context, heterosexual counselors can be inhibited in their ability to be allies to homosexual and bisexual clients.

ABLE-BODY-ISM

People with disabilities have a long history of being discriminated against (Fulton & Sabornie, 1994). An understanding of this type of discrimination is enhanced by an assessment of the doing-mastery-over-fate orientation descriptive of American society. The U.S. culture places inordinate emphasis on youth and fitness and preoccupation with the body beautiful. A disability is seen as an imperfection, which is contrary to the cultural values of control and domination, inherent in this country's fabric. A clear bias for the able-bodied exists. How much thought do most able-bodied people give to the ability to access a house or other building? Because most buildings have been constructed for able-bodied persons, persons without disabilities are often oblivious to their unearned privileges. Architectural space and design are outgrowths of cultural attitudes and assumptions that are biased against persons, and in particular, women with disabilities. Weisman (1992) said,

> Placement in barrier-free housing and rehabilitation services favors
> men. . . . Disabled women are not usually thought of as wives and mothers
> who often manage households with children and husbands. The wheel-
> chair-accessible two- and three-bedroom unit is a rarity. (p. 118)

The myth that people with disabilities are childlike, dependent, and depressed contributes to maltreatment, ignorance from the larger society, and denial about the fact that, at any time, able-bodied people can and most likely will become disabled if they live long enough. Multiculturally competent counselors have the ability to regard clients with disabilities as whole human beings wherein the disability is understood as a component of identity and not the entire focus of the counseling event or an exhaustive account of the client's essence (Fowler, O'Rourke, Wadsworth, & Harper, 1992). The counselor's facility at beholding the client's multiple spiritual, occupational, sexual, and social identities is commentary about the counselor's moral and ego development.

CONSEQUENCES OF ABLE-BODY-ISM AMONG THE ABLE-BODIED Society was created for persons who are able-bodied. Our society of concrete can be very uninviting and even hostile toward persons with disabilities and for able-bodied people as well.

How many of us who are able-bodied have struggled with opening a new bottle of ibuprofen or battled with the emergency brake after having our cars serviced?

Stereotypes abound regarding people with disabiliites. One of the most pernicious is that persons with disabilities desire to be able-bodied. This mistaken belief is similar to the belief that people of color desire to be White or that women desire to be men. Equating the experience of having a disability with living a lesser life is problematic for at least two reasons. First, such an attitude is not characteristic of a multiculturally competent counselor who possesses accurate beliefs and attitudes of diverse client populations. Second, this attitude is arrogant and psychologically restrictive for able-bodied persons, who at any time can become disabled. Although having a disability can deflate a sense of self and depress self-esteem (Livneh & Sherwood, 1991), this is not the experience of all persons with disabilities. For this reason, Weeber supports the development of a model of identity disability (J. Weeber, personal communication, August 20, 1997).

CLASS ELITISM

Much of the formal training counselors receive in traditional counselor education programs emanates from a middle-class bias. This bias is characterized by emphasis on meritocracy, the Protestant work ethic, Standard English, and adherence to 50-minute sessions (Sue & Sue, 1990). The difficulty with this type of partiality is that it can alienate counselors from particular clients. Persons who have limited access to material wealth in a materialistic culture are not perceived as being psychologically viable. The acronym *YAVIS* refers to clients who are *y*oung, *a*ttractive, *v*erbal, *i*ntelligent, and *s*uccessful (Schofield, 1964). A dangerously close relationship exists between self-worth and income. Thus, the poor, regardless of their work ethic, tend to be perceived as being lazy and even immoral (Gans, 1992). Conversely, the rich are esteemed and admired, often independent of their moral conduct.

The relationship between class and power is dubious (Pinderhughes, 1989). Low-income status is not valued in a consumeristic society and may provoke feelings of powerlessness and depression (Pinderhughes, 1989); however, similar feelings are felt among middle-class persons who experience discrimination (see the Storytelling "Seeing Hue").

CONSEQUENCES OF CLASS ELITISM   Because socioeconomic class converges with gender, race, ability, and personal power, as well as other identity constructs, it is simplistic to conclude that being able-bodied or male or having a high income is automatically associated with feelings of safety, security, less tendency to depression, and less pain. Counselors in particular are mistaken in assuming that not having high status is correlated with feelings of less power, thus ascribing low status to non-White persons, ethnic group members, and persons who have low income (Gibbs, Huang, & Associates, 1989).

AGEISM

Ageism refers to discrimination against people because of their age. This discrimination is often aimed at the middle-aged or the elderly (Nuessel, 1982). Ageist

STORYTELLING
Seeing Hue

A few years ago, a (struggling) European American graduate student revealed an example of privilege that had recently occurred. She and a dark-skinned Cuban American friend, who was upper-middle income, went to a drug store and purchased some items. At the checkout counter, the student wrote a check for her items and was not asked to show any identification. When her friend went to write a check, the clerk asked for identification. On seeing the discrepancy, the White student asked the clerk why she was not asked for identification but her friend was. The clerk then informed the student that she had seen her in the store before and had waited on her. The student explained to the clerk that this was her first time in the store.

This story reveals the assumptions made about the class status of people on the basis of their skin color.

Tracy

terms vary and include primarily negative expressions, although a few are neutral and less positive. Examples are *crotchety, fuddy-duddy, fart, senility, wizened, golden-ager, graybeard,* and *Lawrence Welk generation* (Nuessel, 1982).

Atkinson and Hackett (1995) stated that "delineating the elderly as being 65 and over is a purely arbitrary separation" (p. 192). Its genesis is in the decades-old Social Security system, which was instituted when people did not live as long as they now do. For instance, in 1900, elders made up roughly 4% of the U.S. population. In 1990, they represented more than 12%. "While the total United States population grew 13.5 percent from 1970 to 1982, the 65 and over age group grew 34.3 percent" (p. 12).

Ageism is confounded with other layers of discrimination. For instance, until very recently, limited attention had been devoted to the study of breast cancer. On the surface, this lack of focus can easily be attributed to sexism; however, is ageism also imputed? Does the fact that the majority of women survivors of breast cancer are not in their 20s or 30s, but rather in their 50s, contribute to the dearth of research on this disease? Is it less important for an aging woman to lose the commodity of beauty that esteems her with worth and power as it is associated with sexuality? These questions are disturbing, yet counselors need to know how adversely affected they are by the intersecting layers of discrimination.

Elders ought not be treated as monoliths. Doing so greatly impedes the delivery of effective services. Differences exist between a 65-year-old healthy person and a 90-year-old elder whose health has begun to decline. Atkinson and Hackett (1995) described the "young-old" and the "old-old" (p. 14). The young-old is in fairly good health with stable financial supports. The old-old is experiencing deficits in several psychological, physical, social, and financial resources.

Counselors need to be mindful of the social supports available to the elderly client. Sturdy social supports with both friends and family results in less dependency on formal psychological help (Phillips & Murrell, 1994). Part of a counselor's assessment, then, should be an examination of an elder's level of involvement in meaningful and purposeful social activity. The elder's sense of personal autonomy or control over life is also an important component of overall wellness. Some illnesses, such as Alzheimer's disease, will require that the counselor work in sync with other caregivers to maximize the quality of living during a stressful, disquieting, and potentially chaotic time. Age biases contribute to some counselors seeing little merit in providing psychotherapy to aging persons. One weakness of psychoanalytic theory is that it is not seen as viable for persons of age 50 or older (Corey, 1991). Focusing on the client's strengths, regardless of the presenting problem, is a crucial step in facilitating growth or bolstering coping abilities.

CONSEQUENCES OF AGEISM FOR THE NON-ELDERLY   Unlike most traditional cultures where the elderly tend to be respected and valued, in the U.S. culture, inordinate emphasis is placed on youthfulness. The societal significance attached to doing, productivity, and maintaining mastery over nature may explain this cultural preoccupation with youth and the herculean effort to defy and, in some instances, deny aging. Aging appears to be viewed as a loss of control and of diminishing power. Discrimination against a segment of the population that is composing a higher percentage of the total and that all people will be members of, if they are fortunate, culminates in fear-based stereotypes about the experience of being an elder. It is heartening to see how a culture of menopausal women is redefining hot flashes as power surges and recognizing the "change" in life as a time of ascendancy and coming into one's own.

IMPLICATIONS FOR COUNSELORS

Not understanding the meaning of race in one's life, the racial self does not become well defined. This lack of clarity about a core identity construct adversely affects counselors' empathy toward their clients. American society socializes people into attitudes that are often not honoring of difference. Counselors need to recognize these and other biases within themselves and not allow shame to fan denial. The ongoing process of unlearning these attitudes is tumultuous, but the good news is that it is possible. Counselors need to ascertain whether they are able to work effectively with a variety of clients (see the Storytelling "Counselor, Know Thyself").

Counselors have a professional and ethical obligation to refer clients to other professionals when they are unable to provide necessary assistance (see the case study "Multiple and Textured Identities"). However, the counselor who is highly judgmental toward a White woman involved in an interracial relationship needs to determine whether such intolerance also extends to persons who, say for example, do not practice her same religious affiliation.

STORYTELLING
Counselor, Know Thyself

One of my students once told me she could not and would not work with men who had sexually assaulted women. Her personal experiences as a survivor of rape affected her ability to do so. Her honesty was not an indication of unfinished business as much as of a clarity of boundaries and personal limitations we all need to recognize.

Tracy

CASE STUDY
Multiple and Textured Identities

Bryan Wong is a 28-year-old Chinese American gay male. He was raised in a medium-size city in California. His father is a minister and has been married to Bryan's mother for nearly 30 years. Bryan has two younger sisters. As a certified public accountant, Bryan earns a very good salary. Ever since he was a boy, his father wanted him to be a minister. For 2 years, Bryan went to Bible college but left prior to graduation because he did not want to be a minister. Bryan has not disclosed his sexual orientation with his parents but has confided in one of his sisters. He wants to talk with his parents but is afraid of their reaction. Lately, his mother has been talking about the importance of grandchildren to continue the family name. Bryan has been in a monogamous and satisfying relationship with his male partner for 2 years. He presents to his counselor, James Lee, on the recommendation of his partner, with feelings of depression, guilt, anger, and sadness.

QUESTIONS FOR DISCUSSION

1. What would contribute to Bryan's feelings of depression? Guilt? Anger? Sadness?
2. On which identity constructs might an inexperienced counselor focus?
3. What are the unearned privileges to which Bryan is not entitled?
4. How might James help Bryan disclose his feelings if Bryan is reluctant to talk?
5. Would a counselor need to approach Bryan differently if he were from a different racial group? Low-income? If so, how and why?

DISCUSSION AND INTEGRATION
The Client, Bryan

Bryan has to contend with homophobia, "coming-out" issues, and racism, but also with normal development issues that people his age encounter—developing commitments to work and love. One primary conflict is how he can remain true to his sexual orientation, given that its revelation will most likely hurt the people he loves dearly. Because Bryan lives in a heterosexist and patriarchal world, with the assumptions that he is heterosexual, will marry a woman, father children, and presumably lead a household. Most Asian American families, too, have this expectation of their male children (Greene, 1994).

Gay men of color, according to Loiacano (1989), do not receive the same degree of psychological privileges from the gay community that White gay men receive. "Because of the overwhelming fear of rejection and stigmatization" (p. 19), Chan (1989) stated, many Asian American gay men and lesbians are not likely to "come out" to their parents. In addition, psychological research has not attended to the intersections of sexual orientation and ethnicity (Greene, 1994).

Because of the underlying assumption that persons who share gender are monolithic, use of the phrase "men in general" is problematic (Carrigan, Connell, & Lee, 1987). Although Bryan is able-bodied, male, and middle class, he does not enjoy the privileges that heterosexual and White men do. Bryan has middle-class status and as a result enjoys certain privileges associated with this status, such as purchasing power, choice about living conditions, and not having to contend with prevailing myths that surround the poor, such as lacking ambition, being lazy, and untrustworthy. Undoubtedly, similar stereotypes may emanate from Bryan's other identity—namely, his sexual orientation.

Bryan's dilemma is very real as he struggles with multiple identities. One dilemma is finding validation in the gay community, which is certainly not free of racism. Some gay men of color appear to perceive more racism among White gay men than among the general White population (Loiacano, 1989). About Black gay men Loiacano (1989) said, "The benefits that Black gay men receive from the predominant White gay and lesbian community can be diminished by bias-related practices and beliefs related to race" (p. 24). Chan (1989) found discriminatory practices evident among gay and lesbian Asians. One woman indicated, "It is a problem to find my support only within the lesbian community, because I feel that I am either seen as 'exotic' and stereotyped, or unaccepted because I am Asian and not like the majority of White lesbians" (p. 19).

Another theme in Bryan's life is finding validation in the Asian community. One Asian man interviewed by Chan (1989) discussed the enormous pressure he felt to be secretive about his homosexuality. He said

> I wish I could tell my parents—they are the only ones who do not know about my gay identity, but I am sure that they would reject me. There is no frame of reference to understand homosexuality in Asian American culture. (p. 19)

About internalized oppression, one woman interviewed by Loiacano (1989) remarked that the "horizontal violence" perpetuated within the gay community on gay persons can be very oppressive toward others who are gay (descriptive and internalized oppression). This process interferes with members' ability to harness collectively their energies toward combating discrimination.

Finally is the need to integrate both race and sexual identities. This challenge can lead many people to feel that sanity is slipping away from them, particularly for those people being told they are "freaky," "crazy," "stupid" (Loiacano, 1989), and in enough religious circles, "the anti-Christ" or "demon possessed." Such societal hostility contributes to problems among many lesbians and gay men, such as depression, poor self-esteem, and chemical addiction (Rudolph, 1989).

The Counselor, James

In a study of Chinese Americans in the Bay Area of California, factors found to be associated with a more positive attitude regarding help-seeking for a nervous or emotional problem were better English ability, age (e.g., younger persons), marital status (e.g., being married), and SES (e.g., coming from a lower socioeconomic background; Ying & Miller, 1992). Although Bryan is neither married nor from a low socioeconomic background, he is young, and English is his native language.

Bryan has enormous strengths, and as an effective counselor, James is sensitive to these. Bryan engaged in self-care when he left Bible school. This learning environment and the subject matter were inconsistent with his personal desires. Bryan also evidenced persistence in that he reenrolled in college and eventually completed a degree in an area of his choosing.

Commitment is another area where Bryan is strong. He has been in a satisfying relationship for nearly 2 years despite the assumption that homosexuality is linked with sexual appetite, craving, and promiscuity. Courage is an extremely important factor to identify because asking for psychological assistance is particularly difficult for men who espouse the traditional male role (Good et al., 1989). Bryan cares for others. He loves his parents and knows that revealing his sexual orientation will create confusion in the family and within the church community once the membership discovers that the minister's son is gay. Instead of focusing on weaknesses and powerlessness, James can assist him by realizing that he is vulnerable (because of his conflicts) and yet still has choices. This knowledge can ultimately be empowering.

James helps Bryan explore the options of either coming out to his parents or remaining closeted. Waiting to decide which course of action to take is also an option and can be seen as a source of a strength. That one sister knows Bryan is gay may decrease some of Bryan's feelings of secrecy and inauthenticity with his family. Such feelings contribute to guilt feelings and anger in that a significant part of who he is has been kept a secret from his parents.

According to Rudolph (1989), "a large percentage of counselors perceive homosexuality as pathological and less desirable than heterosexuality, although many display some willingness to accept homosexuality in other people" (p. 81). James unravels any feelings of homophobia and, if need be, supplements self-knowledge on homosexuality, religion, and its convergence with other identity constructs. Reading across these and other related topics; consulting with colleagues; attending professional meetings; and without seeming too void of information about the client's culture, asking appropriate questions conducive to the therapeutic event are helpful strategies.

If Bryan is unwilling to disclose his personal feelings, James must consider how culture contributes to this reluctance. Uba (1994) said, "In addition to concerns about stigma and traditional coping strategies, there are other reasons that Asian Americans are reluctant to discuss their problems" (p. 223). It is not uncommon for many Asian Americans to perceive talking about themselves or disclosing private personal information to a stranger as reflective of low maturity and lack of discipline. However, in a study by Lin (1994) on 145 adult Chinese Americans, when qualified ethnic and language-matched therapists were provided, the Chinese Americans were found to stay in therapy as long as the general American public.

Although formal assessments could be helpful to ascertain Bryan's depression level, stress level, and coping skills, Uba (1994) stated that "just as there are few normative data on the behaviors of Asian Americans, there often are not data on normative responses of Asian Americans to various tests" (p. 165).

Professional counselors, as well as counselor trainees, can enhance their efficacy by recognizing that the "isms" in society affect not only the group being discriminated against. Empowered persons who are members of devalued groups operate from a place of power, as opposed to victimization. Personal power does not come from denying injustice or oppressive acts, but rather comes from recognizing them, realizing one's vulnerabilities (Pinderhughes, 1989). It is crucial that the counselor avoid assumptions of Bryan's individual empowerment based on a cursory assessment of his income, occupation, and gender.

SUMMARY

In this chapter, the presentation of human differences as status variables was explored through an examination of the Robinson model on discourses. Hughes's (1945) work on the dilemmas and contradictions of status was also useful. The consequences of hierarchical socialization were presented, and the advantages of a model based on cultural pluralism was envisioned. The importance of counselors recognizing systems of inequity was articulated, and a case study allowed readers to synthesize the ideas presented.

REFERENCES

Atkinson, D. R., & Hackett, G. (1995). *Counseling diverse populations.* Madison: Brown and Benchmark.

Bem, S. L. (1993). *The lenses of gender: Transforming the debate on sexuality inequality.* New Haven, CT: Yale University Press.

Bronstein, P., & Quina, K. (1988). *Teaching a psychology of people.* Washington, DC: American Psychological Association.

Carrigan, T., Connell, B., & Lee, J. (1987). Toward a new sociology of masculinity. In H. Brod (Ed.), *The making of masculinities: The new men's studies* (pp. 63–100). Boston: Allen and Unwin.

Chan, C. S. (1989). Issues of identity development among Asian American lesbians and gay men. *Journal of Counseling & Development, 68,* 16–20.

Corey, G. (1991). *Theory and practice of counseling and psychotherapy* (4th ed.). Pacific Grove, CA: Brooks/Cole.

Fowler, C., O'Rourke, B. O., Wadsworth, J., & Harper, D. (1992). Disability and feminism: Models for counselor exploration of personal values and beliefs. *Journal of Applied Rehabilitation Counseling, 23,* 14–19.

Fulton, S. A., & Sabornie, E. J. (1994). Evidence of employment inequality among females with disabilities. *Journal of Special Education, 2,* 149–165.

Gans, H. J. (1992, January 8). Fighting the biases embedded in social concepts of the poor. *Chronicle of Higher Education,* p. A56.

Gibbs, J. T., Huang, L. N., & Associates. (1989). *Children of color: Psychological interventions with minority youth.* San Francisco: Jossey-Bass.

Gollnick, D. M. (1980). Multicultural education. *Viewpoints in Teaching and Learning, 56,* 1–17.

Good, G. E., Dell, D. M., & Mintz, L. B. (1989). Male role and gender role conflict: Relations to help seeking in men. *Journal of Counseling Psychology, 36,* 295–300.

Good, G. E., & Mintz, L. B. (1990). Gender role conflict and depression in college men: Evidence for compounded risk. *Journal of Counseling & Development, 69,* 1, 17–21.

Greene, B. (1994). Ethnic-minority lesbians and gay men: Mental health and treatment issues. *Journal of Consulting and Clinical Psychology, 62,* 243–251.

Grubb, H. J. (1992). Intelligence at the low end of the curve: Where are the racial differences? In A. Burlew, W. Banks, H. McAdoo, & D. Azibo (Eds.), *African American psychology: Theory, research, and practice* (pp. 219–228). Newbury Park, CA: Sage.

Haider, R. (1995). *Gender and development.* Cairo, Egypt: American University in Cairo Press.

Herrnstein, R. J., & Murray, C. (1994). *The bell curve: Intelligence and class structure in American life.* New York: Free Press.

Hughes, E. C. (1945). Dilemmas and contraditions of status. *American Journal of Sociology, 50,* 353–357.

King, N. (1988). Teaching about lesbians and gays in the psychology curriculum. In P. A. Bronstein & K. Quina (Eds.), *Teaching a psychology of people: Resources for gender and sociocultural awareness* (pp. 168–174). Washington, DC: American Psychological Association.

Lin, J. C. H. (1994). How long do Chinese Americans stay in psychotherapy? *Journal of Counseling Psychology, 41,* 288–291.

Livneh, H., & Sherwood, A. (1991). Application of personality theories and counseling strategies to clients with physical disabilities. *Journal of Counseling & Development, 69,* 525–538.

Loiacano, D. K. (1989). Gay identity issues among Black Americans: Racism, homophobia, and the need for validation. *Journal of Counseling & Development, 68,* 21–25.

McBride, M. C. (1990). Autonomy and the struggle for female identity: Implications for counseling women. *Journal of Counseling & Development, 69,* 22–26.

McIntosh, P. (1989, July/August). White privilege: Unpacking the invisible knapsack. *Peace and Freedom,* pp. 10–12.

Myers, L. J., Speight, S. L., Highlen, P. S., Cox, C. I., Reynolds, A. L., Adams, E. M., & Hanley, P. (1991). Identity development and worldview: Toward an optimal conceptualization. *Journal of Counseling & Development, 70,* 54–63.

Nisbett, R. (1995). Race, IQ, and scientism. In S. Fraser, *The bell curve wars: Race, intelligence, and the future of America.* New York: Basic Books.

Nuessel, F. H. (1982). The language of ageism. *Gerontologist, 22,* 273–276.

Phillips, M. A., & Murrell, S. A. (1994). Impact of psychological and physical health, stressful events, and social support on subsequent mental health help seeking among older adults. *Journal of Consulting and Clinical Psychology, 62,* 270–275.

Pinderhughes, E. (1989). *Understanding race, ethnicity, and power: The key to efficacy in clinical practice.* New York: Free Press.

Renzetti, C. M., & Curran, D. J . (1992). *Women, men, and society.* Boston: Allyn & Bacon.

Reynolds, A. L., & Pope, R. L. (1991). The complexities of diversity: Exploring multiple oppressions. *Journal of Counseling & Development, 70,* 174–180.

Robinson, T. L. (1999). The intersections of dominant discourses across race, gender, and other identities. *Journal of Counseling & Development, 77,* 73–79.

Rogers, J. A. (1967). *Sex and race.* St. Petersburg, FL: Helga Rogers.

Rudolph, J. (1989). Effects of a workshop on mental health practitioners' attitudes toward homosexuality and counseling effectiveness. *Journal of Counseling & Development, 68,* 81–85.

Schofield, W. (1964). *Psychotherapy: The purchase of friendship.* Upper Saddle River, NJ: Prentice Hall.

Skovholt, T. M. (1993). Counseling and psychotherapy interventions with men. *Counseling and Human Development, 8,* 263–283.

Sue, D. W., & Sue, D. (1990). *Counseling the culturally different: Theory and practice.* New York: John Wiley.

Swanson, J. L. (1993). Sexism strikes men. *American Counselor, 1,* 10–13, 39.

Takaki, R. (1994). *From different shores: Perspectives on race and ethnicity in America.* New York: Oxford University Press.

Tolman, D. L. (1991). Adolescent girls, women, and sexuality: Discerning dilemmas of desire. *Women & Therapy, 11,* 55–69.

Uba, L. (1994). *Asian Americans: Personality patterns, identity, and mental health.* New York: Guilford Press.

Weisman, L. K. (1992). *Discrimination by design: A feminist critique of the man-made environment.* Urbana: University of Illinois Press.

Ying, Y., & Miller, L. S. (1992). Help-seeking behavior and attitude of Chinese Americans regarding psychological problems. *American Journal of Community Psychology, 20,* 549–556.

Chapter 4

Converging Race

Y por eso los grandes amores de muchos colores me gustan a mí. (And so the loves of many colors are pleasing to me.)

"De Colores" (from an old song)

Being a multiculturally competent counselor means having the ability to image race as an identity construct through a developmental lens. It also means understanding that race converges with other identity constructs. These intersections have implications for the counseling event and represent an understudied area in counseling (Robinson, 1993).

Chapter 3, on statused identities, posited that race is a primary status trait. An example of this is as follows:

> *Darren Yasamura is a third-generation Korean American. He is a lawyer. A trial judge assumes that because of Darren's race (Asian) and his ethnicity (Korean), he is quiet, timid, and speaks limited English. This type of assessment of Darren is an example of race and ethnicity, or A dimensions, serving as primary traits for evaluation rather than Darren's achieved traits (J.D., Ph.D., criminal lawyer, author, and professor), or B dimensions.*

The good news is that not all trial judges would make the same error. Racial identity theory helps explain this particular trial judge's self-knowledge and subsequent perceptions of others. Throughout this chapter, racial identity theory is discussed. First, the discussion expands race beyond the limiting contexts of oppression and/or privilege (Smith, 1991). Second, it helps explain that race, in itself, is an inappropriate identity construct for predicting counseling success.

RACE AND SCIENCE

Much of the attitudes about race has been affected by notions of race and science. A substantial portion of the dialogue about race includes conceptual frameworks that argued the inferiority of African and Semitic people attributable to inherent biological deficiencies (see Pedersen, 1994). Charles Darwin's (1859) work *The Origin of Species by Means of Natural Selection* was used to support the genetic intellectual superiority of Whites and the genetic inferiority of non-Whites, who were referred to as the "lower races." Professional organizations such as the American Association of Physical Anthropologists contested this information and the use of outdated 19th-century notions of race (see Pedersen, 1994).

Despite the claims to racial purity and the superiority of one race over another, everyone comes from the same source (Zuckerman, 1990; see also the Storytelling "One Spirit"). Still, outdated racial categories such as Negroid, Mongoloid, and Caucasoid remain. Given that human beings are products of migratory patterns and world conquests throughout the centuries, the argument of a pure race does not exist and is illogical (Dobbins & Skillings, 1991).

As early as 1870, the U.S. Bureau of the Census divided the U.S. population into five races: White, Colored (Black), Colored (mulatto), Chinese, and Indian (Root,

STORYTELLING
One Spirit

I was enjoying the splendor of one of the most magical cities I had ever visited—Venezia, Italy. After walking leisurely through one of the many plazas, I heard the church bells ringing loudly. I noticed that people were scurrying to enter a tiny church off one of the cobblestone streets. I followed them and soon realized they were gathering for evening Mass. I studied Italian for 3 years in high school, but I understood little of the Catholic Mass. Not comprehending the spoken language was of little concern to me. What I experienced was the presence of spirit that united me with the Italian Catholics kneeling on either side. Being neither Catholic nor Italian, I was enormously grateful for this blessed experience to transcend race, ethnicity, culture, class, language, and religion. In this little Catholic Italian church, we were One Spirit.

Mary

1992). Since this time and in the present day, controversy among biologists, anthropologists, and other scholars has surrounded the topic of number of races.

Gossett (1963) said,

> Linnaeus had found four human races; Blumenbach had five; Curvier had three; John Hunter had seven; Burke had sixty-three; Pickering had eleven; Virey had two "species," each containing three races; Haeckel had thirty-six; Hurley had four; Topinard had nineteen under three headings; Desmoulins had sixteen "species"; Deniker had seventeen races and thirty types. (p. 82)

To clarify many misconceptions surrounding racial differences, Zuckerman (1990) reported that, in his analysis of 18 genetic systems (blood groups, proteins, and enzymes) in 40 populations within 16 subgroups around the world, "the major component of genetic diversity is between individuals in the same tribe or nation; it accounts for 84% of the variance. Of the remaining variance, 10% is accounted for by racial groupings and 6% by geographic regions" (p. 1300).

Alan Goodman, dean of natural science at Hampshire College, said that, depending on which trait is used to distinguish races, "you won't get anything that remotely tracks conventional race categories" (cited in Begley, 1995, p. 67). Spickard (1992), a scholar on biracial identity, argued, "The so-called races are not biological categories at all. Rather, they are primarily social divisions that rely only partly on physical markers as skin color to identify group membership" (p. 17).

Considerable uncertainty surrounds racial origins. Rogers (1967), a historian, wrote that "for us of the present day, the earliest history of all peoples and nations is lost in a fog" (p. 21). Agreement among reputable historians and archaeologists is that the color of primitive humans was Black. Zuckerman (1990) concurred and wrote, "although there is considerable speculation on the origin of races, little can be proved other than that a species, *Homo sapiens,* gradually evolved from its predecessor *Homo erectus* about 200,000 years ago in East Africa and spread through Africa and Eurasia" (p. 1297). On the basis of an examination of skeletons and art on the continents, early humans might have lived anywhere from 600,000 to 8,000 B.C. Rogers (1967) said that these people were of

> small stature, probably from four and a half to five feet tall. Their nearest living descendants are believed to be the Bushmen of South Africa; the Mincopies of the Andaman Islands off the coast of India; the hill-folk of Southern India; the Tapiro of New Guinea; and the Negritos of the Philippines. (pp. 28-29)

If the origins of the human race are Black, where did Whites originate? Rogers (1967) cited several scholars who submitted that the White race is a function of lack of pigmentation, lost over time because it was not needed in cold environments. For this reason, Sergi, of the University of Rome, stated that European man was African man transformed by European environmental effects. Within this line of reasoning, the correct term is *Eur-African,* of which there are three categories: "(a) the African with red, brown, and black pigmentation, (b) the Mediterranean or brunette complexion, inhabiting the great basin, including part of Northern Africa . . . and finally, (c) a Nordic variety of blond skin and hair, blue or gray eyes, most universally represented as Scandinavia, North Germany, and England" (Rogers, 1967, pp. 29-30).

RACE AS A SOCIAL CONSTRUCTION

Race has been criticized as nebulous because biology is often based on phenotypic appearances, such as skin color, hair type and color, eye color, stature, and head shape. Clearly, these characteristics alone do not accurately assign one to a particular racial classification (Zuckerman, 1990; see also the Storytelling "Right Research, Wrong Researcher"), yet race represents one of the most salient identity constructs for all people. It is used as a marker by police, bankers, judges, teachers, employers, potential suitors, and others throughout society to assign people who share certain phenotypic characteristics to racial group membership. Assumptions about these assignments ensue and affect the ways people experience daily life. Although race labeling may be fraught with problems, particularly in a climate where it is argued that race does not have legitimate biological properties, this information may be irrelevant to the dark-skinned African American man who is challenged in getting a taxi to stop for him at night in New York City.

For a long time, race has made a key difference in society and is filled with sociopolitical overtones (Cornell & Hartmann, 1997). In discussing the attitudes of the English toward Africans in the 16th century, Jordan (1994) wrote, "White and Black connoted purity and filthiness, virginity and sin, virtue and baseness, beauty and ugliness, beneficence and evil, God and the devil" (p. 42). Several centuries later, some of these demeaning attitudes linger and are embedded in the fabric of the American quilt, although they are contrary to the espoused values of democracy and equality.

At the time in U.S. society when the census listed five races, to be Colored (Black or mulatto) was not just a source of difference. Race functioned as a status variable. More specifically, the experience of being "Colored" meant no voting rights, no educational access to predominantly White institutions, extreme vulnerability to being lynched, and no legal protection under the law. Yet, the mere classification of races was not solely responsible for differential treatment. Attitudes about race were pivotal to the creation of a social structure where institutional policy bestowed privilege and conferred disadvantage on persons because of race (Hughes, 1945; McIntosh, 1988; Pinderhughes, 1989). The 1990 census, too, listed five races, but they were White, Black, Asian, Hispanic, and Indian (Cornell & Hartmann, 1997).

To address racial inequality, affirmative action was created through the provision of opportunity for groups that had been targets of historical discrimination. Many misbelieve that affirmative action seeks to impose quotas, which results in unqualified people (often regarded as people of color and women) taking jobs away from those who are qualified (often regarded as White males). The goal of affirmative action was to encourage employers to create opportunity for people of color, given their exclusion. Eventually, this provision extended beyond racial classification to include gender, sexual orientation, physical disability, and religion. About this controversial issue, Takaki (1994) said,

> Affirmative action is actually designed to address the legacy of past racial discrimination and existing inequality by training and identifying qualified individuals of excluded racial minorities and allowing them greater access to equality and opportunity in education and employment. (p. 7)

RACIAL IDENTITY DEVELOPMENT

Given that more differences exist within groups than between them (Cornell & Hartmann, 1997), differences in racial identity, attitudes, and value orientations are to be expected among racially similar people. Unique experiences and knowledge of self as racial and cultural beings influence identity development and contribute to intragroup variation. One benefit of racial identity development models is that they attest to the reality of psychological differences within racial and ethnic groups. Although given different names, racial identity development models assume within-group heterogeneity and maintain that early levels of development have the potential to change over time as individuals encounter dissonance to existing cognitive schema (Robinson, 1999). Discouraged, then, is a monolithic perspective when seeking to understand racially similar people. By integrating racial identity into the discussion, we conceptualize race as one component of psychosocial identity, with the goal of moving it beyond a discussion of privilege and oppression. Toward this end, several racial identity development models are discussed below.

CROSS'S NIGRESENCE MODEL

Cross's (1991) theory of racial identity development, called the **Negro-to-Black conversion experience,** or **nigresence,** is the most widely used racial theory about African Americans. It presumes a sociopolitical perspective and refers to the process of developing healthy racial collective identities, given discrepancies in sociopolitical power as a function of racial membership. In Cross's work, a distinction is made between *personal identity (PI)* and *reference group orientation (RGO)*. The former refers to self-esteem and interpersonal competence; the latter refers to racial identity and racial self-esteem. Cross's work on Black racial identity has been extremely influential in the development of models related to other aspects of identity, such as racial and cultural identity (Sue & Sue, 1990) and the womanist identity model (see Ossana, Helms, & Leonard, 1992).

Within Cross's (1991) theory, identity development is a maturation process whereby external negative images of the self are replaced with positive internal conceptions. Cross's five-stage nigresence model—(a) preencounter, (b) encounter, (c) immersion and emersion, (d) internalization, and (e) internalization and commitment—refers to "a resocializing experience" that "seeks to transform a preexisting identity (a non-Africentric identity) into one that is Africentric" (p. 190). Robinson and Howard-Hamilton (1994) discussed **Africentricity** as a conscious ideology with a strong connection to one's spirituality and kinship via African culture, culminating in the shared belief "I am because we are and since we are, therefore I am." An optimal Africentric worldview can be measured by an instrument called the Belief Systems Analysis Scale (BSAS), developed by Fine and James-Myers (1990). Although discussed in Chapter 2, *Africentrism* involves an awareness of Black identity, knowledge of cultural customs and traditions, liberating psychological resistance strategies, and an understanding of oppression and strategies to resist it (Dana, 1993; Robinson & Howard-Hamilton, 1994).

At *preencounter,* the African American views the world through the lens of the White dominant culture. Essentially, race has low salience. When people are asked to describe themselves, identifiers other than race, such as work, church, profession, and club affiliation, surface as key descriptors. Cross (1991) maintained that many preencounter African Americans are psychologically healthy and that anti-Black attitudes among African Americans in this stage are rare, although they do exist. Despite indices of psychological health among African Americans at this base stage of racial identity, Cross stated, "Preencounter Blacks cannot help but experience varying degrees of miseducation about the significance of the Black experience" (p. 192). African Americans in this first stage are more likely to operate from a Eurocentric cultural perspective in evaluating beauty and art forms.

At the *encounter* stage, one's new view of the world, as a result of a shocking personal experience, is inconsistent with the old. According to Cross (1991), the two aspects of this stage are (a) experiencing an encounter and (b) personalizing it. In every year of a person's life, myriad encounter experiences could encourage move-ment from preencounter to encounter. If the experiences are not internalized and personalized, however, movement up to this next stage cannot occur. Other identity constructs, such as religion, class, and education, can delay racial identity forma-tion, particularly when similarity with the referent group (e.g., being Christian, mid-dle-class, academically gifted) is encouraged and differences (e.g., race) that may be perceived as threatening or divisive are ignored (Robinson, 1999).

In the *immersion and emersion* stage, the focus is on being Black to the exclu-sion of others, particularly Whites. Cross (1991) indicated that this is a transitional stage with respect to identity transformation: "The person's main focus in life becomes a feeling of 'togetherness and oneness with people'" (p. 207).

The fourth stage of Cross's model, *internalization,* is characterized by more peace and calm. At this juncture, dissonance regarding an emerging identity has been resolved, evidenced by high salience attached to Blackness.

Internalization and commitment persons seek to eradicate racism for all oppressed people. According to Cross, this stage is similar to the internalization stage but is reflective of sustained long-term interest and commitment, as opposed to a brief period in one's life. At the higher stages of Cross's model, the African American is more able than at the lower stages to reconceptualize the self outside the narrow confines of oppression. At initial stages, the African American has little awareness of racial oppression because race has minimal importance.

THE RACIAL/CULTURAL IDENTITY DEVELOPMENT MODEL

The **racial and cultural identity development model (R/CID),** developed by Sue and Sue (1990), incorporates the experiences of people of color, various ethnic groups, and European Americans. The R/CID model has five stages: (a) conformity, (b) dissonance, (c) resistance and immersion, (d) introspection, and (e) integrative awareness. The lower stages reflect ethnocentric attitudes and cognitions. Accurate awareness about self and others as racial beings is limited. In contrast, the higher stages advance multicultural attitudes in that people are committed to racial equity for all persons and the eradication of racism.

Conformity is the first stage. White culture is regarded as superior. This stage is the essence of White racism. Thus, people of color unequivocally prefer the domi-nant culture's values over their own and esteem White cultural values and institu-tional standards as superior. Attitudes toward self, toward members of the same group, and toward other people of color tend to be depreciating. Low self-esteem is characteristic, and shame is associated with physical characteristics or traditional modes of dress. The denial mechanism often used is "I'm not like them" (other peo-ple of color), or "I've made it on my own," or "I'm the exception." The White person's attitudes are very ethnocentric, and the person has minimal awareness of self as a racial being, as well as limited accurate knowledge of other ethnic groups. White superiority and minority inferiority are accepted.

In the *dissonance* stage, denial gradually begins to break down because of situa-tions that contradict internalized beliefs. A traumatic event, however, can move people more rapidly into this second stage. Ultimately, conflict occurs between self-depreciating and self-appreciating attitudes and beliefs. For people of color, this is a fatiguing stage as tremendous energies are used to resolve conflicts toward the self, the same racial group, and the group in the majority. The person becomes aware that racism exists and that stereotypes associated with other people of color are questioned. Among Whites, movement occurs when culture is examined and the person acknowledges her own Whiteness. The person also recognizes personal racism and her role in being oppressive. Conflict results, and feelings of guilt, shame, and anger are common. Yet, rationalizations are common, such as "I'm just one person. What can I do about racism?"

In the *resistance and immersion* stage, people of color completely endorse minority-held views and reject the dominant values of society. Feelings of guilt and shame for having devalued one's racial group and anger for having been miseducated over an extended period of time are strong. Generally, people have affirming attitudes toward self and group. They have a hunger to discover their history and culture. Unlike in the first stage, attitudes toward the dominant group are depreciating. Often evident are enormous racial pride, a strong sense of identification with one's own racial and/or ethnic group, and a genuine desire to eliminate oppression of one's own racial group. For some, interaction may be restricted as much as possible to members of the same group. Among Whites, the person challenges her own racism and for the first time realizes what racism is all about. It is seen everywhere. Consequently, anger is projected at institutions and parents for espousing democratic values that are not truly practiced. Negative feelings about being White develop. Persons may become paternalistic or overidentify with a group of color.

Fourth is the *introspective* stage. Here, the person focuses on individual autonomy and expression and becomes more critical of group ideology. By this stage, many European Americans have migrated through two extremes—of naïveté and/or disdain about anything non-White to rejection of Whiteness. Many people of color have less energy invested in being angry with European Americans. An attempt is made to contact other groups of color to ascertain their personal and group experiences with oppression. In short, there is "an independent search for goals and direction beyond merely reacting to White racism" (Sue & Sue, 1990, p. 116).

Integrative awareness is the last stage in the R/CID model. It is accompanied by an inner sense of security, autonomy, and racial pride. The person of color has a strong desire to eradicate oppression in any shape or form, regardless of similarity to the individual's minority group. The person realizes that each culture has acceptable and unacceptable aspects, that each member of any group is an individual, and that European Americans are also victims of racism. Among European Americans, a nonracist identity begins to emerge, as does a search for aspects of White culture that are self-affirming.

ADDITIONAL MEASURES OF IDENTITY

Other measures of identity for various ethnic groups are available. For example, the Ethnic Identity Questionnaire measures preferences of Japanese kinship ties, sex roles, interracial attitudes, and personality characteristics (Dana, 1993). The Acculturation Rating Scale for Mexican Americans has been used to "represent Hispanic cultural origins" (Dana, 1993, p. 122). This 20-item scale looks at ethnicity of friends, language preference, and contact with Mexico. A similar scale, the Hispanic Acculturation Scale, has 12 items and examines three factors: (a) language use and ethnic loyalty, (b) electronic media preferences, and (c) ethnic social relations.

The Indian Assimilation Scale was developed in 1937–38 and is considered the best example of a pan-Indian measure. It includes attitudes toward native customs, marriage preferences, participation in organizations, and desire to become assimilated (Dana, 1993).

Although not developed for any particular racial or ethnic group, the Cultural Adaptation Pain Scale (CAPS), developed by Sandhu, Portes, and McPhee (1996), assesses the cultural adaptation and psychological pain associated with becoming acculturated. Fifteen major themes of psychological pain are explored. The four factors identified were (a) pain, (b), learned helplessness, (c), positive adaptation, and (d) bigoted.

BIRACIAL IDENTITY DEVELOPMENT

Poston (1990) developed a biracial identity development model, given the increasing percentage of persons who are biracial. Furthermore, many existing models assume racial homogeneity among persons; thus, a biracial model is greatly needed.

The stages in Poston's model are (a) personal identity, (b) choice of group categorization, (c) enmeshment/denial, (d) appreciation, and (e) integration. In *personal identity,* persons are very young, and awareness of membership in any ethnic group is new. Reference group orientation (RGO) attitudes are virtually nonexistent, and the emphasis is on personal identity attitudes, such as self-esteem. In the *choice of group categorization* stage, persons may feel pressure to choose an identity of one ethnic group in order to have a sense of belonging. Factors that influence choices concerning either a multicultural existence or one parent's race as dominant include the status of parents' ethnic background, acceptance within a particular culture, and physical appearance. In *enmeshment/denial,* persons are confused and feel guilt about the perceived need to choose one identity over another. In *appreciation,* persons have begun to appreciate the multiple identities that make up their existence. The group of persons with whom they identify is also broadened. In the last stage, *integration,* persons now feel a sense of wholeness as they are able to esteem their diverse identities and have developed a coalesced self-concept.

WHITE RACIAL IDENTITY DEVELOPMENT

Traditional conceptions of race refer to people of color, but European Americans also have race and experience racial identity. It is an infrequent experience or encounter, however, that would encourage a White person to assess her or his attitudes about being a racial being (Pope-Davis & Ottavi, 1994). Helms (1984, 1995) developed a White racial identity model that offers insight. Helms has been the primary voice in the development of a model of White racial identity development, and Ponterotto (1988) and Hardiman (1982) have done crucial work in this area as well.

It is important to explore this understudied area because Whites are racial beings and are shaped by the construct of race in their lives and also experience adverse consequences because of racism (Pinderhughes, 1989).

In a society where unearned skin color advantages are conferred, European Americans need to develop a positive racial identity that does not emanate from oppression and domination. This transformation may be difficult for many European Americans for at least two reasons. First, it is possible for White people to live in this society without having to acknowledge or give much consideration to the meaning of being White. Second, denial about one's own race impedes self-awareness, a crucial factor in racial identity development.

Helms's (1984, 1995) model has six stages (statuses) of (a) contact, (b) disintegration, (c) reintegration, (d) pseudoindependence, (e) immersion-emersion, and (f) autonomy. Helm's revised model includes information processing strategies such as obliviousness (IPS) or flexibility which "reflect the various attitudes, behaviors, and feelings that White people have developed as a result of being socialized to engender a white racist attitude" (Pack-Brown, 1999, p. 89).

A person enters the *contact* stage (status) from encountering the idea or actuality of Black people. Family background and environment affect whether the attitude toward Black people is one of trepidation or naive curiosity. In contact, the European American automatically benefits from institutional and cultural racism without the conscious awareness of doing so.

European Americans in the contact stage (status) tend to have positive self-esteem. They are idealistic about the equal treatment of African Americans; however, in actually interacting with them, they may experience some anxiety or arousal. Through interaction with African Americans, the European American realizes that, independent of economic conditions, clear distinctions exist in the treatment of people across race. Continuing to have socialization experiences will move the person into Helms's second stage (status), disintegration.

Entry into *disintegration* is characterized by conscious conflict that has its origins in dissonance. The European American in this stage (status) realizes that African and European Americans are not valued in the same way in this society.

The third stage (status) is *reintegration,* which is entered as the European American realizes that, within the dominant culture, the covert and overt belief of White superiority and African American inferiority exists. Yet, the person has a desire to be accepted by her or his White racial group. It is important in reintegration that a racial identity be acknowledged. Here, White privilege is protected even though it is unearned. People of color are not entitled to it because they are of inferior social, moral, and intellectual status. Because honest dialogue about race between racially different people does not often take place, it is fairly easy for a person to fixate in this stage (status). A jarring event can trigger movement into the fourth stage (status), however—*pseudoindependence.*

According to Helms (1990), "Pseudoindependent is the first stage of redefining a positive White identity" (p. 61). This stage (status) is primarily one of intellectualization wherein the person acknowledges responsibility for White racism. Although the negativity of the earlier stages does not exist, White norms continue to be used to interpret cultural or racial differences. Socially, the person is met with suspicion by both Whites and Blacks. Discomfort with the ambiguous racial identity may move the person into the fifth stage (status).

This fifth stage (status), *immersion-emersion,* is characterized by the replacement of old myths and stereotypes with accurate information. It is a period of unlearning. Here, the person may participate heavily in White-consciousness groups in which the goal is to help the person abandon a racist identity. Thus, attention is not on changing African Americans, but rather on seeking to change White people. The successful resolution of this stage (status) requires that the individual recycle or reexperience earlier emotion that was distorted or repressed.

Autonomy, the sixth and last stage (status) of Helms's (1984, 1995) model, is an ongoing process. In this stage, internalizing and experiencing new ways of being a racial being learned from previous stages are primary goals. In this stage (status), race is not a threat, as the person is not acting myopically. As is consistent with Cross's (1991) work, a variety of personality types are found in this last stage (status).

Helms (1990) posited that the first phase of her model, abandonment of racism, begins with the conflict stage and ends with reintegration. The second phase, development of a nonracist White identity, begins with the pseudoindependent stage and ends with the autonomy stage.

Sabnani, Ponterotto, and Borodovsky (1991) reviewed White racial identity models. One model was Ponterotto's racial consciousness development model. It has five stages and resembles other stages of identity development with respect to the emergence of emotions and cognitive awareness: (a) preexposure, (b) exposure, (c), zealot (half of zealot-defensive), (d) defensive (half of zealot-defensive), and (e) integration. The first stage, *preexposure,* describes persons who give little thought to multicultural issues and have not explored their own racial and/or ethnic identity. The second stage, *exposure,* characterizes persons who are required to examine their own cultural values, confront the harsh realities of racial inequity, and subsequently feel guilt and anger. The *zealot* half of the zealot-defensive stage is entrenched in minority issues and is a strong advocate for "minority" concerns. The fourth stage, the *defensive* half of zealot-defensive, indicates a different type of emotional energy altogether. Persons retreat from multicultural issues and find safety in same-race relationships. The fifth and last stage, *integration,* which is the same name of the last stage for several identity models, reflects a sense of harmony and balance. Persons exhibit an openness and receptivity to cultural differences.

OPTIMAL THEORY APPLIED TO IDENTITY DEVELOPMENT (OTAID)

Myers et al. (1991) developed a theory of optimal identity that is neither linear nor categorical. In criticizing some psychosocial identity models, she observed that they have limited the role of the individual in the identity process, did not consider people with multiple identities, and were based on a Eurocentric worldview. Myers maintained that the dichotomy of the spirit world and matter within American society makes it difficult to attain a positive self-identity in the United States, regardless of race, because self-worth is based primarily on external validation. Persons who turn outside themselves for meaning, peace, and value have adopted a suboptimal worldview. According to Myers, within an optimal perspective, self-worth is intrinsic in being. Thus, the purpose of life is becoming clearer about how the self is connected with all of life. Spiritual development is an integral part of identity development (see the Storytelling "One Spirit").

In Phase O, known as *absence of conscious awareness,* the person lacks awareness of being. This is regarded as an infancy stage. Phase 1 is *individuation.* Here, the world is the way it is in that people simply lack awareness of any view of self other than the one to which they were initially introduced. They rarely assign meaning or value to the various aspects of their identity. Phase 2 is *dissonance;* persons begin the exploration of their true self and affectively explore dimension of the self that may be demeaned by others. In Phase 3, *immersion,* one's energy is focused on those who are regarded as similar. Phase 4, *internalization,* occurs as people feel good about who they are and have successfully incorporated feelings of self-worth. Phase 5, *integration,* happens as people's deeper understanding of themselves allows them to change their assumptions about the world. The self is more secure internally, and peaceful relationships are a manifestation of this. The final stage, Phase 6, is *transformation.* The self is redefined toward a sense of personhood that includes ancestors, the unborn, nature, and community. The universe is understood as benevolent, orderly, and personal.

A BIRD-EYE'S VIEW OF THE RESEARCH

An abundance of research on racial identity has been done with a predominantly college and graduate student population. The purpose here is to examine some of the research to identify common themes related to identity development.

Poindexter-Cameron and Robinson (1997) conducted research on racial identity, womanist identity, and self-esteem among 84 African American college women attending both historically Black and predominantly White institutions. Instruments used to access racial identity, womanist identity, and self-esteem were the Racial Identity Attitudes Scale, long form, developed by Helms and Parham (1984); the Womanist Identity Attitude Scale, developed by Ossana et al. (1992); and the Rosenberg Self-Esteem Inventory (Rosenberg, 1965), respectively. Pearson-moment product correlation indicated a negative correlation between self-esteem and preencounter, the lowest level of racial identity. Conversely, a positive correlation was noted between internalization, a high stage of racial identity, and self-esteem. Although high at both campuses, self-esteem among Black women at the predominantly White institution was higher than among the Black women of the historically Black institution. These data suggest that the conceptual scheme of this identity model is consistent with assumptions about self-esteem—namely, that the higher stages of identity are related to higher levels of self-esteem and vice versa.

Parks, Carter, and Gushue (1996) conducted a study of racial identity among 214 Black and White women to investigate the constructs of racial identity and womanist identity. White racial identity was assessed using the White Racial Identity Attitude Scale (WRIAS; Helms & Carter, 1990). Black racial identity was assessed using the Racial Identity Attitudes Scale (RIAS; Helms & Parham, 1984). The Womanist Identity Attitude Scale (Ossana et al., 1992) measured womanist identity. Using canonical correlation analysis, these researchers found that, among Black women, higher levels of attitudes associated with the womanist attitudes were related to higher levels of internalization. Similar to the Poindexter-Cameron and Robinson (1997) study, internalization is correlated with dimensions of high identity. For White women, no relationships were found between racial and womanist identity.

Although in another study of African American college students preencounter levels on the RIAS were predicted to be correlated with stress, this hypothesis was not confirmed in the Neville, Heppner, and Wang (1997) study of 90 students. These researchers found that immersion/emersion attitudes were related to negative problem solving. This finding suggests that this particular stage may be characteristic of compromised levels of psychological functioning.

Brown, Parham, and Yonker (1996) conducted research with 35 European American trainees in a 16-week graduate-level cross-cultural course. The course included three phases: (a) self-awareness, (b) knowledge about other cultures, and (c) skill development. The researchers used the WRIAS (Helms & Carter, 1990) to measure White racial identity. They found that, on average, the cross-cultural counseling course changed the racial identity attitudes of White counselors-in-training. Noteworthy gender differences were found as well. An increase in pseudoindependence scores between the pre- and posttests was found among women, who in this stage may endorse the importance of assimilation to achieve a multicultural society. The European American male students had obtained higher autonomy scores by the end of the semester. Autonomy is the highest stage of Helms's conceptual model, and persons with these attitudes more "freely espouse and practice a multicultural mentality" (p. 515).

Research conducted by Robinson (1994) with African American and European American educators in the Southeast found that, independent of race, people favor multicultural education and want cross-cultural friendships. However, stands against racism and sexism describe different behaviors. This research found that African Americans and women were more socially proactive against racism and sexism than were European Americans and men.

IMPLICATIONS FOR COUNSELORS

The higher stages of racial identity facilitate reconstructing the self beyond oppression because of accurate subjective knowledge, the essence of true knowledge (Myers, 1991). Effectiveness in the counseling relationship is influenced by the com-

STORYTELLING
Right Research, Wrong Researcher

It was my student Ada's first professional conference. She was so excited about presenting her master of science research at this predominantly Black conference. I was proud of Ada; she was an excellent student and had done a thorough job on her master's thesis. I had cautioned her that some people might take issue with the fact that she was a White woman doing research on Black women. After our presentation—and Ada did a lovely job—she was approached by several audience members who congratulated her. One woman was unhappy and asked Ada why she was doing this type of research. This woman thought Ada was an inappropriate researcher because of her skin color. Ada's mind and heart were oriented toward equity and justice, and she was historically aware that some White researchers had done research on African Americans that depicted them in stereotypical and demeaning ways. In addition, I was her thesis supervisor and a Black woman. All this woman from the audience saw was color, Ada's white skin. It was the most salient characteristic of Ada. That sounds like racism to me.

Tracy

patibility of racial identity development between the client and the counselor. For example, clients of color in conformity and preencounter, the first stages of two of the models discussed above, are more likely to prefer a White counselor over a counselor of color. The belief exists that "Whites are more competent and capable than members of one's own race" (Sue & Sue, 1990, p. 108). In this scenario, if the counselor is European American, the client will typically be overeager to identify with the counselor. If the counselor is non-White, then the counselor will experience feelings of hostility from the client even if the client and the counselor are of the same race. Regardless of the counselor's race, "there is an obligation to help the client sort out conflicts related to racial/cultural identity through some process of reeducation" (p. 109). Understandably, the counselor is incapable of doing this if personal unawareness of racial themes is pervasive.

During the encounter and dissonance stages, clients are preoccupied with questions concerning the self and identity. They may still prefer a White counselor; however, counselors can take advantage of clients' focus on self-exploration toward resolution of identity conflicts. During the immersion/emersion, resistance and immersion stage, clients of color tend to view their psychological problems as an outgrowth of oppression and racism. In this stage, clients of color are prone to prefer counselors of their own race. In fact, people of color may tend to perceive White counselors as enemies. Thus, it is important for European American counselors not to personalize any attacks from clients of color because many statements regarding the unjust sociopolitical nature within the United States have legitimacy. It is also wise for counselors to anticipate that resistance/immersion clients will test them, as this stage is one of great volatility. Finally, counselors are apt to be more effective with a client when they use action-oriented methods aimed at external change.

Even during the introspection stage, clients may accept a counselor of a different race while preferring one of their own race. Ironically, persons at this stage may resemble persons at earlier stages, as there is conflict between the desire to identify with one's own group of color and the need to exercise a greater degree of personal freedom and choice.

Clients of color at the last stages of racial identity, integrative awareness and internalization commitment, experience an inner sense of security regarding their self-identities. They are able to choose counselors, not on the basis of race, but on the basis of ability to be empathic and understanding of the issues clients bring to counseling. Sue and Sue (1990) indicated that "attitudinal similarity between counselor and client is a more important dimension than membership-group similarity" (p. 112).

Regardless of race, counselors need to recognize their biases and assess their personal readiness prior to engaging in multicultural counseling (Robinson, 1993). To not do so is to place the client in jeopardy. Richardson and Molinaro (1996) found that the reintegration counselor may be impatient toward clients of different races and less likely to establish rapport with clients. Cook (1994) suggested that White counselors may also engage in ethnocentric behavior if they operate at Helms's reintegration stage and recognize their own race as standard for "normal" behavior of the client. Not until the immersion/emersion stage do White counselors acknowledge clients' race, respect cultural influences, and examine the sociopolitical implications. At the pseudoindependence stage, the White counselor will discuss racial issues but only when interacting with persons of color (Cook, 1994). Generalized assumptions still frame people's thinking.

The importance of a supervisor assisting with a supervisee's racial identity has been researched by Ladany, Brittan-Powell, and Pannu (1997). They found in their research of 105 raciallly diverse counselors that when supervisees and supervisor were at parallel levels of high racial identity stages, agreement about the supervision process was higher. In addition, when supervisor and supervisees had high levels of racial identity or when the supervisor had a higher level of racial identity than the supervisees, the supervisees' perception of the supervisor's multiculutral development influence on them was greater.

Ultimately, our beliefs and attitudes will inform the quality of our listening and our talking. Delpit (1990) eloquently said,

> We do not really see through our eyes . . . but through our beliefs. To put our beliefs on hold is to cease to exist as ourselves for a moment—and that is not easy . . . but it is the only way to learn what it might feel like to be someone else and the only way to start the dialogue. (p. 101)

Regardless of race, counselors who are uncomfortable about racial meanings and the various layers of their identity and unwilling to face their biases are poor candidates for helping anyone (see the case study "Biracial, Not Binary").

CASE STUDY
Biracial, Not Binary

Shannon Ester is an academically gifted 21-year-old biracial Native American and European American senior at Lonell University, a prestigious, predominantly White private school in the Southeast. Shannon has dark brown eyes, straight black hair, and caramel skin. She does not resemble her fair-skinned European American mother, who is a homemaker. Shannon's architect father is Cherokee. They reside in upstate New York.

During first-year-student orientation, a pre-med faculty member, on seeing her, assumed she had inadvertently wandered into the wrong advising group. Shannon was a mathematics major at the time. Without talking with her, he informed her that the social sciences orientation was on the east side of campus. When she asked her classmates about joining math study groups, she was told they were all full. She discovered that some of her classmates assumed she would lower the curve. A campus newspaper run by a predominantly White staff published an article accusing the university of relaxing admission standards for students of color and thereby lessening the reputation of the university by admitting affirmative action students.

During her first semester, some Native American students asked Shannon to join the Union of Asian, Hispanic, African and Native American Students (AHANA). She declined because she could not understand why they wanted to segregate themselves. After all, "people were people." During autumn of her sophomore year, she decided to join AHANA. During the second semester of her sophomore year, Shannon, on the advice of a friend, started seeing Dr. Emerson, a European American male counseling psychologist, to discuss her depression and her desire to leave college.

At first, Shannon was resistant to see Dr. Emerson, thinking that he, along with many other White people, did not understand ethnic and race matters. Sensing Shannon's hesitancy and lingering hostility, Dr. Emerson asked Shannon how she felt about counseling with him. This question allowed Shannon to share some of her concerns about discrimination and provided an opportunity to discuss the growing salience of her ethnicity, to which Dr. Emerson was very sensitive. Dr. Emerson suggested that she do a genogram to learn more about her family history and encouraged her to continue with AHANA, as he recognized that it was a source of support to her. Dr. Emerson also suggested that Shannon and her parents consider family counseling at some point to work through Shannon's anger at them for raising her to be blind about her ethnicity.

For a year, Shannon has been dating James Ribno, a Native American student in mathematics. Prior to college, Shannon had had no dating experiences with Native men because she dated only European Americans. Last year, she told James, "I realize that I was raised not to want to know who I am as an Indian." Growing up, she was taught that if people simply worked hard and were nice, then they would be treated fairly. Last Christmas, she told her parents she felt robbed of her ethnic heritage and announced that she was working on an Indian reservation in New Mexico during the summer to do an internship with her people. Last year, Shannon was president of AHANA and was very vocal about the racial and sexual discrimination on campus. Now she is campus liaison to the dean on concerns for all students of color. Next year, she will attend Yale Medical School on a full academic scholarship to focus on health care for Native Americans.

QUESTIONS

1. According to the R/CID model, on entering college, Shannon was most likely in which stage?
2. After her first year, Shannon was most likely in which stage of the R/CID model?
3. After her first year, Shannon was most likely in which stage of Myers's model?
4. As a senior, Shannon is most likely in which stage of the R/CID model?
5. When Dr. Emerson first counseled Shannon, at what stage in his development, according to the R/CID model, would he have been least effective with Shannon?

6. Where do you think Dr. Emerson is in his racial/ethnic identity development?

7. Does race always have to be important in the counseling event?

DISCUSSION AND INTEGRATION
The Client, Shannon

Shannon comes from a middle-class family. She has been adversely affected by the dearth of affirming media images, the lack of positive role models in positions of power, and the promotion of negative expectations and stereotypes regarding Native Americans. Shannon's isolation from other Native people interrupted her positive racial identity development (Robinson, 1999). The upper class among Native Americans is a very small group and is distinguished by its wealth and prominence.

Shannon has cycled through several developmental stages of racial and cultural identity as a result of her experiences in college as a biracial person. Such movement is precisely one of the real treasures of college in that students are afforded the opportunity to experience themselves anew, challenge earlier scripts and injunctions given by parents, and establish for themselves an ideology for life.

On the basis of her naiveté about her own identity as a Native American, Shannon arrived at college in the conformity stage of development. She appeared to be very assimilated with respect to her endorsement of the dominant culture and separation from her Native American heritage. She stated that "people were people." Cross (1991) maintained that, in addition to having an encounter, one must internalize it. For Shannon, several encounter experiences took place. The pre-med faculty member assumed she had wandered into the wrong advising group, without ascertaining her major. His assessment was based on her gender and race, which served as primary status traits over her achievement of placing into the pre-med track at this prestigious private college.

In Myers's 1991 model, Shannon was in the first phase of individuation. She lacked awareness of the world as being any other way than the way she had initially been introduced to it. Also, she did not assign meaning or value to the various aspects of her identity, such as race or ethnicity.

When Shannon asked about joining math study groups, classmates informed her they were all full, and some classmates assumed she would lower the curve. Myths about affirmative action abound, as some of the students have learned not to expect academic excellence from people of color.

Although some Native American students invited Shannon to join AHANA during her first year, she declined because she could not yet understand why they wanted to segregate themselves from the other students. Because "people were people," Shannon failed to see the significance of ethnic identity in shaping overall development. She joined a year later. During the spring semester of her sophomore year, Shannon started counseling to deal with her depression. Her cognitive dissonance stemmed from the way she had traditionally conceptualized herself in the world. This view was constantly being challenged, and depression was a consequence.

Because of the stigma often associated with seeking professional counseling and the inadequate experiences that many people of color have had with mental health professionals, it is not uncommon for people to battle with depression on their own for long periods prior to getting any professional help, if at all. Consistent with classical developmental theory, appropriate support is conducive to personal growth. In its absence, immobilization or stagnation can result. If Shannon had remained in the conformity stage, she might have had difficulty in therapy with a counselor of color because people of color in this stage are characterized by believing that "White cultural, social, institutional standards are superior" (Sue & Sue, 1990, p. 101). That Shannon was reluctant to counsel with Dr. Emerson is a strong indication that she had moved out of the conformity stage and was transitioning into the dissonance stage. Attitudes and beliefs toward members of the wider society often reflect conflict during this period (Sue & Sue, 1990).

By her junior year, Shannon had moved into the resistance/immersion stage of the R/CID model. Her agitation at administrative forces on campus perceived as racially unjust gives some indication of this, although such behavior could occur in more advanced stages as well. By her senior year, it seems that Shannon has moved into the introspective stage of the R/CID model. She is committed to accurate, subjective knowledge of the self that has not been externally packaged and promoted. Shannon is committed to working on an Indian reservation as a way of giving back to her people and connecting with them at the same time.

Shannon grew up in a middle-class family and enjoyed the benefits of her parents' earned class privileges. It is important to recognize, however, that her racial socialization left her without accurate cultural and racial knowledge about a primary aspect of her identity—race. For this reason, her socialization, despite the obvious privileges, can be considered oppressive. She was robbed of cultural knowledge and ignorant of the rich Cherokee legacy of which she is part. Gunn Allen (1994) spoke about memory and tradition:

> The American idea that the best and the brightest should willingly reject and repudiate their origins leads to an allied idea—that history, like everything in the past, is of little value and should be forgotten as quickly as possible. (p. 192)

Counselors need to understand this seeming contradiction, look beneath the alleged power and glamour of socioeconomic class and privilege, and avoid being blinded by their allure. It is essential that counselors perceive the underlying racial and cultural woundedness that some clients of color bring to the counseling event when they are denied accurate racial knowledge. Neither counselors of color nor European Americans who are at less sophisticated stages of racial identity can engage in this type of exploration with a client.

Shannon might have been more susceptible to depression because of her disconnectedness from her Cherokee ethnicity. Smith (1991) indicated that persons who are more embedded in their culture tend to be more "ethnically hardy" (p. 183). She also stated that persons who are embedded in their culture may be protected from developing a negative identity or a feeling of inferiority and helplessness (Camilleri & Malewska-Peyre, 1997). Some data reported earlier (Poindexter-Cameron & Robinson, 1997) provide empirical support that low racial identity levels are related to compromised self-concepts.

A discussion of heritage-consistent and -inconsistent styles among Indian/Alaskan people (Zitzow & Estes, as cited in Sue & Sue, 1990) may illuminate Shannon's situation. The heritage-inconsistent Native American (HINA) is described as being in denial and lacking pride in being a Native American. Although most Indians/Alaskans maintain some traditional connections (Dana, 1993), there is pressure to adopt majority cultural values. As a biracial person, Shannon certainly feels pressure to align herself with one racial group over another (Poston, 1990). Wilson (1992) addressed the issue of identity within American Indians and stated that concern over blood quantum is common independent of urban or rural status. It appears that Shannon did this by not seeing her Native American connections. This absent referent group orientation helps explain some of the guilt feelings she experienced over not participating in her Indianness. When Shannon started college, her lifestyle was more descriptive of the HINA. Her various encounter experiences moved her into many of the characteristics of the heritage-consistent Native American (HCNA). As Shannon's security in her heritage grew, she became more comfortable with and actively sought out community with other Native Americans. What is also important to attend to is the realization that Shannon is like so many millions of Americans who are multiracial yet live in a society that too often requires one's identification with one racial group (Root, 1992).

The Counselor, Dr. Emerson

Dr. Emerson is obviously not in the conformity stage of his development because he saw the significance of Shannon being involved with AHANA and understood the growing salience of Shannon's ethnicity. Had he been in this first stage of the R/CID model, he could not have been sensitive to the importance of Shannon's ethnicity in her own recovery. The suggestion for family counseling to work through some of Shannon's feelings toward her parents might have been overlooked as well. Yet, seeing the value of family connections is respectful of Shannon's cultural orientation despite her feelings of disappointment with her parents. Herring (1990) stressed the importance of network therapy with Native American populations. This therapy stresses the collateral relationships descriptive of Indian/Alaskan families. The family, tribe, clan, and other community affiliations are valued and need to be included as a means of working with the client (LaFromboise, Trimble, & Mohatt, 1990). Although Shannon has become bicultural, Dana (1993) main-

tained that, in counseling with Indians/Alaskans, a nondirective approach that focuses on mutuality may be helpful. Respect for the cultural value structure and not interrupting the client are also important components of the therapeutic event.

Dr. Emerson appears to be at higher stages of development (e.g., introspective or integrative awareness), given his ability to identify ethnicity and race as potential conflicts. He was aware that race and culture are crucial to healthy identity formation (Ward, 1989). He was neither afraid nor ignorant of the ethnic differences between himself and Shannon yet appreciated that differences need not impede effective multicultural counseling. His acknowledgment of these differences allowed him to create a counseling climate that was appreciative of Shannon and himself.

SUMMARY

Dismantling socialization patterns that have contributed to the unearned validation and unjust devaluation of people because of racial group membership is a crucial component of a multicultural society. Understandably, this process is difficult, yet a relationship exists between higher stages of racial identity development and advanced stages of moral development (Painter, 1993). It is conceivable that multicultural attitudes are related to higher levels of moral development, with the lower stages of development characterized by denial, defensiveness, and racist ideology. Encounter experiences that challenge current ways of thinking are crucial to development and, though dissonance provoking, provide individuals with an opportunity to move from traditional ways of perceiving the world and their place in it. The higher stages of racial identity characterize persons who are committed to eradicating racism and dedicated to creating a world where racial and cultural differences are valued and respected.

The purpose of this chapter was to establish that race is a status variable. Other multiple constructs were also considered in relationship to race in an effort to provide an understanding of the saliency of race as an identity construct that intersects with other multiple identities. Also discussed in this chapter were primary stage models on racial identity development and attending attitudes. Implications for efficacy in multicultural counseling were considered. Despite the differences between the models, they communicate that race attitudes exist on a continuum. More specifically, a multicultural and inclusive framework has as its most fundamental premise a celebration and acknowledgment of differences and is reflective of the more advanced stages of development. In contrast, the lower levels of stage models characterize ethnocentric and suboptimal ideologies in that self-awareness is relatively untapped. Clearly, counselors and teachers are by no means exempt from harboring attitudes that make them vulnerable to engaging in discriminatory practices.

REFERENCES

Begley, S. (1995, February 13). Three is not enough. *Newsweek,* pp. 67–69).

Brown, S. P., Parham, T. A., & Yonker, R. (1996). Influence of a cross-cultural training course on racial identity attitudes of White women and men: Preliminary perspectives. *Journal of Counseling & Development, 74,* 510–516.

Camilleri, C.,& Malewska-Peyre, H. (1997). Socialization and identity strategies. In J. Berry, P. Dasen, & T. S. Sarawathi (Eds.), *Cross-cultural psychology* (Vol. 2, pp. 41–68). Boston: Allyn & Bacon.

Cook, D. A. (1994). Racial identity in supervision. *Counselor Education and Supervision, 34,* 132–241.

Cornell, S., & Hartmann, D. (1997). *Ethnicity and race: Making identities in a changing world.* Thousand Oaks, CA: Pine Forge Press.

Cross, W. E. (1991). *Shades of Black: Diversity in African American identity.* Philadelphia: Temple University Press.

Dana, R. H. (1993). *Multicultural assessment perspectives for professional psychology.* Boston: Allyn & Bacon.

Darwin, C. (1859). *The origin of species by means of natural selection.* New York: Modern Library.

Delpit, L. D. (1997). The silenced dialogue: Power and pedagogy in educating other people's children. In A. Halsey, H. Lauder, P. Brown, & A. Wells (Eds.), *Education: Culture, economy, society* (pp. 582–594). Oxford, UK: Oxford University Press.

Dobbins, J. E., & Skillings, J. H. (1991). The utility of race labeling in understanding cultural identity: A conceptual tool for the social science practitioner. *Journal of Counseling & Development, 70,* 37–44.

Fine, M. A., & James-Myers, L. (1990). The development and validation of an instrument to assess an optimal Afrocentric worldview. *Journal of Black Psychology, 17*(1), 37–54.

Gossett, T. (1963). *Race: The history of an idea in America.* New York: Schocken.

Gunn Allen, P. (1994). Who is your mother? Red roots of White feminism. In R. Takaki (Ed.), *From different shores: Perspectives on race and ethnicity in America* (2nd ed., pp. 192–198). New York: Oxford University Press.

Hardiman, R. (1982). *White identity development: A process-oriented model for describing the racial consciousness of White Americans.* Unpublished doctoral dissertation, University of Massachusetts, Amherst.

Helms, J. E. (1984). Toward a theoretical explanation of the effects of race on counseling: A Black and White model. *Counseling Psychologist, 12*(3), 153–165.

Helms, J. E. (1990). *Black and White racial identity: Theory, research, and practice*. New York: Greenwood Press.

Helms, J. E. (1995). An update of white and people of color racial identity model. In J. G. Ponterotto, J. M. Casa, L. A. Suzuki, & C. M. Alexander (Eds.), *Handbook of multicultural counseling* (pp. 181–198). Thousand Oaks, CA: Sage.

Helms, J. E., & Carter, R. T. (1990). Development of the White Racial Identity Inventory. In J. E. Helms (Ed.), *Black and White racial identity: Theory, research, and practice* (pp. 67–80). Westport, CT: Praeger.

Helms, J. E., & Parham, T. A. (1984). *Racial Identity Attitude Scale*. Unpublished manuscript.

Herring, R. (1990). Understanding Native American values: Process and content concerns for counselors. *Counseling and Values, 34,* 134–137.

Hughes, E. C. (1945). Dilemmas and contradictions of status. *American Journal of Sociology, 50,* 353–357.

Jordan, W. (1994). First impressions: Libidinous Blacks. In R. Takaki (Ed.), *From different shores: Perspectives on race and ethnicity in America* (2nd ed., pp. 41–51). New York: Oxford University Press.

Ladany, N., Brittan-Powell, C. S., & Pannu, R. K. (1997). The influence of supervisory racial identity interaction and racial matching on the Supervisory Working Alliance and Supervisee Multicultural Competence. *Counselor Education and Supervision, 36,* 284–304.

LaFromboise, T. D., Trimble, J. E., & Mohatt, G. V. (1990). Counseling intervention and American Indian tradition: An integrative approach. *Counseling Psychologist, 18,* 628–654.

McIntosh, P. (1988). *White privilege and male privilege: A personal account of coming to see correspondences through work in women's studies* (Working Paper, No. 189). Wellesley, MA: Wellesley College Center for Research on Women.

Myers, L. J. (1991). Expanding the psychology of knowledge optimally: The importance of worldview revisited. In R. Jones (Ed.), *Black psychology* (2nd ed., pp. 15–28). Berkeley, CA: Cobb & Henry.

Myers, L. J., Speight, S. L., Highlen, P. S. Cox, C. I., Reynolds, A. L., Adams, E. M., & Hanley, P. (1991). Identity development and worldview: Toward an optimal conceptualization. *Journal of Counseling & Development, 70,* 54–63.

Neville, H. A., Heppner, P., & Wang, L. (1997). Relations among racial identity attitudes, perceived stressors, and coping styles in African American college students. *Journal of Counseling & Development, 75,* 303–311.

Ossana, S. M., Helms, J. E., & Leonard, M. M. (1992). Do "womanist" attitudes influence college women's self-esteem and perceptions of environmental bias? *Journal of Counseling & Development, 70,* 402–408.

Pack-Brown, S. P. (1999). Racism and white counselor training: Influence of white racial identity theory and research. *Journal of Counseling & Development, 77,* 87–92.

Painter, L. (1993). *A study of the relationship between moral development and racial identity among White college students*. Unpublished master's thesis, North Carolina State University at Raleigh.

Parks, E. E., Carter, R. T., & Gushue, G. V. (1996). At the crossroads: Racial and womanist identity development in Black and White women. *Journal of Counseling & Development, 74,* 624–631.

Pedersen, P. (1994). *A handbook for developing multicultural awareness*. Alexandria, VA: American Counseling Association.

Pinderhughes, E. (1989). *Understanding race, ethnicity, and power: The key to efficacy in clinical practice*. New York: Free Press.

Poindexter-Cameron, J., & Robinson, T. L. (1997). Relationships among racial identity attitudes, womanist identity attitudes, and self-esteem in African American college women. *Journal of College Student Development, 38,* 288–296.

Ponterotto, J. G. (1988). Racial consciousness development among White counselor trainees: A stage model. *Journal of Multicultural Counseling & Development, 16,* 146–156.

Pope-Davis, D. B., & Ottavi, T. M. (1994). The relationship between racism and racial identity among White Americans: A replication and extension. *Journal of Counseling & Development, 72,* 293–297.

Poston, W. S. C. (1990). The biracial identity development model: A needed addition. *Journal of Counseling & Development, 69,* 152–155.

Richardson, T. Q., & Molinaro, K. L. (1996). White counselor self-awareness: A prerequisite for developing multicultural competence. *Journal of Counseling & Development, 71,* 238–242.

Robinson, T. L. (1993). The intersections of gender, class, race, and culture: On seeing clients whole. *Journal of Multicultural Counseling & Development, 21,* 50–58.

Robinson, T. L. (1994). *What a difference difference makes.* Unpublished manuscript.

Robinson, T. L. (1999). The intersections of identity. In A. Garrod, J. V. Ward, T. L. Robinson, & B. Kilkenney (Eds.), *Souls looking back: Stories of growing up Black.* New York: Routledge.

Robinson, T. L., & Howard-Hamilton, M. (1994). An Afrocentric paradigm: Foundation for a healthy self-image and healthy interpersonal relationships. *Journal of Mental Health Counseling, 16,* 327–339.

Rogers, J. A. (1967). *Sex and race.* St. Petersburg, FL: Helga Rogers.

Root, M. P. P. (1992). Within, between, and beyond race. In M. P. P. Root (Ed.), *Racially mixed people in America* (pp. 3–11). Newbury Park, CA: Sage.

Rosenberg, M. (1965). *Society and the adolescent self-image.* Princeton, NJ: Princeton University Press.

Sabnani, H. B., Ponterotto, J. G., & Borodovsky, L. G. (1991). White racial identity development and cross-cultural counselor training: A stage model. *Counseling Psychologist, 19,* 76–102.

Sandhu, D. S. Portes, P. R., & McPhee, S. A. (1996). Assessing cultural adaptation: Psychometric properties of the cultural adaptation pain scale. *Journal of Multicultural Counseling & Development, 24,* 15–25.

Smith, E. J. (1991). Ethnic identity development: Toward the development of a theory within the context of majority/minority status. *Journal of Counseling & Development, 70,* 181–187.

Spickard, P. R. (1992). The illogic of American racial categories. In M. P. P. Root (Ed.), *Racially mixed people in America* (pp. 12–23). Newbury Park, CA: Sage.

Sue, D. W., & Sue, D. (1990). *Counseling the culturally different: Theory and practice.* New York: John Wiley.

Takaki, R. (1994). *From different shores: Perspectives on race and ethnicity in America.* New York: Oxford University Press.

Ward, J. V. (1989). Racial identity formation and transformation. In C. Gilligan, N. P. Lyons, & T. J. Hanmer (Eds.), *Making connections: The relational worlds of adolescent girls at Emma Willard School* (pp. 215–232). New York. Troy Press.

Wilson, T. P. (1992). Blood quantum: Native American mixed bloods. In M. P. P. Root (Ed.), *Racially mixed people in America* (pp. 108–126). Newbury Park, CA: Sage.

Zuckerman, M. (1990). Some dubious premises in research and theory on racial differences. *American Psychologist, 45,* 1297–1303.

Chapter 5

Converging Gender

Depression serves a woman as it presses down on her, forcing her to leave behind that which was not of herself, which had influenced her to live a life alien to her own nature. Her suffering, now substantial, insists that she no longer deny its truth.

Judith Duerk, **Circle of Stones**

Gender shapes each of our lives in primary ways. It influences core information regarding what we and others come to believe about ourselves. Across race, class, culture, and sexual orientation, some common gender themes seem to exist for men and women. Yet, among people of color, gender is often obscured by race, in that race appears to vie for more attention as the salient identity construct.

In this chapter, gender as both a social construct and a status characteristic are emphasized. It is acknowledged that gender differences exist between men and women and within groups of women and men. This truth is neither refuted nor regarded as problematic. However, the way gender inequity is perpetuated as a primary status characteristic within society is examined. Selected literature is presented on gender roles and sex role typology. The subsequent impact on gender identity is also investigated, as is gender from a biological perspective. Myths about biological differences between males and females are exposed.

GENDER AND BIOLOGY

In each human body cell, chromosomes are the genetic material carried. Except for the reproductive cells (sperm and ova) and mature red blood cells, each cell has 46 chromosomes arranged into 23 pairs. Twenty-two pairs of chromosomes, called **autosomes,** are matching sets in both males and females. The 23rd pair, called **sex chromosomes,** differs between the two sexes. Among genetically normal males, the sex chromosomes are XY; among genetically normal females, they are XX (Moir & Jessel, 1991).

As curious as it may seem, from conception to about the 6th week in utero, all human embryos are anatomically identical. During the 6th week, sexual differentiation begins. The genetic information in the Y chromosome stimulates the production of a protein called *H-Y antigen.* This protein promotes the change of the undifferentiated gonads into fetal testes. The fetal testes synthesize myriad hormones known as **androgens.** Two important androgens are *Mullerian inhibiting substance (MIS)* and *testosterone.* MIS is involved in the degeneration of the female duct system (Renzetti & Curran, 1992). Testosterone promotes further growth of the male Wolffian duct, the duct system that leaves the testes; it is often referred to as the aggression, dominance, and sex hormone (Moir & Jessel, 1991).

In the 8th week, the hormone dihydrotestosterone encourages the formation of external genitals. It is suggested that, for the female, the lack of testosterone may prompt the undifferentiated gonads of an XX embryo to transform into ovaries around the 12th week of gestation (Renzetti & Curran, 1992).

THE POLITICS OF HORMONES

Although biological differences attributable to gender are not a function of social constructions, the medical and scientific communities have influenced public thought and perceptions of biochemistry. For example, boy babies are more vulnerable than girl babies; however, fathers tend to play more roughly with boy children because male infants are perceived as being hardier than female infants. Actually, girls are sturdier and less vulnerable to infectious diseases than boys. Clearly, stereotypes run smack in the face of reality. Fausto-Sterling (1992) stated that biological differences lead adults to interact differently with babies. This has been documented in empirical studies in which subjects were unaware of an infant's gender. In one study in particular, a baby was startled by a toy and began to cry. Subjects who concluded that the baby was male associated the crying behavior with anger due to being startled. Subjects who concluded that the baby was female indicated that "she" began to cry because she had been frightened. More sex differences have been noted in babies. Moir and Jessel (1991) wrote that, at just a few hours old, girls appear to be more sensitive to touch than boys, are more sensitive to noise, and show greater interests in communicating with people. Boys appear to be more active than girls.

Another example extends farther through the developmental pipeline. More than 600,000 hysterectomies are performed in the United States each year, yet very few of these operations are performed because of life-threatening situations. Some are even suspected of being unnecessary. Interestingly, per capita, "half as many hysterectomies are performed in Great Britain as in the United States (Balch & Balch, 1997, p. 337). Could the historical devaluation of women and their bodies among the male-dominated medical community contribute to this extremely high rate of costly hysterectomies?

The quality of research findings, their interpretation, and scientific inquiry are affected by personal and political ideology. Take the naturally occurring conditions of menstruation and menopause, for example. Much of the research and studies done in these areas express deep hatred and fear of women and their bodies. Menstruation has been perceived of as an impediment and an illness, and menopause has been labeled a disease and a social problem. In fact, because women's bodies are different from men's, they have too often been regarded as abnormal.

Not only, then, is menopause big business, so is weight loss, the eating disorders of anorexia and bulimia, and liposuction and other forms of plastic surgery. The medical community has used estrogen against women to support a belief that this hormone is essential for femininity and youth. Conversely, this same chemical has been viewed as responsible for erratic and strange behavior. How often are the social, life history, and family contexts that characterize middle-aged women's lives investigated as more important variables than emotional changes occurring during the years of the climacteric (Fausto-Sterling, 1992)?

GENDER ROLE SOCIALIZATION

Although sometimes used interchangeably, *sex roles* and *gender roles* do differ. Typically, **sex roles** are behavioral patterns culturally approved as more appropriate for either males or females (Worell & Remer, 1992); however, in this work, *sex roles* refer to roles related to the function of one's biology, such as erection, ejaculation, menstruation, ovulation, pregnancy, and lactation. **Gender roles** are a consequence of society's views regarding appropriate behavior based on one's biological sex, such as diaper changing, garbage takeout, spider killing, dinner making, and primary breadwinning. The meaning of the term **gender** varies among different cultures and changes throughout time; nonetheless, the most common definition is the culturally determined attitudes, cognitions, and belief systems about females and males. Haider (1995) said, "the focus of gender is on social roles and interactions of women and men rather than their biological characteristics which is sex. . . . gender is a matter of cultural definition as to what is considered to be masculine or feminine" (p. 35). **Masculinity** refers to traditional societal roles, behaviors, and attitudes prescribed for men, whereas **femininity** references traditional societal roles, behaviors, and attitudes prescribed for women (Mintz & O'Neil, 1990).

Although an individual's personality develops through the interplay of both biological inheritance and social experience, at birth males and females are ascribed certain roles, characteristics, and behaviors associated with explicit values and expectations according to a constructed gender role that is socially generated (Haider, 1995). Undoubtedly, confusion arises when the sex category to which one should be assigned is ambiguous. With the application of rigorous criteria that are socially derived, people are placed within indigenous categories as male or female, man or woman (West & Zimmerman, 1991). West and Zimmerman (1991) said, "not only do we want to know the sex category of those around us (to see it at a glance, perhaps), but we presume that others are displaying it for us in as decisive a fashion as they can" (p. 21).

Gender is a status characteristic that manifests in multiple ways throughout society. Males tend to enter into the world as the preferred sex. It is not uncommon for couples with just girl children to keep having children until a male child is born.

Far too often, society places men's work on a higher level for remuneration and recognition. Even in female activities, male involvement gives men expertise. In coaching positions at colleges and universities, men can be hired as coaches for women's sports; however, it is very rare for women to be hired as coaches for men's sports.

The devaluation of women is culturally rooted. Several authors have noted that highly valued traits within the culture are typically deemed masculine—competitiveness, assertiveness, high achievement, and goal directedness (Burnett, Anderson, & Heppner, 1995). Not only are males valued in this culture over women, but masculinity also has greater "social utility" in U.S. culture than does femininity. This, according to Burnett, Anderson, and Heppner (1995), is known as the "masculine supremacy effect" (p. 323). These authors said, "this position suggests a cultural bias toward masculinity such that individuals who are masculine receive more positive social reinforcement and hence develop higher self-esteem" (p. 323). In this study, masculinity was viewed as more valuable not only for men but also for women. More specifically, "within this high press for masculinity, the person-by-environment interaction suggest, especially for women, those low in individual masculinity were at particular risk for decreased self-esteem" (p. 325).

The process of preparing boys to be masculine men and girls to be feminine women is largely an unconscious one. Socializing influences include parents, grandparents, the extended family, teachers, the media, and other children. The family influences children in their most important identity formation, the gender role (see the Storytelling "He's a Boy"). Usually, parents ensure that children are exposed to games, activities, and household chores compatible with the children's gender—and they are rewarded for acting appropriately. These rewards may be in the form of toys, accolades, encouragement, playing with the children, or actually offering advice and instructions. For example, a mother may serve as a role model and show her daughter how to vacuum the floor; thus, the daughter is being prepared for caring for the upkeep of a home. Pressure is put on girls to be obedient, good mothers, selfless, dependent, and trustworthy (McBride, 1990). Girls tend to be socialized to direct activity either in the home (cleaning, cooking) or close to it, and they often have a difficult time dealing with the new and unexpected because they tend to be protected and sheltered.

The range, then, of behaviors that are permissible for women is narrower than for men. From childhood, boys are taught to be outgoing, independent, and assertive. In addition, on the playground, girls and boys spontaneously participate in sex-differentiated games. Girls participate in extremely structured, turn-taking games that include fewer players, are governed by a set of rules, and less often require alternative strategies.

There has to be a relationship between these types of gender socialization experiences and the tendency of girls to attribute their success to luck, as opposed to skill (Sadker, Sadker, & Long, 1993).

SEX DIFFERENCES

Fausto-Sterling (1992) discussed the societal myths of gender as it relates to biology. She proffered that if sex differences do exist, they are very small. Additionally, complex environmental factors influence the development of the areas in which boys and girls are often seen as differing (e.g., visual and spatial skills).

Although there are exceptions, sex differences have been found in several areas (Young, 1981). The first area is *aggression*. Boys seem to engage in more antisocial behavior, such as fighting. Television is a major influence here. A second area is

STORYTELLING
He's a Boy

I deliberated long about telling this story and having it appear in print. I realize the tremendous power in both the spoken and written word. Part of my reluctance is the result of a desire not to malign my mother's memory. She was an excellent mother, and I know, beyond a shadow of a doubt, that the woman I am today is attributable primarily to my angel mother. My mother raised me to be independent, to trust God, and to get a good education. We always lived in a house, and Mom always worked. One day, the choices for dinner for myself, my sister, and my brother were fish sticks and steak. I assumed that the steak would be shared. Once I made my assumptions known, my mother intervened and said that my brother alone would have the steak. I protested loudly and queried her until I received the quintessential stare that most African American children grow accustomed to receiving from their mothers. This penetrating gaze basically told me to cease and desist. Even though I knew that my mother would literally get the upper hand, I continued to ask why my brother should get the steak. Could we not share the steak and fish? I wanted to understand but did not. Her behavior was so different from what I had ever experienced. Eventually, I was told that the steak was for my brother because "he is a boy." I was horrified, angry, and very confused. On the one hand, I had been taught to be my best and to do what I wanted to do; on the other hand, I was being told that the better quality of meat was reserved for my brother simply because he had been born a male and I had not. I watched my brother eat the steak. He seemed oblivious to my disgust, most likely because he perceived me to be as I was—powerless. My thoughts were not kind, and in my defeated 10-year-old heart I wished he would choke as I ate my tasteless fish sticks (which are loaded with fillers). I wanted more than anything else for justice to reign; I knew I had been wronged by no fault of my own.

Tracy

activity. Boys play outdoors more and play more actively. For many, sitting still is a problem. Boys are more curious, explorers. *Impulsivity is* the third area. Males are more impulsive than girls and have a difficult time resisting temptation. This may explain why accident rates are higher among males, given that they are more prone to take more chances. The fourth area is *anxiety.* Females are more fearful and anxious than boys. They are also more compliant and feel pressure to do the right thing. With regard to *social relationships,* females tend to be more nurturing—playing with dolls and babies. Females also show more concern with the welfare of the group and tend to compromise. Males have a more external network of friends. *Self-concept* differs as well. Males view themselves as more powerful, as having more control over events in the world. Males see themselves as instrumental, effective, ambitious, and assertive—as able to make things happen. Unfortunately, females tend not to share this perception of themselves. Yet, men often feel like workhorses and are also trapped in traditional roles of provider and breadwinner (Swanson, 1993). *Achievement* is the last area where differences between the sexes have been found. Males expect to do better. Whereas females tend to blame failure on themselves, males blame failure on external circumstances (Young, 1981).

To interpret differences between the sexes, it is important to look at the variation between a whole group rather than within a group. An example is spatial ability; 5% can be attributed to sex differences, but 95% can be attributed to individual differences or the richness of environmental experiences (Fausto-Sterling, 1992).

SEX ROLE TYPOLOGY

Why are restrictive and traditional sex roles that limit the range of behaviors available to people adopted and perpetuated? This question was asked by psychologist Sandra Bem, who developed the concept of **androgyny.** She also designed the Bem Sex Role Inventory, which has been used in hundreds of research studies to help in understanding the concept of *gender role socialization* and androgyny. *Androgyny* is from the Greek *andro,* meaning "male," and *gyne,* meaning "female" (Bem, 1993). Androgyny has been conceptualized as synonymous with a world where people as gendered beings can fully develop without restricting and confining sex roles.

Psychological differences between the sexes are not biological destiny, but rather are learned after birth through the sex role socialization process (Cook, 1987). Although this is the case, a uniformity myth tends to make sex synonymous with gender roles. Often, men are connected with masculine characteristics that are instrumental, agentic, and goal-oriented in nature. Emphasis is placed on self-development and separation from others. Masculine characteristics are related to goal directedness, achievement, and recognition by others for one's efforts.

Research suggests that masculinity has a more positive impact on how positively one sees oneself (Burnett et al., 1995). Women, though, are associated with the feminine characteristics of expressiveness and communality, with a focus on emotionality, selflessness, sensitivity, and interpersonal relationships. Femininity may influence how others respond to a person, but it is not surprising that masculinity is seen as strongly related to various indexes of psychological health (Burnett et al., 1995). As was discussed in Chapter 2, the U.S. culture is a masculine culture in that competition, independence, and assertiveness—traditional masculine traits—are valued. Similar to this is the concept of **androcentrism**, which is a traditional systematic construct in society wherein the worldview of men is used as the central premise of development for all individuals (Worell & Remer, 1992). Bem (1993) said that the central image underlying the concept of *androcentrism* is males at the center of the universe, looking out at reality from behind their own eyes and describing what they see from an egocentric—or androcentric—point of view.

Although masculinity and femininity are associated with biological sex, sex role typology, which references a psychological dimension, is not predicated on sex. Men can be feminine and women can be masculine. Sex-typed persons (e.g., men ascribing to a strictly masculine role, women being feminine), however, have internalized society's sex-appropriate standards for desirable behavior to the relative exclusion of the other sex's typical characteristics. This can contribute to narrow and restricted behaviors. An example of this is seen in research conducted by Stevens, Pfost, and Potts (1990). They found that "masculine-typed men and feminine-typed women reported the most avoidance of existential issues, with sex-typed persons indicating the least openness to such concerns . . . the findings also complement evidence of behavioral rigidity among sex-typed individuals" (p. 48).

Bem (1993) hypothesized that an individual with both masculine and feminine characteristics would be more flexible and function more productively than a sex-typed individual. Androgynous persons demonstrate a lack of statistically significant differences between masculinity and femininity scores, thus showing a blend of both dimensions. (*Androgynous* refers to persons who are high in both feminine and masculine psychological and behavioral traits, not to persons' biological, male or female, physical characteristics.) Spence and Helmreich (1978) critiqued a bipolar orientation to understanding masculinity and femininity. They said, "while the bipolar approach to the psychological aspects of masculinity and femininity has been dominant, dualistic conceptions have also been proposed: masculinity and femininity are separate principles and may coexist to some degree in every individual, male or female" (p. 18). Masculinity or femininity should refer to behaviors, not physical makeup. The androgynous person, less bound to the restrictive sex-appropriate standards for behavior, is theoretically able to develop psychologically to the fullest and respond receptively to a wide range of situations, perhaps in ways that the less integrated person is unable to do. Undifferentiated persons, whose scores on the Bem Sex Role Inventory are low on both masculine and feminine dimensions, tend to be disadvantaged. They report psychological problems, poorest social interactions, and low self-esteem.

ORTHOGONAL AND BIPOLAR MODELS

Bem (1993) describes masculinity and femininity within a bipolar model. The **orthogonal model,** in contrast, describes masculinity and femininity as meeting at complementary right angles, rather than as antagonistic or unrelated groups of psychological characteristics. A person has a range of characteristics, behaviors, and traits available to use freely. Cross-culturally, the concepts of *masculinity* and *femininity* have been represented as complementary domains, traits, and behaviors for thousands of years. For example, the yin-yang theory of the harmony and balance of forces in nature is based in Confucian thought and Chinese cosmology. Uba (1994) said that the yin is representative of feminine, negative, inferior, and weak, whereas the yang is symbolic of masculine, positive, superior, and strong. "If this supposedly natural balance is upset (e.g., if a wife domineers over her husband), the equilibrium within the family would be disrupted" (p. 29).

Western philosophy dictates that masculinity and femininity be mutually exclusive or dichotomous. Common language used when referring to the two genders is "the opposite sex," or reference is made to one's partner as "the other half." Masculinity in the Western worldview is associated with an instrumental orientation, a cognitive focus on getting the job done, or as solving problems. Femininity, in contrast, is associated with a concern for others and harmony with the group. Other adjectives used to describe masculine and feminine behavior are as follows:

MASCULINE	FEMININE
Autocentric	Allocentric
Selfish	Selfless
Inner	Outer
Assertive	Submissive
Independent	Dependent
Cognitive	Affective
Aggressive	Passive
Instrumental	Expressive
Agency	Communion

Bem (1993) said that an individual can be both masculine and feminine; expressive, instrumental, and communal; and compassionate and assertive, depending on the situation. Limiting oneself to one domain could be dangerous to human potential. Individuals are encouraged to mitigate agency with communion, strength with yielding. Bem stated that this is necessary because extreme femininity untempered by a sufficient concern for one's own needs as an individual may produce dependency and self-denial, just as extreme masculinity untempered by a sufficient ability to ask for help from others may produce arrogance and exploitation.

WOMEN AND SEX ROLE TYPOLOGY

Characteristics commonly associated with femininity on the Bem Sex Role Inventory include yielding, gullibility, being childlike, and not using harsh language. For the most part, the culture encourages women to sacrifice their development and needs for the benefit of others', usually men's. Yet, women who sacrifice their own development to meet the needs of others often inhibit the development of self-expression, self-knowledge, and self-esteem (McBride, 1990). This socialization process of being selfless can contribute to women equating self-care with being a destructive and selfish person. In fact, research on 218 Black and White female college students found that White women who questioned traditional notions of womanhood and valued women were more likely to exhibit psychological symptomatology, such as depression, anxiety, and paranoia (Carter & Parks, 1996).

Several models help in understanding women's development (Enns, 1991). These models seek to highlight the relational strengths that woman embody and, according to Enns (1991), to attempt "to correct the inadequacies of mainstream theories and conceptualize women's experiences in their own terms" (p. 209). Women's psychosocial development is different from men's. For instance, Gilligan (1982) criticized major identity development theorists who depict women as inferior to men because of important gender differences. According to Gilligan, women's development "relies more on connections with others, on relatedness rather than separateness" (p. 271). Erikson (1968) has been observed as focusing the majority of his attention on the masculine version of human existence. The primacy of men in the human life event reflects the sexism of the time (Horst, 1995). Recently, other psychologists have written about the unique experience of women and the implications of this on their development. Nelson (1996) commented that relational skills are highly functional and involve a complex array of competencies essential to preserving family and culture.

Although it has been stated that women may emphasize relationships over men, the importance of autonomy for women cannot be underestimated. McBride (1990) argued that **autonomy** refers to being able to define oneself, rather than being defined by others. Autonomy can mean interdependence, mutual cooperation, and individuation. Citing Chickering's definition, McBride stated that **instrumental autonomy** refers to the ability to act on the world, carry on activities, cope with problems, and take action to meet one's needs. **Emotional autonomy** is the freedom from pressing needs for approval and reassurance. Women are often unaware of how much energy they invest in doing things for others versus developing healthy interdependence.

What are the benefits of masculinity for women (McBride, 1990)? Women with androgynous and masculine (instrumental) gender role orientations have been found to have higher levels of self-esteem than women with more feminine (expressive) and undifferentiated gender role orientations. Low self-esteem (Burnett et al., 1995) and avoidance of existential issues (Stevens et al., 1990) have been reported for women who are low in masculinity.

The capacity to commit to concrete affiliations and partnerships and to develop the ethical strength to abide by such commitments even though they may call for significant sacrifices and compromises is a source of strength. From a developmental perspective, this embodies Erikson's (1968) discussion of the balance between the *sytonic,* which references healthy identity, and *dystonic,* or confusion and crises. Horst (1996) said that balancing identity and identity confusion results in a capacity for fidelity and that balancing intimacy and isolation results in a capacity to love. The significance of this balance is that passing through a crisis wherein one becomes committed to a particular set of values represents identity.

MEN AND SEX ROLE TYPOLOGY

Gender socialization exists for both males and females. Boys are encouraged to be assertive, independent, strong, and self-reliant and to restrict emotion. One consequence of this socialization pattern is that men's restrictive emotionality seems to be related to depression and to more negative attitudes toward seeking professional psychological help (Good & Mintz, 1990).

Another way of understanding restrictive emotionality on men's lives is by comparing an underused muscle to the difficulty many men have in receiving assistance during emotional stress (Skovholt, 1993). Men's tendency to avoid expressing affection toward other men is associated with increased likelihood of depression. Boys are also prepared to engage in the world and explore it and to play by themselves. In doing so, they develop improvisational and problem-solving skills and are given important practice in the art of negotiation. Achievement and success are emphasized for boys, which may explain why boys enter an activity with a premise that they can master, create, and make a difference. This conflicted and rigid behavior is categorized as **gender role conflict,** which "describes the detrimental consequences of gender roles either for the person holding them or for those associated with this person" (Mintz & O'Neil, 1990, p. 381). Good, Robertson, Fitzgerald, Stevens, and Bartels (1996) conducted research on the relationship between masculine role conflict and psychological distress among a group of male university clients. These authors stated that the instrument used to measure masculine role conflict, the Gender Role Conflict Scale (GRCS), is

> based on the theoretical notion that the traditional gender socialization of boys demands more than they can deliver; that is to be regarded as adequately masculine, men must be powerful and competitive; not show vulnerability, emotions, or weakness; control themselves, others, and their environments; be consistently rational; be sexually skilled; and be successful in their work. The impossibility of successfully meeting all these demands is hypothesized to lead to distress. (p. 45)*

Four subscales of the GRCS examine men's conflict with traditional masculine roles: (a) achieving success, (b) experiencing emotions, (c) sharing affection with other men, and (d) balancing work and family relations. In the Good et al. (1996) study, masculine role conflict was associated with psychological distress, such as paranoia, psychoticism, obsessive-compulsivity, depression, and interpersonal sensitivity. According to Good et al., four behavioral patterns emerge when men experience gender role conflict. The first behavioral pattern is *restrictive emotionality,* which refers to men's reluctance or difficulty that men have expressing their emotions. The second behavioral pattern is *restrictive affectionate behavior between men.* Men may also be afraid of sharing a full range of emotions for fear of being seen as gay (Good, Dell, & Mintz, 1989). Gertner (1994) said that men may also be limited in how they express their sexuality and affection to others. *Obsession with achievement and success* is the third behavioral pattern, which references a disturbing and persistent preoccupation with work, accomplishment, and eminence as a means of demonstrating value. Understandably, seeking help may be experienced as antithetical to being in control and having power. This may help explain why men

---

* *From "The Relation Between Masculine Role Conflict and Psychological Distress in Male University Counseling Center Clients," by G. E. Good, J. M. Robertson, L. F. Fitzgerald, M. Stevens, and K. M. Bartels, 1996, Journal of Counseling & Development, 75, p. 45. Copyright 1996 by the American Counseling Association. Reprinted by permission.*

remain less likely than women to seek therapeutic assistance (Gertner, 1994). It is not that women are more psychologically distressed than men; it is just that men's socialization patterns do not encourage them to seek needed psychological help. Further, feeling sad or depressed may be seen as unmanly (Good et al., 1989). *Balancing work and family relations* is the fourth behavioral pattern. Because men are socialized to focus on achievement, other areas of life, such as home and leisure, can easily be ignored or sacrificed or both. These four behavioral patterns have been related to depression (Good & Mintz, 1990). Gertner (1994) added homophobia and health care problems to this as well.

Despite the disturbing findings regarding the correlation between depression and masculine role conflict, healthy male development can be accomplished with the expansion of gender roles and the abolishment of limited scripts for appropriate masculinity (Skovholt, 1993). Skovholt (1993) said that "this narrow funnel of acceptable masculinity may give males a solid sense of gender identity, but it can, in time, also become a prison that constricts personal growth and development" (p. 13). Men are fearful of being perceived as or labeled feminine, which is part of the narrow funnel through which they must conduct their lives. From a psychosocial perspective, this fear stems from the arduous task men must complete: separate from their mothers toward developing their male identities (Skovholt, 1993). This particular socialization process dictates that men should never engage in opposite-sex behaviors and attitudes.

Men travel through their developmental paths unduly conflicted yet trying to maintain power over women and other men (Pleck, 1984). A key task of the men's movement was to articulate the male experience of power and powerlessness (Swanson, 1993). Often, it is falsely assumed that female powerlessness translates into male power. Swanson (1993) articulated that sometimes men feel like success objects. Not only are women assailed for leaving traditional roles, but men, too, are attacked as irresponsible for abandoning their provider role.

One disadvantage of rigid gender socialization pertains to emotional expression. Many men are restricted emotionally, which may represent a compounded risk of the likelihood of depression, coupled with a decreased use of greatly needed psychological services. Because many men leave intimacy to women, they may need to be educated on the benefits of emotional expression. Certainly, men have basic needs to love and to be loved, to care and to be cared for, to know and to be known, but socially prescribed gender roles tend to require men to be inexpressive and competitive with one another. Evaluating life success in terms of external achievements rather than interdependence is also emphasized.

Good and Mintz (1990) also found significant relationships between depression and factors of gender role conflict. Although college men were examined, the results may have implications for older men, given components of the male role that appear to be consistent over time. These researchers found that boys' games, though rule-governed, rewarded creativity, improvisation, and initiative and involved teams composed of a larger number of peers and encouraged both cooperation and competition.

Until gender-roles ascribed by society change, and the inherent sexism is transformed, men and women alike will be constricted and suffer from the consequences of inequities based on biological sex and accompanying socially constructed roles (Gertner, 1994). The wounds of patriarchal power and control damage men as well as women (Brown, 1994). The roles for men need to be transformed so that men become "acutely aware of their power to influence self and to break the bonds to patriarchy, emotional handcuffs in the form of assumptions and interpretations that favor patriarchal values about the worth of human beings and the meaning of their experiences" (Brown, 1994, p. 118).

IMPLICATIONS FOR COUNSELORS

One reverberating point throughout this text is that U.S. society is highly gendered and has rather rigid notions about appropriate modes of being for men and women (Kaplan, 1987). Thus, the power of the therapeutic event is found in the interpersonal relationship between client and therapist. The importance of clinical skills and training is not being minimized; however, the relational bond is primary.

It is important for counselors to note that, over time, women and men maintain and modify their sex role-related perceptions, attitudes, and behaviors. Counselors also need to remember that sex role typology is complicated. Individual differences in determining sex role must be allowed for so as not to stereotype people. Yet, it is important to incorporate an understanding of gender role socialization in working with clients. For instance, practitioners need to know that men usually feel comfortable with side-by-side intimacy and that face-to-face intimacy, to many men, feels like an invasive and aggressive, highly confrontational experience (Swanson, 1993). Although counselors need to understand that the gender dyad makes a difference in the counseling event, often the male and client roles are rather discontinuous. For instance, the personal characteristics of the male role often focus on physical strength and accomplishment, whereas the client role emphasizes acknowledgment of weakness. In the male role, men are often punished for seeking help, whereas in the client role, help seeking is reinforced (Skovholt, 1993). Gender can add another dimension to the therapeutic process. Good and Mintz (1990) found that, between two men, a male counselor and a male client, restricted emotionality and homophobia present themselves as issues. As unfortunate as it is, homophobia may prevent male counselors from showing concern and care for male clients, and a male client may feel tremendous angst and fear may surface if he experiences warmth toward a male counselor. It is also likely that a male counselor could be embarrassed at his feelings toward another man's emotional expressions. The client could also be ashamed to disclose.

When the counselor is male and the client is female, a different dynamic can surface. One form of bias is for male counselors to respond to female clients as sex objects. Moreover, because of socialization, a male counselor may adapt a one-up type of position with the client. The client may also have difficulty expressing to the counselor emotion that she may subconsciously feel is intolerable. About this particular dyad, Kaplan (1987) found that women with male therapists saw themselves as less self-possessed, less open, and more self-critical than did the women with female therapists.

Certain reactions to women in therapy are the product of socialization. Bernardez (1987) found three specific reactions to women in therapy: (a) the discouragement and disapproval of behavior that did not conform with traditional role prescriptions, such as mother; (b) the disparagement and inhibition of expression of anger and other "negative" affects, such as anger and bitterness; and (c) the absence of confrontation, interpretation, and exploration of passive-submissive and compliant behavior in the client. Despite these reactions from therapists, Bernardez reported that female therapists showed greater empathy and ability to facilitate self-disclosure than males. Male therapists may be more inclined to reproduce the dominant-subordinate position by unconscious encouragement of the female's compliance, submissiveness, and passivity.

A problem for both sexes is the strong gender role prohibition against female anger, criticism, rebellion, or domination. Anger is often equated with hatred, destructiveness, or bitterness. Helping clients realize that they have the right to take care of themselves even if those in their environment tell them they are hurting others is an important step on the road to self-mastery.

Female counselor-male client represents the typical care-giving pattern in society. Yet, men may be very challenged entering therapy and abdicating power to a woman. If a woman is uncomfortable with her power, given some of her socialization tapes that maintain the power of men over women, she may fidget or acquiesce her power.

Female counselor-female client is probably one of the most emotionally intense dyads. These dyads were found to allow for a fuller exploration of childhood experiences. Female clients, because of socialization, may challenge the female counselor and question her competence. Because of gender role socialization, therapists of both genders have difficulties with a whole array of aggressive behaviors in their women clients (Kaplan, 1987).

Regardless, then, of the gender of the counselor or the client, empathy is the key ingredient in the counseling event (Pinderhughes, 1989). According to Kaplan (1987), **empathy** is the ability of the therapist to surrender him- or herself to the affect of another while cognitively structuring that experience so as to comprehend its meaning in terms of other aspects of the client's psyche (p. 13). It requires that the counselor be comfortable and familiar with the world of affect and the nature of connections between people. If the counselor is uncomfortable, a typical response is to ignore, discard, or discourage communication.

Therapists may disapprove of women who show power and controlling, competitive, and autonomous behavior while disliking behavior typically regarded as feminine (e.g., self-depreciation, submissiveness). Some male therapist may subconsciously dread women dominating them and fear their own vulnerability to female aggression. Female therapists may also fear the eruption of their own anger toward men, which can have an adverse impact on the therapeutic relationship.

Although female therapists may be less inhibited than their male colleagues, women helpers may internalize the split-off anger of the client, which can interfere with the client's experience of these feelings in her own life. It is also possible that some therapists are afraid to experience the powerlessness that comes with examining social injustice (Bernardez, 1987).

Given the research on college men, depression, and low likelihood of their seeking out psychological services, college counseling centers are in a prime position to do outreach (residence halls, orientations, classrooms, student development). Helping people reclaim the parts of themselves they have forfeited in order to conform to society's role expectations, both at home and at work, may enhance development. In addition, men can be encouraged to reframe their notions of counseling. Good and Wood (1995) said that "changing men's view of counseling might consist of efforts to emphasize that participating in counseling is an activity involving personal courage and strength that is displayed through facing and sharing one's concerns" (p. 73).

Regardless of race, ethnicity, and sexual orientation, male and female children and adolescents receive similar gender-appropriate messages. Poor White men and upper-class men of color are socialized to function and be in positions of control (whether they actually are is a different matter). For this reason, seeking help is incompatible with the masculine role. Middle-class White women and poor women of color are socialized to emphasize the needs and wants of others, usually before their own (see the case study "Redefining Womanhood" at the end of this chapter). Despite the similarities, more research is needed on the specific effects of class and other sources of differences as mediating traditional gender role messages.

The value of both masculine and feminine characteristics for men and women is tremendous. Practitioners need to recognize that some changes evidenced by clients may not be indicative of deviation or even of sex atypicality. Individual differences must be accounted for. A primary theme articulated throughout this work is that more differences are found within groups than between them.

CASE STUDY
Redefining Womanhood

Valerie is a widowed 39-year-old African American woman. She has two children—a 12-year-old daughter and a 10-year-old son. Valerie is a secretary and earns a modest salary. Five years ago, her husband died in a car accident. Valerie is very involved in her Baptist Church as a member of the Missionary Society and a member of the choir. Last month, she was diagnosed with breast cancer. Her doctor strongly recommended a mastectomy (removal of the entire breast) and removal of the lymph nodes because of the advanced nature of the cancer. Although Valerie had felt a lump for several years, she ignored it because she was frightened and did not like going to the doctor. Besides, at times she simply did not have adequate medical

insurance and chose to take her children to the doctor instead of meeting her own medical needs. Valerie finally went to the doctor because her breast had become disfigured and she could no longer deny that something was wrong. When Valerie decided to have the surgery, the doctor told her that the surgeon might have to remove a portion of the second breast if the cancer had spread. On awaking from the surgery, the doctor informed her that she had had a radical mastectomy on one breast and a lumpectomy on the other. One month after the surgery, Valerie has not revealed to the man she has been dating for 6 months why she was ever admitted to the hospital, although he has been very kind and supportive of her. Valerie is contemplating end-ing the relationship with him. She believes that he will not want a woman who looks the way she does. Valerie's doctor has informed her that she can return to work, but Valerie is reluctant to be around people, given that she will look different. She is concerned that people are talking about her.

QUESTIONS

1. Does Valerie's race/ethnicity affect Valerie's problem orientation?
2. Does Valerie's race/ethnicity affect the way a counselor should interact with her?
3. What type of gender issues are operating in Valerie's case?
4. Are Valerie's reactions appropriate, given her substantial loss?
5. Could a male counselor be effective in counseling Valerie?
6. How might a counselor help Valerie disclose her feelings if Valerie is reluctant to talk?

DISCUSSION AND INTEGRATION
The Client, Valerie

Although Valerie survived her breast surgery with her life, her severe depression in reaction to multiple and significant losses at one time is understandable. Valerie needs to know that her mourning and consuming sadness are normal reactions to devastating loss and disappointment.

Valerie is mourning the loss of one breast and surgical changes to the other. Since puberty, Valerie has lived in a body with two breasts. The routine tasks of bathing, dressing, running, and sexual activity were all visual, sensual, and visceral reminders of her womanhood. Valerie's body image and satisfaction have undeniably been affected by her surgery, given that society places such a premium on physical attractiveness for women (Okazawa-Rey, Ward, & Robinson, 1987).

In addition to the pressures of society about body perfection, a mastectomy and lumpectomy greatly alter the shape, feel, and image a woman has of her body. Valerie is also feeling some anxiety that her new body detracts from her sexual desirability and may even be antithetical to it. Furthermore, she worries that her new body makes her less attractive to herself, to the man she has been dating, and to other men as well. Valerie may believe that her changed body makes her a less desirable candidate for a long-term, fulfilling, romantic relationship.

According to Bernardez (1987), depression is often associated with selfless, sacrificial behavior and the expectation that women should put others first and discount their own personal needs. Limited financial resources contributed to Valerie's decision to put her children's medical needs before her own. Like many African American women, Valerie is among some of the lowest paid workers in the nation's workforce. And in actuality, racism and sexism subject Black women to considerable discrimination (Evans & Herr, 1991). Napholz (1994) said that "in comparison to White women, Black women are hindered by mean earnings that are lower than those of White women, by overrepresentation in low-status occupations and by a disproportionately low level of education" (p. 469).

Although Black women develop breast cancer less frequently than White women, Black women are more likely to die from it. Often, higher mortality rate is attributable to inadequate health care (White, 1994). This is the case with Valerie. Access to proper medical care was not always available to her; at times, her employer did not offer adequate coverage. Her current secretarial job, however, provides full medical benefits for herself and her children. Fear of something being wrong with her body was immobilizing. This is understandable. Far too often, women's power comes from their beauty and physical allure. Within this context, having a "perfect" body is key to a woman's desirability (Okazawa-Rey et al., 1987).

Women also tend to be socialized not to express anger (sadness and fear tend to be more readily tolerated). Valerie may also be afraid to tap into some of the anger or rage she feels. Some of these feelings may be self-directed, partly because of her frustration for not acting sooner on her own behalf. Although Valerie needs to stop condemning herself for not attending to the lump that she had felt for a few years, her inaction might be valuable information for the counselor.

Valerie's husband died suddenly 5 years ago. This event may help explain her decision not to act any sooner on her behalf. Depression or even post-traumatic stress may account for Valerie's lack of action. That African American women are less likely than White women to seek treatment for mental health issues through formal systems (Reed, McLeod, Randall, & Walker, 1996) exacerbates the problem. Valerie also is a member of the Black community, which has historically been treated poorly by the medical establishment. For example, as part of a medical research study, the federal government withheld treatment from Black men who had syphilis.

Research conducted by Napholz (1994) on 113 African American women, aged 18 to 65, may also offer insight into Valerie. Napholz found that sex-typed women (e.g., feminine) had more depression and lower self-esteem than women who were psychologically androgynous.

Women who sacrifice their own development to meet the needs of others often inhibit the development of self-expression, self-knowledge, and self-esteem (McBride, 1990). Depression is often associated with the behavior of women, such as Valerie, constantly putting others' needs first and discounting their own needs. Environment also plays a role. Reed et al. (1996) said, "African American communities are often devoid of community support resources (e.g., hospitals, physician offices, shopping centers, recreation facilities, and public transportation)" (p. 11). Even though it may be tempting to blame Valerie for behaving selflessly, her socialization patterns influenced her overall identity development (Lemkau & Landau, 1986). For many women, choosing to care for the self is a terrifying proposition, as it is likened to the denial of others (McBride, 1990).

Far too often, women are unaware of how much energy they invest in doing things for others versus developing healthy interdependence (McBride, 1990). For years, Valerie has lived and worked in environments where she was encouraged to meet other people's needs and attend to their well-being and was even rewarded for it. However ironic, Valerie's cancer and surgery now allow Valerie the opportunity to take care of herself, probably for the first time ever and to examine critically her life and priorities. Valerie must also ask herself what she wants out of life and what she is able to offer life. To create a new rhythm different from anything she has ever experienced, Valerie needs tremendous energy and support. With therapy and perseverance, Valerie will arrive at the place where she will eventually honor her choices to survive with her life regardless of how unacceptable her life appears to her now.

Valerie, as are many African American Christians, may be reluctant to go to a secular European American counselor. They are concerned about the counselor's ability to relate. Although Valerie needs counseling, she is burdened by the cultural stigma that counseling bears: Counseling is an undesirable option and benefits primarily the weak who are incapable of rising above their problems on their own. Anxiety over a counselor's willingness to maintain confidentiality or feelings of disloyalty about sharing family secrets in light of the emphasis on self-disclosure within the Western paradigm may plague Valerie and other potential newcomers to counseling.

The Counselor, Jill Sayers

Judith Duerk (1994) is quoted at the opening of this chapter: "Depression serves a woman as it presses down on her, forcing her to leave behind that which was not of herself, which had influenced her to live a life alien to her own nature. Her suffering, now substantial, insists that she no longer deny its truth" (p. 32). Valerie is a depressed woman and, as such, needs a warm and empathic space where she can tell her story. To stand in the presence of her fear, self-pity, confusion, and self-contempt, an effective counselor is essential. Her crying spells, irritability, changes in appetite, excessive sleeping, and other symptoms are characteristic of depression.

A sensitive female counselor is recommended—one who is not afraid to help Valerie wrestle with some very real emotions. A male counselor could be ideal for Valerie, more so than a female counselor, in helping Valerie explore the areas of her life that feel untouchable. Valerie may not feel silenced by a man who is not perceived as being threatened by her loss and pain. Hays (1996) discussed how clients "may exclude information that they assume the counselor will not understand or include details designed to counteract the counselor's presumed prejudices" (p. 36). Jill would not be effective if she has not confronted discourses around death, beauty, womanhood, and loss in her own life. Any negative reactions to Valerie's feelings may protect the female therapist from similar feelings in herself of which she may disapprove (Kaplan, 1987). The very exploration of bitterness and resentment can lead to the identification of sources of dissatisfaction. Eventually, movement can be made toward resolving unrest.

Whereas Jill may need to refer Valerie to her minister to talk about existential and spiritual concerns—life, freedom, responsibility, and meaning—she can assess the role of Valerie's spirituality as a tool for coping. In doing so, she can encourage Valerie's faith and help strengthen her psychological resistance skills (Robinson & Howard-Hamilton, 1994). Such skills would include knowing that she is not alone, that she will be all right despite how things appear, and that there is a purpose to her life and living. Although seemingly paradoxical, Valerie's spiritual beliefs may be a source of strength for her, as well as a source of internal conflict. On the one hand, Valerie may believe that God is her source of strength. On the other hand, she may wrestle with a crisis of faith. If God is her protector, then why did God allow her cancer?

In addition to assessing Valerie's internal coping strategies, Jill should also appraise the type of support systems available to Valerie as she endeavors to make sense of her life, which is now in crisis. Jill needs to assist Valerie in understanding her tendency to deny her own needs. It also appears that Valerie somehow subscribes to the mistaken notion that her silence will protect her. Her inability to dialogue with herself about the lump that she felt for years contributed to her inaction; if the cancer had been diagnosed sooner, the outcome might have been very different. In addition, not talking to her boyfriend is destructive to her relationship and disallows him the opportunity to provide her with much-needed support.

Because multicultural counseling recognizes that personhood includes various dimensions of identity such as gender, religion, sexual orientation, race, and social class, an effective counselor is sensitive to the role of these and other constructs in Valerie's life. Poindexter-Cameron and Robinson (1997) said that African American women can relate to White women and Black men on certain issues and to neither group on certain other issues. Far too often, race issues tend to be masculinized, and gender issues are viewed from a Eurocentric framework. In relating to Valerie, Jill needs to consider a both/and (convergence of identities) perspective rather than a dualistic, either/or perspective.

Valerie has a low-paying, traditionally female job, and like many African American women, she contends with economic exploitation and historical sexism and racism. According to Jones (1985), "the vast majority of Black female wage earners were barred from peacetime factory labor and from the traditional (White) female occupations of secretarial and sales work until well into the 1960s" (p. 4). In a society that far too often equates self-worth with body perfection, she deals with yet another type of objectification.

With regard to treatment modalities, Valerie could be encouraged to consider traditional as well as alternative therapies. She might find group counseling with other women who have survived breast cancer to be helpful. Channeling anger and sadness through peaceful movement such as dance could be tremendously therapeutic. The expressive arts of poetry, music, clay work, mask making, and drawing are excellent media for releasing emotion. Work with clay may be particularly therapeutic because Valerie would be able to sculpt and pound (Gladding, 1997).

Valerie is concerned about her children. School-age children can be assisted in the recovery process by encouraging them to express their emotions. The children could "act out" the feelings of anger, fear, and confusion. Psychoeducational groups for children can also be helpful as children (a) share with others in a similar situation, (b) learn about cancer and its various treatments, and (c) expand their arsenal of coping strategies (Johnson, 1997).

From a behavioral perspective, journaling about her feelings and examining the reasons behind her choice not to consult a physician when she first noticed the lump several years ago may assist Valerie in honoring the decisions she made. Because she may not be cognizant of how much time and energy she invests in others, Jill could introduce the tissue exercise: First, Valerie is given a piece of tissue and then is asked to tear off pieces of it that represent the amount of time she gives to the various activities and people in her life (e.g., her children, work, church). She is then asked to indicate how much time, on average, she allocates to herself. For many women, the size of the remaining tissue is very small or nonexistent, yet it serves as a visual indicator of the way women often engage in selfless behaviors. Self-care becomes less of a priority than care for others. Counseling, however, needs to help Valerie value her strong interpersonal skills while assisting her with self-declaration (Nelson, 1996).

Cognitive restructuring might be very helpful for Valerie. For instance, one of Valerie's thoughts might be, "A man will not want me now that I am deformed." Jill could help Valerie expand her notions of life, beauty, intimacy, sexuality, and relationships and challenge those self-defeating thoughts with the belief, "My sexuality is greater than having both of my breasts" (Henderson, 1997).

Narrative therapists would use externalizing conversations by asking Valerie, "What effect has the breast cancer had on your life?" "What issues does breast cancer raise for you?" and "What other issues are raised for you, such as health issues and the effects on the body?" (G. Monk, personal communication, November 16, 1998). These questions are very different from "How long have you had this problem (or disease)?" In the first instance, the problem is externalized. In the second, the problem is seen as internal to Valerie, which invites self-blame and recrimination (Monk, Winslade, Crocket, & Epston, 1997).

SUMMARY

In this chapter, the construct of gender in women's and men's lives was considered. The socialization process, as well as biological dimensions, was explored. Counselors need to be aware of the consequences of gender socialization on their personal lives and on those of their clients. Not to do so is to ignore the powerful role of gender in life.

REFERENCES

Balch, J. F., & Balch, P. A. (1997). *Prescription for nutritional healing.* Garden City Park, NY: Avery.

Bem, S. L. (1993). *The lenses of gender: Transforming the debate on sexuality inequality.* New Haven, CT: Yale University Press.

Bernardez, T. (1987). Gender-based countertransference of female therapists in the psychotherapy of women. In M. Braude (Ed.), *Women and therapy* (pp. 25–39). New York: Haworth Press.

Brown, L. (1994). *Subversive dialogues: Theory in feminist therapy.* New York: Basic Books.

Burnett, J. W., Anderson, W. P., & Heppner, P. P. (1995). Gender roles and self-esteem: A consideration of environmental factors. *Journal of Counseling & Development, 73,* 323–326.

Carter, R. T., & Parks, E. E. (1996). Womanist identity and mental health. *Journal of Counseling & Development, 74,* 484–489.

Cook, E. P. (1987). Psychological androgyny: A review of the research. *Counseling Psychologist, 15,* 471–513.

Duerk, J. (1994). *Circle of stones: Woman's journey to herself.* San Diego, CA: Lura Media.

Enns, C. Z. (1991). The "new" relationship models of women's identity: A review and critique for counselors. *Journal of Counseling & Development, 69,* 209–217.

Erikson, E. (1968). *Identity: Youth and crisis.* New York: Norton.

Evans, K. M., & Herr, E. L. (1991). The influence of racism and sexism in the career development of Africa.

Fausto-Sterling, A. (1992). *Myths of gender: Biological theories about women and men.* New York: Basic Books.

Gertner, D. M. (1994). Understanding and serving the needs of men. *Counseling and Human Development, 27,* 1–16.

Gilligan, C. (1982). *In a different voice.* Cambridge, MA: Harvard University Press.

Gladding, S. (1997). *Community agency counseling.* Upper Saddle River, NJ: Merrill/Prentice Hall.

Good, G. E., Dell, D. M., & Mintz, L. B. (1989). Male role and gender role conflict: Relations to help seeking in men. *Journal of Counseling Psychology, 36,* 295–300.

Good, G. E., & Mintz, L. B. (1990). Gender role conflict and depression in college men: Evidence for compounded risk. *Journal of Counseling & Development, 69,* 1, 17–21.

Good, G. E., Robertson, J. M., Fitzgerald, L. F., Stevens, M., & Bartels, K. M. (1996). The relation between masculine role conflict and psychological distress in male university counseling center clients. *Journal of Counseling & Development, 75,* 1, 44–49.

Good, G. E., & Wood, P. K. (1995). Male gender role conflict, depression, and help seeking: Do college men face double jeopardy? *Journal of Counseling & Development, 74,* 1, 70–75.

Haider, R. (1995). *Gender and development.* Cairo, Egypt: American University in Cairo Press.

Hays, P. A. (1996). Addressing the complexities of culture and gender in counseling. *Journal of Counseling & Development, 74,* 332–338.

Henderson, P. A. (1997). Psychosocial adjustment of adult cancer survivors: Their needs and counselor interventions. *Journal of Counseling & Development, 75,* 188–194.

Horst, E. A. (1995). Reexamining gender issues in Erikson's stages of identity. *Journal of Counseling & Development, 73,* 271–278.

Johnson, L. S. (1997). Developmental strategies for counseling the child whose parent or sibling has cancer. *Journal of Counseling & Development, 75,* 417–427.

Jones, T. (1985). *Labor and love, labor and sorrow: Black women, work, and the family from slavery to present.* New York: Basic Books.

Kaplan, A. G. (1987). Reflections on gender and psychotherapy. In M. Braude (Ed.), *Women and therapy* (Vol. 6, pp. 11–24). New York: Haworth Press.

Lemkau, J. P., & Landau, C. (1986). The "selfless syndrome": Assessment and treatment considerations. *Psychotherapy, 23,* 227–233.

McBride, M. (1990). Autonomy and the struggle for female identity: Implications for counseling women. *Journal of Counseling & Development, 69,* 22–26.

Mintz, L. B., & O'Neil, J. M. (1990). Gender roles, sex, and the process of psychotherapy: Many questions and few answers. *Journal of Counseling & Development, 68,* 381–387.

Moir, A., & Jessel, D. (1991). *Brain sex: The real difference between men and women*. New York: Delta.

Monk, G., Winslade, J., Crocket, K., & Epston, D. (1997). *Narrative therapy in practice: The archaeology of hope*. San Francisco: Jossey-Bass.

Napholz, L. (1994). Sex role orientation and psychological well-being among working Black women. *Journal of Black Psychology, 20,* 469–482.

Nelson, M. C. (1996). Separation versus connection: The gender controversy. *Implications for Counseling Women, 74,* 339–344.

Okazawa-Rey, M., Ward, J. V., & Robinson, T. (1987). Black women and the politics of skin color and hair. In M. Braude (Ed.), Women and therapy (pp. 89–102). New York: Haworth Press.

Pinderhughes, E. (1989). *Understanding race, ethnicity, and power: The key to efficacy in clinical practice*. New York: Free Press.

Pleck, J. H. (1984). Men's power with women, other men, and society: A men's movement analysis. In P. P. Ricker & E. H. Carmen (Eds.), *The gender gap in psychotherapy: Social realities and psychological processes* (pp. 79–89). New York: Plenum Press.

Poindexter-Cameron, J., & Robinson, T. L. (1997). Relationships among racial identity attitudes, womanist identity attitudes, and self-esteem in African American college women. *Journal of College Student Development, 38,* 288–296.

Reed, M. K., McLeod, S., Randall, Y., & Walker, B. (1996). Depressive symptoms in African American women. *Journal of Multicultural Counseling & Development, 24,* 6–14.

Renzetti, C. M., & Curran, D. J. (1992). *Women, men, and society*. Boston: Allyn & Bacon.

Robinson, T. L., & Howard-Hamilton, M. (1994). An Afrocentric paradigm: Foundation for a healthy self-image and healthy interpersonal relationships. *Journal of Mental Health Counseling, 16,* 327–339.

Sadker, M., Sadker, D., & Long, L. (1993). Gender and educational equity. In J. Banks & C. McGee-Banks (Eds.), *Multicultural education* (pp. 111–128). Boston: Allyn & Bacon.

Skovholt, T. M. (1993). Counseling and psychotherapy interventions with men. *Counseling and Human Development, 25,* 1–16.

Spence, J. T., & Helmreich, R. L. (1978). *Masculinity and femininity: Their psychological dimensions, correlates, and antecedents*. Austin: University of Texas Press.

Stevens, M. J., Pfost, K. S., & Potts, M. K. (1990). Sex role orientation and the willingness to confront existential issues. *Journal of Counseling & Development, 68,* 47–49.

Swanson, J. L. (1993). Sexism strikes men. *American Counselor Counseling and Development, 68,* 21–25.

Uba, L. (1994). *Asian Americans: Personality patterns, identity, and mental health*. New York: Guilford Press.

West, C., & Zimmerman, D. H. (1991). Doing gender. In J. Lorber & S. A. Farrell (Eds.), *The social construction of gender* (pp. 13–37). Newbury Park, CA: Sage.

White, E. C. (1994). *The Black women's health book: Speaking for ourselves*. Seattle, WA: Seal Press.

Worell, J., & Remer, P. (1992). *Feminist perspectives in therapy: An empowerment model for women*. New York: John Wiley.

Young, V. L. (1981). *Secret of the sexes: An eye-opening look at the sex roles we teach our children* [Video]. Stamford, CT: NOVA Library.

Chapter 6

Converging Sexual Orientation

**Wouldn't it be great
just to have sex and not worry about dying?**

Statement made by a man in the video Finding Our
Way: Men and Sexuality

This chapter focuses on sexual orientation. One goal is to expose readers to the heterosexual bias that exists in this culture and how an assumption of heterosexuality can be very damaging to lesbian and gay clients. If counselors are not aware of their own biases, service delivery can be seriously hampered; yet, far too often counselors do not receive adequate training in this area. Although they feel inadequately trained and lack knowledge about gay, lesbian, and bisexual clients, most therapists are willing to treat these clients. Clearly, this is a direct violation of the ethical standards of the American Counseling Association (ACA) (Dworkin & Gutierrez, 1989).

Behavioral/fantasy exercises are provided as a means to help readers identify their attitudes and biases concerning sexual orientation. First, definitions are provided, and, as customary, a case study concludes the chapter.

DEFINITIONS AND TERMINOLOGY

To eliminate confusion, appropriate language and terminology particular to therapy with gay and lesbian clients is provided (Dworkin & Gutierrez, 1992). "As with any group, language has a strong impact on gay and lesbian culture. As times change and as words develop new connotations, some words fall out of favor" (Hunt, 1993, p. 2). The following terms are considered nonbiased and accepted terminology among gay men, lesbians, and bisexuals. These terms are used as the standard terminology in this chapter.

Heterosexism is the belief that everyone is heterosexual and that heterosexual relationships are preferred and necessary for the preservation of the family, particularly the nuclear family. Heterosexism is institutionalized through religion, education, and the media and leads to homophobia (Pharr, 1988). It describes the institutionalization of antigay, antilesbian, and antibisexual beliefs, attitudes, and behaviors. Heterosexism is the deeply ingrained notion that heterosexuality is the superior sexual orientation (Wall & Evans, 1992). Pharr (1988) stated that heterosexism has been defined as a worldview, a value system that prizes heterosexuality, that assumes it is the only appropriate manifestation of love and sexuality, and that devalues homosexuality and all that is not heterosexual.

Although similar to heterosexism, **homophobia** is the irrational fear of anyone gay or lesbian or of anyone perceived to be gay or lesbian. Homophobia is a weapon of sexism because it works to keep men and women in rigidly defined gender roles (Pharr, 1988). *Homophobia* comes from the Latin *homo,* meaning "same" (in this case, referring to same-gender attraction), and *phobia,* meaning "fear of"; thus, the term's original application to individuals was an extreme and persistent fear and loathing of homosexuals (King, 1988; Pharr, 1988).

Homosexual defines attraction to the same sex for physical and emotional nurturance and is one orientation on the continuum from homosexual to bisexual and heterosexual. This term has become associated with the historical belief that homo-

sexuality is unnatural, a sin, and a sickness. For this reason, females who are homo-
sexual/gay often prefer the term **lesbian** to describe their sexual orientation. The difference in terminology, which arose during the feminist movement, reflects the difference between gay men and lesbians. The term *lesbian* gets its origins from the
Greek poet Sappho (c. 600 B.C.), who lived on the Greek island of Lesbos in the
Aegean Sea. Sappho's poems are exclusively about women.

Someone who acknowledges her or his homoerotic preference and incorporates
this knowledge into her or his identity and carries this identity into interpersonal relationships is defined as **gay.** The term *gay* signifies more self-awareness, self-acceptance, and openness than the term *homosexual.* Often, in developmental literature,
the process of coming to terms with one's sexuality involves moving from being
homosexual to becoming gay.

One consequence of homophobia is **internalized homophobia.** It is produced by
the negative messages about homosexuality that lesbians and gay men hear
throughout their lives. Because gay men and lesbians are stereotyped, uninformed,
or fed inaccurate, distorted information about homosexuality, the messages are
internalized and result in low self-esteem. Internalized homophobia can lead to self-
hatred and other psychological problems (Dworkin & Gutierrez, 1989).

When gay men and lesbians come to accept being gay or lesbian as a salient
component of their identities, it is descriptive of the process of **coming out.** Numerous developmental models discuss the stages of the coming out process, such as
those of Cass (1979) and Coleman (1982).

Gay and lesbian people have struggled throughout history with the notion that
their sexual identity was a choice—and the wrong choice. Because of socialization,
gay men and lesbians have behaved heterosexually even though their identity was
gay or lesbian. Many remember feeling different at an early age and see this as
stemming from their gay and lesbian orientation. For this reason, the term **sexual
orientation,** rather than *sexual preference,* is preferred. By owning this orientation,
gay men and lesbians make a conscious choice to let their behavior conform to their
orientation, just as a heterosexually oriented person makes a choice not to behave in
a homosexual manner.

Heterosexism affects everyone, covertly and overtly, in this society. It is not only
harmful to the victims but to the perpetrators as well. According to Smith (1982),
heterosexism is intimately associated with other discriminatory practices (e.g. classism, sexism, racism, ageism) in our society. She stated that verbal and behavioral
expressions of heterosexism are acceptable and go uncontested in contexts where
other discriminatory comments or gesticulations (e.g. racist, sexist, or anti-Semitic
remarks) would be challenged or prohibited.

Sexual politics ensures the dominance of males over females and the dominance
of heterosexuals over persons who are gay and lesbian (Pleck, 1984). Within a system of **hegemony** (refers to a historical situation where power is won and held) and
androcentrism, where the complementary of women and men implies women's
subordinate social position to men, homosexuality becomes a threat for heterosexual men. Heterosexual men are socialized into believing that in order to reject anything that remotely resembles homosexuality, they must oppress women. For this

reason, "any kind of powerlessness, or refusal to compete among men becomes involved with the imagery of homosexuality" (Pleck, 1984, p. 84). Within heterosexuality, a central dimension of the power that men exercise over women is found. Clearly, sexism and homophobia are interlocking paradigms.

Sexual inequality and heterosexuality cannot be discussed without addressing sociopolitical power dynamics within society, such as the suppression of women's sexuality, forced sexuality through incest and rape, the idealization of heterosexual marriage, and the contradicting and confusing roles of motherhood.

Traditionally, a healthy or ideal personality has included a concept of *sexual identity* with three basic components: (a) a sexual preference for members of the opposite sex, (b) a sex role identity as either masculine or feminine, depending on one's gender, and (c) a gender identity that is a secure sense of one's maleness or femaleness. Bem (1993) set out to refute these components by stating that sexual preference ought to be considered orthogonal to notions of mental health. She also indicated that the terms *heterosexual* and *homosexual* should be used to describe acts rather than persons.

A "Guided Phantasy" is provided below so that readers can visualize/role-play how a heterosexual would feel in a gay, lesbian, or bisexual world.

GUIDED PHANTASY

This "guided phantasy" process is similar to guided imagery, which is a common therapeutic technique. The process is simple but very powerful because it elicits deep and internalized emotional responses from participants. Participants are not allowed to debate the responses from others in the group, and it is important that the leader create a safe environment for all voices to be heard. The purpose of this exercise is to get participants to confront their homophobic and heterosexist attitudes and beliefs. The facilitator guides the dialogue so that everyone can discuss the emotional turmoil they may be experiencing.

PROCEDURE

To reduce any fears, anxiety, or tension the participants may be feeling at the time, the leader tells the group what is about to take place. The leader tells the participants to find a comfortable area in the room and to take a few moments to clear their minds of other thoughts, close their eyes, relax, and concentrate on their breathing. After everyone has become comfortable, the facilitator begins the reading process (excerpted below) in a slow, methodical, and deliberate manner. After the process is over, the leader pauses for a few moments to allow participants to digest their responses, and then asks them to volunteer their reactions during the process. It is up to the facilitator to guide the participants gently but firmly in remaining focused on their feelings and not intellectualizing the process.

Imagine a world very different from the way the real world is now. This phantasy is not real, nor will it ever be real. Rather, it is a process of the imagination designed to increase your awareness of your own reactions. Note your reactions—whether they be in the form of a thought, an image, a feeling, an emotion, or a sensation in your body—take whatever you get, allow it to be there, do not try to change it or to make it go away. There is no right or wrong in this process—even nothing is a reaction. If you start intellectualizing, go back to where you can again sense your reactions.

Take deep breaths. Close your eyes. Clear your mind.

Consider reversing the world order as we now know it. Think of the world's population composed primarily of gay men, lesbians, and bisexuals, with only 10% to 12% of the population heterosexual. Feel that, and sense the meaning for you as a heterosexual woman or man; as a lesbian woman or gay man.

Think of it as always being this way, every day of your life. Feel the ever-presence of gay, lesbian, and bisexual individuals; feel the nonpresence of heterosexuals. Absorb what it tells you about the value of being heterosexual and of being homosexual.

Imagine that almost everything you have ever read used only homosexual characters and descriptions, virtually ignoring reference to heterosexuals. The overwhelming number of personalities on radio, in films, and on television news, commercials, and situation comedies are presented as gay, lesbian, or bisexual. Textbooks make no reference to heterosexuals in history. No heterosexuals are portrayed in the media.

Imagine that only two openly heterosexual legislators have been elected to national office in the history of this country. Gays, lesbians, and bisexuals are the visible leaders, at the center of power—and rightfully so, as they have the stable character and moral responsibility to be the guardians of social order and of the natural balance of humans and nature.

Consider that long ago, before the use of artificial insemination by gay men, lesbians, and bisexuals, the promiscuous sexual activity of heterosexuals violated the social order and natural law through irresponsible over-population, incest, abortion, and sexual abuse of children. These violations gave rise to contempt for heterosexuality, and therefore all who engaged in this abomination became outcasts. They were called:

BREEDERS—WEIRDOS—PIGS—HETS

These are names that freeze the hearts of heterosexuals. It means that you are different, unacceptable, an outcast. No "normal" person would want to associate with one, let alone *be* one. Heterosexuals are stigmatized by all social institutions: churches, the courts, educational institutions, politics, and the military.

Imagine how fearful you were of playmates who called you "breeder" in teasing fun. They didn't even know the real meaning of the word, but you did. And so you learned to be distrustful and wary of everyone to prevent anyone from learning your terrible secret: You were attracted to a school-mate or teacher of the opposite sex!

Imagine that your entire adolescence is spent learning gay, lesbian, and bisexual social behavior; all dating preparation, social events, and adult training is gay, lesbian, or bisexually directed. You had desperately wanted to appear "normal," so you went to the Junior Prom with an attractive gay, lesbian, or bisexual to avoid suspicion. You may have even kissed or had sex to "prove" your gay, lesbian, or bisexual identity—all the while secretly thinking of your forbidden heterosexual infatuation.

For a while, you may have believed that you were the only heterosexual in the world—if you had even heard this word to describe your feelings. In time, however, you met someone else like you. Cautiously at first, because you could be wrong, you began to develop a friendship and then the friendship turned to love. You were ecstatic; you wanted to tell everyone you knew how lucky you were. But you couldn't. You had to keep it a secret from your parents, or else they would have been disappointed and hurt; a secret from your neighbors and coworkers, or else you would have been evicted or fired. And no matter how happy you were, you never forgot that you could be attacked for any public display of affection—even hand holding.

Imagine that there are laws against many sexual behaviors practiced by gay men, lesbians, bisexuals, and heterosexuals but that, in practice, they are only used as excuses to arrest and convict heterosexuals. Similarly, the vast majority of clergy preach love for each other but are vehement in condemning you and your love to eternal hell.

Imagine that you want to make a commitment to the person you love but that there is no legal or cultural way to sanction that commitment. Even if you live together for 50 years, you will have no legal right to visit your partner in the intensive care unit of a hospital, to make emergency medical/legal decisions, or even to make funeral arrangements according to your partner's wishes or to inherit mutual property without family survivors contesting it.

Imagine reading about a 17-year-old heterosexual boy who was attacked by four gay, lesbian, and bisexual football players as he left a hidden bar where heterosexuals could secretly meet to socialize. It was a completely unprovoked attack in which he was beaten to death. Nevertheless, when the jury found the attackers guilty, the judge sentenced them to "probation" so as not to interrupt their college football careers.

This and all other forms of oppression of heterosexuals is present in every social institution. Some forms are very subtle; some, like the celebrities—Orange Juice Queens, political and religious leaders—who often campaign to wipe out heterosexuality in the name of God and country, are direct and dangerous.

Consider now, for a moment, the tensions and anxieties you might experience from having to confront these questions and pressures. You could become clinically anxious or depressed or both, requiring psychotherapy. The therapy, of course, will be administered by a gay, lesbian, or bisexual therapist who has been trained to perceive all your symptoms as relating to your underlying psychological conflict—that is, your hetero-sexuality! Group therapy is recommended. You will be the only openly het-erosexual person in the group. The gay, lesbian, or bisexual group leader will ask you to express your deep feelings.

What feelings do you experience? [PAUSE]

Keep your eyes closed for a few more moments. Take a deep breath. And when you are ready, open your eyes.

FIRST IMPRESSIONS EXERCISE

Directions: Consider your responses to the following questions, noting how your impressions of gays and lesbians may be affected. Discussing these with colleagues can enhance the experience.

1. What was the first reference to gays or lesbians you ever remember hearing?
2. What do you remember about the first person you ever saw or met who you identified as gay or lesbian?
3. What type of treatment did gay and lesbian clients receive in your therapy or counseling course?
4. How were gay or lesbian student therapists treated in your training program? Gay or lesbian supervisors or instructors?
5. Do you currently have friends or acquaintances whom you know to be gay or lesbian? If not, why do you think this is so? Who do you think might be gay or lesbian?
6. If so, what are they like? Do you think they are typical of gays or lesbians?
7. What is the most memorable same-sex experience of your life? The most traumatic? The most meaningful and/or eye-opening? (Falco, 1991, p. 174)

DEVELOPMENTAL PROCESSES

Coping strategies vary for the gay client. Often, a therapist can assess the gay client's level of identity development in the coming out process. According to the Cass model (1984), the gay identity formation process occurs in six stages, begin-ning with the individual having a sexual self-portrait that is heterosexual. For exam-ple, if the client were talking about a female, she would see herself and her behavior as a heterosexual. She would also see others viewing her as a heterosexual. For the most part, the person's sexual self-portrait is consistent or congruent with heterosex-uality. At some point in life, however, a change occurs. It might happen in childhood, in adolescence, in early adulthood, in middle age, or even very late in life. This developmental process can take several years.

THE DEVELOPMENTAL PROCESS OF COMING OUT

O'Bear and Reynolds (1985) suggested a developmental process for lesbians and gay men. A 16-year gap exists between awareness of homosexual feelings and the development of a positive gay/lesbian identity (see the following list). An 8- to 10-year gap exists between first awareness of same-sex feelings and self-labeling as homosexual. Coming out professionally seems to be the most difficult process, occurring almost 18 years after first awareness of one's orientation.

	AGE OF GAY MEN	AGE OF LESBIANS
Became aware of homosexual feelings	13.8	12.8
Understood what homosexual was	15.6	17.2
Had first same-sex sexual experience	19.9	14.9
Had first homosexual relationship	22.8	21.9
Considered self homosexual	23.2	21.1
Acquired positive gay identity	29.7	28.5
Disclosed identity to spouse	26.7	33.3
Disclosed identity to friends	28.2	28.0
Disclosed identity to parents	30.2	28.0
Disclosed identity professionally	32.4	31.2

CASS'S MODEL OF GAY, LESBIAN, AND BISEXUAL SEXUAL IDENTITY FORMATION

Vivian Cass (1979) developed a model to assess the growth, development, and awareness of gay, lesbian, and bisexual individuals. It is highlighted here; however, Sullivan (1998) developed an identity model that combines Cass's model with a racial identity development model. An overview of each stage in Cass's model is provided below.

Stage 1 is *identity confusion.* It is characterized by a growing awareness of thoughts, feelings, or behaviors that may be homosexual in nature. These self-perceptions are incongruent with earlier assumptions of personal heterosexuality and constitute the first developmental conflict of this model. How individuals perceive these characteristics or behaviors will influence the way they seek to resolve the incongruence, either through repression (identity foreclosure) or by moving into Stage 2.

In Stage 2, *identity comparison,* individuals begins to investigate those qualities first experienced in the first stage. As they begin to gather information and seek out contacts with gay others, there is increased congruence between self-perceptions and behaviors but increased conflict with others. As a sense of conflict heightens, individuals may move to Stage 3.

Identity tolerance, Stage 3, is marked by increased contact with the gay community, leading to greater empowerment. At this point, individuals hold an increasingly strong homosexual self-image but continue to present themselves (outside the community) as heterosexual.

At Stage 4, *identity acceptance,* the conflict between the self and nongay others' perceptions is at an intense level. This conflict may be resolved through passing as "straight," having limited contact with heterosexuals, or selectively disclosing to significant (heterosexual) others. Those who find that these strategies effectively manage the conflict may stay at this level comfortably; otherwise, the continuing conflict pushes individuals into Stage 5.

In Stage 5, *identity pride,* the conflict is managed through fostering a dichotomized homosexual (valued) and heterosexual (devalued) worldview. This stage is marked not only by strong pride in the gay community and identity but also by intense anger directed toward, and isolation from, the heterosexual society. How others, particularly those who are not gay, respond to the expression of these feelings influences whether individuals move to the final stage.

Identity synthesis is the last stage. Movement most likely occurs when individuals experience positive reactions from heterosexual others, creating new incongruence in their perception. Individuals at this Stage 6 perceive similarities and dissimilarities with both homosexuals and heterosexuals and see sexuality as one part of their total identity. Although some conflict is always present, it is at the lowest and most manageable point in this stage.

Most counselors will work with a gay, lesbian, or bisexual client at some juncture during their professional careers. The Cass model is provided as a guideline for assessing a client's level of development. It is important to note, however, that the client may remain "stuck" in a given stage, skip certain developmental levels, or regress from a higher stage to a lower stage, depending on the events that occur in her or his life.

A more detailed explanation of the Cass model, with specific examples of possible client reactions and proposed counselor statements, are provided next.

STAGE 1: IDENTITY CONFUSION Examples of questions a person in Stage 1 may be asking are "Who am I?" "Am I homosexual?" and "Am I really a heterosexual?" The individual sometimes feels, thinks, or acts in a homosexual way but would rarely, if ever, tell anyone about this. The individual is fairly sure that homosexuality has something to do with her or him personally. *Occurs when there is continuing personalization of information regarding homosexuality.*

Entrance into this stage begins with the conscious awareness that information regarding homosexuality is somehow personally relevant. When the continuing personalization of this information can no longer be ignored, the individual's sexual self-portrait feels inconsistent, or incongruent. The process of gay identity formation has begun.

The person begins privately to label her or his own behavior (or thoughts or feelings) as possibly homosexual. The person maintains a self-image as heterosexual and perceives others as maintaining the same image. To deal with this incongruity that has been introduced into the sexual-self-portrait, the person adopts one or more of the following three strategies (Berzon, 1988). The first is the *inhibition strategy,* which is descriptive of the person who regards the definition of her or his behavior (thoughts, feelings) as correctly homosexual but finds this definition undesirable and unacceptable. Several actions are taken: The person restricts information regarding homosexuality (e.g., I don't want to hear, read, or know about it) or inhibits behavior (e.g., It may be true, but I'm not going to do anything about it). Denying the personal relevance of information regarding homosexuality is also an action taken (e.g., It has nothing to do with me). Becoming hypersexual (e.g., within the context of heterosexual interactions) or becoming asexual wherein the person seeks a "cure" describe other possible behaviors. Another action is to become an antigay moral or religious crusader. If the inhibition strategies employed are completely successful in enabling the person to inhibit or redefine or disown responsibility for homosexual behavior, a foreclosure of gay/lesbian identity will occur at Stage 1.

Personal innocence strategy is a second strategy. Here, the person rejects either the meaning or the context of the homosexual behavior so as not to have to own it. She or he then redefines the meaning or context of the behavior. For example, in U.S. society, gentle contact between males is acceptable in a variety of situations without the participating individuals being defined as homosexuals. Little boys have "circle jerks." Men confined for long periods of time without access to women have genital contact with one another, and they are not necessarily defined as homosexuals. The shift occurs in the contextual meaning when males develop emotional attachments to the other males with whom they are having sex or when they have repeated contacts with the same male, increasing the possibility of emotional involvement. Therefore, males in the process of redefining the meaning or content of their behavior would be careful to keep sexual contacts free of emotional involvement and avoid repeated contacts with the same person. The sexual contact is then explained as just fulfilling a physical need.

For females in U.S. society, just the opposite is true. Girls can be inseparable, experience deep emotional involvement with one another, and spend more time with each other, even into adulthood, than they do with the men in their lives, and they are not defined as homosexuals. The shift occurs when they have genital contact in addition to their emotional involvement, which is considered to be homosexuality but may not be. Quite a bit of same-sex sexual experimentation occurs in adulthood among persons who had been or currently are in heterosexual marriages. It is possible that defining one's identity as homosexual may not be altogether accurate. Qualitative research is needed in this area.

Women in Stage 1 who adopt a personal innocence strategy would be careful to keep relationships with women strictly nonsexual no matter how emotionally involved they are (defining it as just a good friendship). Another example of the personal innocence strategy is categorized as redefining context. The individual disowns responsibility for her or his homosexual behavior by redefining the context in which it occurred. Examples of these rationalizations are "I was just experimenting," "I was drunk," "I just did it for the money," "I did it as a favor for a friend," "It was an accident," and "I was taken advantage of."

Success in the use of the inhibition and personal innocence strategies depends on the individual's ability to avoid provocative situations and to employ the psychological defense of denial. Nevertheless, it is impossible to avoid erotic dreams and physiological responses to persons of the same sex to whom the individual is attracted. In this instance, these strategies will be only partially successful, and the individual may very well experience the beginning of a negative or self-rejecting sexual identity.

The person in the *information-seeking strategy* is likely to adopt this third strategy if the meaning attributed to her or his homosexual behavior is perceived as correct, or at least partially acceptable. Now the individual seeks more information-in books, in therapy, or in talking with anyone who might have expertise or experience related to this topic. The question being addressed is "Am I homosexual?" This strategy of seeking more information moves the person along to Stage 2.

Implications for Counselors. The several helping strategies that counselors can employ include (a) being aware of personal feelings toward gay men and lesbians, (b) validating confusion, (c) providing a safe, supportive environment conducive to the exploration of this struggle and confusion, (d) exploring what it means to be homosexual, (e) disputing myths about homosexuality, and (f) suggesting readings.

STAGE 2: IDENTITY COMPARISON   "I feel like I probably am homosexual, although I am not definitely sure. I feel different. I think I may want to talk with someone, maybe someone gay about feeling different, but I'm not sure if I really want to or not." *Occurs when the person accepts the possibility that she or he may be homosexual.*

The individual begins to examine the wider implications of being homosexual. Whereas in Stage 1 the task was to handle the self-alienation that occurs with the first glimmerings of homosexuality, the main task of Stage 2 is to handle the social alienation that is produced by feeling different from peers, family members, and society at large. A particularly troubling aspect of relinquishing one's heterosexual identity is the giving up of behavioral guidelines and the expectations for one's future that accompany them. If marriage and family are not in one's future, then what is? What will give form, structure, and a sense of normalcy to one's life? With the letting go of a perception of a self that is clearly heterosexual, one can experience a profound feeling of loss.

Implications for Counselors. Counselors are encouraged, as with any loss, to help the client move beyond the grief by acknowledging and expressing it. At this stage of identity development, grieving the loss of that heterosexual blueprint for life is an inescapable part of what is going on. By helping the individual acknowledge and talk about feelings of loss, the sooner it can be worked through and prevented from becoming a chronic, underlying theme in the person's intimate partnerships.

Certain conditions heighten the feeling of alienation from others: (a) living in geographic isolation with no other gay people or resources available and (b) being from a family that is deeply religious and with strong convictions about homosexuality as a sin.

Cass (1984) described three approaches that people take in coping with alienation. In the first approach, an individual may react positively to being different and devalue the importance of heterosexuals in her or his life. This occurs because the individual has always felt different due to homosexual feelings, and now it is a relief to know that others have the same experience and that one might get support and understanding from them. The individual has always been nonconforming regarding interest in marriage or parenting, and this behavior may explain this particular coping style. The individual may actually find being different special and exciting.

Devaluing the importance of heterosexuals in one's life works if one is able to avoid negative confrontation from heterosexuals regarding one's homosexuality. In other words, one needs to be able to pass or pretend heterosexually. This passing strategy works if the person can avoid threatening situations, such as social gatherings where one is expected to be accompanied by an opposite-sex partner. Other passing strategies include controlling personal information, as in dressing and behaving carefully to avoid being typed as a homosexual; deliberately cultivating and presenting a heterosexual image (supermacho man, the ultrafeminine woman); and disassociating from anything homosexual.

In the second approach that people take in coping with alienation, the person accepts the homosexual definition of her or his own behavior but rejects a definition of self as homosexual in order to feel less alienated from important heterosexuals in her or his life. Here are four strategies the individual may employ to reject homosexual self-definition while continuing homosexual behavior:

1. *Special Case.* The person characterizes what is happening as the product of the liaison with one person and this one person only.
2. *Ambisexuality.* The person says she or he can do it with anybody; it doesn't matter what gender the other person is.
3. *Temporary Identity.* The person regards her or his homosexuality as only temporary: "I could be heterosexual again any minute."
4. *Personal Innocence.* The person blames her or his homosexuality on anyone or everyone else.

In these four strategies, the individual tends to compartmentalize sexually, keeping it separate from other aspects of life.

In the third approach used in coping with social alienation in the identity comparison stage, the person accepts self and behavior as homosexual but fears negative reactions from others to the extent that overt homosexual behavior is inhibited, homosexuality is devalued, and heterosexuality is given much positive weight. The most common example is the gay man or lesbian who is heterosexually married and seeks anonymous sex under covert conditions. It is also possible for the person to reduce the fear of negative reaction from others by moving to another city or country to remove her- or himself from the scrutiny of particular heterosexuals about whom there is concern.

When any of the previous approaches for coping with social alienation are employed successfully, sexual identity is likely to foreclose at Stage 2. If any of these approaches are only partially successful, a self-hating identity is likely to be perpetuated. The person is most likely to move into the next stage when any of these approaches break down.

Counselors are encouraged to become familiar with local resources for gay men, lesbians, and bisexuals and to suggest supportive organizations and assist the client in building a support structure within the gay community.

STAGE 3: IDENTITY TOLERANCE "I feel sure that I'm homosexual, and I tolerate it. I see myself as homosexual for now, but I'm not sure about the future." *Occurs when the person has come to accept the probability that she or he is a homosexual and recognizes the sexual/social/emotional needs that come with being homosexual.*

With more of a commitment to a homosexual identity, the individual is now free to pursue social, emotional, and sexual needs. Doing this accentuates the difference between the person and heterosexuals even more. To deal with the increased social alienation from heterosexuals, the person seeks out gay people and the gay subculture. Involvement in the gay/lesbian community has distinct advantages in terms of the individual's movement toward a more positive gay/lesbian identity. According to Berzon (1988), it (a) contributes to a ready-made support group that understands and shares the individual's concerns, (b) provides opportunities to meet a partner, (c) gives access to positive gay and lesbian role models, and (d) provides opportunities to practice feeling more at ease as a lesbian or a gay man. However, if the person has poor social skills, is very shy, has low self-esteem, has strong fear of exposure (of sexual identity), or has a fear of the unknown, positive contacts are made more difficult.

Implications for Counselors. Counselors are encouraged to assist the client in overcoming barriers to positive socialization. A negative experience may occur if the individual encounters gay men and lesbians who are still employing the inhibition and denial strategies of Stages 1 and 2. These lesbians and gay men will be perceived as unhappy, self rejecting individuals with whom one would not want to be affiliated. However, individuals at this stage will be empowered by people who are accepting of their own gay and lesbian identities. A shift occurs when the individual's significant others become homosexuals rather than heterosexuals.

If the contacts made are experienced as negative, a reduction of involvement with gay subculture is probable, resulting in a foreclosure at Stage 3, identity tolerance. If contacts are perceived as positive, it is likely that the strategies employed have broken down and that the individual will want to explore further. This breakdown of strategies will result in movement into Stage 4. In any case, the commitment to gay identity is now sufficient for the person to say, "I am a homosexual."

STAGE 4: IDENTITY ACCEPTANCE   "I am quite sure that I am gay/lesbian, and I accept this fairly happily. I am prepared to tell a few people about being gay/lesbian (e.g., friends, family members), but I carefully select whom I tell." *Occurs when the person accepts, rather than tolerates, a homosexual self-image and contact with the gay/lesbian subculture continues and increases.*

The individual now has a positive identification with other gay people. The questions of earlier stages (What am I? Where do I belong?) have been answered. Attitudes toward sexual orientation of the gay men and lesbians with whom the person becomes associated are crucial at this point. If these individuals regard being gay as partially legitimate (being gay is okay in private, but being public about it is not okay), then the person is likely to adopt this attitude as her or his own philosophy and to live a compartmentalized, "passing" gay life.

To reduce the stress involved in interfacing with a homophobic society, the person has less and less to do with heterosexuals. Some selective disclosure of gayness to nongay family, friends, and coworkers occurs, but as much control as possible is exercised over the potentially discrediting information. The emphasis is on fitting into society and not making waves. If, on the one hand, this strategy is successful, the person forecloses at this identity acceptance stage. If, on the other hand, the person comes to associate with people who regard being gay as fully legitimate (in private and public), this attitude is likely to be adopted. Feeling that being gay is legitimate tends to increase the distance the person feels from a society that is still, for the most part, antigay. Homophobic attitudes are now particularly offensive.

To deal with the anger toward the antigay society, in combination with the increasing self-acceptance that is occurring, the person moves into Stage 5.

Implications for Counselors. Counselors are encouraged to help the client create a support system within the gay/lesbian community before coming out to heterosexual significant others.

STAGE 5: IDENTITY PRIDE "I feel proud to be a gay/lesbian and enjoy living as one. I am prepared to tell many people about being gay/lesbian and make no attempt to hide this fact. I prefer to mix socially with other gay men/lesbians because heterosexuals are typically antigay." *Occurs when, accepting the philosophy of full legitimation, the person becomes immersed in the gay/lesbian subculture and has less and less to do with heterosexual others.*

As identification with the gay/lesbian community deepens, pride in accomplishments of the community increases. However, daily living still requires continuing encounters with the heterosexual world and its homophobic attitudes. These encounters produce feelings of frustration and alienation. The combination of anger and pride energizes the person into action against the heterosexual establishment and creates "the activist."

Confrontation with the heterosexual establishment brings the person more into public view, and earlier strategies to conceal sexual orientation must be abandoned. Doing so precipitates disclosure crises with significant heterosexuals, such as family and coworkers. It is better to tell the folks yourself than to let them hear that you are gay as you are interviewed on the 6 o'clock news.

What becomes crucial at this point is whether those significant heterosexuals in the individual's life react negatively to the disclosure as expected or react positively. If the reaction is negative, confirming the person's expectations that it would be so, the view of the world as being divided into gays (who are okay) and nongays (who are not okay) gets reinforced. In this instance, the person forecloses at the identity pride stage. If the reactions of the heterosexuals to whom the person discloses are positive and inconsistent with her or his negative expectation, the person tends to change those expectations, which moves her or him into Stage 6.

Implications for Counselors. Counselors are encouraged to assist in dispelling the dichotomous worldview. Caring and supportive heterosexuals in the individual's life, including a heterosexual counselor, need to be highlighted.

STAGE 6: IDENTITY SYNTHESIS "I am prepared to tell anyone that I am gay/lesbian. I am happy about the way I am but think that being gay/lesbian is not the most important part of me. I mix socially with fairly equal numbers of gay men/lesbians and heterosexuals and anyone who is accepting of gay men and lesbians." *Occurs when the person develops an awareness that the "them and us" philosophy, in which all heterosexuals are viewed negatively and all homosexuals positively, no longer holds true.*

The individual now acknowledges that some nongay people are as supportive of her or his gay identity as other gay people are. Because heterosexuals as a class are no longer seen as hostile, it is no longer necessary to sustain the high level of anger of Stage 5. Increasing contact with supportive nongays produces more trust. The need to dichotomize the world into gays who are okay and nongays who are not is gone. The gay/lesbian aspect of one's identity can now be integrated with all other aspects of self.

Implications for Counselors. Counselors are encouraged to be sensitive to the impact a gay/lesbian identity may have on the context surrounding the problems and issues faced by the individual. How would the individual's situation be different if she or he were heterosexual?

ADDITIONAL COUNSELING STRATEGIES

What can counselors do to work effectively with gay, lesbian, and bisexual clients? Having some type of gay, lesbian, or bisexual literature on the bookshelf helps. Display something as small as a pin (one pin available for heterosexuals says "Straight but not narrow"), a poster, or a quote that depicts a multicultural and nonbiased view of the world. Or you may want to display on your wall pictures of you with same-sex friends. Counselors need to read, study, and attend workshops on counseling gay men, lesbians, and bisexuals and not assume that everyone is heterosexual. Being informed about local gay events, attending them, and making contacts to heighten awareness can also be very helpful. Finally, volunteer work needs to be done at AIDS/HIV blood centers and gay and lesbian hotlines.

It is imperative that all persons have an opportunity to receive the services of a mental health professional. These services should not be offered by a few sympathetic counselors in the field, but rather be available from therapists who seek to empower and enhance their clients' identity development.

RATIONALE FOR A FOCUS ON GAY AND LESBIAN ISSUES IN COUNSELING

It is essential that counselors receive adequate training in counseling persons who are gay, lesbian, and bisexual. Rudolph (1990) projected that approximately 25% to 65% of the gay, lesbian, and bisexual population seek psychotherapy, a percentage two to four times higher than in the heterosexual population. Moreover, a significantly larger percentage of gay men and lesbians report dissatisfaction with their treatment, compared with heterosexuals. Even though there is a need to provide psychotherapy in the gay/lesbian community, many mental health professionals have not been provided the appropriate training to assist gay men, lesbians, and bisexuals effectively through their coming out or identity development process (see the case study "Slowly Coming Out of the Closet" at the end of the chapter). Survey and anecdotal literature reveals that the source of dissatisfaction often is the counselor's ignorance or prejudice toward homosexuals (Bell & Weinberg, 1978). Just as counselors must be aware of their racial biases regarding cultural and racial groups, they must also assess their biases as they relate to gay, lesbian, and bisexual clients (Pope, 1995). Counselors, too, have been influenced by living in a society that socializes people toward racist and homophobic attitudes (see the Storytelling "Being Free").

Caroline Pace (1991) conducted an in-depth study on the attitudes of mental health professionals and graduate students in training programs toward gay men and lesbians. She found that "counselors, like other individuals socialized by heterosexist institutions in the United States, hold negative attitudes toward lesbians and gays" (p. 73). The mental health professionals and counselors-in-training scored in the "low grade homophobic" range of the Index of Attitudes Toward Homosexuals Scale, which was developed by Hudson and Ricketts (1980). This scale has been used in studies designed to measure attitudes toward gay men and lesbians in several populations.

Gays, lesbians, and bisexuals experience homophobia not only in the counselor's office, which should be a safe place to explore one's identity issues, but by the general public as well. For example, 90% of gay men and lesbians polled have experienced some form of victimization because of their sexual orientation (Task Force on Gay/Lesbian Issues, 1982). Additionally, in an environment that should support the universe of expression, ideas, and exploration, colleges and universities have been bastions of heterosexist and homophobic activity. In a study of homophobia on college campuses, researchers found that, among persons who were gay, lesbian, and bisexual, 45% to 65% experienced verbal assaults, 22% to 26% were followed or chased, 12% to 15% were sexually harassed or assaulted, 16% to 25% experienced threats of physical violence, 35% to 58% feared for their safety, and over 90% expected to experience further acts of homophobic harassment while in college (Beryl, 1989).

Other crucial issues that face the gay population are substance abuse, depression, runaways, HIV and AIDS, partner abuse, and attempted suicide. Researchers maintain that substance abuse among lesbians and gay men is high. The gay bar may be the most accessible and visible place to persons who are "out" to interact with others who are also "out" (Rothblum, 1994). Gay men and lesbians attempt suicide two to seven times more often than heterosexual comparison groups (Durby, 1994; Hammelman, 1993). Gay youths have a plethora of problems during adolescence, such as intensified feelings of isolation, depression, and lack of healthy role models (Browning, Reynolds, & Dworkin, 1994). School counselors should be aware of, and be prepared to work with, a diversity of youths because an estimated 3 million adolescents across the country are gay, lesbian, or bisexual (O'Connor, 1992). Unfortunately, because of the lack of role models and sympathetic support systems, another 20% to 35% of these young individuals attempt suicide (O'Connor, 1992).

STORYTELLING
Being Free

When Ellen DeGeneres "came out of the closet" regarding her sexual orientation, I felt proud and inspired. Despite the homophobic society in which we live, she decided that she was no longer going to be silent about a salient component of her identity. She let go of that which was toxic in her life and a source of bondage—the secrecy, the hiding, and the shame. Because as human beings we are more similar than we are different, I confronted myself about how I, too, needed to come out of that which led to a lesser life. As a heterosexual, I have unearned sexual orientation privilege. Benefits and assets are readily available to me on a daily basis simply because I am heterosexual. Yet, such privilege does not negate the need for me to liberate myself. Several years ago, I quickly became free of other people's thoughts that I should wait until I get married before I bought my house. As a free woman, I have come out of shoes that, though pretty, hurt my feet and make my life miserable. What is sexy about a look of pure anguish on my face because my feet hurt? I had learned through a variety of socializations that I looked better (e.g., sexy, thinner, taller) in high heels. Because I wanted to be appealing to others, particularly men, I was willing to be extremely uncomfortable. I am convinced that no American woman with feet has not done similarly. In the words of Aretha, ask yourself, "Think, what are you trying to do to me?" I have come out of relationships, with men and women, that pinch and distress my life. In doing so, I have made room for delightful treasures that are a source of pure joy. I no longer buy or wear clothes that leave indentations on my stomach and that restrict my mobility. Regardless of sexual orientation, there are tremendous benefits to coming out and being free.

Tracy

COUNSELING GAYS, LESBIANS, AND BISEXUALS OF COLOR

According to Dworkin and Gutierrez (1992), identity development is an important component of the adjustment process among persons who are gay, lesbian, or bisexual. In a recent research study of 50 gay men and lesbians of color, Hefty (1994) found no significant differences in the mean level of self-esteem, self-criticism, spirituality, and connection to family among African American gay, lesbian, and bisexual and heterosexual African Americans.

African American gay men and lesbians encounter homophobia within their own racial communities and racism within the White gay community. These experiences are found among other cultures as well. For example, Asian American gay men and lesbians find themselves "caught between two conflicting cultural values, between Asian and western influences" (Chan, 1992, p. 116). Asian American and Native American Indian gay men and lesbians also contend with strong traditional family roles, subsequent expectations, and community values that are often collectivistic, as opposed to individualistic, in orientation (Greene, 1994a). It is important for therapists who work with Asian clients to ask themselves the following questions:

Is the client an immigrant or American born?
To what ethnic group does the client belong?
What are the specific cultural values of this group? Of the client's family? Of the client?
How strongly does the client follow traditional customs?
What is the client's socioeconomic status?
What is the client's level of bilingualism?

Similarities are found between the Native American Indian and Asian American cultures. Greene (1994a) said that "bearing some similarity to Asian cultures, gender roles are clearly delineated among Indian families, and obedience to parents is expected" (p. 247).

In working with Native American Indian gay clients, the devastation of colonialism and Western influences needs to be considered in interpreting sexuality. It is crucial that Spirit, and not the material world, be held as sacred in traditional Native American Indian cultures. Allen (1992) talked about the gynecentric societies, which value the centrality of women, honor the young, and revere all of life that is part of the whole. In traditional society, there were sacred places for men and women who were embodied by Spirit and did not want to marry persons of the other gender, and there were men who dressed and lived like women. Concerning contemporary Native American Indians who are gay, Greene (1994a) stated that acceptance may be less on reservations than in large urban centers.

Similar issues arise when working with Latino clients. Morales (1992) stated,

> The life of a Latino gay and Latina lesbian in the United States often means a life that is lived within three communities: the gay and lesbian community, the Latino and Latina community, and the predominantly White heterosexual mainstream society. (p. 126)

The resolution and recognition of these multiple identities, according to Morales, is the movement through five "states reflective of cognitive and lifestyle changes" (p. 131). Morales contends that an individual can move through several of these states simultaneously, as opposed to in a linear stage model, in which an individual needs to resolve one stage successfully before moving into another. Morales's sexual identity formation states (pp. 131–134) are described below:

1. *State 1: Denial of Conflicts.* The individual believes that she or he is viewed and treated the same as others, acts of discrimination are minimized, and the use of denial helps relieve the burden of overt oppression. The person identifies with the gay, lesbian, or bisexual lifestyle but has primarily White lovers. The therapist is encouraged to focus on helping the client perceive how multiple identities can be personality and lifestyle assets.

2. *State 2: Bisexual Versus Gay or Lesbian.* The preference for the bisexual label is a way to avoid being categorized, labeled, or ostracized. The Latino/Latina gay, lesbian, or bisexual also finds comfort in the Latino community because the White gay community is perceived as hostile. Therapists should focus on clients' feelings of hopelessness, despair, and depression, which are a direct result of their feelings of conflict.

3. *State 3: Conflicts in Allegiances.* The consciousness-awakening process in which the multiple identities are recognized (Latino/Latina/male/female) could provoke dissonance. Thus, in therapy, the counselor should focus on recognizing and prioritizing these allegiances, rather than on choosing sides.

4. *State 4: Establishing Priorities in Allegiance.* Emergence of cultural pride in this state is strong. The person prefers being called Latino or Latina to form an attachment, personally and culturally, with the community. The term *minority* has an oppressive connotation (Morales, 1992, p. 133). The therapeutic strategies in this state should be to enhance the client's Latino and Latina gay contacts.

5. *State 5: Integrating the Various Communities.* The gay or lesbian Latina/Latino is comfortable with the multicultural identity and needs to continue to develop contacts and advocates in the community. Self-confidence needs to be heightened so that the client can expand these personal contacts and feel comfortable in doing so.

CASE STUDY
Slowly Coming Out of the Closet

The following case study is provided to allow an integration of the material discussed throughout this chapter. Case study material is a reliable tool to assist counselors in training and practitioners in their understanding of heterosexism (Greene & Herek, 1994).

Paula Day is a 34-year-old European American woman who has recently divorced Bill, her husband of 7 years. They have a 6-year-old daughter, Rae, who lives with Paula. Paula is a career counselor at a community agency. Currently, she is facilitating a group composed of people whose workplaces have been downsized, and they are looking to settle into new careers. Paula left her husband because she found the marriage to be troubled and constantly conflictual. She also found her attraction to other women to be unrelenting. When she married Bill shortly after graduate school, she figured that these feelings for other women would subside. Once she had a child, she also thought her life would be full

with being a wife, mother, and career woman; at least that's what her mother told her. For the last 6 months, Paula has had a relationship with Betty, a woman she has known since graduate school. At first, they started having lunch a few times a week. Recently, they have been spending more time together on weekends, and their relationship has evolved into a sexual one. Betty and Rae get along well, but Paula is reluctant to reveal to Rae the nature of her relationship with Betty. She fears that if her ex-husband were to find out about her sexual relationship with Betty, it might jeopardize the custody arrangement she has with Rae. Paula has revealed her sexual orientation to some colleagues at work who are gay, lesbian, bisexual, or homosexual allies, and she has received support from them. Paula maintains that, for the first time in her adult life, she feels a freedom and peace she never had before. When Paula was in college, she had a covert sexual relationship with a woman at another college, but it ended after her friend left college to attend a school farther away. Paula tried to discuss her same-sex attraction with her very religious mother years ago when she was a teenager and then again before she married, but she encountered great resistance. Her mother admonished her to pray, get her mind out of the gutter, and do the right thing by marrying Bill. Paula and Betty have a growing number of friends who are gay, lesbian, and bisexual.

QUESTIONS

1. Where would you classify Paula in Cass's (1979, 1984) model?
2. How does the O'Bear and Reynolds (1985) model apply to Paula?
3. Would a heterosexual counselor be appropriate for Paula?
4. What types of issues might emerge if Paula were a person of color?
5. What types of therapeutic techniques could be used?

DISCUSSION AND INTEGRATION
The Client, Paula

According to O'Bear and Reynolds (1985), Paula's experiences are consistent with the developmental processes of lesbians. When Paula was a teenager, she was aware that she had homosexual feelings. During college, she had her first homosexual relationship. Paula is a bit behind the model with regard to the acquisition of a positive gay identity and disclosure to spouse about one's sexual orientation. Other influences in Paula's life, such as custodial concerns, fear of rejection from her family, and limited exposure to positive role models, ultimately affect her identity development. Paula has revealed her orientation to some colleagues at work, which albeit risky, suggests that she feels a certain safety in disclosing. It appears that Paula is in the identity acceptance, or Stage 4, of Cass's (1979) model. At this stage, persons admit that they are quite sure they are gay/lesbian and are at a place of acceptance with a fair degree of happiness and peace. Although they are still rather cautious and selective about to whom they disclose, they are willing to tell

a few people about being gay/lesbian. At this stage, people do not merely tolerate a homosexual self-image, but rather increase contact and interaction with the gay/lesbian subculture. Paula now has a partner who is also gay, is out to some of her colleagues at work, and enjoys a social life with people who share her sexual orientation.

Even though it took several years, Paula now has a positive identification with other gay people. She has resolved some of the nagging questions characteristic of earlier stages, such as "What am I?" and "Where do I belong?" It appears that Paula has both a private and a public life as they relate to her gay identity. In a sense, her life is compartmentalized in that she is passing as a heterosexual around her mother. Given her family situation, this may be the best decision Paula could make at the present time. Although Paula wants her life to work (all of us do, regardless of our sexual orientation), it is likely that her legitimate and positive contacts with members of the gay community and her partner may increase her dissonance about the compartmentalized nature of her life. As stated earlier, feeling that being gay is legitimate tends to increase the distance people feel from a society that is homophobic.

To deal with her anger with an antigay society, along with her enhanced self-acceptance, Paula may move into Stage 5, identity pride. At this stage, people have pride at being gay/lesbian and enjoy living as gay/lesbian persons. In fact, no attempt is made to hide this fact, and there is even a preference to mix socially with other gay men/lesbians.

Paula may question whether she is lesbian or bisexual, given her heterosexual-like behavior with her husband and her homosexual activity with Betty. Rothblum (1994) cited a model of sexual orientation formation in which the various levels of identity are regarded as multidimensional, congruent, and/or incongruent. For example, Paula may say that she is lesbian, has sex with Betty, but is not yet a member of the lesbian community. Again, it is important to reiterate that heterosexual behavior is not synonymous with a heterosexual identity. Like so many others in this heterosexist society, it is possible that Paula engaged in heterosexual behavior and assumed a heterosexual identity within the context of marriage, given its acceptability within her immediate family and society at large. Paula needs to be commended for being honest with herself and others about who she is.

If Paula were a person of color, the multiple layers of her gender, sexual orientation, and race would need to be considered, particularly within the context of societal racism, sexism, and homophobia (Greene, 1994b). Even though African American gay men, lesbians, and bisexuals exhibit high levels of self-esteem (Hefty, 1994), a tremendous amount of oppression and isolation exists within communities of color around homosexuality. The impact of having multiple identities that are devalued in society represents a severe lack of support by both communities of color and the White-dominated gay and lesbian populace. Even in gay and lesbian generally supportive social communities, people of color who are gay and lesbian are often repressed and do not receive the affirmation that White American members receive (Loiacano, 1989).

The racism and oppression faced by gay men and lesbians of color often urge them to turn to their same-race communities for potential support, the development of coping techniques, and help with maintaining a positive identity (Icard, 1986). Because of the level of homophobia, few gay men and lesbians of color actually find needed support psychologically and socially. The African American community often has the attitude that homosexuality is inconsistent with being Black (Riggs, 1994). For instance, African American lesbians experience tremendous difficulty finding acceptance among the African American population because lesbianism is largely incompatible with female role expectations based on "traditional" African American values (Loiacano, 1989). Similarly, African American gay males are faced with a problem of complying with male role expectations that include propagating the race and holding allegiance to the African American community, which generally maintains an antihomosexual attitude (Icard, 1986).

The Counselor, Toni Swain

Although it may be tempting to focus solely on Paula's sexual orientation, Toni, as an effective coun-

selor, bears in mind that multiple and simultaneous identities describe Paula's life. She is a mother, daughter, career woman, and partner. She is White, a baby boomer, middle class, and has been shaped by certain historical events (e.g., the assassinations of President John F. Kennedy and Martin Luther King, Jr.; the impeachment of Richard Nixon).

Toni, as a heterosexual counselor, could be effective with Paula but not unless she had worked through her own homophobic attitudes, which counselors, along with others, are socialized into (Holahan & Gibson, 1994). Chojnacki and Gelberg (1995) connected Cass's model to developmental stages of heterosexual counselors. A counselor who is at Stage 1, confusion, may not clearly apprehend the oppressive contexts in which gay, lesbian, and bisexual persons live. Therefore, such a counselor may not understand the need for clients to be in a support group. Counselors in the latter stages, such as Stage 5, identity pride, begin to feel pride about the quality of the services they provide to their clients and recognize the importance of understanding "the history, culture, ethics, jargon, and sense of community that define the gay and lesbian culture"(Pope, 1995, p. 302). Counselors at this stage also begin to experience greater alienation from colleagues perceived to be homophobic. Where Toni is in her own identity development will have profound implications for her ability to be an ally for Paula (Greene & Herek, 1994).

Many gay and lesbian clients are cautious about entering therapy because they are aware of the homoprejudice among society at large and even among members of the helping profession (Rothblum, 1994). Paula and other gay, lesbian, or bisexual persons are disadvantaged when the helping professional is ignorant of sexual orientation, developmental processes, identity development, counseling techniques, and overall challenges with which this population contends on a daily basis. Referring a client to a different counselor who can be more effective is the standard course of action. This is particularly the case when the first counselor is unable or not adequately trained to provide the necessary support the client needs. Yet, counselors may want to ascertain whether their unwillingness to work with persons who are gay and lesbian is indicative of an intolerance for other sources of diversity, such as race, class, and, ability.

To relax, Toni could encourage Paula to do breathing exercises. Cognitive-behavioral techniques may also be beneficial, wherein Paula can identify and then dispute some of the thoughts she is having that create emotional distress, such as "I am not a fit mother if I am a lesbian." It is most important that Toni be warm, nonjudgmental, skilled as a clinician, and knowledgeable about gay/lesbian issues. It may be helpful for Toni to disclose that she is heterosexual and yet talk about her expertise and openness in this area. Toni and other counselors are encouraged to help clients create a support system within the gay/lesbian community before the clients come out to heterosexual significant others.

SUMMARY

This chapter examined sexual orientation and acknowledged that it exists on a continuum. Definitions were provided, and developmental processes, identity models, and implications for counselors, particularly in working with gay, lesbian, and bisexual clients, were discussed. A case study allowed readers to apply the material contained throughout. The importance of studying this topic was provided. Clients of color who are gay, lesbian, or bisexual were also discussed in an effort to help the reader in understanding the convergence of multiple identities.

REFERENCES

Allen, P. G. (1992). *The sacred hoop: Recovering the feminine in American Indian traditions.* Boston: Beacon Press.

Bell, A., & Weinberg, M. (1978). *Homosexuality: A study of human diversity among men and women.* New York: Simon & Schuster.

Bem, S. L. (1993). *The lenses of gender: Transforming the debate on sexuality inequality.* New Haven, CT: Yale University Press.

Beryl, K. (1989). Antigay violence and victimization in the United States: An overview. *Journal of Interpersonal Violence, 5,* 274–294.

Berzon, B. (1988). *Permanent partners: Building gay and lesbian relationships that last.* New York: E. P. Dutton.

Browning, C., Reynolds, A. L., & Dworkin, S. H. (1994). Affirmative psychotherapy for lesbian women. *Counseling Psychologist, 19,* 177–196.

Cass, V. C. (1979). Homosexual identity formation: A theoretical model. *Journal of Homosexuality, 4,* 219–235.

Cass, V. C. (1984). Homosexual identity: A concept in need of definition. *Journal of Homosexuality, 9,* 105–126.

Chan, C. S. (1992). Cultural considerations in counseling Asian American lesbians and gay men. In S. H. Dworkin & F. J. Gutierrez (Eds.), *Counseling gay men and lesbians: Journey to the end of the rainbow* (pp. 115–124). Alexandria, VA: American Association for Counseling and Development.

Chojnacki, J. T., & Gelberg, S. (1995). The facilitation of a gay/lesbian/bisexual support-therapy group by heterosexual counselors. *Journal of Counseling & Development, 73,* 352–354.

Coleman, E. (1982). Developmental stages of the coming out process. *American Behavioral Scientist, 25,* 469–482.

Durby, D. D. (1994). Gay, lesbian, and bisexual youth. *Journal of Gay and Lesbian Social Services, 1*(3/4), 1–37.

Dworkin, S. H., & Gutierrez, F. (1989). Introduction to special issue. Counselors be aware: Clients come in every size, shape, color, and sexual orientation. *Journal of Counseling & Development, 68,* 1, 6–8.

Dworkin, S. H., & Gutierrez, F. (1992). *Counseling gay men and lesbians: Journey to the end of the rainbow.* Alexandria, VA: American Association for Counseling and Development.

Falco, K. L. (1991). *Psychotherapy with lesbian clients: Theory into practice.* New York: Brunner/Mazel.

Greene, B. (1994a). Ethnic-minority lesbians and gay men: Mental health and treatment issues. *Journal of Consulting and Clinical Psychology, 62,* 243–251.

Greene, B. (1994b). Lesbian women of color: Triple jeopardy. In L. Comas-Diaz & B. Greene (Eds.), *Women of color: Integrating ethnic and gender identities in psychotherapy* (pp. 389–427). New York: Guilford.

Greene, B., & Herek, G. M. (1994). *Lesbian and gay psychology: Theory, research, and clinical applications.* Thousand Oaks, CA: Sage.

Hammelman, T. L. (1993). Gay and lesbian youth: Contributing factors to serious attempts or considerations of suicide. *Journal of Gay and Lesbian Psychotherapy, 2*(1), 77–89.

Hefty, D. L. (1994). *Layered identities: Self-esteem and sexual orientation among African American gays, lesbians, and bisexuals.* Unpublished manuscript, University of Florida, Gainesville.

Holahan, W., & Gibson, A. A. (1994). Heterosexual therapists leading lesbian and gay therapy groups: Therapeutic and political realities. *Journal of Counseling & Development, 72,* 591–594.

Hudson, W. W., & Ricketts, W. A. (1980). A strategy for the measurement of homophobia. *Journal of Homosexuality, 5,* 357–372.

Hunt, B. (1993). What counselors need to know about counseling gay men and lesbians. *Counseling and Human Development, 26*(1), 1–12.

Icard, L. (1986). Black gay men and conflicting social identities: Sexual orientation versus racial identity. In J. Gripton & M. Valentich (Eds.), Social work practice in sexual problems [Special issue]. Journal of Social *Work and Human Sexuality, 4*(1–2), 83–93.

King, N. (1988). Teaching about lesbians and gays in the psychology curriculum. In P. A. Bronstein & K. Quina (Eds.), *Teaching a psychology of people: Resources for gender and sociocultural awareness* (pp. 168–174). Washington, DC: American Psychological Association.

Loiacano, D. K. (1989). Gay identity issues among Black Americans: Racism, homophobia, and the need for validation. *Journal of Counseling & Development, 68,* 21–25.

Morales, E. S. (1992). Counseling Latino gays and Latina lesbians. In S. H. Dworkin & F. J. Gutierrez (Eds.), *Counseling gay men and lesbians: Journey to the end of the rainbow* (pp. 125–140). Alexandria, VA: American Association for Counseling and Development.

O'Bear, K., & Reynolds, A. (1985). *Opening doors to understanding and acceptance: A facilitator's guide for presenting workshops on lesbian and gay issues.* Manual presented at the American College Personnel Association Convention, Boston.

O'Connor, M. F. (1992). Psychotherapy with gay and lesbian adolescents. In S. H. Dworkin & F. J. Gutierrez (Eds.), *Counseling gay men and lesbians: Journey to the end of the rainbow* (pp. 3–22). Alexandria, VA: American Association for Counseling and Development.

Pace, C. (1991). *A description of factors affecting attitudes held by mental health professionals and students toward lesbians and gays.* Unpublished master's thesis, University of Florida, Gainesville.

Pharr, S. (1988). *Homophobia: A weapon of sexism.* Little Rock, AR: Chardon.

Pleck, J. H. (1984). Men's power with women, other men, and society. In P. P. Ricker & E. H. Carmen (Eds.), *The gender gap in psychotherapy: Social realities and psychological processes* (pp. 79–89). New York: Plenum Press.

Pope, M. (1995). The "salad bowl" is big enough for us all: An argument for the inclusion of lesbians and gay men in any definition of multiculturalism. *Journal of Counseling & Development, 73,* 301–304.

Riggs, M. (1994). *Black is . . . Black ain't* [Video]. San Francisco: California Newsreel.

Rothblum, E. D. (1994). "I only read about myself on bathroom walls": The need for research on the mental health of lesbians and gay men. *Journal of Consulting and Clinical Psychology, 62,* 213–220.

Rudolph, J. (1990). Counselors' attitudes toward homosexuality: Selective review of the literature. *Journal of Counseling & Development, 65,* 165–168.

Smith, B. (1982). Toward a Black feminist criticism. In G. Hull, P. Scott, & B. Smith (Eds.), *All the women are White, all the Blacks are men, but some of us are brave* (pp. 157–175). Old Westbury, NY: Feminist Press.

Sullivan, P. (1998). Sexual identity development: The importance of target or dominant group membership. In R. C. Sanlo (Ed.), *Working with lesbian, gay, bisexual, and transgender college students: A handbook for faculty and administrators* (pp. 3–12). Wesstport, CT: Greenwood Press.

Task Force on Gay/Lesbian Issues. (1982). *Homosexuality and social justice.* San Francisco: Archdiocese of San Francisco.

Wall, V. A., & Evans, N. J. (1992). Using psychosocial development theories to understand and work with gay and lesbian persons. In N. J. Evans & V. A. Hall (Eds.), *Beyond tolerance: Gays, lesbians, and bisexuals on campus* (pp. 25–28). Alexandria, VA: ACPA.

Chapter 7

Converging Physical Attractiveness, Ability, and Disability

When asked whether
she had any regrets about her life,
Eleanor Roosevelt replied, "Just one. I
wish I'd been prettier."

This chapter explores, with an ever-steady gaze on cultural values, the inordinate emphasis on external standards of perfection. Cultural values of independence, thinness, physical strength, and athleticism pervade U.S. society. One primary medium for the transmission of images is advertisements, both print and audiovisual (Covell, 1992). Chronic dieting among women, preoccupation with body sculpting among men, even to the point of damaging the body with steroids, and eating disorders, such as anorexia and bulimia, are common and even epidemic within the culture. These behaviors seem to have their genesis in cultural images and values that far too often place a greater premium on physical attractiveness than on developed inner character strength. Implications for self-esteem development based on possession of valued physical characteristics are also examined. Race, gender, and body size are integrated into this discussion of physical attractiveness. The need for counselors to be aware of the salience of physical attractiveness as a status variable in everyday life is crucial to understanding clients as whole beings. That narrow definitions of physical attractiveness have implications for mental health attitudes, body validation, and the development of coping strategies to cope meaningfully with both unanticipated and normal maturational changes in physical appearance and body ability is articulated. Integrated into this discussion is an examination of the culture's clear preference for the able-bodied and intolerance for persons with disabilities. Implications for the development of a healthy relationship with the body, regardless of being able-bodied or having a disability, are presented. Multiple components of physical attractiveness exist and encompass facial beauty, skin color, physical ability and strength, visible signs of aging, height, weight, and hair length and texture. The discussion of physical attractiveness is broadened to include personal empowerment.

PHYSICAL ATTRACTIVENESS AS A STATUS VARIABLE

It has been said that literature reveals life. If this is so, the literature clearly supports a reality that societal distinctions are made between those persons who are regarded as physically attractive and those who are not (Cash & Duncan, 1984; Downs, 1990; Unger, Hilderbrand, & Madar, 1982; Webster & Driskell, 1983). Numerous research findings have consistently shown a pattern across all age-groups where people react more favorably to attractive infants, children, and adults than they do to individuals perceived as unattractive (Ponzo, 1985). Physical attractiveness has even been linked to assumptions of moral character, intelligence, marital satisfaction, dating frequency, and quality of life (Dion, Berschid, & Walster, 1972; Webster & Driskell, 1983).

As highly valued traits in this society, beauty and physical attractiveness influence the assumptions held about individuals and the choices made about with whom to associate. Ponzo (1985) stated, "We desire to be with those who are physically beautiful because we have bought the 'beauty is good' hypothesis. We also believe that we will be viewed more positively by association" (p. 483).

Because of the hierarchical relationship that emerges between those who are perceived to have the commodity of attractiveness and those who are not, physical attractiveness is a **status variable.** More specifically, the attractive have more social power, meaning that, as with other forms of privilege, they are able to exercise this power on a daily basis to negotiate their lives more effectively.

Hahn (1988a) discussed beauty power and its close association with mate selection and sexual intimacy. She said, "As long as physical beauty determines sexual choices, human relations will be guided by fortuitous pleasing compositions of bone, muscle, and skin" (p. 27). Hahn observed that inner beauty and character will take a back seat in the competition for partners. Perceived as a prized commodity, beauty operates to "snare a mate who can give her the opportunity to live out her biological and social destiny" (Hutchinson, 1982, p. 60).

Although definite privileges and benefits are associated with physical attractiveness, physical attractiveness can be a hindrance to healthy interpersonal relationships. Attractive people may be perceived to be more vain and egotistical, to feel less sympathetic toward the oppressed, and to be more bourgeois in their attitudes than persons who are not as attractive (Okazawa-Rey, Robinson, & Ward, 1987). These and other perceptions and, arguably, prejudices toward attractive persons may adversely affect approachability and the cultivation of trusting alliances with them.

THE CONVERGENCE OF PHYSICAL ATTRACTIVENESS WITH GENDER AND RACE

Undoubtedly, race and skin color are variables in the beauty business. From a cultural perspective, female beauty is often based on European American standards of blond-haired, blue-eyed European ideals of beauty regardless of the fact that women's physical features are often very different from this standard. It is duly noted that the physical features of many White women often differ from societally based rigid beauty standards as well.

To get closer to the beauty ideal has meant different things for women. Emmons (1992) found that African American teenage girls were more likely than any other race and gender group examined to use laxatives as a dieting ploy. In contrast, European Americans were more likely to vomit to lose weight. Research conducted by Lester and Petrie (1998) on 139 female Mexican American college students found evidence of bulimia nervosa among 1.4% to 4.3% of the sample. Emmons's research points to an erroneous assumption about eating disorders—that they are rare among people of color. The stereotypes about which groups are affected by eating disorders and the dearth of people of color doing research on eating disorders contribute to this mistaken belief. Root (1990) stated that a relationship may exist between increasing opportunities for social mobility for women of color and increasing vulnerability to disordered eating despite strongly entrenched beliefs about the protective aspects of race. Despite African American youths' positive self-esteem (Gibbs, 1985; Gibbs, Huang, & Associates, 1989; Ward, 1989), however, feeling enormous pressure to look and be perfect according to European ideals may adversely affect self-concept among women of color; they may feel compelled to change hairstyles, dress, body size, and makeup to be accepted and thus keep the doors of opportunity wide open. Robinson and Ward (1991) indicated that obesity among many African American women may be a quick-fix coping strategy to deal with the pressures and frustrations of daily existence.

Oppressive stereotypes about women of color are pervasive throughout the media. For instance, Root (1990) identified that

> Women of color are either fat and powerless (African American and Latina women); fat, bossy, and asexual; corrupt and/or evil (Asian/Pacific Island Americans, and African Americans); obedient, quiet, and powerless (Latinas and Asian/Pacific Americans); exotic (Asian Americans, mixed race); or hysterical and stupid. (p. 530)

In an effort to conform to accepted standards of beauty, many women of color will seek to fulfill European-centered beauty standards equated with status, acceptance, and legitimacy. Some Asian women have undergone plastic surgery to make their eyes appear more round and Western looking. This drastic physical change may be fueled by Uba's (1994) statement, "There is evidence that Asian Americans have lower self-concepts than Euro-Americans do when it comes to physical appearance" (p. 83). Rhinoplasty to obtain a nose that is smaller, narrower, and finer is a path many Jewish women have traveled. African American women have been known to bleach their skin, and there is the monumental issue of hair, on which African American women spend an inordinate amount of time and money (see the Storytelling "Loving Ourselves, Head to Toe"). Many of them, along with their Jewish sisters, have for decades been "relaxing" their hair by applying chemicals to make it straight and less naturally coiled or curly. The author Alice Walker refers to this relaxing process as "oppressing" the hair.

Skin color has social power and status (Okazawa-Rey et al., 1987). Mullins and Sites (1984) found that the inheritance of light skin color, which generally came from the mother, who tended to be lighter than the father, along with the mother's education, occupational attainment, and income, served to bolster a family's social position over time. Intraracial conflict around the issue of **colorism**, or stereotyped attributions and prejudgments based on skin color, has been documented in the literature (Okazawa-Rey et al., 1987; Robinson & Ward, 1995). Colorism is often manifested as a preference for lighter skin tones over darker ones, being that color-consciousness is rooted in the social, political, and economic conditions that existed during slavery; however, discrimination against persons with lighter skin tones occurs as well.

More recently, Robinson and Ward (1995) found that although African American adolescents reported high levels of self-esteem, students who were at the extremes of skin color, lighter or darker than most African Americans, were less satisfied with their skin color than students who were somewhere in the middle. This finding from

STORYTELLING
Loving Ourselves, Head to Toe

Several years ago when at Harvard graduate school, two of my friends (Margo and Janie) and I assembled a group of African American women graduate students together to talk about hair, skin color, race, and self-concept. Our interest in this topic emanated from informal discussions at the local campus pub regarding our hair—what to do with it and, of great importance, how to pay for what was done. We became fascinated at the rather significant space these issues occupied in our lives over time, both as young women and as girls. Motivated by an opportunity to gather with sisters and broaden our understanding of psychosocial identity issues in our lives, we invited other women to join us. The gathering was enlightening, powerful, and moving. African American women talked about the enormous significance of hair—its length and texture—as well as skin color in the formation of individual attitudes about personal beauty and that of others. Of issue were family members' comparisons among children concerning the possession of desired or devalued physical traits. One dark-skinned woman shared that she thought *black* and *ugly* were synonymous because these were the words a male adult family member constantly used to describe her—black and ugly. She smiled triumphantly as she proudly announced that recently, on turning 40, she had arrived at the inner place where she could look at her external self in the mirror and see dignity and beauty. Her unlearning process took four decades. I reflected on this story when, a few years later, I was getting my hair cut in a natural style in North Carolina and the hairdresser informed me that God told her to tell me not to cut my hair. I informed this woman that I had a good relationship with God and that if God wanted me to know something, then God would tell me.

Tracy

among a sample of more than 100 is consistent with other literature. Skin color extremes (being very light- or very dark-skinned) are least preferable to the majority of respondents (Neal & Wilson, 1989; Porter, 1991). Essentially, students at either end of the skin color continuum had lower levels of satisfaction with their skin color, compared with students who self-reported skin color as somewhere in between. Of the three categories of students, those students classified as "in-between" had a 68% satisfaction rate with skin color, in comparison with the darker- and lighter-skinned adolescents, 42% and 50%, respectively. Moreover, "lighter" students were most likely to express a desire to be darker than students categorized as "darker" or "somewhere in-between," and darker students were more likely to express a desire to be lighter than others. This study suggests that students at either extreme of the skin color continuum may be more vulnerable to dissatisfaction with their skin color than students who are not at color extremes.

Colorism in the African American community may be a double-edged sword, affecting those who are seen perhaps as "too black" and those who may not be seen as "black enough." Furthermore, being considered different in any context may invite feelings of insecurity. Among the other major findings was a positive relationship between satisfaction with skin color and self-esteem. Despite the confirmation of this hypothesis, it should be remembered that self-esteem is a multidimensional construct and that traditional self-esteem inventories do not typically access this. Moreover, skin color attitudes are connected to several variables, including the particular ethnic group, group cohesiveness, and its status in society, and factors such as family, school, and peers (Phinney & Rosenthal, 1993). More research is needed with a larger sample of students across skin color hues to interpret this finding most accurately. Given that skin color issues are connected to broader themes of racial identity and an awareness of the sociopolitical context of race in America, adolescents' perspectives on skin color seem to be linked to their knowledge of their African heritage, lineage, and racial validation. As African American people celebrate Blackness across various hues, skin color as an intrapersonal and interpersonal issue may take on less significance.

Although appearance is important to both genders, personal beauty is frequently considered the most important virtue a woman can possess. According to Lakoff and Sherr (1984), "beauty is power," and many women have gained social success banking on the social marketability of their perceived physical attractiveness. The socialization process in this culture equates self-worth with mobility, thinness, beauty, and, far too often, dress size. From a very early age, little girls are conditioned, in both subtle and overt ways, that fulfillment in life is hugely dependent on being physically beautiful. As children, many Africa American women remember being cautioned by their mothers that unless their newly washed hair was done (which usually meant being pressed and curled but sometimes braided), they could not go outside. The implicit message in this statement was that being in one's unaltered, natural state was synonymous with being unpresentable.

In addition to learning that beauty is a valuable commodity, young girls learn passivity from the pressure imposed on them to stay clean and neat, correlates of femininity, purity, and acceptability. Grown women continue the legacy by restricting their movement, in an effort to be socially desirable, by oppressing themselves in fashions that are uncomfortable, tight, or even painful. Probably few, if any, America women have not worn uncomfortable shoes just because they accompany an outfit, add height, slenderize the entire body, and elongate the legs. The bunions, corns, and other foot problems that millions of women suffer are often a result of this socialization standard.

Even though this commentary has focused on women, it does not suggest that men are not engrossed in the task of adorning themselves in an effort to appeal to others. Men's bodies appear to be less dependent on external beauty standards as a key component of not only self-definition but validation.

It is not surprising that many women behave in a manner that suggests beauty is something to be acquired and at any cost (Okazawa-Rey et al., 1987). Billions of dollars are spent annually on products and services in Herculean effort to beautify and defy the aging process. Understand that looking one's best is not being assailed. What is problematic is the excessive emphasis placed on physical attractiveness, which is synonymous with being able-bodied as a key component of self-esteem, life-satisfaction, and self-worth.

Although standards of beauty have been different over time, across cultures, and among racial groups, age is most likely the one identity construct that has the greatest bearing on beauty. **Ageism,** or discrimination against middle-aged and elderly people, differs between men and women. Although Nuessel (1982) stated that "ageism is distinct from other forms of discrimination because it cuts across all of society's traditional classifications: gender, race, religion, and national origin" (p. 273), ageism affects women in that, in the normal and inevitable maturational process, men mature and become refined, whereas women wilt and wither. This is an example of how having membership in a group that is valued is disadvantaging and ultimately levies a high toll (Robinson, 1999). With punitive gaze, people are being watched for their allegiance to the commodity of beauty. More universal policies are needed for the entire population that is "at risk" for both chronic illness and disability (Zola, 1989).

Regarding age and beauty, isn't it interesting that as women mature and develop a sense of personal power and internal locus of control, many are perceived as having less of the commodity of beauty? Power in this context is associated with being able to make desired events happen and having sufficient control over self and others. Women who have learned that selflessness is a less desirable trait than responsible care and respect for the self are in a position of power. They have come to critique and challenge externally defined constructions of beauty.

SEX ROLE TYPOLOGY, BODY IMAGE, AND SATISFACTION

Attitudes about body image and subsequent levels of satisfaction are socially constructed and can be deconstructed or challenged and changed so that new discourses about their meanings are created (Monk, Winslade, Crocket, Epston, 1997). For instance, research (Jackson, Sullivan, & Rostker, 1988; Unger et al., 1982) strongly suggests that a masculine sex role type, as opposed to a feminine one, may be related to a more favorable body image. This could be a function of the psychological nature of masculinity. More specifically, masculine individuals, according to the Bem Sex Role Inventory, yield a higher score on traits such as self-reliance, assertiveness, making decisions easily, and independence (Bem, 1974). Such attributes appear to contribute to autonomy in self-definition in that there is less reliance on others to validate or legitimate the self. A person's high dependence on external validation of the self contributes to depressed self-esteem and external locus of control (McBride, 1990).

In other research conducted on the attractiveness of the androgynous male, researchers found that masculinity, too, is a double-edged sword. Masculine subjects were rated less favorably than androgynous males; however, androgynous men who were seen as too feminine were rated as less likable (Cramer, Cupp, & Kuhn, 1993).

Although some literature reveals many positive social and psychological benefits of femininity (Cook, 1987), feminine persons have been found to exhibit lower self-esteem than masculine persons (Burnett, Anderson, & Heppner, 1995). Masculinity appears to be a greater indicator of overall well-being, in comparison with femininity. Research documents this finding as well. Napholz (1994) found in her study of African American working women that sex role orientation was associated with both depression and self-esteem. The sex-typed group (e.g., feminine) had significantly higher depression and lower self-esteem scores than the androgynous group. Those who were undifferentiated had significantly higher depression and lower self-esteem scores when compared with the androgynous and cross-typed groups (e.g., masculine).

Other research related to sex role type has found that, among children, both boys and girls, those who are rated as more attractive are more likely to play with feminine-typed toys and less likely to play with masculine-typed toys, in comparison with children rated as unattractive (Downs, 1990). Regarding older children, attractive adolescents were more likely to hold on to traditional sex-typed values for themselves and others (Downs & Abshier, 1982). Being regarded as attractive may affect one's ability to develop an androgynous sex role type. Females judged as attractive may be challenged in their development of a masculine sex role. Attractive men may have difficulty developing a feminine one. This concern is important, given the effect of androgyny on self-esteem, attitudes about success, and ability to cope with existential issues (Cano, 1987; Cook, 1987; Stevens, Pfost, & Potts, 1990).

Despite the noble efforts of the women's movement, negative body image continues to be with us into the 21st century. According to Hutchinson (1982), "body image is not the same as the body, but is rather what the mind does to the body in translating the experience of embodiment into its mental representation" (p. 59). Birtchnell, Lacey, and Harte (1985) indicated three aspects of body image: (a) *physiological,* which involves the brain's ability to detect weight, shape, size, and form; (b) *conceptual,* which is the mental picture of one's own body; (c) and *emotional,* which refers to the feelings about one's body weight, shape, and size. Brouwers (1990) argued that the emotional aspect of body image is the crux of the eating disorder known as **bulimia,** characterized by recurrent episodes of binge eating and feelings of lack of control over eating behavior during binges. This makes sense, given that intense dissatisfaction with body image and strong hatred of one's body is correlated with bulimia. Such strong negative emotion regarding the body often elicits severe feelings of depression and powerlessness.

Where does such intense dislike for the body originate? For young girls, they are socialized that their primary role in life is to please and to be pleasing to others, tending to be much more anxious than boys and worrying about being socially desirable. If the body deviates from acceptable cultural standards, and it often does, dissatisfaction may ensue when the girl child is not empowered to celebrate her body and the joys of it. Often, adult women, too, are incapable of assisting young girls in this celebration process if, as older women, they cannot honor their own bodies. Tolman (1991) maintained that, among most adolescent girls, a discourse regarding their natural sexual desires is missing. Women's inability to name and give voice to their own sexual hunger interferes with dialogue between women cross-generationally.

A closer relationship exists among beauty, thinness, success, power, acceptance, and self-worth for girls and women than it does for boys and men. In fact, one study found that overall body dissatisfaction was higher among girls than among boys

(Paxton et al., 1991). This finding may explain why 87% of persons undergoing plastic surgery are women (Steinem, 1992). In the United States, over 90% of persons suffering from **anorexia nervosa,** or self-starvation of the body, are young females (Andersen, 1986). Adolescents are particularly vulnerable to eating disorders because anorexia nervosa has its highest incidence at the beginning of adolescence and bulimia nervosa has its highest incidence at the end (Emmons, 1992). From a psychodynamic perspective, the earlier scripts that are set in motion will have a powerful impact on behavior and cognition unless early information is replaced with new information. Arrival to adulthood does not ensure clarity about the existence or elimination of dysfunctional tapes. With respect to eating disorders, Chernin (1985) said that they "must be understood as a profound developmental crisis in a generation of women still deeply confused after two decades of struggle for female liberation, about what it means to be a woman in the modern world" (p. 17).

Family of origin has a pivotal role in the life of the girl who has an eating disorder. Brouwers (1990) reported that negative attitudes toward the body begin in the family and that, after self-body evaluation, the daughter's belief that the mother was critical of the daughter's body was the second biggest predictor of bulimia in female college students. Research by Kashubeck, Walsh, and Crowl (1994) indicated that campus factors or values may influence who is vulnerable to eating disorders at different schools. One school research site emphasized physical appearance, attention to fashion, and participation in the sorority-fraternity system. The other school was a liberal arts institution that emphasized political activism and intellectual talent. Although the rate of eating disorders did not differ between the two sites, the study found that

> different factors were associated with eating disorder symptomatology at
> each school. At the first school, factors related to eating-disordered think-
> ing and behavior were perceived pressure to dress fashionably, to be intel-
> lectual, and depressed grade point averages. At the second school, the
> strongest predictors of eating disorder symptomatology were having low
> masculine gender role identity and being female. (p. 643)

Toward the important work of identity formation and declaration, one task of adulthood is to unlearn many of the negative tapes received during childhood and adolescence and to replace them with tapes that affirm the self and are more reflective of who the individual has sculpted the self to be. The media, church, educational institutions, other women, family members, and men create an environment wherein men "construct the symbolic order" within which gender inequity and male supremacy are reproduced.

In this system, women (and, arguably, men because the privilege to define reality often comes with a price tag) become detached from their bodies in a warring fashion. This is particularly true when a gap exists between perception of body image and approximation to the socially constructed standard. In short, intense body dissatisfaction and a sense of disembodiment can ensue when one's body does not conform to the standard. Hutchinson (1982) stated, "The body is experienced as alien and lost to awareness. . . . The body has broken away or has been severed from the mind and is experienced as a foreign object, an albatross, or a hated antagonist" (pp. 59-60).

Alienation from the body interferes with the important work of appreciating and ultimately accepting the multiple identities of the self regardless of how it is configured. Perceptions of the body amid parts that cause pain, create difficulty, or are defined by society as unattractive and therefore deemed unacceptable can be transformed and embraced through deliberate paradigm shifts. New discourses or ways of bringing meaning to bear on the value of the body can emerge and take root interpersonally (Monk et al., 1997).

MEN AND BODY IMAGE

American society places an inordinate amount of emphasis on thinness as a criterion for physical attractiveness in women more than in men (Downs, 1990). Whereas the majority of American women seek to lose weight, American men seem to be equally split between those who desire to lose weight and those who wish to gain some (Davis, Stuart, Dionne, & Mitchell, 1991). **Patriarchy,** women's dependence on men for economic gain, and the objectification of women's bodies are partly responsible for this dynamic. But men, too, are affected by societal notions of attractiveness. Athletic leanness (Emmons, 1992) and a sculpted, muscular body (Gillett & White, 1992) are often the criteria for men's attractiveness and social acceptability. Thus, men are now more concerned with their body image and physical appearance than they were a few decades ago (Davis et al., 1991). This standard is evidenced in advertising that often depicts men in erotic poses with emphasis on their bulging muscles and the phallic symbol (Kervin, 1989).

Although adult men are affected by societal dictates, adolescents tend to be more vulnerable, in part, because of the dramatic physical changes that take place during puberty. To achieve an ideal body image, teenagers have been known to resort to a variety of methods that include fasting, dieting, using laxatives, and purging. Although females represent the majority of eating disorder cases, boys and men are not immune to these disorders. Andersen (1986) stated that although similarities are found between males and females with eating disorders, some differences are found with respect to pre-illness weight, psychotherapeutic needs, and modality themes. Overall, males are less conscious of the desire to achieve a certain weight or clothing size. Instead, they place greater emphasis on muscle definition and avoiding fat and flab on the body. Boys are socialized to believe that masculinity is synonymous with being a protector, provider, and worker. Athleticism and body strength create the basis for virility. Men with physical disabilities often struggle with oppressive and internalized notions of masculinity that tend to be inconsistent with the presence of disability. Emmons (1992) found that boys, too, were engaging in dieting behaviors, meaning that adolescent males, as a group, are under considerable pressure to shape and sculpt their bodies to fit societal standards. Perhaps greater emphasis on fashion advertisements and product lines wherein the young, muscular male body is revered (Mishkind, Rodin, Silbersein, & Striegel-Moore, 1987) has contributed to this pressure.

The male body and its muscles are associated with strength and power. It is argued that, in times of psychocultural stress, through bodybuilding and maintenance of a health regime a male can gain discipline over the body, which is a form of salvation in itself (Gillett & White, 1992). Moreover, masculinity is reclaimed by attaining a hypermasculine body image through bodybuilding. Pumped muscles demonstrate strength, power, and authority. Psychologically for men, bodybuilding may be a way to resist perceived oppression or as a counteraction to the accomplishments of women.

To achieve the ideal body, steroids are often employed, not only among professional athletes but also among high school seniors (Ham, 1993). Anabolic-androgenic steroid hormones can enhance body size toward achieving the "chiseled" body look, increase speed, and boost performance. They also have been known to cause adverse effects on the liver, cardiovascular and reproductive systems, and even psychological health. Both men and women are subject to increased risks of cancer, liver dysfunction, kidney disorders, and heart disease (Ham, 1993). Despite the risks and the potential lethal effects of steroids, they are often used to achieve an ideal body image. Clearly, culture's obsession with beauty comes with a heavy price tag.

DISABILITY AND EXPERIENCES IN AND OF THE BODY

Having an able body is so highly valued in U.S. society that persons with disabilities are discriminated against, stereotyped, ignored, and in many instances presumed to be biologically inferior. Hahn (1988a) said,

> The most salient features of many disabled persons are bodily traits similar
> to skin color, gender, and other attributes that have been used as a basis
> for differentiating people for centuries and without which discrimination
> would not occur. (p. 26)

Hahn (1988b) observed that disabled men and women, unlike groups of color, have been unable to refute discrimination-based notions of biological inferiority.

Zola (1991) stated that preference for specific body types over others represents another societal "ism." In this work, this form of discrimination has been termed "able-body-ism" (see Chapter 3). Just as being male is a biological fact, so is having a disability. Being handicapped, however, is a psychosocial outgrowth of this biological reality (Weeber, 1992). Considerable silence surrounds the experiences of those who have disabilities. This is particularly relevant among able-bodied persons who assume that lack of membership in the disability community entitles them to ignorance or apathy.

Societal attitudes toward disability are numerous and degrading. Many persons perceive the disability to be the only salient element in a person's life. Fowler, O'Rourke, Wadsworth, and Harper (1992) said, "When one's physical and/or mental abilities are considered as the primary status for characterizing individuals, the resulting polarity implicitly divides all persons into two groups: the able and the unable" (p. 14). Much like race, physical disability can be elevated to a primary status trait, where it overrides other characteristics, even achieved ones, and can produce feelings of invisibility. Often, people with disabilities are seen as helpless, childlike, dependent, asexual, and economically subordinate. In addition to such dangerous myths, able-bodied people are too often embarrassed when it comes to talking about or associating with those who have disabilities (Weeber, 1992).

As with other identity constructs, disability intersects with gender. In a society where masculinity is often equated with virility, strength, sexuality, and self-reliance, it is understandable how men with physical disabilities can be perceived as a contradiction to hegemonic masculinity. Gerschick and Miller (1994) stated that "men with physical disabilities are marginalized and stigmatized because they undermine the typical role of the body in United States culture. . . . Men's bodies allow them to demonstrate the socially valuable characteristics of toughness, competitiveness, and ability" (p. 35). To arrive at the place of acceptance of one's self in one's body, there has to be, as Collins (1989) indicated, (a) a confrontation of the societal standard that maintains that masculinity is not only narrowly defined but also in contradiction to the disabled man's body, (b) repudiation of this socially constructed norm, and (c) affirmation of the self through a recognition that the norms and discourses, and not the person, are problematic. From this perspective, the man is able to reconstruct, for himself, alternative gender roles and practices (Gerschick & Miller, 1994).

Real-life stories in which people experience dramatic and sudden changes in their bodies are numerous (see the case study "Redefining Manhood" at the end of this chapter). Wendell (1989), for example, wrote powerfully about the sudden overnight process of going from being able-bodied to being disabled as a result of a disabling chronic disease:

> In 1985, I fell ill overnight with what turned out to be a disabling chronic disease. In the long struggle to come to terms with it, I had to learn to live with a body that felt entirely different to me—weak, tired, painful, nauseated, dizzy, unpredictable . . . I began slowly to identify with my new, disabled body and to learn to work with it. (p. 63)

Waiting to return to her original state was indeed dangerous because the likelihood of this occurrence was remote. So, in time, she was required to learn how to identify and coexist with her new disabled body but not without struggle. Within a culture where normalcy and disability are regarded as contradictory, Wendell (1989) wrote, "Disabled women struggle with both the oppressions of being women in male-dominated societies and the oppressions of being disabled in societies dominated by the abler-bodied" (p. 64).

Both Wendell (1989) and Zola (1991) maintained that a theory on disability and the body is needed. Because of the strong cultural assumptions of able-bodiedness (see the Storytelling "The Unthinkable") and physical attractiveness, such a theory is beneficial to all, regardless of current or, better yet, temporary physical status.

One way that many people with disabilities experience their bodies is through pain. Wendell (1989) stated that persons who live with chronic pain can teach the general public what it means to share space with that which hurts. Crucial questions emerge, such as how a person welcomes pain into his or her life, especially if it is feared. In turn, are people with chronic pain feared and loathed by those who are reminded of their own vulnerability? Feeling the pain, as opposed to endeavoring to medicate it away (Wendell, 1989), meditating on the pain, and engaging in visual imagery and thereby making peace with it are examples of being in, listening to, and embracing one's body for what it is. Indeed, this increased consciousness is a gift of pain. Such a gift can move a person to a place of unconditional acceptance of his or her body despite the circumstances. Writer Audre Lorde (1994) once said, "There is a terrible clarity that comes from living with cancer that can be empowering if we don't turn aside from it" (p. 36). It is in the not turning away, the bold and yet humble confrontation of the source of pain, that strength is found for the journey. Note how all of us can benefit from this lovely truth because pain, in its various hues, is a feature of living and is independent of physical ability status.

Although the wisdom from people with disabilities may benefit many able-bodied persons, the psychological tendency to regard persons who differ from a societal referent point as "other" can interfere with receiving life lessons. Yet, how would this culture be enhanced by listening to dismissed or silenced voices? Wendell (1989) stated that "if disabled people were truly heard, an explosion of knowledge of the human body and psyche would take place" (p. 77). Many persons with disabilities have much to teach the able-bodied about this process of acceptance, dignity, and empowerment (see the Storytelling "Being Ourselves").

STORYTELLING
The Unthinkable

Able-bodied persons enjoy unearned privileges in a society constructed for them. Unless I am lugging audiovisual equipment, I do not have to think about how I am going to get to my class that meets on the seventh floor in the event (likelihood) that the elevator decides not to work. When getting ready to purchase my home, I did not have to inquire about wheelchair accessibility (none of my friends at the time enabled me to think about this). When arranging for a taxi, van, or shuttle, I do not have to ask myself or anyone else, Can I get in? How does not thinking about these unearned privileges affect my accessibility to myself and others?

Tracy

STORYTELLING
Being Ourselves

I called her Mazick. Her name was Maurie Mazicki. She was my friend, running partner (e.g., hanging out, not jogging), and study mate. Maurie had cerebral palsy. This meant that, in her labored speaking voice, most people made assumptions about her intelligence because of how she sounded and looked while she spoke. I understood Mazick and found her to be funny, loving, articulate, and much smarter than anyone of us. She called her wheelchair Freedom. I would catch a ride on the back of Freedom, and we would squeal like children, especially going down a hill. Maurie helped me experience a place of worship that refers to reckless abandon. I've not seen Maurie since the summer we graduated from college in 1982. I miss her and want to, from the words of Sly and the Family Stone, thank her for letting me be myself again and again and again. I know that she continues to live in a society that does not afford her the same decency.

Tracy

IMPLICATIONS FOR COUNSELORS

Helping professionals are not exempt from attitudes that favor children and adults regarded as attractive over those regarded as unattractive (Ponzo, 1985). Guidance counselors need to be particularly mindful of the power of words in shaping children's constructions of themselves. Lerner and Lerner (1977) wrote, "Evidence suggests that when compared to the physically attractive child, the unattractive child experiences rejecting peer relations, the perception of maladjustment by teachers and peers, and the belief by teachers of less educational ability" (p. 586). Professionals are encouraged to ascertain their own beliefs about body image and physical attractiveness. Some professionals may be more inclined to gravitate toward YAVIS (*y*oung, *a*ttractive, *v*erbal, *i*ntelligent, and *s*uccessful) clients. In doing so, they are discriminating against clients who do not conform to these characteristics. Because the counseling event is supposed to be empowering, this bias is dysfunctional for the client and a discredit to the profession.

As with other areas, such as race and gender, effective multicultural counselors need to examine their own attitudes and beliefs about weight and appearance (Brouwers, 1990). Not to do so is to disadvantage the client because the counselor is operating from a limited knowledge base regarding the self. Myers et al. (1991), said, "According to optimal theory, our purpose in being is to gain self-knowledge" (p. 58). Not to know self is to operate from a suboptimal framework, which is a huge hindrance to healing and empowerment in counseling.

CASE STUDY
Redefining Manhood

Larry is a 28-year-old handsome, athletic Mexican American male from a working-class family. Professionally, he is a pipe layer. While driving his motorcycle one evening, he was hit by a drunk driver, lost control of the cycle, and slid into a tree. The impact left Larry paralyzed from the waist down. Doctors say Larry will never walk again. Larry is very depressed and angry. He has withdrawn from his family and his fiancée, Melanie. Prior to the accident, he was very physically active and competed in professional squash tournaments. At the time of the accident, he and Melanie were planning to be married in 5 months.

QUESTIONS
1. How can a counselor help Larry heal?
2. How does Larry's status as a paraplegic affect his masculinity and, more specifically, his sexuality?
3. How important is Larry's ethnicity in approaching his orientation to the problem?
4. How much time does Larry need to feel angry?
5. Can a woman effectively counsel Larry?

DISCUSSION AND INTEGRATION
The Client, Larry

Understandably, Larry is angry and depressed. He has suffered a major loss—unplanned, unwelcome, and unfair changes in his body—because of someone else's gross irresponsibility. Larry needs time to heal physically, psychologically, socially, and emotionally. First, he must mourn, and only he can decide how long this process will take.

Larry's life after the accident can continue to be meaningful, but first Larry has to redefine success, attractiveness, masculinity, desirability, and sexuality. Fowler et al. (1992) indicated that "a disability is a characteristic which carries sufficient conceptual power to stereotype an individual, regardless of whether the disability was present at birth or acquired later in life" (p. 102). Thus, Larry's conceptualization of self must shift. Part of this shifting self-conceptualization encompasses notions of what it means to be a man.

Regarding Larry's ethnicity, does being Latino have any bearing on Larry's problem orientation and its resolve? Because ethnicity is a primary identity construct, the answer is yes. Knowing the salience of ethnicity in Larry's life would certainly help answer this question. Without this specific information, however, a sensitive counselor could consider common values held by many Latinos, which include religion (traditionally Catholicism), submission to and/or respect of nature, close family ties, and *personalismo. Orgullo,* or pride, is also a primary value among many Latinos. Some of Larry's issues stem from damage to his pride as an able-bodied man who has depended on his body professionally, sexually, and socially. For example, Guttman (1994) indicated that "in social science as well as popular literature, the Mexican male, especially if he is from the lower classes, is often portrayed as the archetype of 'machismo' which however defined invariably conjures up the image of virulent sexism" (p. 21).

In a patriarchal society that is designed by men for men, U.S. cultural values of the Protestant work ethic, individualism, capitalism, and self-reliance become inextricably bound to notions of physical attractiveness, power, mobility, strength, and domination over one's body. The belief is that the body can be controlled—that somehow illness and perhaps subsequent disability are a result of the individual's doing. For this reason, "the body beautiful" is central to self-expression (Gillett & White, 1992). An insatiable hunger to be alluring, lovely, and desired permeates the culture.

These values about physical attractiveness emanate from a conceptual framework. Myers et al. (1991) stated that, in society today, with all of its isms, "the very nature of the conceptual system is itself inherently oppressive and that all who adhere to it will have a difficult time developing and maintaining a positive identity" (p. 55). Essentially, a suboptimal system operates within a paradigm where self-worth is attached to external factors separate from the self. Optimally, self-worth is intrinsic to the self. Given that accidents and illness can suddenly change the ability of one's body and one's control over it, such myths should be easily dispelled but they are not. Grappling with existential issues is stress producing, and research suggests that high-masculine men and high-feminine women are adversely affected in their ability to cope (Stevens et al., 1990).

Larry will need to reconstruct the meanings of existential concepts. One possible interference with engaging in this existential process is sex role orientation. Stevens et al. (1990) found that masculine-typed men and feminine-typed women reported the most avoidance of existential issues, such as the meaning of life, death, and personal choice. By comparison, androgynous men appeared particularly receptive to life's challenges.

The Counselor, Andres Vermellian

An effective counselor, Andres understands the essential process of mourning, anger, and depression associated with a major life crisis. Larry is in the recovery process. At the appropriate time, Andres can serve as an educator helping Larry critique traditional notions of masculinity. For instance, physical strength is associated with manhood. Men with disabilities are often not perceived by society as strong because a large part of this strength and manhood equation is having an able body. Andres could help Larry see different types of strength, physical as well as character, that are not typically identified by society.

Asking for psychological help is a form of strength, and so is having spiritual and human resources that radiate love and acceptance. Research has shown that supportive social networks are associated with psychological well-being and adjustment to one's disability (Belgrave, 1991; Swanson, Cronin-Stubbs, & Sheldon, 1989). Prior to the accident, Larry had a very active life involving the full use of his legs. As the healing progresses, it is hoped that Larry will continue to be physically, socially, and sexually active. Although he is unable to walk, he can develop his upper body strength. He can also be mobile even if it is via the use of a wheelchair, which is another way of getting around. Zola (1989) indicated that a shift in society's perceptions of a wheelchair would have far-reaching implications for society.

Andres, as a multiculturally sensitive counselor, can be effective in working with Larry by helping him expand his concepts of self-worth by embracing his new appearance. In assisting Larry through a variety of personal and physical rehabilitation work, Andres is in a better position to help him value his body and his life despite narrow societal constructions. The goal is that, eventually, the way Larry's body feels and its multiple functional properties can be identified and esteemed. Because body strength, appearance, and, for many, able-bodiedness are transient, less emphasis needs to be placed on looks and more energy needs to be placed on nurturing appreciation for inner character.

Through journaling, within small groups, or both, Larry can collectively begin to unravel the strongholds of socially constructed notions of beauty and attractiveness and how these have had an enormous impact on self-concept and well-being. Counselors need to reframe meanings of strength, realizing that persons who have disabilities can and do exhibit strength through their lived experiences of dignity, interdependence, and peace. It is also crucial to remember that what is perceived as attractive is a cultural dictate mediated by the values of society. Gunn Allen (1992) stated,

If American society judiciously modeled the traditions of the various Native Notions, the place of women in society would become central, the distribution of goods and power would be egalitarian, the elderly would be respected, honored, and protected as a primary social and cultural resource, the ideals of physical beauty would be considerably enlarged to include "fat" strong-featured women, gray-haired, and wrinkled individuals, and others who in contemporary American cultured are viewed as "ugly." (p. 211)

Because Larry is an individual first, Andres needs to investigate the significance of ethnicity and other factors in his life while understanding that because of this major life transition, values are steadily changing. Although not essential for counseling effectiveness, that Andres is a Latino man (from Costa Rica) can greatly benefit his ability to empathize in this situation. Regardless of his religious denomination, it would be important to examine whether Larry believes that the accident occurred because of some "sin" in his life or because of God's judgment. Religion represents the core of most people's lives. For Larry, it may very well have a major bearing on his orientation to, and coping with, his situation. Andres needs to assess his sense of guilt for the accident. Vulnerability and uncertainty do not coexist well in a society that values empiricism, domination, and conquest. Wendell (1989) stated, "The demand for control fuels an incessant search for the deep-layered explanations for causes of accidents, illness and disability" (p. 72).

Many of the issues Larry is grappling with are sensitive and related to his sexual impotence. Thus, a woman would most likely be an inappropriate counselor. Nonetheless, the woman counselor-male client dyad represents the typical care-giving pattern in society. Second, homophobia interferes with the ability of many men to share intimately with other men. Larry will undoubtedly have major concerns about his sexuality. How will he experience sexual gratification? He may also wonder about the ability to provide sexual pleasure without an erect penis, How will he satisfy his fiancée or any other person? Fortunately, a series of technological devices are available that assist couples with achieving satisfying sex lives in the event of spinal cord injuries, medication-induced impotence, and other barriers to erection. Penile implants made of silicone or polyurethane can be surgically installed. One type consists of two semirigid but bendable rods; the other type consists of a pump, fluid-filled reservoir, and two cylinders into which the fluid is pumped to create an erection. Vacuum devices can also be also used to increase blood flow to the penis (Balch & Balch, 1997, p. 340).

Larry has the use of his body above his waist. His body, mind, spirit, and heart are sources of giving and receiving intense pleasure. Notions of what is a normal sex life have to be altered if Larry is going to seek and eventually find meaning in his life. Besides, too much emphasis is placed on genital sex, anyway.

SUMMARY

This chapter examined the culture's fascination and preoccupation with physical attractiveness. Included in this discussion was a case study that examined able-bodied-ism in a male client who had become disabled as a result of a motorcycle accident. Regardless of attractiveness or disability, it is important that clients reconstruct notions of physical beauty and strength. Implications for counselors were discussed with respect to the convergence of physical attractiveness, race, and gender. Data on colorism, or discrimination based on skin color hue, were also presented.

REFERENCES

Andersen, A. E. (1986). Males with eating disorders. In F. E. F. Larocca (Ed.), *Eating disorders* (pp. 39–46). San Francisco: Jossey-Bass.

Balch, J. F., & Balch, P. A. (1997). *Prescription for nutritional healing.* Garden City Park, NY: Avery.

Belgrave, F. Z. (1991, January-March). Psychosocial predictors of adjustment to disability in African Americans. *Journal of Rehabilitation, 37–40.*

Bem, S. L. (1974). The measurement of psychological androgyny. *Journal of Consulting and Clinical Psychology, 42,* 155–162.

Birtchnell, S. A., Lacey, J. H., & Harte, S. (1985). Body image distortion in bulimia nervosa. *British Journal of Psychiatry, 47,* 408–412.

Brouwers, M. (1990). Treatment of body image dissatisfaction among women with bulimia nervosa. *Journal of Counseling & Development, 69,* 144-147.

Burnett, J. W., Anderson, W. P., & Heppner, P. P. (1995). Gender roles and self-esteem: A consideration of environmental factors. *Journal of Counseling & Development, 73,* 323–326.

Cano, L. (1984). Fear of success: The influence of sex, sex role identity, and components of masculinity. *Sex Roles, 10,* 341–346.

Cash, T. S., & Duncan, N. C. (1984). Physical attractiveness stereotyping among Black American college students. *Journal of Social Psychology, 1,* 71–77.

Chernin, K. (1985). *The hungry self: Women, eating, and identity.* New York: Harper & Row.

Collins, P. H. (1989). The social construction of Black feminist thought. *Signs, 14,* 745–773.

Cook, E. P. (1987). Psychological androgyny: A review of the research. *Counseling Psychologist, 14,* 471–513.

Covell, K. (1992). The appeal of image advertisements: Age, gender, and product differences. *Journal of Early Adolescence, 12,* 1, 46–60.

Cramer, R. E., Cupp, R. G., & Kuhn, J. A. (1993). Male attractiveness: Masculinity with a feminine touch. *Current Psychology, 12,* 142–150.

Davis, C., Stuart, E., Dionne, M., & Mitchell, I. (1991). The relationship of personality factors and physical activity to body satisfaction in men. *Personality and Individual Differences, 12,* 689–694.

Dion, K., Berschid, E., & Walster, E. (1972). What is beautiful is good. *Journal of Personality and Social Psychology, 14,* 94–108.

Downs, A. C. (1990). Physical attractiveness, sex-typed characteristics, and gender: Are beauty and masculinity linked? *Perceptual and Motor Skills, 71,* 451–458.

Downs, A. C., & Abshier, G. R. (1982). Conceptions of physical attractiveness among young adolescents: The interrelationships among self-judged appearance, attractiveness stereotyping, and sex-typed characteristics. *Journal of Early Adolescence, 2,* 57–64.

Emmons, L. (1992). Dieting and purging behavior in Black and White high school students. *Journal of the American Dietetic Association, 92,* 306–312.

Fowler, C., O'Rourke, B., Wadsworth, J., & Harper, D. (1992). Disability and feminism: Models for counselor exploration of personal values and beliefs. *Journal of Applied Rehabilitation, 23,* 14–19.

Gerschick, T. J., & Miller, A. S. (1994). Gender identities at the crossroads of masculinity and physical disability. *Masculinities, 2,* 34–55.

Gibbs, J. T. (1985). City girls: Psychosocial adjustment of urban Black adolescent females. *Sage: A Scholarly Journal on Black Women, 2,* 28–36.

Gibbs, J. T., Huang, L. N., & Associates. (1989). *Children of color: Psychological interventions with minority youth.* San Francisco: Jossey-Bass.

Gillett, J., & White, P. G. (1992). Male bodybuilding and the reassertion of hegemonic masculinity: A critical feminist perspective. *Play and Culture, 5,* 358–369.

Gunn Allen, P. (1992). The sacred hoop: Recovering the feminine in American Indian traditions. Boston: Beacon Press.

Guttman, M. C. (1994). The meanings of macho: Changing Mexican male identities. *Masculinities, 2,* 21–33.

Hahn, H. (1988a, Winter). Can disability be beautiful? *Social Policy, pp.* 26–32.

Hahn, H. (1988b). The politics of physical differences: Disability and discrimination. *Journal of Social Issues, 44*(1), 39–47.

Ham, E. L. (1993, August). Steroids: Wrestling with the issues. *Trial,* pp. 36–42.

Hutchinson, M. G. (1982). Transforming body image: Your body—friend or foe? In *Current feminist issues in psychotherapy* (pp. 59–67). New York: Haworth Press.

Jackson, L. A., Sullivan, L. A., & Rostker, R. (1988). Gender, gender role, and body image. *Sex Roles, 19,* 429–443.

Kashubeck, S., Walsh, B., & Crowl, A. (1994). College atmosphere and eating disorders. *Journal of Counseling & Development, 72,* 640–645.

Kervin, D. (1989, Winter). Advertising masculinity: The representation of males in *Esquire* advertisements. *Journal of Communication Enquiry, 14*(1), 51–70.

Lakoff, R. T., & Scherr, R. L. (1984). *Face value: Politics of beauty.* Boston: Routledge, Kegan, & Paul.

Lerner, R. M., & Lerner, J. L. (1977). Effects of age, sex, and physical attractiveness on child-peer relations, academic performance, and elementary school adjustment. *Developmental Psychology, 13,* 585–590.

Lester, R., & Petrie, T. A. (1998). Prevalence of disordered eating behaviors and bulimia nervosa in a sample of Mexican American female college students. *Journal of Multicultural Counseling & Development, 26,* 157–165.

Lorde, A. (1994). Living with cancer. In E. C. White (Ed.), *The Black women's health book: Speaking for ourselves* (pp. 27–37). Seattle, WA: Seal.

McBride, M. C. (1990). Autonomy and the struggle for female identity: Implications for counseling women. *Journal of Counseling & Development, 69,* 22–26.

Mishkind, M. E., Rodin, J., Silbersein, L. R., & Striegel-Moore, R. H. (1987). The embodiment of masculinity: Cultural, psychological, and behavioral dimensions. In M. S. Kimmel (Ed.), *Changing men: New directions in research on men and masculinity* (pp. 37-52). Newbury Park, CA: Sage.

Monk, G. D., Winslade, J. S., Crocket, C., & Epston, D. (1997). *Narrative therapy in practice: The archeology of hope.* San Francisco: Jossey-Bass.

Mullins, E., & Sites, P. (1984). Famous Black Americans: A three-generational analysis of social origins. *American Sociological Review, 49,* 672.

Myers, L. J., Speight, S. L., Highlen, P. S., Cox, C. I., Reynolds, A. L., Adams, E. M., & Hanley, P. (1991). Identity development and worldview: Toward an optimal conceptualization. *Journal of Counseling & Development, 70,* 54–63.

Napholz, L. (1994). Sex role orientation and psychological well-being among working Black women. *Journal of Black Psychology, 20,* 469–482.

Neal, A. M., & Wilson, M. I. (1989). The role of skin color and features in the Black community: Implications for Black women and therapy. *Clinical Psychology Review, 9,* 323–333.

Nuessel, F. H. (1982). The language of ageism. *Gerontologist, 22,* 273-276.

Okazawa-Rey, M., Robinson, T. L., & Ward, J. V. (1987). Black women and the politics of skin color and hair. *Women & Therapy, 6,* 89–102.

Paxton, S. J., Wertheim, E. H., Gibbons, K., Szmukler, G. I., Hillier, L., & Petrovich, J. L. (1991). Body image satisfaction, dieting beliefs, and weight-loss behaviors in adolescent girls and boys. *Journal of Youth and Adolescents, 20,* 361–379.

Phinney, J., & Rosenthal, P. A. (1993). Ethnic identity in adolescence: Process, context, and outcome. In F. Adams, R. Montemayor, & T. Oulotta (Eds.), *Advances in adolescent development* (Vol. 4, pp. 145–172). Newbury Park, CA: Sage.

Ponzo, Z. (1985). The counselor and physical attractiveness. *Journal of Counseling & Development, 63,* 482–485.

Porter, C. (1991). Social reasons for skin tone preferences of Black school-age children. *Journal of the American Orthopsychiatric Association, 61,* 149–154.

Robinson, T. L. (1999). The intersections of dominant discourses across race, gender, and other identities. *Journal of Counseling & Development, 77,* 73–79.

Robinson, T. L., & Ward, J. V. (1991). A belief in self far greater than anyone's disbelief: Cultivating resistance among African American adolescents. *Women & Therapy, 11,* 87–103.

Robinson, T. L., & Ward, J. V. (1995). African American adolescents and skin color. *Journal of Black Psychology, 21,* 256–274.

Root, M. P. P. (1990). Disordered eating in women of color. *Sex Roles, 22,* 525–536.

Steinem, G. (1992). *Revolution from within: A book of self-esteem.* Boston: Little, Brown.

Stevens, M. J., Pfost, K. S., & Potts, M. K. (1990). Sex role orientation and the willingness to confront existential issues. *Journal of Counseling & Development, 68,* 47–49.

Swanson, B., Cronin-Stubbs, D., & Sheldon, J. A. (1989). The impact of psychosocial factors on adapting to physical disability: A review of the research literature. *Rehabilitation Nursing, 14,* 64–68.

Tolman, D. L. (1991). Adolescent girls, women, and sexuality: Discerning dilemmas of desire. In C. Gilligan, A. Rogers, & D. L. Tolman (Eds.), *Women, girls, and psychotherapy: Reframing resistance* (pp. 55–69). New York: Haworth Press.

Uba, L. (1994). *Asian Americans: Personality patterns, identity, and mental health.* New York: Guilford Press.

Unger, R. K., Hilderbrand, A., & Madar, T. (1982). Physical attractiveness and assumptions about social deviance: Some sex-by-sex comparisons. *Personality and Social Psychology Bulletin, 8.*

Ward, J. V. (1989). Racial identity formation and transformation. In C. Gilligan, N. P. Lyons, & T. J. Hanmer (Eds.), *Making connections: The relational worlds of adolescent girls at Emma Willard School* (pp. 215–232). New York: Troy Press.

Webster, M., Jr., & Driskell, J. E., Jr. (1983). Beauty as status. *American Journal of Sociology, 89,* 140–164.

Weeber, J. (1992). *The importance of a disability identity theory: Implications for gender.* Unpublished manuscript.

Wendell, S. (1989). Toward a feminist theory of disability. *Hypatia, 4,* 63–81.

Zola, I. K. (1989, October-December). Aging and disability: Toward a unified agenda. *Journal of Rehabilitation,* 6–8.

Zola, I. K. (1991). Bringing our bodies and ourselves back in: Reflections on a past, present, and future "medical sociology." *Journal of Health and Social Behavior, 32,* 1–16.

Chapter 8

Converging Socioeconomic Class

> People everywhere
> brag and whimper about the woes of their
> early years, but nothing can compare with
> the Irish version: the poverty; the shiftless,
> loquacious alcoholic father; the pious,
> defeated mother moaning by the fire;
> pompous priests; bullying schoolmasters;
> the English and the terrible things they did
> to us for eight hundred years.
>
> *Frank McCourt,* Angela's Ashes: A Memoir of a
> Childhood

This chapter was difficult to write. This difficulty was partly attributable to the dearth of material available on socioeconomic class and its effects on psychosocial identity development within counselor education. It was also a challenge extrapolating the effects of class on my (Tracy's) own life. Considering that class, race, and gender are inextricably connected made this process even more challenging.

Frank McCourt's (1996) words were helpful and powerful. His multiple identities (growing up poor, Catholic, Irish, the child of an alcoholic, and oppressed by the English and schoolmasters) enable us to see how these simultaneous identities intersected to shape him and his reflections of his boyhood life. This chapter is dedicated to an examination of the effects of class on identity. A case study is provided for the purposes of integrating material discussed throughout the chapter and linking the implications for counseling and counselor education. In addition, this chapter attempts, within the context of the U.S. culture, to explore both the meanings and the implications of a middle-class bias on the training of counselors in counselor education programs nationwide.

CLASS: AN IDENTITY CONSTRUCT

Class is an identity construct that has a significant impact on identity development. Consider the research conducted by McLoyd and Wilson (1992), who found that working- and lower-class parents placed less emphasis on happiness during the rearing of their children. This research zeroed in on the psychological effects of class on people's lives. Although I (Tracy) understood that class is fluid and prone to change throughout a person's life, I was intrigued at how one's childhood experiences within a particular class group shaped identity. In the case of these parents, survival issues took precedence over being happy, which may have been regarded as a luxury.

In my quest to explore the effects of class, I did not want to arbitrarily equate being middle-class with feelings of power, security, and privilege and being poor with feelings of anxiety, depression, and low self-esteem. Yet, I was interested in just what some of the long-term effects of class were. As is customary, others are crucial to the process of self-discovery (see the Storytelling "Class Behaviors?").

Part of my making sense of class and its influence on development was to query friends. I noticed that, among some who grew up in working-class families, as middle-class urban-dwelling adults they had a tendency to buy in bulk. In asking about this behavior, I was told it was related to their childhood experiences of constantly running out of regularly used items (because of limited resources). As adults, they simply did not have to tolerate this annoyance endured as non-income-earning children. Clearly, research in this area is needed.

STORYTELLING
Class Behaviors?

Recently, in a university lecture, cultural critic bell hooks spoke about growing up poor. She commented on the tendency of poor people (e.g., working class/lower middle class) to save things and delay wearing or using new purchases. This reflection of her experience resonated with me. I, too, had engaged, albeit unconsciously, in this same behavior as a child, adolescent, and even young adult. What was it about belonging to this particular class group that influenced behavior? Was it related to the perception that resources were scarce, hard to come by, not readily replenishable, and thus had to be savored? How did being African American and female also shape this tendency to behave in this way? Once my status as middle class became more solid and secure, these familiar tendencies did not automatically disappear. I was motivated to deliberately change some assumptions implicit in my thinking. A low-grade anxiety was mixed in with the perception that supply was limited. Fortunately, I made another discovery: There is freedom in placing a demand before the universe and knowing that supply is adequate to meet this demand.

Tracy

THE NEGLECT OF CLASS AS A STATUS VARIABLE

Other disciplines, such as sociology and anthropology, have devoted ample attention to class issues, particularly within the context of educational equity (Fine, 1991; Lareau, 1997; Ogbu, 1997). Class as a status variable, however, has been largely neglected in the counselor education literature. Effects of socioeconomic class on students' career identities and vocational choices have been explored (see McWhirter, McWhirter, McWhirter, & McWhirter, 1995; Rojewski, 1994). Socioeconomic class as a psychosocial identity construct has received scant attention in the counselor education literature. Recently, Ladany, Mellincoff, Constantine, and Love (1997) discussed at-risk urban high school students' commitment to career choices. They stated,

> In the context of at-risk urban high school settings, students are often
> forced to make vocational decisions regarding their intent to go to college
> or to identify options for employment, while simultaneously contending with
> poverty, unstable family structures, and inhospitable environments. (p. 46)

These authors also discussed the significance of considering how class issues (e.g., extreme financial hardship) may impinge on students' ability to pursue career choices or even to contemplate them seriously. Their work underscored the effects of class on career commitment and vocational identity, given that students who tended to be uncommitted to their career choices also experienced difficulty in other vocational areas.

The major emphasis in cross-cultural counseling has been on race, ethnicity, and, more recently but to a lesser extent, gender. Career choices, vocational identity, and other occupational themes are usually regarded as job measures or class indicators. This may explain why the majority of the research on class has focused in this area. Yet, class converges with each of these identity domains and affects the ways people develop, engage in self-definition, and construct meaning in their lives.

MIDDLE-CLASS BIAS AND COUNSELOR TRAINING

Although a self-confessed radical, Alinsky (1990) referred to three class groups that are useful for understanding class distinctions in society: (a) the haves, (b), the have nots, and (c) the have a little; want mores. He said that the purpose of the haves (e.g., the middle class) is to maintain the status quo, and the have nots (the poor) to seek to change it—by appealing often to laws that are above and beyond man-made laws (e.g., religiosity). For the most part, counselor educators receive very little information about socioeconomic class as it relates to influences on identity development and subsequent implications for counseling. Moreover, the training caters to the haves, as opposed to other social classes (e.g., working and lower classes).

Part of this bias is related to the nature of graduate education itself, which is steeped in privilege. Graduate students are college graduates who have distinguished themselves from others as capable of meeting the rigors of an academic program. Just being in graduate school is an esteemed position in society that carries middle-class connotations independent of students' varied class-linked childhood socialization experiences. In other words, the graduate school environment acculturates its members in a middle-class direction with its emphasis on success, competition, and individualism. Furthermore, graduate students are preparing themselves for jobs that will designate them as having middle-class social standing. Although it is hoped that students' salaries will reflect their elite standing, such is not always the case in the counseling profession.

Despite the privileged status of graduate school, some students make considerable financial sacrifices (e.g., working and going to school, borrowing money from family, securing a school loan) to attend school. Nonetheless, the majority of graduate students in the United States could be described as having embodied traditional values anchored within a middle-class framework: success, motivation, perseverance, self-reliance, Standard English, and delayed gratification. Although this middle-class bias has been identified, it is important to clarify what it means for a middle-class bias to pervade the training of counselors.

It seems possible that the effects of socioeconomic class on psychosocial identity have been neglected in the counseling literature because the pervasiveness of middle-class bias has obscured awareness of it. The counselor education training culture itself has been shaped within a middle-class framework, given the culture's materialistic leanings. Sue and Sue (1990) identified two aspects of middle-class bias within counselor training. The first pertains to the emphasis on Standard English within society at large. The second refers to the 50-minute counseling sessions that typically characterize the counseling event.

Standard English represents a class issue because dialect, accent, and use of English are often used in drawing conclusions about a person's educational, occupational, income, and ultimately class status. In this regard, the use of Standard English becomes a form of power within society because its proper usage dictates which people are able to access certain positions in society.

Delpit (1997) discussed the relevance of power embodied in language style. Although she argued against obliterating the unique cultural or speaking style of a group, she advocated educating people about the sociopolitical context that has standards and rules regarding the status quo:

> To imply to children or adults that it doesn't matter how you talk or how
> you write is to ensure their ultimate failure. Tell them that their language
> and cultural style is unique and wonderful but that there is a political power
> game that is also being played, and if they want to be in on that game
> there are certain games that they too must play. (pp. 590-591)

Delpit emphasized the dialectic: a both/and perspective, where on the one hand the cultural style is embraced and esteemed, while on the other hand students understand that others perceived as powerful (e.g., teachers, prospective employers) may denigrate it. This means having knowledge about the appropriate contexts where one's language style can be celebrated and where it will not.

Judgments and evaluations about people are made on the basis of their proximity to normative standards of behavior. These norms include gender, race, sexual orientation, physical and mental ability, and use of Standard English (Reynolds & Pope, 1991). **Cultural encapsulation,** or defining reality on the basis of a limited unidimensional cultural orientation (Wrenn, 1962), can contribute to counselors being biased toward certain normative standards in society. For this reason, Schofield's (1964) use of the acronym YAVIS (*y*oung, *a*ttractive, *v*erbal, *i*ntelligent, and *s*uccessful) helps counselors see their tendency to favor this type of client. Perhaps it is because such a client is thought to be more similar to the counselor's actual or imagined sense of self.

Such a middle-class bias is highlighted in the emphasis on monetary success. Some counselors could, rather innocently but easily, regard clients from lower socioeconomic groups as less preferred and more difficult to be with in counseling relationships because of noticeable differences in communication and behavioral styles (e.g., the use of slang, street talk, or non-Standard English). If counselors are thinking in this way, then how is their best practice extended to such a client, particularly if the counselors are subconsciously lamenting (annoyed) that the client is on a sliding scale and not paying full fare for the hour of counseling time? Did their elite graduate school educations prepare them for such work?

These questions point to the second aspect, the 50-minute counseling session, that Sue and Sue (1990) discussed as a reflection of a middle-class bias within counselor training. The American Counseling Association (ACA) code of ethics does not dictate 50- or 60-minute counseling sessions. Sometimes clients, depending on the type of work they do, have work schedules that fluctuate from week to week. For example, a client may work the 11:00 p.m. to 7:00 a.m. shift at a gas station or hospital one week but from 3:00 p.m. to 11:00 p.m. the next week. Moreover, this information may not be posted until a few days prior to the beginning of a new shift. For some clients, a 90-minute session every other week or so might be preferred. Fortunately, this adjusted schedule applies to people across various socioeconomic groups (e.g., highly paid physicians on call, as well as poorly paid shift workers). Essentially, one could argue, then, that a middle-class bias does not encompass the full class continuum: the very poor or the extreme elite. Instead of being able to write down an appointment and reserve a particular time for a client, the counselor must be flexible and accommodating. Admittedly, this can feel haphazard for the counselor. Which client, however, might heighten the professional's feelings of esteem and status, and which client might contribute to the professional's feelings of frustration and aggravation?

These types of class issues are not discussed in counselor training because of a focus on that which is normative. An expectation, albeit implicit, that clients have jobs and conventional work hours based on standard work fuels this oversight. Yet, what about clients who do not own cars, live in cities where reliable public transportation is essentially nonexistent, or are unable to get a bus that puts them in the counseling chair on time? How considerate are we as counselors of the difficulty clients face to get to us, given the many challenges in their path that are a function of the ways class shapes their lives and ours? Do we subtract the time from their hour, even if another client is not scheduled immediately, because of the middle-class cultural adage that "time is money"? Although we as counselors need to make a living like everybody else, do we need to recruit paying clients to balance the ones who do not pay? Conversely, if clients appear for their appointments in an expensive car and have very elite jobs, are we intimidated by their wealth? Given that components of class culture include art, music, tastes, religion, food, and furniture (Bordieu, 1984), how conspicuous do we become of the surroundings of our offices or of our proximity to middle-class status if high-status clients appear? And how might our intimidation or being impressed detract from our ability to extend to these wealthy clients our best professional practice? Clearly, socioeconomic class is an identity construct because of its enormous meanings within the culture. It influences our meaning of status, legitimacy, and power.

A middle-class bias is seen in the very basic tenets of counseling, such as confidentiality. Students learn early in their programs that counselors can even be sued for violating a client's confidentiality. Pedersen (1997) said,

> In an individualistic culture, personal space and personal time are valued
> as property to be privately owned, and any infringement of those bound-
> aries is considered a form of theft. . . . In other more collectivistic cultural
> contexts, . . . personal privacy is less valued and may even be perceived as

selfish or self-centered in ways that are destructive to the welfare of the community. (p. 25)*

Another middle-class bias exists in the expectation that clients will self-disclose. Actually, this is a hallmark of Rogerian counseling. It assumes that, after disclosure, people experience a measurable and identifiable benefit and catharsis. Clearly, the roots of positivism are at work. Isn't it possible for some clients actually to feel violated, given the unidirectional nature of the counseling exchange that could be conceived of as inconsistent with community and reciprocity? Another assumption embedded in disclosure is that an individual will be articulate (in Standard English) and should, after rapport has been developed, feel comfortable enough to discuss private and personal issues with a professional stranger independent of family and/or community involvement or support. Many poor people, because of limited education or migrant status, do not speak Standard English. Inability to speak Standard English is not synonymous with lack of intelligence or the ability to learn.

The roots of a middle-class cultural bias are also reflected in the official documents used to standardize the profession and provide its membership with rules and guidelines for their professional practice. For example, the ACA code of ethics (Section A.10c) discourages bartering for services. It reads as follows:

> Counselors ordinarily refrain from accepting goods or services from clients in return for counseling services because such arrangements create inherent potential for conflicts, exploitation, and distortion of the professional relationship. Counselors may participate in bartering only if the relationship is not exploitative, if the client requests it, if a clear written contract is established, and if such arrangements are an accepted practice among professionals in the community. (Cottone & Tarvydas, 1998, p. 28)

This position is steeped in a middle-class framework (see the Storytelling "Christmas Sharing"). Pedersen (1997) critiqued this position and said,

> This presumes a money economy to be more "fair" in every cultural context even though money, like goods, may mean something quite different for the very poor and the very rich. The emphasis should be more on fair and equitable exchange range than the particular, in this case money, medium of exchange. (p. 27)†

In certain contexts, money may not be as readily available or even esteemed in the same ways as other forms of currency. A woman may not be able to afford $90 an hour

---

*   From "The Cultural Context of the American Counseling Association Code of Ethics," by P. B. Pedersen, 1997, Journal of Counseling & Development, 76, p. 25. Copyright 1997 by the American Counseling Association. Reprinted by permission.

†   From "The Cultural Context of the American Counseling Association Code of Ethics," by P. B. Pedersen, 1997, Journal of Counseling & Development, 76, p. 27. Copyright 1997 by the American Counseling Association. Reprinted by permission.

STORYTELLING
Christmas Sharing

For about 5 months, I had been facilitating a support group for women survivors of incest. To show their appreciation, they invited me to dinner (it was Christmastime). Given that I was not charging them for the group, they pitched in and gave me $100. I gladly accepted the money despite my awareness of ACA ethical guidelines (not accepting gifts from clients). It would have been a cultural violation for me not to receive their gift and would have had adverse implications for the success of the support group.

Tracy

for counseling (or even a greatly reduced amount based on a sliding scale), but she may value doing housework, gardening, or providing child care as an expression of gratitude and as a means of giving back to the one who helped her in a time of need.

Interesting but not surprising, the ACA code of ethics does not encourage dual relationships. Again, in certain contexts, such as the size of the community and the availability of resources, dual relationships may not be easily avoided. It is a middle-class bias that presumes such avoidance is preferred. Pedersen (1997) spoke on this issue: "To the extent that a collectivistic culture depends on overlapping relationships of roles in the fabric of society, role diffusion is unavoidable. Most cultural contexts inevitably involve conflicting roles for participants, including the counselor" (p.26).* If there are few counselors of color in a community (urban and rural), it is likely that clients of color and the select counselors will frequent the same churches and community and recreational activities and may even have the same employer. Thus, the clear division of roles assumes an abundance of resources that are diverse enough so as not to overlap. The assumption is that clients and their counselors are possibly in different social/political circles. This simply is not the case in some rural communities, communities of color, and/or ethnic communities—where, for instance, the family rabbi might also be the marriage counselor and the child's Hebrew tutor.

Elaboration on key values within American society allows one to understand why a middle-class bias prevails in the training of counselors. Competition, the Protestant work ethic, and self-reliance all stem from the individualistic culture that truly defines the West (Sue & Sue, 1990). Yet, some communities are more collective, wherein greater dependence on others is the norm (see the Storytelling "Hurricane Fran"). Perceptions of dependence also seem to be fostered by class status. Perhaps it is easier to live without cultivating a relationship with neighbors if one is not dependent on them for the use of a telephone, for borrowing sugar, for helping with child care, and for offering companionship within walking distance. Although economically motivated need may not be the primary motivation behind relationship development and maintenance within neighborhoods, patterns of interacting are influ-

---

* *From "The Cultural Context of the American Counseling Association Code of Ethics," by P. B. Pedersen, 1997,* Journal of Counseling & Development, 76, p. 26. *Copyright 1997 by the American Counseling Association. Reprinted by permission.*

enced by class. Class also affects one's ability to provide for personal material needs independent of others.

The communities in which Mary and I were reared were very collective and collaborative. Although I grew up in California and Mary in Illinois, in both communities neighbors borrowed household products from one another, helped one another with child care, shared resources, and even watched television in one another's home when someone's "tube" was in the shop for repair. My family did not have a car, so much of the friendships my family had were within the school and community itself and in walking distance. Having middle-class status, particularly within an individualistic context, may make it much easier not to be in relationships with persons in close proximity to oneself. This is most likely different from poor or collectivistic communities (independent of class differences), where value is placed on the community being in relationship with one another. Moreover, within such a collectivistic context, values of unity and sharing of resources and of one's personal self are embedded within the culture.

CULTURAL LINKS AND CLASS EFFECTS

Just as middle-class status has value in society, the opposite is also true. Being poor in American society has certain meanings and discourses (social forms of communication) around it. Being poor and then becoming rich is often admired because the values of hard work, pulling oneself up by one's bootstraps, change, and perseverance are showcased. Being poor and staying that way, however, is looked upon with a cer-

STORYTELLING
Hurricane Fran

When hurricane Fran hit North Carolina in September 1996, neighbors became neighborly—in many cases, for the first time. The power was out, so people put their food on a grill, cooked it before it spoiled, and shared what they had with one another. They also shared ice, batteries, telephones, showers, words of encouragement, and information about how to get the necessary services in the face of the disaster that had swept the state. I remember one of my neighbors informing me to go the fire station to get water because, in my neighborhood, everyone was on a community well, which meant that if the electricity was out, so was the water. Irrespective of class, the residents of Wake and several other counties were deeply affected. By candlelight and flashlight, people met and talked at each other's homes. The individualism of the culture seemed to vanish for just a moment. And amid the devastation, people made friendships and established connections they would not have otherwise.

Tracy

tain disdain because such a position does not mirror the American values of competition, success, change, and progress. It appears that the inability to alter significantly, or rather rise above, one's station in life is not indicative of core American values.

Differences across socioeconomic class groups are not meant to be categorized in disparate fashion, given their fluidity and tendency to overlap. For example, in many working-class families, values characterize a middle-class perspective (e.g., education, hard work, money management, perseverance, delayed gratification), although indicators of material acquisition might be lacking. Ogbu (1997) described this as follows:

> Because the basis for membership in class groups can be acquired by an individual during a lifetime, social classes are open entities. Although they are more or less permanent, the entities have no clear boundaries; furthermore, their membership is not permanent because people are continually moving in and out of them. (p. 768)

Ogbu helps us appreciate that the prospering can become the homeless in a relatively short time.

Bordieu's (1984) notion of *cultural capital* is helpful in understanding preparedness toward a middle-class orientation. He maintained that certain cultural experiences within the home assist children in their adjustment to school. The home environment, along with a host of other socializing agents (e.g., school, church, neighborhood, extracurricular activities), serves to socialize children toward a middle-class perspective. Linguistic structures, styles of interacting, and authority patterns of interacting characterize cultural resources that can be turned into highly beneficial and socially lucrative cultural capital. This information has enormous significance for school counselors and counselors in community agencies working with school-age populations.

Lareau (1997) conducted research on two very different school populations. At the first school, 60% of parents were professionals, compared with 1% at the other. The majority of the professional parents had college degrees, and many fathers had advanced degrees. Parents in the unskilled jobs had either a high school education and or had dropped out of high school. Only 1% of parents at the first school were unskilled workers, compared with 23% at the second one. Lareau found that interactions between professional parents and teachers were more frequent and comfortable. Professional parents were also more involved in the academic preparation of their children. Parents at the school where the majority of parents were semiskilled or unskilled tended to have uncomfortable and infrequent interactions with teachers. Also, many unskilled parents left the training and education of their children to teachers, although both sets of parents truly valued educational success and achievement. Lareau wrote, "In the middle-class community, parents saw education as a shared enterprise and scrutinized, monitored and supplemented the school experience of their children" (p. 712). This difference could be a reflection of the parents' lack of confidence in their own ability to be of academic assistance to their children. Children from middle-class families had greater cultural capital than children from lower income families. This is not to say that the family-school relationship among the middle class was better for children in comparison with children from the working class. Lareau stated, however, that "the social profitability of middle-class arrangements is tied to the school's definition of the proper family-school relationship" (p. 713).

School counselors need to be mindful of the ways culture may work against the accessible nature of schools for working-class parents and for the children themselves. What may appear to be apathy from parents may actually be feelings of fear and uncertainty. For many of these parents, the quality of interactions with school personnel is linked to the discourses predominant from their own educational contexts that were perhaps alienating and fraught with shame and difficulty. Brantlinger (1993) said,

> In my own interviews with low-income parents, I discovered strong feelings and well-formulated opinions about a number of school-related issues. Although asked to discuss their children's school experiences, these parents inevitably launched into lengthy and emotional accounts of their own school careers, detailing a profusion of humiliating and painful experiences. Even elderly parents recalled conversations and events that had happened many years earlier. It was clear that school had been a setting of great significance and that the parents carried the mental baggage of their own problematic school careers into parenting. (p. 11)

RACE, GENDER, AND CLASS

Within a materialistic and consumeristic society, the structural inequities that can work against a person's best efforts to be successful can be overlooked. It is perhaps easy to blame people for failing to transcend their situations despite structural and institutional forces. For instance, women systematically earn less money than men. Often, men in nontraditional jobs (e.g., nursing) earn more money than their female counterparts (Chusmir, 1990). Among people of color, class does not operate as a primary status trait particularly because race and gender tend to be more conspicuous than class and can override it (see the Storytelling "The Laundromat").

Defining **racial stratification** as "the hierarchical organization of socially defined 'races' or groups on the basis of assumed inborn differences in status honor or material worth, symbolized in the United States by skin color" (Ogbu, 1997, p. 768), Ogbu argued that "the inequality between Blacks and Whites is one not of class stratification but of racial stratification" (p. 766).

Membership in groups that tend to be more valued functions as a mediating variable in conjunction with membership in groups that tend to be less valued (Robinson, 1999). As African American women, Mary and I share the experiences of African American women who are poor; however, our educational status and university fac-

STORYTELLING
The Laundromat

When I was a doctoral student at North Carolina State University, I had an encounter with covert racism and sexism while I was washing my clothes at the neighborhood Laundromat. I had just finished reading a chapter in my textbook and had gotten up from my chair to remove my clothes from the washer and put them into the dryer. I completed this last mundane task and headed back to my chair. Before I could take my seat, a young White male stopped me and said, "Would you please give me change and a box of soap powder." Despite my lack of proximity to a laundry-attendant station and all the symbolism associated with studenthood—my eyeglasses, book bag, university sweatshirt, coffee mug—I had been mistaken for the Laundromat attendant. I told the young man that I did not work at the Laundromat and was there to wash my clothes. He looked at me and walked away. No apology for the mistake, no look of embarrassment, just disappointment that he could not receive his change.

Mary

ulty positions afford us certain benefits in a variety of sectors we can and do cash in. Essentially, mediating variables affect the quality of one's lived experiences and shape notions of power, privilege, and vulnerability.

Race, gender, and disability, all status variables, need to be discussed in the context of class. In 1996, 32.6% of female-headed households were in poverty; 40% of White female-headed households were in poverty; and half (50.9%) of all Latino female-headed households were in poverty (Lamison-White, 1997). The higher unemployment, underemployment, and incarceration rates of men of color have an adverse affect on women of color, who are most likely to be in relationships with these men. Failure to look at the situation from this perspective can lead to locating pathology within women of color who are raising their children on their own.

Success in American society is often defined and measured by material acquisition. Homes, cars, boats, jewelry, and other "things" are indicators of income and occupation, which are often suggestive of even moral attributes such as being honest, hard working, smart, happy, and morally good. Given this, it is not surprising that socialization practices, particularly of males but inclusive of females, promote the idea that proper manhood is tied into being a provider and having success in one's chosen career (Swanson, 1993). The inability to be successful in this fashion has and continues to have far-reaching implications for men who, for a variety of personal and systemic reasons, are unable to be successful in this way. Washington (1987) talked about this issue as it relates to Black men: "Economic stressors such as unemployment, underemployment, job losses, health catastrophes, loss of personal property, and gross indebtedness also exert an unacceptable level of chronic stress" (p. 194). The stress is tied into not being able to achieve society's clear standards about manhood, which are synonymous with career and material success.

Other literature on class has examined sex role type and its connections to a family's socioeconomic class level. Weitzman (1979) stated, "All the studies have found that persons in the higher social classes tend to be less rigid about sex distinctions" (p. 26). Research conducted by McCandless, Lueptow, and McClendon (1989), however, does not support the hypothesis that sex role differentiation is more pronounced in the lower socioeconomic status (SES) groups. These researchers were interested in further examining the relationship between sex role differentiation and family SES. Through analyzing attitudinal and behavioral data of 5,600 high school seniors to determine the validity of the hypothesis that sex role differentiation is greater among persons in lower SES groups, they actually found that sex role differentiation is greater among *higher* SES groups. This finding could be linked with Alinksy's (1990) statement about "the haves" being oriented to maintaining the status quo.

Race affects the ways gender messages are communicated. For instance, Renzetti and Curran (1992) cited research that stated Black boys and girls tend to be more independent than White boys and girls. Parents' strong emphasis on hard work and ambition and the less frequent gender stereotyping among many Black children may explain this finding.

Kenway (1988) conducted research on privileged girls in private schools in Australia, also a Western nation. She was interested in looking at self-esteem within an educational context. In talking with the girls about their experiences, Kenway found that the girls used words such as *proper, right, perfect, education, manners,* and *success* to describe their status as upper class. Kenway said,

> There is a tendency to equate high self-esteem with the confidence which many private school girls exude, but such confidence may be illusory, as the girls have learned that "what we appear to be is what people think we are." . . . Self-esteem may be bought via the right "casual-chic" designer label. In the culture of consumption within which private schools are immersed, success also can be bought alongside approval, acceptance, and social honour. (p. 155)

Kenway encouraged her readers to see the costs to these young girls in their efforts to maintain an image based on elite class distinctions as measured by an exclusive school environment.

IMPLICATIONS FOR COUNSELORS

It is important that counselors seek to unravel for themselves the effects of class on their own lives. Dominant discourses within society and particularly within the nation's training programs pertain to the relationship between class and worth. Far too often, the poor are regarded as lazy, unmotivated, and intellectually inferior, whereas the nonpoor are seen as the referents for society. Counselors need to appreciate the influence of class when listening to their clients' stories and to help their clients make important connections between their identity development and the effect of class on their lives (see the case study "Poor, Not Impoverished"). For example, an adult client from a working-class family might be reluctant to take certain occupational risks because of socialization experiences that emphasize security, saving for a rainy day, and being practical about the future. The counselor could ask the client, "What is the effect of growing up poor on your willingness now to change jobs?" or "What kinds of messages did you receive about being poor?" Anxiety about change and taking risk could be increased among persons who experienced difficulty as children and even as adults when endeavoring to meet basic needs. This is not to say that middle-class clients would not evidence some reluctance about the uncertainty of change, but having access to other resources (e.g., trust funds, the family home, inheritance) and other financial catch nets may make it more psychologically comfortable to engage in risk-taking behavior.

Acquiring middle-class status or becoming poor in one's life does not erase the effects of early conditioning. These issues can easily be missed, however, if it is assumed that all clients and their counselors have had similar and consistent socialization experiences from childhood to adulthood. Persons who are from a middle-class background can move into a lower income level because of unemployment, disability, or other changes in life circumstances. Such movement depicts the fluidity and permeability of class. A change in income does not equate a loss of values into which one has been socialized.

CASE STUDY
Poor, Not Impoverished

Georgia Winters is a 27-year-old European American community agency counselor. She has an M.Ed. in counselor education. Her class background is solid middle class (her mother was a teacher, her father an engineer). She has been married for 2 years and is pregnant with her first child. After conducting an in-service training for child care workers through her church, to which she is very committed, Georgia was approached by Lydia, a woman who attended the session. Lydia, 25 and also European American, was requesting counseling services.

Lydia grew up on a farm in a rural community. She has three children, ages 2 to 7. Two of the children were fathered by Lydia's ex-husband (she married when she was 17). The youngest child has a different father, who resides nearby. Michael, Lydia's boyfriend, is an orderly at the local hospital. They have been dating for a year. Lydia desires counseling because she is pregnant with Michael's child and does not want another child, but her Christian

beliefs (she is a born-again Christian) do not support abortion. Michael is excited about the baby as it is his first child.

Michael is an alcoholic and has amassed thousands of dollars in unpaid gambling debts. Sometimes Lydia helps him out by lending him money, which he has never repaid. Lydia receives assistance from the state (e.g., subsidized public housing, food stamps). She also works in a child care facility during the day and earns minimum wage; her earnings are below the poverty line for a family of four. Georgia even has to call Lydia at work because often Lydia's telephone is disconnected for an unpaid telephone bill.

To accommodate Lydia's time-scheme, Georgia schedules Lydia as her last appointment during the day. Lydia's limited health insurance will not cover Georgia's hourly fee, so Georgia is seeing her on a sliding fee scale. Lydia pays $12 per hour. Periodically, Lydia is late to counseling because she is unable to get a ride from Michael, who should not be driving because his driver's license was suspended (for driving while intoxicated on several occasions). At other times, Lydia catches the bus. Lydia catches the bus at night, but she is not afraid (she was in fights often prior to being expelled from school); she has the ability to defend herself. Although she is sometimes late, Lydia has never missed a counseling session and consistently does the homework assignments Georgia asks her to do. Lydia did not complete high school, but she would like to get her GED (general education diploma) and a degree (associate of arts) working with young children.

QUESTIONS

1. How might some of the class differences between Georgia and Lydia be manifested?
2. How might the class differences between Georgia and Lydia affect the counseling event?
3. What types of adjustments has Georgia made to accommodate her client?
4. To what extent are Lydia's behaviors a function of a collectivistic culture?
5. How might Lydia's behaviors be confused with *enmeshment,* or undifferentiated emotional attachment in which boundaries are neither acknowledged nor defined?

DISCUSSION AND INTEGRATION
The Client, Lydia

On the basis of her education, income, and job, Lydia is in a lower income class. The fact that she is receiving government assistance classifies her within a particular class group (e.g., below the poverty line) to be eligible for this type of aid. It is likely that Georgia has not had much training in her counselor education program in working with Lydia.

Although it is clear from the case study that Lydia has some confusion about her pregnancy, to equate her with feelings of powerlessness because of her financial situation and low educational level is wrong (Robinson, 1993). Yet, Georgia needs to bear in mind the vulnerability that poor people often face in society, given society's general disdain for the poor and the fact that poor people are more vulnerable before institutional structures, such as school and the police (Robinson, 1999). For instance, if Lydia is able to get a credit card, then it is likely that her interest rates would be very high (over 18%), which can maintain her in a state of indebtedness and financial dependence. Another example of poor adults not being given the same regard as nonpoor adults is seen in the behavior of some public housing facilities: Men are not allowed to visit freely or even to spend the night. Specific visiting times monitor their presence.

Lydia's vulnerability, in addition to the stress of working at a day care facility, being pregnant, and having three young children, can take a toll on Lydia's mental health. She certainly needs to be commended for asking Georgia for help and for continuing with her counseling relationship. Lydia has many strengths that could easily be overlooked because of the other hardships she is facing: She is a young, divorced, single mother with three children and another child on the way. She has no high school education, receives welfare, resides in public housing, and is working in a relatively low-status and low-paying job at a day care. Her significant other has both substance and gambling addictions. Nevertheless, Lydia is extremely determined. She always presents for her counseling sessions, despite the fact that she comes to them after working a full day, catching a bus, and arranging for child care. Fortunately, Lydia's neighbor watches her children, and Lydia provides care for her neighbor's children on the weekend.

The Counselor, Georgia Winters

Georgia might help Lydia explore where she acquired important skills of persistence. Lydia's experiences on the farm and growing up in a family that struggled hard but stayed together might have fueled many of her current values. In many respects, Lydia possesses characteristics—determination and commitment—that would assist her in meeting her goals. Yet, Georgia needs to be careful of imposing her middle-class Christian values of marriage, self-reliance, individualism, sex after marriage, education, and antiabortion onto Lydia. Georgia's own pregnancy might also color her conceptions of acceptable behavior regarding Lydia's pregnancy. Respecting Lydia's choice and lifestyle may be very difficult for Georgia to do, given the considerable differences between Lydia's and Georgia's lifestyles. Georgia's power position as counselor could make it relatively easy for her to assume a position of authority and judgment in her interaction with Lydia. Georgia would do well to help her client identify personal strengths. Listening to what Lydia desires for her life will hugely benefit Lydia, particularly because she is constantly providing care to needy and dependent others all day and night. Georgia could also help Lydia clarify some of her goals and then ascertain whether the choices she is making (e.g., a pattern of unprotected sex, giving her limited and hard-earned money to a man who has compulsive addictions) are servicing her and her goals. Clearly, Lydia has strengths and has learned how to survive. Yet, she spends more time taking care of others and not devoting attention to herself.

Lydia's financial situation is rather tenuous, yet it is important for her to pay something for her counseling, no matter how meager this amount may be. Although bartering, as the ACA guidelines stipulate, can be problematic for the counseling relationship, Lydia could be asked to pay for her counseling services in the amount that she thinks is respectful to her. It is also possible that growing up in a close-knit rural community fostered within Lydia the collectivistic values of sharing resources. Valuing the strength of the community differs from codependence, which may be a feature in Lydia's relationship with Michael.

Georgia's accommodation of her client's time-scheme (scheduling Lydia as the last client of the day) is to be noted, commended, and encouraged by other helping professionals. Such a position does not mean that the counselor is seeking to rescue the client as much as it is an effort to respect diversity within the counseling event. In this case, class diversity truly represents a cross-cultural counseling situation. It would not be professionally inappropriate for Georgia to offer Lydia a ride home or closer to home if they are leaving at the same time. House calls might also be an option for Georgia if she is comfortable doing this. Above all, it is important that Georgia not become overwhelmed by Lydia's life by seeing Lydia as "a poor, pregnant woman who has all those kids and a boyfriend with all these problems out at night catching a bus, living in public housing and on welfare and only 25!" Helping Lydia avoid feelings of being overwhelmed should be a professional goal for Georgia; nonetheless, Lydia's life has a lot of stress. At the same time, however, she does have support systems (her neighbor, Michael, Georgia, and her children are a tremendous source of pride and joy for her).

Lydia has a lot to teach Georgia about living in the world with tenacity and strength amid multiple challenges. Even her belief that she can protect herself at night, if necessary, is a feature of her life experiences that she honors.

SUMMARY

This chapter on class explored the neglect of class within the literature as a psychosocial variable. The middle-class bias in counselor education training programs was discussed at length. Work conducted by sociologists on school inequity was an important link in this discussion. A case study about a client from a low-income background seeking counseling from a middle-income counselor was provided for the purpose of integrating material discussed throughout. Implications for counselors were also explored.

REFERENCES

Alinsky, S. D. (1990). *Rules for radicals: A primer for realistic radicals.* New York: Random House.

Bourdieu, P. (1984). *Distinction: A social critique of the judgment of taste.* Cambridge, MA: Harvard University Press.

Brantlinger, E. A. (1993). *Politics of social class in secondary schools: Views of affluent and impoverished youth.* New York: Teachers College Press.

Chusmir, L. H. (1990). Men who make nontraditional choices. *Journal of Counseling & Development, 69,* 1, 11–16.

Cottone, R. R., & Tarvydas, V. M. (1998). *Ethical and professional issues in counseling.* Upper Saddle River, NJ: Merrill/Prentice Hall.

Delpit, L. (1997). The silenced dialogue: Power and pedagogy in educating other people's children. In A. Halsey, H. Lauder, P. Brown, & A. Wells (Eds.), *Education: Culture, economy, society* (pp. 582–594). Oxford, UK: Oxford University Press.

Fine, M. (1991). Invisible flood: Notes on the politics of "dropping out" of an urban public high school. *Equity and Choice, 8,* 30–37.

Kenway, J. (1988). *High-status private schooling in Australia and the production of an educational hegemony.* Unpublished doctoral dissertation, Murdoch University, Western Australia.

Ladany, N., Mellincoff, D. S., Constantine, M. G., & Love, R. (1997). At-risk urban high school students' commitment to career choices. *Journal of Counseling & Development, 76,* 45–52.

Lamison-White, L. (1997). Poverty in the United States: 1996. *Current Population Reports* (P. 60-198). Washington, DC: U.S. Bureau of the Census.

Lareau, A. (1997). Social-class differences in family-school relationships: The importance of cultural capital. In A. Halsey, H. Lauder, P. Brown, & A. Wells (Eds.), *Education: Culture, economy, society* (pp. 703–717). Oxford, UK: Oxford University Press.

McCandless, J. N., Lueptow, A., & McClendon, D. (1989). Family socioeconomic status and adolescent sex-typing. *Journal of Marriage and the Family, 51,* 625–635.

McCourt, F. (1996). *Angela's ashes: A memoir of a childhood.* New York: Scribner.

McLoyd, V. C., & Wilson, L. (1992). Telling them like it is: The role of economic and environmental factors in single mothers' discussions with their children. *American Journal of Community Psychology, 20,* 419–444.

McWhirter, J. J., McWhirter, B. T., McWhirter, A. M., & McWhirter, E. H. (1995). Youth at risk: Another point of view. *Journal of Counseling & Development, 73,* 567–569.

Ogbu, J. U. (1997). Racial stratification and education in the United States: Why inequality persists. In A. Halsey, H. Lauder, P. Brown, & A. Wells (Eds.), *Education: Culture, economy, society* (pp. 765–778). Oxford, UK: Oxford University Press.

Pedersen, P. B. (1997). The cultural context of the American Counseling Association code of ethics. *Journal of Counseling & Development, 76,* 23–28.

Renzetti, C. M., & Curran, D. J. (1992). *Women, men, and society.* Boston: Allyn & Bacon.

Reynolds, A. L., & Pope, R. L. (1991). The complexities of diversity: Exploring multiple oppressions. *Journal of Counseling & Development, 70,* 174–180.

Robinson, T. L. (1993). The intersections of race, gender, and culture: On seeing clients whole. *Journal of Multicultural Counseling & Development, 21,* 50–58.

Robinson, T. L. (1999). The intersections of dominant discourses across race, gender, and other identities. *Journal of Counseling & Development, 77,* 73–79.

Rojewski, J. W. (1994). Career indecision types for rural adolescents from disadvantaged and nondisadvantaged backgrounds. *Journal of Counseling Psychology, 41,* 356–363.

Schofield, W. (1964). *Psychotherapy: The purchase of friendship.* Upper Saddle River, NJ: Prentice Hall.

Sue, D. W., & Sue, D. (1990). *Counseling the culturally different: Theory and practice.* New York: John Wiley.

Swanson, J. L. (1993). Sexism strikes men. *American Counselor, 1,* 10–13, 39.

Washington, C. S. (1987). Counseling Black men. In M. Scher, M. Stevens, G. Good, & G. Eichenfield (Eds.), *Handbook of counseling and psychotherapy* (pp. 192–202). Newbury Park, CA: Sage.

Weitzman, L. (1979). *Sex role socialization.* Palo Alto, CA: Mayfield.

Wrenn, C. G. (1962). The culturally encapsulated counselor. *Harvard Educational Review, 32,* 444–449.

Chapter 9

Images of Diversity in Schools

A teacher cannot give you the truth. The truth is already in you. You only need to open yourself—body, mind, and heart—so that his or her teachings will penetrate your own seeds of understanding and enlightenment. If you let the words enter you, the soil and the seeds will do the rest of the work.

Thich Nhat Hanh, The Heart of the Buddha's Teaching: Transforming Suffering Into Peace, Joy, and Liberation

This chapter examines the constructs of race, gender, and class and their intersections with educational access, quality, teachers' expectations, and perceptions of opportunity. Tracking as a method for segregating students into instruction groups is explored, as is the long-term effects of tracking assignments on students' occupational choices, literacy skills, and self-concepts. Subtle ways in which children are exposed to a "hidden curriculum" are also examined. Recent research on gender is reviewed in light of Title IX of the Education Amendments of 1972, which state that no person should be discriminated against on the basis of sex in any educational program that receives federal funds (Bailey, 1993). Finally, multicultural education, its definitions and objectives are also presented.

DIVERSITY AND INTEGRATION

American schools exhibit tremendous diversity across race, ethnicity, class, and religion. Despite this diversity, diverse schools are not synonymous with multicultural ones. Diversity does not ensure the integration of schools that are based on equitable distribution of resources for all children. Despite improvements toward integration since the historic 1954 *Brown v. Board of Education* court case, in which the U.S. Supreme Court justices ruled that segregated public schools were unlawful, schools are now showing increased concentration along racial lines (Valsamis, 1994). Orfield (cited in Valsamis, 1994) also found that socioeconomic class is a factor in integration. African American and Latino students are much more likely than White students to be located in poverty-concentrated schools. More specifically, "poverty is systematically linked to educational inequality" (p. 6.)

The implications of socioeconomic class on not only education but also occupational aspirations are far-reaching. Flanagan (1993) reported a positive relationship between parents' occupational and educational attainments and the achievements of their children, even when adolescents are aware of a variety of occupational choices. Gender also has a major impact on occupational choices. Females are more willing than males to accommodate their careers around family considerations (Flanagan, 1993).

TRACKING

Tracking has been employed since the 19th century for sorting children into specified groups for instructional purposes. Darling-Hammond (1997) said,

> Strategies for sorting and tracking students were developed to ration the
> scarce resources of expert teachers and rich curricula, and to standardize

teaching tasks and procedures within groups. . . . The goal was to instill in
the masses of students the rudimentary skills and the basic workplace
socialization needed to follow orders and conduct predetermined tasks
neatly and punctually.

Tracking greatly increased during the 1920s and 1930s, when numerous immigrants
settled in the United States. Although some researchers distinguish between ability
grouping and curriculum differentiation, these two forms of segmenting students
share common characteristics: (a) Students deemed as different are segregated from
others and placed with those who are deemed similar, (b) group placement is based
on criteria such as standardized test scores, students' race and gender, and teachers'
grades, recommendations, or opinions about students (Banks & Banks, 1993, p. 78).

Given its long history, tracking has become a popular activity, particularly in
schools where lower class students predominate and less so in upper middle private
schools located in suburban areas (Banks & Banks, 1993). Students of color and
ethnic minority students are overrepresented in special education placement and
greatly underrepresented in gifted and talented programs (Carey, Fontes, &
Boscardin, 1994).

Much controversy surrounds the efficacy of tracking. Some researchers maintain
that children in lower ability groups, sometimes referred to as at-risk, are often
seated farther away from teachers, asked to do less work, rewarded for inappropriate
behavior, interrupted more often, given less eye contact and other nonverbal communication of attention and responsiveness, and questioned primarily at the knowledge and comprehension levels. Described as nonachievers, marginal, impoverished, remedial, slow learners, and low socioeconomic status (SES) (Lehr & Harris,
1988), low-ability and at-risk students also tend to be associated with a narrow range
of interest, short attention span, discipline problems, and lack of motivation. Ultimately, labels have a profound impact. This applies to both teachers' and counselors' expectations of children's behaviors and professionals' behavior toward children (Fine, 1988; Rosenthal & Jacobsen, 1968). In such climates, the self-esteem of
students identified as at risk and behaviorally handicapped is often adversely
affected (Fine, 1988; Oakes, 1985). This is not difficult to understand, considering
that their educational processes are characterized largely by less instruction time,
lowered expectations, an overall sense of alienation from the school process, and
diminished excitement from the teacher and other helping professionals (Fine,
1988; Oakes, 1985). When much is expected of children, they will hold high expectations in return (Gross, 1988; Rosenthal & Jacobsen, 1968).

Students' academic and vocational choices, as well as the quality of the classroom climate, are largely a function of teachers' race, gender, and socioeconomic
class expectations (Fine, 1987; Oakes, 1985; Sadker & Sadker, 1987). Evidence of
this was found in research conducted by Moore and Johnson (1983). In their multi-
variate analysis of teachers' classifications of students, Black students from lower
socioeconomic backgrounds were more likely than students from other ethnic
groups with similar grades and socioeconomic backgrounds to be assigned to the
unskilled laborer category when they presented with low grades; however, they were
less likely to be assigned to the professional category when their grades were high. A

different scenario existed regarding high-ability groups. Banks and Banks (1993) reported that high-ability groups spent more time on tasks during class, that teachers used more interesting teaching methods and materials, and that higher expectations were held for these students. Persell (1977) also found that, with abler students, independent projects were encouraged and greater emphasis was placed on conceptual learning. Not surprisingly, the aptitude of students in higher groups tends to develop more than the aptitude of students in lower groups, and high-achieving students have more confidence in their ability (Gross, 1988).

The implications of tracking on a child's educational career are long term. An assessment that takes a week can have a lifelong impact on choices in high school, college, and subsequent vocational decisions (Quality Education for Minorities Project, 1990). Because of its long-term effects, tracking should be based on careful measures. Unfortunately, deliberate assessment from valid and reliable measures does not always occur. According to Oakes (1985), tracking often "results from unquestioned and almost automatic responses" (p. 193). For example, high school students in college-preparatory programs receive better trained teachers, exceptional curriculum materials, relevant field trips, and quality laboratory facilities. The education of lower ability students is of lower quality, with less care and fewer resources. According to Persell (1977), "a major result of tracking is differential respect from peers and teachers with implications for both instruction and esteem" (p. 91). Oakes (1985) and Slavin and Madden (1987) concluded that students do not derive consistent benefits from being segregated by learning ability. Amid traditional arguments that students need to be in homogenous groups with others of similar intelligence, Slavin and Madden asserted that all children learn more in a cooperative, interactive learning climate regardless of their particular learning level. This type of classroom was humane in its celebration of diversity, fun, and improved students' self-esteem and race relations among students. Because tracking has implications for one's entire educational tenure, it can also create a climate for cumulative failure experiences (Fine, 1988).

Just as socioeconomic class is a factor in school integration, it also plays a role in tracking assignments and other educational outcomes, such as school dropout rates and quality of school life. Researchers have found that even when lower income students have IQ scores comparable with those of their middle-class counterparts, they are more likely to be placed in nongifted classes (Banks & Banks, 1993). Moreover, middle-class status has been found not to automatically cancel out effects related to gender and racial bias (Gross, 1988). A study conducted in an affluent Maryland school district involving 28,000 public school children in grades 1 to 12 found that, by the end of the third grade, as many as half of the district's African American and Latino children lagged behind Asian and White children in mathematics skills. According to the National Science Foundation, once students fall behind, it becomes more difficult to catch up. Moreover, Latinos and African Americans, who were disproportionately low achieving, received less effective instruction characterized by rote learning and drill.

Some students of color may have a more difficult time with school learning that may be linked to power issues as a reflection of their minority status. Ogbu (1993) argued that numerical representation is not the only factor to be referenced when discussing the term *minority*. Power relations between groups is an essential variable that also requires consideration. **Power** addresses the sociopolitical processes that characterize one group's interactions with others. In short, autonomous groups of color are different from voluntary or immigrant minorities who differ from involuntary or caste-like people of color, such as African Americans (which is a different ethnic group from West Indians), Native Americans, and Mexican Americans (Ogbu, 1993).

School failure disproportionately affects some groups in comparison with others. The Hispanic Policy Development Project (1987) found that low-income students who left school prior to graduation were more likely to describe teachers as not interested in students than did those who eventually graduated. For many urban students, whose lives are often characterized by "poverty, academic failure, early death due to poor health care and violence, drug abuse, and addiction, high unemployment rates, teenage pregnancy, gangs, and high crime rates" (Steward et al., 1998, pp. 70–71), survival is a key issue. By contrast, Pollard (1993) found in a study of 361 high- and low-achieving male and female middle and high school Hispanic and African American urban students that high achievers experienced more support from teachers and parents and had higher self-concepts of ability. Pollard indicated that, for many African American students (and presumably other groups of color), interpersonal support is found outside rather than within the school walls.

GENDER, RACE, CLASS, AND EDUCATION

Several years ago, the American Association of University Women (AAUW) published a report documenting the gender inequities in the educational system. This report stated that schools were shortchanging girls, as evidenced by the decline in higher level mathematics skills and measures of self-esteem. Girls outdistance boys in speaking, reading, and counting during the early school grades, but by the time girls graduate from high school, they trail their male counterparts (AAUW, 1992; Sadker, Sadker, & Long, 1993). Such discrepancies were not noted between girls and boys as they first entered school. Sadker, Sadker, and Long (1993) said that "girls are the only group in our society that begin ahead and end up behind" (p. 119).

Most gender bias in American classrooms is subtle. Many teachers do not advocate bias but are simply unconscious of it. Sadker et al. (1993) maintained that boys receive more teacher attention because they are likely to shout out answers. Teachers are also more likely to give boys specific feedback that includes praise and constructive criticism.

As children enter school, they are presented with a "hidden curriculum" (see the case study "Children, Divorce, and Counseling in Schools") Sadker and Sadker (1987) defined the *hidden curriculum* as messages and signals that are covertly sent to children about themselves and others and that are directly related to their gender and race. This covert behavior is projected through the diagrams, verbiage, and material in textbooks, films, and other media. Additionally, the ways teachers, school counselors, and school administrators communicate with children gives them messages about themselves. Furthermore, children come to understand that the role they play in significant school events and the extent to which they come into contact with key role models of their own gender and ethnic background are indicators of their importance to the overall environment. "Curriculum ghettos" subtly train students to make choices based to a great extent on race, gender, and class expectations.

On certain sections of the College Board Achievement Test and on tests for admission to graduate and professional schools, gender differences appear. Although male students seem to have the advantage in testing, female students outperform their male counterparts in college mathematics courses (Bailey, 1993). Several researchers have sought to account for gender differences in students' academic achievement. Race, biology, sociology, psychological self-esteem, and students' attitudes toward a particular topic have been offered as possible causes in test performance (Brusselmans-Dehairs, Hencry, Beller, & Gafni, 1997). A survey of eighth graders found that SES is the best predictor of grades and test scores (Flanagan, 1993).

In school and work achievement, the majority of gender differences are socially constructed, as opposed to biologically created (AAUW, 1992; Sadker & Sadker, 1987). The International Association for the Evaluation of Educational Achievement (IAEEA) concluded from its cross-national comparative studies in a variety of areas that "gender differences in ability and achievement are mainly due to societal and cultural influences and not to biological causes" (Brusselmans-Dehairs et al., 1997, p. 19).

The percentage of women obtaining higher education degrees in the sciences demonstrates that education is a pipeline and extends from the early grades to the later ones. Although women earned 52% of all bachelor's degrees in 1990–91, they earned only 14% of bachelor's degrees in engineering, 31% in the physical sciences, and 47% in mathematics. Not to deflect from the encouraging news about women earning bachelor's degrees in technical fields, but the average woman with a college degree earns approximately the same as a man with a high school diploma (Hanmer, 1996).

Shortly after the turn of the 21st century, an estimated 1 million more engineers and scientists will be needed. Compared with boys, girls tend to have a less positive attitude about science and are less confident of their mathematical ability (Brusselmans-Dehairs et al., 1997; Sadker & Sadker, 1987). Currently, women constitute 18% of engineers and scientists in the United States (Lipson, 1994).

In addition to the academic losses to many females, poor children, and children of color are the losses to self esteem during secondary and postsecondary school. Gilligan, Ward, and Taylor (1988) said that girls enter prepubescence with confidence but that, by the time they arrive at adolescence, many have weakened confidence in self-presentation. In their qualitative research project on nearly 100 girls ages 7 to 18, Brown and Gilligan (1992) discussed this loss of voice in developing young girls:

> Our study provides clear evidence that as these girls grow older they
> become less dependent on external authorities, less egocentric or locked in
> their own experience or point of view . . . yet we found that this developmen-
> tal progress goes hand in hand with evidence of a loss of voice, a struggle

> to authorize or take seriously their own experience—to listen to their own
> voices in conversation and respond to their feelings and thoughts—
> increased confusion, sometimes defensiveness, as well as evidence for the
> replacement of real with unauthentic or idealized friendships. (pp. 5, 6)

The issue of voice is crucial to self-construction. **Voice** refers to the convictions and philosophies that characterize an individual's existence. Voice is the foundation of belief systems and values. Not knowing one's voice or being removed from it seems to increase external locus of control where people believe that reinforcing events occur independently of their actions and that the future is determined more by chance and luck (Sue & Sue, 1990). Certainly, this belief system reduces a young woman's autonomy, which is essential to her sense of freedom.

From an ethnographic study conducted in a "low-income, low-skill New York City school," Fine (1987) enlightened her readers about silencing in schools and its subsequent emotional and psychological effects:

> Silencing constitutes a process of institutionalized policies and practices
> which obscure the very social, economic, and therefore experiential condi-
> tions of students' daily lives, and which expel from written, oral, and nonver-
> bal expressive substantive and critical "talk" about these conditions. (p. 157)

Girls' voices are often silenced and their presence invisible. Gifted girls are also less likely to be identified, in comparison with gifted boys. Among girls of color, Scott-Jones and Clark (1986) stated, "Few research studies have focused on both race and gender" (p. 520). The gap in the research literature concerning the psychosocial and educational experiences of school girls of color is tremendous. Generalization of studies on European Americans to non-European Americans may lead to faulty conclusions (Pollard, 1993). Pollard (1993) discovered in her research that African American boys reported less academic support from teachers than did African American girls, yet the students expressed satisfaction with the type of support received from teachers.

The exclusion of children from the best educational resources because of race, gender, class, and ability factors hinders social justice and multicultural perspectives. If more girls, children of color, and children with disabilities are to be prepared with the requisite technical and socioemotional skills to enter mathematics, science, and engineering careers confidently, more effective intervention programs are needed.

Gender also interacts with socioeconomic class and education. Flanagan (1993) reported that although reasons vary for why male and female high school students drop out of school, pregnancy is not the only reason girls give for dropping out. Flanagan said, "Convergent evidence from several studies points to disproportionate numbers of girls from lower SES groups dropping out for family-related problems including child care and domestic duties at home" (p. 366). It may be true that much of the variance in student performance can be attributed to the converging effects of gender, race, and socioeconomic class. Although gender inequity in schools has been documented, other environments and mediums shape self-concept. Included are family, church, and the media.

Certain groups of girls are more likely to get shortchanged in America's schools, but boys are products of discrimination as well. Sadker and Sadker (1987) indicated that although girls tend to be invisible in the classroom, boys are scolded and reprimanded more. They are also far more likely than girls to be identified with a learning disability, reading problem, or mental retardation. Their performance in writing tends to be below that of girls as well.

In the psychological domain, boys are taught stereotyped behaviors at an earlier age than girls (Sadker et al., 1993). This appears to be related to the stricter sanctions against boys adopting feminine behaviors than exists against girls adopting those deemed as masculine. One consequence of a narrow range of sex-typed behaviors is stress and anxiety, which were found to be high among boys who also scored high on sex-appropriate behavior tests. Masculine, sex-role-traditional men are also least likely than androgynous men to seek help or talk with others about their concerns. Thus, being emotionally restrictive is correlated with depression, as well as with having negative attitudes about seeking psychological help (Good & Mintz, 1990; Good, Dell, & Mintz, 1989).

MULTICULTURAL EDUCATION

In an effort to address educational inequities and disparities among children across diverse race, gender, and socioeconomic class groups, educators have touted multicultural education as a remedy. This educational process of promoting greater equity has many names and multiple meanings. These include "teaching the culturally different," "human relations," "multicultural education," and "education that is multicultural and social reconstructionist" (Sleeter & Grant, 1988). Great diversity, and undoubtedly confusion as well, surrounds the definition of multicultural education (Herring, 1998). Gollnick (1991) describes five primary goals of multicultural education: (a) strength and value of cultural diversity, (b) human rights and respect for cultural diversity, (c) alternative life choices for people, (d) social justice and equal opportunity for all people, and (e) equity distribution of power among members of all ethnic groups (p. 9).

Multiculturalism is often used interchangeably with *cultural diversity,* yet these terms differ conceptually. Gollnick's identification of the goals of multicultural education underscore this point. When mentioning cultural diversity, she refers to respect for and seeing strength and value in it. **Cultural diversity** more aptly describes the event of diverse persons inhabiting shared physical space (Robinson, 1992). Cultural diversity does not speak to underlying attitudes or values concerning diversity. In fact, **monoculturalism** assumes that people come from the same cultural plane and desire the values of the larger culture dictated by those with the most racial and ethnic power (McIntosh, 1990). Even in culturally diverse settings, monoculturalism can still dominate. **Multiculturalism** seeks to celebrate a variety of behaviors and epistemologies so that no one culture has a monopoly on truth and each culture is appreciated.

One belief of multicultural education is that it will reduce race and gender inequity in the classroom. However, discriminatory treatment is often transmitted by way of traditional methods such as films, teachers' expectations, and textbooks. This "hidden curriculum" refers to subtle but prevalent influences on students that are part of the unofficial learning children simply absorb independent of their knowledge (Sadker & Sadker, 1987). Pollard (1993) cited an example of this practice. She reported that elementary school teachers were provided with hypothetical descriptions of students and then were asked to rate their preferences for them, as well as to predict academic performance. Male African American students were viewed more negatively by the teachers than were African American females. As microcosms of society, schools reflect society's cultural attitudes and can thus serve to reproduce inequality (Fine, 1987; Sleeter, 1992).

Another common perception among educators is that multicultural education will help students live more effectively within a heterogeneous society. Actually, limited empirical data exist regarding the benefits of multicultural education (Sleeter & Grant, 1988). Sleeter (1992) found this also to be true for adults who were exposed to multicultural education during staff development. Multicultural education did not necessarily decrease discrimination among people. In fact, exposure to a multicultural education curriculum may leave educators feeling more unsettled than previously about how to incorporate the material into the classroom or counseling event (D'Andrea & Daniels, 1992; Cochran-Smith & Lytle, 1992). Regardless of what is not known about multicultural education, teacher morale may be increased and schools may be restructured to serve students more effectively (Sleeter, 1992; see also the Storytelling "Segregation-Integration").

THE CROSS-CULTURAL AWARENESS CONTINUUM MODEL

Locke and Parker (1994) developed a *cross-cultural awareness continuum model* illustrating the levels of awareness through which school personnel must transition to provide effective and meaningful educational experiences for culturally different stu-

STORYTELLING
Segregation-Integration

I attended a segregated grade school until I entered the second grade at the age of 7. I did not know that I was going to be attending an integrated school in the autumn of 1961 because nothing had been explained to me. All I knew was that I would be in a classroom with strange White faces and a few of my friends from all-Black Dunbar School in Illinois.

I was shocked, devastated, and saddened that I had lost my familiar cohort. So, I withdrew for several weeks by not talking at all. I sat alone during recess in the playground, watching everyone else play. One day, my teacher saw me sitting alone and asked three of my White classmates to come over, talk to me, and invite me to play. They did so, and I was ecstatic; those three little girls remained my good friends into junior high.

Mary

dents. The model is helpful for counselors in that it specifically identifies levels that address the self and others, as well as an integration of knowledge, attitudes, and skills.

The seven levels of the continuum are (a) self-awareness, (b) awareness of one's own culture, (c) awareness of racism, sexism, and poverty, (d) awareness of individual differences, (e) awareness of other cultures, (f) awareness of diversity, and (g) skills and techniques. The first level, *self-awareness,* pertains to careful and close examination of one's thoughts and feelings regarding cultural values, beliefs, and attitudes. Before a person is able truly to understand others, the individual must engage in this first step. Locke and Parker (1994) are careful to mention that "individuals never achieve absolute mastery of the awareness levels" (p. 45). Self-knowledge is ever-evolving.

The second level is *awareness of one's own culture.* School and other counselors have "cultural baggage" they inevitably bring to the educational climate in which they serve. Such baggage does not negate their expertise or their moral integrity. However, culture is an enormous shaper of personhood and can contribute to a person being culturally encapsulated. According to Wrenn (1962), **cultural encapsulation** refers to a narrow standard by which reality is defined and people are largely insensitive to cultural differences between people and assume that their worldview is the only right one. Expecting that all other cultures subscribe to a "doing" mode of human activity over a "being" mode represents a liability in dealing with culturally different persons.

Awareness of racism, sexism, and poverty is the third level. Locke and Parker (1994) stated that because talking about these social realities may evoke some personal defensiveness, a systems perspective may be more proactive. More specifically, recognizing that society makes race, gender, and class distinctions as it pertains to social status is important even if one does not personally subscribe to similar values. Educators need to be aware that far too often, low socioeconomic class is wrongly equated with slothfulness (Gans, 1992).

The fourth level, *awareness of individual differences,* entails an acknowledgment and recognition of the individuality and uniqueness of persons. Yet, it is also crucial that the educator or counselor not treat persons as monoliths and disregard their group affiliations.

The fifth level, *awareness of other cultures,* focuses on understanding language differences among cultures, human activity, social relationships, and gender roles.

The sixth level, *awareness of diversity,* pertains to sensitivity to the various components of diversity, as well as to one's personal attitudes about sources of differences.

Skills and techniques is the seventh and last level. Locke and Parker (1994) said that an educator who has teaching skills and experience may be more effective than a person who has limited teaching competence but an abundance of cross-cultural understanding.

IMPLICATIONS FOR COUNSELORS

Guidance counselors and an increasing number of community agency counselors are working in collaboration with school environments, teachers, and other school personnel. Often, counseling professionals are called on to mediate conflict or to provide training that pertains to issues of race and cultural differences. To create multicultural educational environments and to increase the competence of counselors, counselor education training programs need to be clear about multiculturalism and its varying definitions. A focus exclusively on race or ethnicity does not extend to the often other invisible identities that are equally as important, such as class, religion, and sexual orientation. For instance, in research on conceptions of multicultural counseling conducted with 85 preservice school counselors, Herring (1998) found a wide variety of knowledge levels and perceptions. He stated,

> Based on their responses to the research questions, the level of multicultural counseling in their schools most likely ranges from the most superficial to the most meaningful. Variability in counseling may be considered natural; however, so much disagreement about implementation and outcomes, particularly in relation to multiculturalism, is troubling. (pp. 8, 9)

Herring (1998) suggested that training programs engage in more frequent self-examination of their program policies and practices. He recommended that certain instruments may help in monitoring students' progress. Such empirically tested tools include the Cross-Cultural Counseling Inventory–Revised (CCCI–R; LaFromboise, Coleman, & Hernandez, 1991), the Multicultural Competency Checklist (Ponterotto, Alexander, & Grieger, 1995), and the Multicultural Awareness/Knowledge/Skills Survey (MAKSS; D'Andrea, Daniels, & Heck, 1991).

Attending conferences, workshops, and classes and watching educational media programming are effective ways to help counselors increase their awareness while learning essential skills. Professionals who have not engaged in self-examination about their gender attitudes are less effective role models for young people because self-awareness is the first step to understanding others (Locke, 1991). Although difficult, teachers and counselors need to admit to their sexism and culturally biased assumptions (Pedersen, 1988; Sue & Sue, 1990) while knowing what their role assumptions and expectations are. For instance, a female counselor who struggles with autonomy and believes that girls ought to be "ladylike" may be intimidated by an assertive female student. This may lead to her mislabeling the assertive behavior as aggressive or uncooperative.

In addition to counselors engaging in continuous learning to create equitable learning environments, they can encourage teachers to consider the following recommendations:

1. Educate children about various forms of bias and its harmful societal effects. This will help them recognize it in their textbooks, in their classroom environment, and on television.
2. Implement supplementary materials that may offset the impact of stereotypical curriculum materials.
3. Encourage students to question and dialogue about why they might choose to segregate across race, gender, nationality, and religious lines. This process may help students think about their behavior, talk about sensitive and contro-

versial issues, and realize the beauty of not only cultural diversity but also valuing differences.

4. Teach children that oppression (e.g., racism, sexism), and not identities (e.g., race, gender), is a threat to multiculturalism.

5. Teach children about sexism and its impact on their lives, regardless of gender. One way to accomplish this is to encourage children to pursue traditional and nontraditional careers of interest.

6. Discuss androgyny (see Bem, 1974) with children in a way that makes sense to them. As presented in Chapter 5, *androgyny* maintains that traditional notions of masculinity (e.g., self-reliance, independence, taking a stand for one's beliefs) and *femininity* (e.g., nurturance, ability to yield, caring) can exist in both males and females without negating differences between them. Boys need to know that having and expressing feelings is not solely the domain of girls. Girls need to be aware that autonomy is important and is not a negation of intimacy in relationships. Collages, puppet play, role play, and other forms of innovative classroom instruction and play therapy could be used to communicate these mature concepts to young children. For instance, when a young child has an insight about gender, a "myth musher" animal or toy could be tossed to him or her as a way of acknowledging and celebrating the child's ideas (see Gerler & Locke, 1980).

7. Create multicultural teams to serve students more effectively. When counselors have a grossly imbalanced student-counselor ratio, quality service delivery suffers. The Carnegie Council on Adolescent Development (1989) suggested that schools, particularly middle schools, establish small teams wherein staff (e.g., librarians, maintenance personnel) function as mentors. Ultimately, caring adults are needed to help children develop a healthy vision of a better way in a society that is conflictual and difficult for many youths to negotiate (Harvey, Bitting, & Robinson, 1991). Although professional staffs may not be culturally diverse, the service and maintenance personnel are disproportionately persons of color. Such a discrepancy in who does what type of job can, in itself, foster meaningful dialogue among students and adults concerning demography and occupation (Fine, 1987). Nonprofessional staff would not provide counseling, yet they could serve as valid and valuable support system for students.

CASE STUDY
Children, Divorce, and Counseling in Schools

Dennis is a physically healthy 14-year-old European American male in ninth grade. He has a 5-year-old sister. Recently, their parents divorced, and Dennis's mother was granted full custody of them. Once a month, Dennis and his sister spend time with their father. Since the divorce, the mother's income has suffered. She now works as an administrative assis-

tant during the week and is a telemarketing agent on the weekends. Dennis's father is a cook at a local 24-hour restaurant. He resides nearby with his new wife and three stepchildren. Dennis, his sister, and their mom live in a two-bedroom apartment that is much smaller than the one they occupied before their parents' very messy divorce. Subsequently, there is a lot of contention between the parents. Although Dennis has a history of struggling in school with his reading, his grades have dropped from a B– to a C– average. He also seems disinterested in the athletic activities in which he once excelled. He has been spending time with gang members and has started to drink and smoke. Dennis's responsibilities at home have also increased because his mother depends on him to help with the house and the care of his younger sister. One of Dennis's teachers has noticed the considerable academic and personality changes that have occurred within the last few months. He recommends to the mother that a talk with the guidance counselor, Mr. Burns, would be helpful. Mr. Burns is African American and has worked as a guidance counselor for 9 years.

QUESTIONS

1. How might the "hidden curriculum" be affecting Dennis academically and behaviorally?
2. How does the change in socioeconomic class affect Dennis's situation?
3. Does the convergence of Dennis's identities make him more vulnerable to school failure?
4. How might Mr. Burns be most effective with Dennis?

DISCUSSION AND INTEGRATION
The Client, Dennis

Although social attitudes about female-headed households are changing, a stigma is still associated with children who emerge from these "broken homes." Devaney (1995) said that "whether the reaction is pity, fear, or disapproval, single-parent families are, in our social milieu, aberrations of the 'ideal' nuclear family" (p. 203). Far too often, female-headed households are affected by poverty (Hanmer, 1996).

Ultimately, shifts in family structure and status have a direct impact on children, their coping strategies, and their overall well-being, both in the home and at school. Researchers in adolescent development have well documented the significant advances in physical, cognitive, and social growth signaled by the advent of puberty and the subsequent development of sexual maturity (Erikson, 1968; Gibbs, Huang, & Associates, 1989; Gilligan et al., 1988; Sprinthall, 1988). Thus, it is normal that Dennis would be experiencing emotional distress over the loss of the home unit that had characterized his life as he knew it.

Part of the dilemma in assessing Dennis is the multiplicity of his issues. Foremost is the obvious emotional distress and stress over the divorce, which is significant. Recently, Prelow and Guarnaccia (1997) found in their research on life stress among high school adolescents that White adolescents reported more total events having a negative impact than Black and Latino adolescents. The authors suspect that "the higher life stress scores of White adolescents may be that they experienced more events related to family discord (e.g., parental fights, divorce, etc.)" (p. 448). It is clear that Dennis is having and has had family discord over which he has no control. In addition, the normal emotional shifts characteristic of this turbulent period of adolescence need not be overlooked.

Typical of many males across age and racial groups is a socialization pattern that encourages the repression of feelings as they enter mid-adolescence. Dennis has become socially withdrawn except for his recent affiliation with gang members. Although there is a need for him to connect with supportive others, his connections with the gang may be a way to fill the void in his family life. Although his efforts to be in the community are noteworthy, such affiliation can hinder his development if used to replace whatever is broken and has gone awry in his life. Dennis needs to be encouraged; his losses are profound but he need not, on his own, seek to replace what has changed. Often, young people have a difficult time understanding that their parents divorced each other, not the children.

The Counselor, Mr. Burns

Flanagan (1993) reported that a high percentage of girls from low SES groups leave school for family-related problems. In some contexts, this can apply to boys as well. Dennis is at risk of leaving school prior to graduation, as is evident from his declining academic performance, alcohol intake, smoking, gang involvement, and poor school attendance. Mr. Burns needs to intervene immediately and effectively.

As a multiculturally competent counselor, Mr. Burns understands that Dennis's behavioral changes are largely connected to stress and depression. His father, whom he sees much less of now, often works double shifts to make money to provide for his new family and for Dennis and his sister. His mother is usually exhausted when she comes home in the evenings and is also overwhelmed by changes in her family, financial, and emotional structure. Less money is also available in the family since the divorce; this places enormous strain on Dennis's mother as the primary caretaker. Dennis is distraught that the divorce has occurred, but he is not talking openly about this situation with an adult. His younger sister is not a viable confidant.

Having considerable experience in the schools, Mr. Burns knows that Dennis's academic decline might be related to the school's inability to offer real assistance to children experiencing family problems. Schools can sometimes place children at further risk because of the ways they often hold lower expectations for poor children, girls, children in trouble, troubled children, and children who are academically challenged. Fine (1991) said,

> The category "family problems" is one repeated often by educators and policymakers as a primary reason that low-income youngsters drop out. . . . In many cases, however, "family problems" is offered as the reason that students drop out of high school precisely because the high school experience has been discouraging, unengaging, and disinviting and because schools have been structured in ways that do not accommodate students experiencing family problems. (p. 35)

Dennis's issues are multiple, and a school that is not equipped to respond is not poised to offer much-needed assistance to Dennis and other children in his situation. Although Dennis is a White male and does not face the heavy rates of suspen-

sion and expulsion that describe adolescents of color (Fine, 1991), he may not have the type of advocacy from his parents to appeal an expulsion or any other trouble in which he most likely will find himself. He is experiencing major challenges that, without immediate adult intervention, can prove to be hazardous.

Low class status combined with academic struggles can increase Dennis's vulnerability to being a casualty, and Mr. Burns knows this. Mosley and Lex (1990) reported that income level and education are significant predictors of one's coping capacity. More specifically, higher income levels and education provided persons with a greater degree of flexibility for coping with stressful life events. The effect of a covert hidden curriculum must also be assessed. Dennis may not feel very important or central to the school in the light of his academic struggles and behavioral and family difficulties. "Curriculum ghettos" subtly train students to make choices based to a great extent on race, sex, and class expectations.

Divorce occurs in epidemic proportions among our nation's schoolchildren. To help children attend to these enormous transitions, Mr. Burns can be very helpful. Being male may also allow Dennis to connect with a fatherlike figure. Mr. Burns needs to be understanding with Dennis and have appropriate knowledge of his unique situation, as well as an understanding of how the divorce of Dennis's parents has affected him personally.

In addition to showing understanding and empathy, Mr. Burns can link Dennis with additional supports. One possible intervention he can consider is the Refusal and Resistance Skills (RRS) program (Herrmann & McWhirter, 1997). The purpose of this program is to effect prosocial change in both children and adolescents. Behaviors often targeted include sexual activity, smoking, and use of alcohol and other drugs. Dennis has begun to smoke, which is not uncommon for children his age. More than 3,000 teenagers become regular smokers each day in the United States. The RRS program encourages students to develop refusal skills when they are invited or pressured to smoke. RRS has reduced tobacco use among adolescents who had previously experimented with cigarettes; however, health education has been more effective among students who had simply not initially experimented with cigarettes. RRS has also had positive results with alcohol and other drugs. Alcohol is the most frequently used drug among teenagers in the United States. RRS training "significantly increased participants' ability to refuse alcohol and enhanced refusal self-efficacy when compared with the other competing prevention modalities" (Hermann & McWhirter, 1997, p. 181). Research has found that information alone about alcohol and other drugs has been less helpful.

Mr. Burns can help Dennis realize that he did not cause the divorce and that his parents still love and care for him. Asking Dennis what he wants for his life and encouraging him to consider more positive and creative approaches to obtaining it would be helpful. A partner program (e.g., Big Brothers, Big Sisters) might also help Dennis. Curriculum assistance is needed as well, to which Mr. Burns can refer Dennis. Mr. Burns can also talk with Dennis's parents and help them be more informed about how their child is doing and the challenges facing him.

SUMMARY

This chapter examined diversity within the educational system. Tracking as a method for separating students into groups for the purpose of instruction was explored, as were the long-term effects of tracking assignments on students' occupational choices and self-confidence. Some research on gender inequity was reviewed, and multicultural education was defined. Strategies for creating gender-fair classrooms were provided.

REFERENCES

American Association of University Women (AAUW). (1992). *How schools shortchange girls: A study of major findings on girls and education.* Washington, DC: Author.

Bailey, S. M. (1993). The current status of gender equity research in American schools. *Educational Psychologist, 28,* 321–340.

Banks, J. A., & Banks, C. A. M. (1993). *Multicultural education: Issues and perspectives.* Boston: Allyn & Bacon.

Bem, S. L. (1974). The measurement of psychological androgyny. *Journal of Consulting and Clinical Psychology, 42,* 155–162.

Brown, L. M., & Gilligan, C. (1992). *Meeting at the crossroads: The landmark book about the turning points in girls' and women's lives.* New York: Ballantine Books.

Brusselmans-Dehairs, C., Hencry, G. F., Beller, M., & Gafni, N. (1997). *Gender differences in learning achievement: Evidence from cross-national surveys.* Paris, France: UNESCO.

Carey, J. C., Fontes, L., & Boscardin, M. L. (1994). Improving the multicultural effectiveness of your school. In P. Pedersen & J. C. Carey (Eds.), *Multicultural counseling in schools* (pp. 239–249). Boston: Allyn & Bacon.

Carnegie Council on Adolescent Development. (1989). *Turning points: Preparing American youth for the 21st century.* New York: Carnegie Corporation of New York.

Cochran-Smith, M., & Lytle, S. L. (1992). Interrogating cultural diversity: Inquiry and action. *Journal of Teacher Education, 43,* 104–115.

D'Andrea, M., & Daniels, J. (1992). Exploring the different levels of multicultural counseling training in counselor education. *Journal of Counseling & Development, 70,* 78–85.

D'Andrea, M., Daniels, J., & Heck, R. (1991). Evaluating the impact of multicultural counseling training. *Journal of Counseling & Development, 70,* 143–150.

Darling-Hammond, L. (1997). Restructuring schools for student success. In A. Halsey, H. Lauder, P. Brown, & A. Wells (Eds.), *Education: Culture, economy, society* (pp. 703–717). Oxford, UK: Oxford University Press.

Devaney, S. B. (1995). Single parents. In N. Vacc, S. DeVaney, & J. Wittmer (Eds.), *Experiencing and counseling multicultural and diverse populations* (pp. 199–215). Bristol, PA: Accelerated Development.

Erikson, E. (1968). *Identity: Youth and crisis.* New York: Norton.

Fine, M. (1987). Silencing in public schools. *Language Arts, 64,* 157–174.

Fine, M. (1988). Deinstitutionalizing educational inequity: Contexts that constrict and construct the lives and minds of public-school adolescents. In Council of Chief State School Officers, *School success for students at risk: Analysis and recommendations* (pp. 89–119). Orlando, FL: Harcourt Brace Jovanovich.

Fine, M. (1991). Invisible flood: Notes on the politics of "dropping out" of an urban public high school. *Equity and Choice, 8,* 30–37.

Flanagan, C. (1993). Gender and social class: Intersecting issues in women's achievement. *Educational Psychologist, 28,* 357–378.

Gans, H. J. (1992, January 8). Fighting the biases embedded in social concepts of the poor. *Chronicle of Higher Education,* p. A56.

Gerler, E. R., & Locke, D. C. (1980). *An approach to elementary counseling* (North Carolina Department of Public Instruction). Matthews, NC: PCA Teleproductions.

Gibbs, J. T., Huang, L. N., & Associates. (1989). *Children of color: Psychological interventions with minority youth.* San Francisco: Jossey-Bass.

Gilligan, C., Ward, J. V., & Taylor, J. M. (1988). *Mapping the moral domain.* Cambridge, MA: Harvard University Press.

Gollnick, D. M. (1991). *Race, class, and gender in teacher education.* Unpublished manuscript, National Council for the Accreditation of Teacher Education.

Good, G. E., Dell, D. M., & Mintz, L. B. (1989). Male role and gender role conflict: Relations to help-seeking in men. *Journal of Counseling Psychology, 36,* 295–300.

Good, G. E., & Mintz, L. B. (1990). Gender role conflict and depression in college men: Evidence for compounded risk. *Journal of Counseling & Development, 69,* 17–21.

Gross, S. (1988). *Participation and performance of women and minorities in mathematics.* Montgomery County, Maryland, Public School District.

Hanmer, T. J. (1996). *The gender gap in schools: Girls losing out.* Springfield, NJ: Enslow.

Harvey, B., Bitting, P., & Robinson, T. L. (1991). Between a rock and a hard place: Drugs and schools in African American communities. In D. J. Jones (Ed.), *Prescriptions and policies: The social well-being of African Americans in the 1990s.* New Brunswick, NJ: Transaction.

Hermann, D. S., & McWhirter, J. J. (1997). Refusal and resistance skills for children and adolescents: A selected review. *Journal of Counseling & Development, 75,* 177–187.

Herring, R. D. (1998). The future direction of multicultural counseling: An assessment of pre-service school counselors' thoughts. *Journal of Multicultural Counseling & Development, 26*(1), 2–12.

Hispanic Policy Development Project. (1987). Disadvantaged young people: In school as adults. *Research Bulletin, 1*(2), 1–3.

LaFromboise, T. D., Coleman, H. L. K., & Hernandez, A. (1991). Development and factor structure of the Cross-Cultural Counseling Inventory-Revised. *Professional Psychology: Research and Practice, 22,* 380–388.

Lehr, J. B., & Harris, H. W. (1988). *At-risk, low-achieving students in the classroom.* Washington, DC: National Education Association.

Lipson, J. F. (1994, Fall). Women in science. In *Outlook.* Washington, DC: American Association of University Women.

Locke, D. C. (1991). The Locke paradigm of cross cultural counseling. *International Journal for the Advancement of Counseling, 14,* 15–25.

Locke, D. C., & Parker, L. D. (1994). Improving the multicultural competence of educators. In P. Pedersen & J. C. Carey (Eds.), *Multicultural counseling in schools* (pp. 39–58). Boston: Allyn & Bacon.

McIntosh, P. (1990). *Interactive phases of curricular and personal revision with regard to race* (Working Paper No. 219). Wellesley, MA: Wellesley College, Center for Research on Women.

Moore, H. A., & Johnson, D. R. (1983). A reexamination of elementary school teachers' expectations: Evidence of sex and ethnic segmentation. *Social Science Quarterly, 64,* 460–475.

Mosley, J. C., & Lex, A. (1990). Identification of potentially stressful life events experienced by a population of urban minority youth. *Journal of Multicultural Counseling & Development, 18,* 118–125.

Oakes, J. (1985). *Keeping track: How schools structure inequality.* New Haven, CT: Yale University Press.

Ogbu, J. (1993, October). *Understanding structural and cultural factors in minority students' school adjustment.* Paper presented at the University of North Carolina at Greensboro.

Pedersen, P. (1988). *A handbook for developing multicultural awareness.* Alexandria, VA: American Association for Counseling and Development.

Persell, C. H. (1977). *Education and inequality: The roots and results of stratification in America's schools.* New York: Free Press.

Pollard, D. S. (1993). Gender, achievement, and African-American students' perceptions of their school experience. *Educational Psychologist, 28,* 341–356.

Ponterotto, J. G., Alexander, C. M., & Grieger, I. (1995). A multicultural competency checklist for counseling training programs. *Journal of Multicultural Counseling & Development, 23,* 11–20.

Prelow, H. M.,& Guarnaccia, C. A. (1997). Ethnic and racial differences in life stress among high school adolescents. *Journal of Counseling & Development, 75,* 442–450.

Quality Education for Minorities Project. (1990). *Education that works: An action plan for the education of minorities.* Cambridge: Massachusetts Institute of Technology.

Robinson, T. L. (1992). Transforming at-risk educational practices by understanding and appreciating differences. *Elementary School Guidance and Counseling, 27,* 84–95.

Rosenthal, R., & Jacobsen, L. (1968). *Pygmalion in the classroom: Teacher expectation and pupil's intellectual development.* New York: Holt, Rinehart & Winston.

Sadker, M., & Sadker, D. (1987). *Sex and equity handbook for schools.* New York: Longman.

Sadker, D., & Sadker, M., & Long, L. (1993). Gender and educational equity. In J. A. Banks & C. A. M. Banks (Eds.), *Multicultural education* (pp. 109–128). Boston: Allyn & Bacon.

Scott-Jones, D., & Clark, M. (1986, March). The school experience of Black girls: The interaction of gender, race, and socioeconomic status. *Phi Delta Kappan, 67,* 520–526.

Slavin, R., & Madden, N. A. (1987). *Effective classroom programs for students at risk.* Baltimore, MD: Johns Hopkins University, Center for Research on Elementary and Middle Schools.

Sleeter, C. E. (1992). Restructuring schools for multicultural education. *Journal of Teacher Education, 43,* 141–148.

Sleeter, C. E., & Grant, B. (1988). *Making choices for multicultural education: Five approaches to race, class, and gender.* Upper Saddle River, NJ: Merrill/Prentice Hall.

Sprinthall, N. (1988). *Adolescent psychology: A developmental view.* New York: McGraw-Hill.

Steward, R. J., Jo, H. I., Murray, D., Fitzgerald, W., Neil, D., Fear, F., & Hill, M. (1998). Psychological adjustment and coping styles of urban African American high school students. *Journal of Multicultural Counseling & Development, 26,* 70–82.

Sue, D. W., & Sue, D. (1990). *Counseling the culturally different: Theory and practice.* New York: John Wiley.

Valsamis, A. (1994, February/March). Study finds school, segregation increasing. *Harvard Education Newsletter,* p. 38.

Wrenn, C. G. (1962). The culturally encapsulated counselor. *Harvard Educational Review, 32,* 444–449.

Chapter 10

Images of Diversity in Family Relationships

I cannot forget my mother. Though not as sturdy as others, she is my bridge. When I needed to get across, she steadied herself long enough for me to run across safely.

Renita Weems, Black Pearls Journal

We think that our children are ours, but they are only our seed. Their reason and purpose has something to do with them, and I don't think we can take credit for that or try to control it.

Don Cherry, Black Pearls Journal

This chapter looks at the gender role socialization relationship between parents and children—specifically, not only motherhood and fatherhood but also the experience of being daughters and sons. Family structure and marital status and different family patterns, such as father-headed households and the extended family, are discussed. Additionally, an overview of family systems, demographic trends, contemporary family issues, and the context of multicultural issues relating to various racial/ethnic families are presented. The goal is to sensitize counselors to the power of gender role socialization, patriarchy, and their impact on family relationships. Techniques for counseling racial/ethnic families are discussed. This chapter follows a slightly different format from the others, with the case study being presented first; a "Discussion and Integration" section is not provided. Mary asks that you create your own and share it with your classmates and instructor.

CASE STUDY
Families in the New Millennium

Randi King-Striker is a 12-year-old outgoing middle school child who has been discussing the issue of race during the family dinner hour quite frequently for the past 3 to 4 weeks. Randi is African American and Latino (biracial) and was adopted when she was an infant by Jo Striker and her ex-husband, Randy King. Jo has been divorced for 7 years and is now married to James Striker, who has two children from a previous marriage. Jo and James are White, ages 44 and 47, respectively. They are an upper middle-class family living in a predominantly White neighborhood in a city with approximately 35,000 inhabitants. The Strikers' other two children are a White male, James Jr., who is 16; and a White female, Lisa, who is 14. Randi is preoccupied with the issues of her skin color and hair, as well as her cultural heritage. She has noticed the paucity of women of color on television and in the magazines her family members read. Randi has a teacher of color and notices how she interacts with many other teachers of color in the school but does not socialize as much with the White teachers. Randi is being bombarded by her friends questioning her ethnicity and

asking, "What are you?" Jo and James tell Randi that she is like them and that they are family. They do not acknowledge or want to discuss "race" at the dinner table and feel very uncomfortable when Randi continues to probe about her cultural lineage. Randi's most recent experience with her biracial issues occurred at a sleep-over where her friends teased her about her copper skin color and thick, curly dark hair.

Jo and James Striker have come to you for assistance in "dealing with Randi's behavioral problems."

QUESTIONS
1. What type of family data would you collect?
2. What type of immediate intervention(s) would you suggest?
3. What type of long-term intervention(s) would you suggest?
4. What immediate presenting problems/issues would you want to address?
5. What additional information or assistance would you need as the counselor to deal with this case?

OVERVIEW OF FAMILY SYSTEMS

Dramatic demographic shifts in the traditional and historical relationship between career and the American family have occurred in the last several decades (Boyer & Horne, 1988; Fenell & Weinhold, 1996; Howard-Hamilton, Echevarria-Rafuls, & Puleo, 1995). The impact of parental career progression on individuals in the family has become a paramount psychosocial issue. Although parental employment status and patterns are clearly associated with family behavior, the nature of that association has become more complex. The traditional nuclear family pattern, with husband as wage earner and wife as homemaker for one or more children, is no longer the norm. Only about 15% of U.S. households currently fit the traditional pattern. In 1959, 70% of U.S. households had the traditional working father-homemaker mother family pattern (Okin, 1997). Today, over half of all wives are employed outside the home, and more than 52% of all children under age 18 have mothers who are actively involved in the workforce.

Politically and economically based transitions in the past two decades have considerably reshaped the family landscape in this country. In particular, family form and structure have been influenced by a host of factors, including the feminist movement, economic insecurity, the increase in dual-earner households, more mothers in the workforce, and the rising rates of divorce, single-parent households, remarriage, and cohabitation (Boyer & Horne, 1988; Fenell & Weinhold, 1996). Dual-earner families in the 1990s replaced the breadwinner-homemaker model in two-parent family in which both partners participate in the job market for pay. In two thirds of all two-parent households, both parents now work, and this will most likely increase as women of childbearing age continue to enter the workforce. The predominance of dual-earner families has occurred both by choice and by necessity. Women have wanted to work, and they have also responded to economic necessity because of declining family incomes (Ingrassia, 1993). According to U.S. Census data, over 70% of mothers of schoolchildren and 60% of mothers of preschool children were part of this country's workforce. In this millennium, remarried families are expected to predominate as the most typical family form (Lott, 1994). According to Visher and Visher (1979) 1,300 new stepfamilies are formed each day in the United States; this has led to approximately one third of the population (33%) living in some sort of stepfamily arrangement (Glick, 1989). Adoptive families led by single parents and couples are also on the rise, as are same-sex families (Calhoun, 1997; Goldenberg & Goldenberg, 1996; Lott, 1994; Midgley & Hughes, 1997). In addition, it is not unrealistic for parents to be burdened with concerns over the safety of their children in today's world. It is not uncommon for caretakers to have a healthy fear that their children might fall victim to societal predators like drugs, violence, prejudice, and poverty, especially in situations where the parents themselves have fallen prey to these experiences.

For the first time in history, more American children live in families with mothers who are working outside the home than with mothers who are full-time homemakers. In fact, the U.S. Department of Labor has identified the married female as a key contributor to the increased role of women participating in the labor force (Boyer & Horne, 1988). Between 1960 and 1980, the proportion of mothers from two-parent families in the workforce doubled (U.S. Bureau of Labor Statistics, 1980).

These trends in maternal workforce participation are dramatic. Their impact, both real and feared, on family functioning, marital relationships, and child development has received national attention. The United States and other Western cultures have experienced significant social, cultural, and economic changes. Marked economic growth increased the number of available jobs. Rising inflation rates increased the cost of living. The women's movement, the civil rights movement, and associated legal actions improved the access of women, individuals with disabilities, and minorities to the workplace.

Technological advances continued to reduce the time required to maintain a household. Personal fulfillment became more important as an individual goal. The sexual revolution was in its prime. Although proving causality is difficult, these factors seem to be associated with the dramatic increase in the number of women who have chosen or felt economic pressure to enter and remain in the workforce.

An additional factor contributing to the increased number of employed mothers is the rapidly rising divorce rate. One in every three or four marriages in the United States ends in divorce. Currently, approximately one of every five children lives with only one parent. Most (90%) of these single-parent families are headed by women. The proportion of single-father families (10%) is small but has remained constant throughout the past decade (Boyer & Horne, 1988). In this millennium, more than half of all children will spend part of their lives in single-parent homes (either single male or single female). By 2010, married couples will no longer form the majority of households, and an increasing number of unmarried women will bear children. These different and potentially unstable societal situations have many counselors, teachers, politicians, and other leaders frantically searching to find a quick fix to the impending problems, rather than realizing that our monocultural therapeutic model needs to be broadened (Howard-Hamilton et al., 1995).

Why are all these statistics and trends important? Simply stated, these are the families that counselors interact with on a daily basis, professionally and personally. The very definition of family has a bearing on the way family policy is constructed and thus on those whom counselors will serve. Current family policy rewards and punishes certain kinds of family forms, as it defines and privileges particular relationships within certain groups (e.g., separating children from significant family ties but not honoring informal adoption and fostering by members of a family's fictive kinship network; Fenell & Weinhold, 1996; Lott, 1994).

The aforementioned statistics on family life reflect relationships and patterns in families a counselor lives and works with as they are influenced by the political, historical, and socioeconomic trends in this country. Clearly, the form and structure of the American family is changing. Much discussion and speculation surrounds losing the traditional father/breadwinner and mother/homemaker pattern to the dual-earner or single-parent family pattern and its impact on child development and family functioning. It often is assumed that the traditional family pattern is best and that nontraditional family patterns, which often include nonfamily-related child care arrangements, are less desirable. But the general trend of research findings does not readily identify one family pattern or child care pattern as clearly superior or inferior to the others in terms of children's adjustment, child-rearing practices, or family functioning.

The traditional family pattern with distinct sex role separations between home-making and wage earning always has been and remains the societal norm. In a compelling historical review of the origins of the traditional family, Lamb (1982) noted that although women universally have had primary responsibility for the care of young children, these responsibilities rarely prevented them from relying to a sub-stantial extent on supplemental child care arrangements or from contributing to the economic survival of the family. When this society was more agrarian and local-com-munity-based, both parents typically worked in the fields or in a location close to home. Most women entered the paid workforce and remained employed except for brief childbearing and child-rearing interruptions. With the Industrial Revolution, work locations moved farther away from the family home, but most women contin-ued their employment.

Economic conditions in the United States have prompted both parents to have careers outside the home for basic survival purposes. Parents adopt various employ-ment patterns that may be accompanied by changes in family structure or in eco-nomic needs. When wage levels increased at the turn of the 20th century, both par-ents had to work outside the home. One must ask how the traditional family belief came into being if the societal trends have dictated otherwise for nearly 100 years. It could be the infusion of the *gender role socialization* concept that has many people believing that what has been the norm (dual-career families) is abnormal.

Family members are also pushed into perfectionistic, materialistic, and the tradi-tional "all American family" wants and desires because of the emphasis on more is better (Howard-Hamilton et al., 1995). No wonder family members are stressed, confused, and dysfunctional because of frequently conflicting work, school, and per-sonal schedules, regimented and chaotic socialized routines, and little or no intimate space with each other to communicate what has been occurring in each other's lives. These situations often create a struggle for the semblance of a shared life; thus, family discord and confusion occur.

> Gender is the basic category by which our species, the family, and all soci-
> eties are organized. True, gender is not the only issue, but the avoidance of
> this most basic issue in family therapy makes it extraordinary. Until we deal
> with the question of gender we are unlikely to transcend it. (Hare-Mustin,
> 1989, p. 74)

Families have been affected by society's infusion of gender role socialization for cen-turies. The socialization process requires that heads of the household and siblings conform to rigid gender role expectations created by a patriarchal system (Golden-berg & Goldenberg, 1996; Nelson, 1997).

> Although the patriarchal structures of intimacy that serve as the hege-
> monic ideal of family are perhaps the structures among all others that have

silenced and exploited women, they are also the structures—or something
like structures—of many feminists' families. (Nelson, 1997, p. 3)

The vast majority of families in this society are affected by the covert and overt models of socialization that ultimately form the framework and functioning in most households (Hanna & Brown, 1995; Lott, 1994).

The literature on gender role socialization discusses the power base of men as providers gaining recognition from sources outside the home, whereas females' power base and recognition come from their work as caregivers and relationship-maintenance providers inside the home (Burck & Speed, 1995; Lott, 1994; Nicholson, 1997). Even when women work, traditional roles such as child care, household chores, as well as sustaining contact and communication with family and friends, continue to be part of their daily routine (Goldenberg & Goldenberg, 1996). These roles are socially sanctioned and imposed on individuals on the basis of their gender. The assumption is that these roles are symmetrical and equivalent in power. However, the inherent inequality of power is based on what is valued most highly in this society—economic stability. "The contribution of women's family work continues to be minimized, perhaps because it does not directly produce income" (Hare-Mustin, 1988, p. 40).

Society imposes certain expectations of behaviors from women and men within families. Women in families often experience a responsibility to uphold the traditions and rituals in those families. Men are expected to be the financial providers and to be emotionally distant in their caring networks (Lott, 1994; McGoldrick, Anderson, & Walsh, 1989). The socially sanctioned roles within families have left behind generations of women and men who have, at different stages in their lives, felt inadequate and isolated from others because of their narrow gender experience.

Women are expected to assume total responsibility for maintaining family relationships and connections. If they do not take on this role and no one else fills in the gap, the connections in the family unit start to break down. The breakdown of family ties leads to women experiencing an overwhelming sense of guilt and inadequacy (Nicholson, 1997). The socialization of women to take on this caretaking role is handed down from generation to generation within families by the demands of an androcratic society (Nicholson, 1997; Okin, 1997). These positions of gender role rigidity continue to restrict the experiences of members within families. They maintain a female's position as responsible for the survival of the family ties while at the same time limit her position outside the family. They maintain a man's position as a stranger to the family whose value is defined through monetary means.

Families in this millennium will be composed of female-headed households, gay/lesbian couples, biracial partners, blended (divorced/widowed) families, and grandparents or extended family members raising their children's children. These new families need to be comfortable with the therapist understanding and acknowledging these differences. This understanding can be accomplished by asking the following questions after the initial interview to explore the family members' issues in depth (Hanna & Brown, 1995, p 97):

1. What family roles or activities did your family stress, overtly or covertly, that were for boys and/or for girls?
2. What family traditions or rituals stressed specific roles or activities for boys and/or for girls?
3. Does your family discuss how gender roles affect girls and/or boys in our society?
4. How do you feel about these unconscious roles or belifs that are surfacing?
5. In what ways, if any, do you think these ideas and traditions might be related to _____ (the presenting problem)?

These are a few questions the counselor can ask during the assessment process. Care should be taken to eliminate any question that does not seem to resonate with the client. The therapist should always keep the factors of race, gender, disability, age, and socioeconomic status in mind when talking with the client because the personal is political. In other words, the family system plays a key part in gathering background information on the client and whether the client has the ability to process her or his innermost thoughts and connect them with the impact of gender role socialization and/or race. This structural approach to family therapy is a theoretical framework that provides a conceptual map to understanding families.

COUNSELING THEORIES FOR FAMILY PRACTICE

The theoretical framework and theorist most commonly used for family issues is the **structural family approach,** developed by Salvador Minuchin. The structural family approach gives the practitioner a concrete, conceptual map of what should be happening in a family if it is to be functional; it also provides maps of what is awry in the family if it is dysfunctional (Becvar & Becvar, 1993). The structural family approach gives students and practitioners definite ideas about the process of therapy that should be carried out. These processes inevitably vary in practice, however, reflecting the personality of the therapist and the particular structure of the family. Structural family therapy is one of the most heavily researched models, and its efficacy has been demonstrated with a variety of what are generally termed "difficult families." Thus, families with juvenile delinquents, families with anorexic members, families with chemically addicted members, families of low socioeconomic status, and alcoholic families (Fenell & Weinhold, 1996) have all been successfully counseled with the structural family approach. The influence of this approach may also be seen in other models of family therapy, particularly the strategic approach.

Structural family therapy sees the family as an integrated whole—as a system. Accordingly, it is also a subsystem in that its members belong to other agencies and organizations in the community of which it is a part and that affect its basic structure and pattern of organization. In the language of the theory, there are three key concepts/constructs: structure, subsystems, and boundaries.

STRUCTURE

Structural family therapy focuses on the patterns of interaction within the family that give clues to the basic structure and organization of the system. **Structure** refers to the invisible set of functional demands that organizes the way family members interact, or the consistent, repetitive, organized, and predictable modes of family behavior that allow the counselor to consider that the family has structure in a functional sense. The concepts of *patterns* and *structure* therefore imply a set of covert rules that family members may not be consciously aware of but that consistently characterize and define their interactions.

The structure of a family is governed by two general systems of constraints. The first constraint system is referred to as *generic,* an observation that all families everywhere have some sort of hierarchical structure according to which parents have greater authority than children. An important aspect of this generic structure is the notion of reciprocal and complementary functions, which can be discerned by the labels applied to family members that indicate their roles and the functions they serve. Members of a family evolve roles (without a conscious awareness of their roles) to maintain the family equilibrium and to keep it functioning.

A second constraint system is that which is *idiosyncratic* to the particular family. Rules and patterns may evolve in a family while the reason for such characteristic processes may be lost in the history of the family. The rules and patterns become a part of the family's structure. Family structure governs a family in that it defines the roles, rules, and patterns allowable within the family.

SUBSYSTEMS

Structural family theory defines three subsystems: the spouse subsystem, the parental subsystem, and the sibling subsystem. The rule among these subsystems for the functional family is that of hierarchy. Theory insists on appropriate boundaries between the generations.

SPOUSE SUBSYSTEM   The *spouse subsystem* is formed when two people marry and thus create a new family. The processes involved in forming the spouse subsystem are known as *accommodation,* which implies adjustment, and *negotiation* of roles between spouses. The early part of the marriage formation of the spouse subsystem necessitates evolving such complementary roles. Although some of these roles may be transitory and others may be more permanent, the keys to the successful navigation of life as a family are negotiation and accommodation, especially as they concern rules and roles. The adjustment for couples may be difficult and slow because each has certain expectations about the performance of various functions and roles. Negotiation and accommodation are enhanced to the degree that each spouse is her or his own person and is not overly tied to the family of origin or its rules, patterns, and roles. Finally, an important requirement of the spouse subsystem is that each spouse be mutually supportive of the other in the development of her or his unique or latent talents and interests. Accordingly, neither spouse is so totally accommodating of the other as to lose her or his own individuality. Both sides give-and-take, each remains an individual, and as each of the spouses accommodates the individuality, resources, and uniqueness of the other, they are respectfully bound together.

PARENTAL SUBSYSTEM   In the *parental,* or executive, *subsystem,* each spouse has the challenge of mutually supporting and accommodating the other to provide an appropriate balance of firmness and nurturance for the children. The parents are in charge, and an important challenge is knowing how and when to be in charge about specific issues. Parents need to negotiate and accommodate changes in the developmental needs of their children. A family is not a democracy, and the children are not equals or peers to the parents. From this base of authority, the children learn to deal with authority and to interact in situations in which authority is unequal.

SIBLING SUBSYSTEM   By establishing the spouse and parental subsystems, structural family theory also defines the sibling subsystem. The *sibling subsystem* allows children to be children and to experiment with peer relationships. Ideally, the parents respect the ability of the siblings to negotiate, to compete, to work out differences, and to support one another. It is a social laboratory in which children can experiment without the responsibility that accrues to the adult. Children also learn to coalesce to take on the parental subsystem in the process of negotiating necessary developmental changes.

BOUNDARIES

Boundaries are invisible, but they nevertheless delineate individuals and subsystems and define the amount and kind of contact allowable between members of the family. Structural family theory describes interpersonal boundaries among subsystems as falling into one of three categories: clear, rigid, and diffuse.

CLEAR BOUNDARIES   *Clear boundaries* are firm and yet flexible. Clear boundaries also imply access across subsystems to negotiate and accommodate situational and developmental challenges that confront the family. Indeed, situations that occur each day are a test in how to live that necessitates negotiation, accommodation, and experimentation with a new structure over and over again until the family gets it "right," only to find its circumstances have changed once more. Clear boundaries in a family increase the frequency of communication between subsystems, and thus negotiation and accommodation can successfully occur to facilitate change, thereby maintaining the stability of the family.

RIGID BOUNDARIES   *Rigid boundaries* refer to the arrangement both among subsystems and with systems outside the family. Rigid boundaries imply disengagement within and between systems. Family members in that instance are isolated from one another and from systems in the community of which the family is a part. Members in such families thus rely on systems outside the family for the support and nurturance they need and desire.

DIFFUSE BOUNDARIES   The family defined by *diffuse boundaries* is characterized by enmeshed relationships. This is the polar opposite of the rigid boundary family. In this case, everybody is into everybody else's business, and the hovering and the providing of support even when not needed is extreme. The parents are too accessible, and the necessary distinctions between subsystems are missing. There is too much negotiation and accommodation; the cost to both the developing children and the parents is a loss of independence, autonomy, and experimentation. The spouse subsystem devotes itself almost totally to parenting functions, and the parents spend too much time with the children and do too much for them. Such children may be afraid to experiment, perhaps to succeed, perhaps to fail. They may feel disloyal to a parent if they do not want to accept what the parent offers. They probably have difficulty knowing which feelings are theirs and which belong to others. The clear boundary is preferred and represents an appropriate combination of rigid and diffuse characteristics.

For Minuchin, the ideal family builds on a spouse subsystem in which each accommodates, nurtures, and supports the uniqueness of the other. The spouses have attained a measure of autonomy from their families of origin. Ideally, in the family of origin, each spouse felt supported and nurtured and yet experienced a degree of autonomy, independence, and responsibility. Similarly, spouses need to be able to maintain a delicate balance between proximity and distance. On this base, the couple negotiates complementary roles that are stable but flexible and through a process of negotiation and accommodation evolves different structures and role complements to deal with changing circumstances. The spouse subsystem maintains itself even when children are born and the parental/executive and sibling subsystems come into existence.

The ideal family will face expected and unexpected crises appropriately by recognizing and facilitating necessary changes in structure. Such behavior requires a great deal of patience and wisdom. So, with the challenge of each new crisis, a new culture (structure) must be evolved—in many cases, a structure and transition process for which the participants have no direct experience to guide them. That is, families are organisms in a continuous process of changing while trying to remain the same.

GOALS

Problem solving is not the goal of structural family therapy. Symptomatic behavior is viewed as a function of the structure of the family; that is, it is a logical response in the family, given its structure. Problem solving will naturally occur when appropriate structural adaptations have been made. Thus, problem solving is the business of the family; structural change so that problem solving can occur is the business of the structural therapist. Symptom removal without the appropriate change in structure would not be successful therapy from the structural perspective.

The structural therapist must join the family and respect its members and its way of organizing itself. Thus, the therapist gets into the family and accommodates to its usual style. Such joining is a necessary prerequisite of attempts to restructure. The structural therapist also respects the hierarchy of the family by asking for the parents' observations first. Problems thus get redefined relative to the family structure. Structural family therapy is action oriented and aimed at influencing what happens in the therapy session.

Becvar and Becvar (1993, pp. 207-208) noted specific techniques and activities the structural therapist might conduct while in therapy:

1. Meet with family members separately to discuss therapeutic boundaries
2. Assist family members who are not communicating effectively toward increasing their dialogue with one another
3. Help specific dyads find ways to end conflictual relationships without intrusion from other family members
4. Help family members find ways to cognitively view themselves differently by embracing a positive frame of reference

Structural family therapy primary processes include being clear about family structure and having respect for the family's efforts to achieve higher levels of functioning. Additionally, the therapist should respect the family's traditional modes of operation, yet provide a healthier model of behavior. This can be achieved by "supporting members, challenging them to try new methods in session and praising them generously when they are successful. There must be an intensity sufficient enough to gain the attention of the family members" (Becvar & Becvar, 1993, p. 208).

MULTICULTURAL THEORETICAL PERSPECTIVES IN FAMILY THERAPY

The structural family approach and multicultural theoretical paradigms should be viewed and implemented as complementary approaches to treatment. Gushue and Sciarra (1995) state that two models currently in the counseling literature provide a framework for the impact of culture on family therapy and family systems: (1) the intercultural dimension and (2) the intracultural dimension, which delineates the issues of (a) acculturation (b) racial/cultural identity, and (c) bilingual theory.

When looking at the *intercultural dimension,* the counselors working with White, middle-class, heterosexual males used this paradigm to guide all work with their clients. But they then began to realize that, for families, too, diversity was normative. Different cultures had differing ways of understanding "appropriate" family organization, values, communication, and behavior. Although the family perspective had revolutionized the individual view of the client by taking family context into account, it now needed to understand its own unit of analysis (the family) in the light of an even larger context: culture.

In the *intracultural dimension,* the counselor must turn to three crucial questions of within-group difference: (a) To what extent does this particular family conform to or differ from the "typical" patterns of family functioning for its culture? (b) What cultural differences may exist within the family itself (among the various subsystems)? and (c) If cultural differences exist within the family, what consequences do these differences have for interactions both among the subsystems and between the various subsystems and the counselor? Answering these questions leads the therapist to the issues of (a) acculturation, (b) racial/cultural identity, and (c) bilingual theory.

Acculturation initially referred to the potentially mutual influence that two cultures have on each other when they come into contact (Ivey, Ivey, & Simek-Morgan, 1997; Mindel, Habenstein, & Wright, 1988; Sue & Sue, 1990). Over the years, however, it has more commonly come to refer to the interaction between a dominant and a nondominant culture in which one is affected much more profoundly than the other.

The models of *racial/cultural identity* (Atkinson, Morten, & Sue, 1989; Cross, 1971, 1991; Helms, 1990, 1995; Sue & Sue, 1990) presented in Chapter 4 are important to integrate into family systems therapy because they provide the therapist with information regarding within-group differences and an individual's psychological orientation to membership in both the dominant and nondominant cultures in the United States.

Bilingual theory questions whether intracultural differences in a given family can be attained by observing and understanding the function of linguistic difference within the family system. As immigration from non-English-speaking countries continues to rise, bilingual persons in therapy will become an increasing phenomenon. Some issues that need to be addressed for the bilingual client are related to the immigration experience, language barriers within the family, and language barriers between therapist and client. "Family therapists must take great care before using norms that stem from the majority cultural matrix in assessing the attitudes, beliefs, and transactional patterns of those whose cultural patterns differ from theirs" (Goldenberg & Goldenberg, 1996, p. 36). The racial/ethnic behaviors described in the next section provide important information the therapist must be keenly aware of to empathize with the personal issues affecting people of color in this country (Goldenberg & Goldenberg, 1996). Beyond these behaviors, the therapist must also understand the unique issues related to the language barriers, racism and stereotypes, hopelessness, cultural shock, powerlessness, and rage.

IMPLICATIONS FOR COUNSELORS

AFRICAN AMERICANS

Dana (1993) stated that Whites once believed that African American families were barbaric and morbid deviations from predominant-culture families. African American families have demonstrated, however, a stability and cohesive functioning that is often culture-specific. Competence among intact inner-city African American families includes shared power, strong parental coalitions, closeness without sacrificing individual ego boundaries, and negotiation in problem solving. The competence of these inner-city families is related to a significantly higher income than that of neighboring families. Nonetheless, many of these competent families are at risk because of economic conditions and the uncertain employment status of family members (Ingrassia, 1993).

As a result of economic conditions, families are often of three-generation composition (Boyd-Franklin, 1989; Ingrassia, 1993; Staples, 1988). They do not necessarily include only blood relations but may have uncles/aunts, cousins, "play sisters," and "home boys/girls." These co-residential extended families make possible an elastic kinship-based exchange network that may last a lifetime. These families exhibit role flexibility and interchangeability in which male-female relationships are often egalitarian because of the presence of working wives, mothers, and grandmothers (Boyd-Franklin, 1989; Staples, 1988). Members of the extended family may also exhibit "child keeping," using an informal adoption network (see the Storytelling "It Takes a Village").

African American men have identity as the nominal heads of households, tied in to their ability to provide for their families. Girls, however, are socialized by their mothers for strength, economic independence, family responsibility, and daily accountability (Boyd-Franklin, 1989). Women are identified as possessing fortitude, perseverance, and strength during adversity. Women are also identified as "mother," and 47% of households have a female head.

Women are also generally more religious than men and function to tie the family into a complete church-centered support system of persons in particular roles, activities, and social life (Boyd-Franklin, 1989). This is especially notable in Baptist churches. Other major religious groups with some similar functions include the African Methodist, Jehovah's Witnesses, Church of God in Christ, Seventh-Day Adventist, Pentecostal, and Nation of Islam sects.

This culture-specific description of the African American family is not intended to suggest that all families are extended and nonconsanguineous in composition. In fact, the recent trend has been toward single life, and marriages have an increasing fragility in the African American community (Boyd-Franklin, 1989; Ingrassia, 1993; Staples, 1988). In addition, many African Americans have opted for identification with the dominant Anglo American culture and are more egocentric in lifestyle and less communal in orientation. As a result, African Americans may show greater within-group differences in egocentrism-sociocentrism than, for example, Native American Indians. To the extent that they become explicitly Africentric, however, middle-class persons especially will deal with their individual life experiences in a collective manner, with a strong emphasis on flexibility, sharing, and consideration for the welfare of other persons within their spheres of responsibility and influence (Boyd-Franklin, 1989; Ingrassia, 1993; Staples, 1988).

ASIAN AMERICANS

Asian Americans typically have patriarchal families with authority and communication exercised from top to bottom, interdependent roles, strict adherence to traditional norms, and minimization of conflict by suppression of overt emotion (Kitano, 1988;

STORYTELLING
It Takes a Village

I was raised in Alton, Illinois, a city of approximately 25,000 inhabitants 25 miles east of St. Louis, Missouri. I was raised by my neighbors, teachers, and relatives, in addition to my biological family. This is the beauty of growing up in the late 1950s through the early 1970s, during a time when emphasis was on the responsibility of an entire community raising and keeping a watchful eye on the children. I will never forget the day I was roller-skating on the cement portion of our open car shelter and fell. It was so sudden that I did not have time to cover my face and break my fall. I bit into my bottom lip and screamed as blood came pouring out of the wound. My neighbor, Mr. Wilson, who lived three distant doors down the street, heard me cry and ran up to our house to check on me. In our world today, a child may scream for hours without one person checking.

When I was growing up, nothing went unnoticed. For example, when a child excelled in school, an athletic achievement was accomplished, or a graduate was heading to college or the military to represent the community, accolades where heaped on those children verbally, with hugs, and in writing (usually in the church bulletin), which raised our level of self-esteem immeasurably.

I often think about the things that contributed to my success, and they were my biological family, church family, extended community family, and teachers. My biological family taught me the importance of culture, racial pride, tolerance, and support. My church family elevated my level of self-esteem when they requested that I lead a prayer, give a speech for the holidays, play my clarinet with my sister accompanying me on the piano, and sing in the choir. My extended community family always noticed when I achieved a major milestone and recognized my efforts publicly and as often as possible. My teachers and counselors were significant in my life; although a few attempted to thwart my success, the vast majority told me that I would be very successful someday. I never internalized the negative rhetoric because my "family" was telling me there was so much for me to accomplish; surely a handful of cynical teachers can't know as much as my wise family elders!

What does it take to maintain a strong family structure? I believe it takes a strong spiritual base. This should be employed in the manner the family feels most comfortable—for example, meditating and reflecting, reading a favorite quote or affirmation from a book, or walking and talking about something that's negative and teaching the technique of reframing the situation. A mentor is needed to be a role model and to provide hope for the future. For example, as a godmother, I communicate with my goddaughter and gave her encouraging words as she entered kindergarten. I also recommend that children be given a diary as soon as they are able to write. I began journaling my "life" when I was 7 years old, and it was a safe place for me to vent my anger, chronicle my day, and visualize my goals. I am quite sure things in everyone's childhood could be attributed to the development of a successful individual. One thing that resonates with everyone is the importance of connection with "family."

Mary

Min, 1988; Sue & Sue, 1990; Tran, 1988; Wong, 1988). Guilt and shame are used to control family members, and obligations to the family take precedence over individual prerogatives (Kitano, 1988; Sue & Sue, 1990; Wong, 1988). Under the aegis of the family, discipline and self-control are sufficient to provide an impetus for outstanding achievement to honor the family. Negative behaviors such as delinquency, school failure, unemployment, or mental illness are considered family failures that disrupt the desired harmony of family life. In addition is the belief in external control, a fatalism that allows an equanimity and acceptance without question of life as it unfolds.

In China and the United States, absolute control by the family as a major ingredient in the formation of a traditional self-concept has not only diminished but is being openly questioned (Wong, 1988). Despite questioning of traditional filial identity, strong evidence suggests, at least among Hong Kong Chinese students, the continued presence of an extended self, or collective orientation.

Similarly, in Japan the emphasis on the importance of collectivity has been increasing, particularly in the form of corporate family effectiveness instead of intrafamily lineal authority or filial piety (Goldenberg & Goldenberg, 1996; Kitano, 1988). However, this collectivity may also be expressed in humanistic or socialist terms.

In the United States, problems faced by first- and second-generation Chinese may differ as a result of inability to express filial piety properly (Goldenberg & Goldenberg, 1996; Sue & Sue, 1990; Wong, 1988). Although first-generation men in particular are required to achieve and/or to be good providers for their families, sufficient achievement to fulfill family expectations has not always been possible for them. Second-generation individuals also may fail to be unquestioningly faithful to the traditional values of their parents. Their self-worth is increasingly defined either by dominant culture values or by pan-Asian values, in which a common response to racism and personal pride may take precedence over filial piety. As a result, individuals in both generations may experience considerable guilt and anxiety. It may be argued that the locus of loyalty within the Chinese community is in the process of shifting from the family, including ancestors, to other collectivities, including the pan-Asian community in the United States. Overall, the traditional Asian American family believes in loyalty and devotion to its values (Goldenberg & Goldenberg, 1996). The primary tradition is **filial piety,** which is the dedication and deference of children to their parents (Goldenberg & Goldenberg, 1996).

LATINOS

The fastest growing group in this country is the Latino American (Becerra, 1988; Sanchez-Ayendez, 1988; Sue & Sue, 1990; Szapocznik & Hernandez, 1988). Personal identity for Latino Americans is sociocentric in nature, with the self and self-interest often subordinated to the welfare of *la casa* and *la familia* (Becerra, 1988; Sue & Sue, 1990). The balance of group and individual prerogatives, however, depends on the individual manner of dealing with the culture in traditional, bicultural, nontraditional, or marginal terms. For traditional and bicultural persons, the balance will often be in favor of needs in the extended family. For nontraditional and marginal persons, the balance may favor more egocentric decisions and actions.

Traditional sex roles are clearly defined by *machismo* for men and *marianismo* and *hembrismo* for women (Becerra, 1988). *Machismo* is more than male physical dominance and sexual availability. It includes the role of a provider responsible for the welfare, protection, honor, and dignity of his family. *Marianismo* refers to the spiritual superiority of women and their capacity to endure all suffering, with reference to the Virgin Mary. After marriage, the *Madonna* concept includes sacrifice and femaleness, or *hembrismo*, in the form of strength, perseverance, and flexibility. These *hembrista* behaviors ensure survival and power through the children.

Personal identity is also associated with being strong. *Strong* refers to inner strength, or *fuerza de espiritu,* characterized by toughness, determination, and willpower (Dana, 1993). A strong person can confront a problem directly and be active in resolving it, thereby delaying admitting that help may be needed. *Controlarse,* or controlling oneself, is the key to being a strong person and includes *aguantarse,* or being able to withstand stress during bad times; *resignarse,* or resigning oneself and accepting fate; and *sobreponerse,* or imposing one's will or overcoming circumstance. A weak person will have little or no self-control and be less able to exercise responsibility or to display *orgullo,* or pride, and *verguenzza,* or shame. As a result, she or he is more easily influenced by people or events and is relatively unable to become strong.

The family name is very important to the Latino American, with a man, along with his given name, adopting both his father's and mother's names. It is often expected, as well as encouraged, that family members will sacrifice their own needs for the welfare of the family (Goldenberg & Goldenberg, 1996). Thus, the family constellation is loyal, committed, and responsible to each other and have a strong sense of honor.

NATIVE AMERICAN INDIANS

Native American Indian children have extended self-concepts by self-descriptions that indicate an emphasis on family ties, traditional customs, and beliefs, and moral worth (John, 1988). The extended family network includes several households (Goldenberg & Goldenberg, 1996; John, 1988). "A non-kin family member through being a namesake of a child, consequently assumes family obligations and responsibilities for child rearing and role modeling" (Goldenberg & Goldenberg, 1996, p. 37). The presence and impact of these strong family ties once made possible the social controls that existed throughout life and that shaped concepts of the self. In some tribes, during earlier periods, control by the family over social behavior and sexuality during all phases of life was absolute (John, 1988). The power of these family ties has been diluted over time, however, and family life for Native American Indians has become more difficult to characterize. The family now has an uncertain composition, and *extended family* refers to a village-type Native American Indian community network in which responsibility is shared.

This shared responsibility includes food, shelter, automobiles, and all available services, including child care (John, 1988). The Native American Indian community expects decisions by tribal consensus, institutional sharing as a source of social esteem, and a characteristic indirection in attempts to control the behavior of others. As a result of an extended concept of self, the community is enabled to enforce values and to serve as a source of standards by using a loose structure or flexible nexus of support. For an example of extended self-concept, *tiospaye,* in Lakota Sioux, is used to refer to family in the broadest sense that is conducive to survival.

Examples of an extended self-concept include obligations to other human beings and to the native community. An extended self-concept serves to provide a continued group identity (John, 1988). This group identity increases the likelihood of prolonged individual survival in an alien and hostile mainstream culture in which the natural and social environments are increasingly less responsive to native persons.

The composition of the self-concept of any individual Native American Indian also may be affected by her or his level of assimilation into the larger culture. Despite education, occupation in nontraditional jobs, and bicultural status, however, many Native American Indians have shown a significant retention of cultural values (John, 1988). As a result, the homogeneity of beliefs among Native American Indians may be greater than is characteristic of other cultural groups in this country. Without some clear understanding of an individual's self-concept in any service setting, it may not be feasible to provide adequate services or even to know which services would be most helpful.

Therapists attempting to develop a process and that will take into account the impact of culture could follow Hanna and Brown's (1995, p. 101) assessment questions of racial and cultural factors:

1. How does your racial/cultural/religious heritage make your family different from other families you know?
2. Compared to other families in your cultural group, how is your family different?
3. What are the values that your family identified as being important parts of your heritage?
4. At this particular time in your (family's) development, are there issues related to your cultural heritage that are being questioned by anyone?
5. What is the hardest part about being a person of color in this culture?
6. When you think of living in America versus the country of your heritage, what are the main differences?
7. What lesson did you learn about your people? About other peoples?
8. What did you learn about disloyalty?
9. What were people in your family really down on?
10. What might an outsider not understand about your racial/cultural/religious background?

SUMMARY

This chapter delineated some complex and intricate issues affecting multicultural families and the role gender plays in the success or failure of this system. The approach presented here emphasized the need to attend to both intergroup and intragroup cultural differences when working with families (Gushue & Sciarra, 1995), as well as noted gender socialization issues, societal trends, and biases the counselor has internalized. It is important to have a factual perspective of the overall worldview and specific values of a given family's culture. Therapists must also take into account their own worldviews and family values and assess how their personal perspectives may influence, bias, or spill over into the therapeutic process. To be effective in cross-cultural contexts, the therapist must be linguistically cognizant and culturally aware. Ethnocentrism, gender bias, and stereotypical beliefs will be infused in the counseling process if multiple perspectives are not taken into account by the therapist. The unfortunate result may be early termination, protracted family strife and dysfunction, and a continuation of such behaviors by the therapist, who then endangers many more families. The case study provided an opportunity for students to think about how they would approach the family presented as a function of integrating material presented. Interactions between and among diverse family members and the therapist can be very rewarding for the persons in the session and society as well.

REFERENCES

Atkinson, D. R., Morton, G., & Sue, D. W. (1989). *Counseling American minorities: A cross-cultural perspective.* Dubuque, IA: W. C. Brown.

Becerra, R. M. (1988). The Mexican American family. In C. H. Mindel, R. W. Habenstein, & R. Wright (Eds.), *Ethnic families in America: Patterns and variations* (3rd ed., pp. 141–159). New York: Elsevier.

Becvar, S. B., & Becvar, R. (1993). *Family therapy: A systematic integration* (2nd ed.). Boston: Allyn & Bacon.

Boyd-Franklin, N. (1989). *Black families in therapy: A multisystems approach.* New York: Guilford.

Boyer, M. C., & Horne, A. M. (1988). Working parents: A family matter. *Counseling and Human Development, 21*(1), 1–11.

Burck, C., & Speed, B. (1995). *Gender, power, and relationships.* New York: Routledge.

Calhoun, C. (1997). Family outlaws: Rethinking the connections between feminism, lesbianism, and the family. In H. L. Nelson (Ed.), *Feminism and families* (pp. 55–68). New York: Routledge.

Cross, W. E. (1971). The Negro-to-Black conversion experience: Toward a psychology of Black liberation. *Black World, 20,* 13–27.

Cross, W. E. (1991). *Shades of Black: Diversity in African American identity.* Philadelphia: Temple University Press.

Dana, R. H. (1993). *Multicultural assessment perspectives for professional psychology.* Boston: Allyn & Bacon.

Fenell, D. L., & Weinhold, B. K. (1996). Treating families with special needs. *Counseling and Human Development, 28*(7), 1–10.

Glick, P. (1989). Remarried families, stepfamilies, and stepchildren: A brief demographic analysis. *Family Relations, 38,* 24–27.

Goldenberg, I., & Goldenberg, H. (1996). *Family therapy: An overview* (4th ed.). Pacific Grove, CA: Brooks/Cole.

Gushue, G. V., & Sciarra, D. P. (1995). Culture and families: A multidimensional approach. In J. G. Ponterotto, J. M. Casas, L. A. Suzuki, & C. M. Alexander (Eds.), *Handbook of multicultural counseling* (pp. 586–606). Thousand Oaks, CA: Sage.

Hanna, S. M., & Brown, J. H. (1995). *The practice of family therapy: Key elements across models.* Pacific Grove, CA: Brooks/Cole.

Hare-Mustin, R. T. (1988). Family change and gender differences: Implications for theory and practice. *Family Relations, 37,* 36–41.

Hare-Mustin, R. T. (1989). The problem of gender in family therapy theory. In M. McGoldrick, C. M. Anderson, & F. Walsh (Eds.), *Women in families: A framework for family therapy.* New York: Norton.

Helms, J. (1990). *Black and White racial identity: Theory, research, and practice.* New York: Greenwood Press.

Helms, J. (1995). An update of Helms's White and people of color racial identity models. In J. G. Ponterotto, J. M. Casas, L. A. Suzuki, & C. M. Alexander (Eds.), *Handbook of multicultural counseling* (pp. 181–198). Thousand Oaks, CA: Sage.

Howard-Hamilton, M. F., Echevarria-Rafuls, S., & Puleo, S. G. (1995). Societal transformation: Ecological issues affecting educational, mental health, and family systems. *Peabody Journal, 70,* 141–159.

Ingrassia, M. (1993, August 30). Endangered family. *Newsweek,* pp. 17–29.

Ivey, A. E., Ivey, M. B., & Simek-Morgan, L. (1997). *Counseling and psychotherapy: A multicultural perspective* (4th ed.). Boston: Allyn & Bacon.

John, R. (1988). The Native American family. In C. H. Mindel, R. W. Habenstein, & R. Wright (Eds.), *Ethnic families in America: Patterns and variations* (3rd ed., pp. 325–366). New York: Elsevier.

Kitano, H. H. L. (1988). The Japanese American family. In C. H. Mindel, R. W. Habenstein, & R. Wright (Eds.), *Ethnic families in America: Patterns and variations* (3rd ed., pp. 258–275). New York: Elsevier.

Lamb, M. E. (1982). Parental behavior and child development in nontraditional families. In M. E. Lamb (Ed.), *Nontraditional families: Parenting and child development.* Hillsdale, NJ: Erlbaum.

Lott, B. (1994). *Women's lives: Themes and variations in gender learning* (2nd ed.). Pacific Grove, CA: Brooks/Cole.

McGoldrick, M., Anderson, C. M., & Walsh. F. (1989). *Women in families: A framework for family therapy.* New York: Norton.

Midgley, M., & Hughes, J. (1997). Are families out of date? In H. L. Nelson (Ed.), *Feminism and families* (pp. 55–68). New York: Routledge.

Min, P. G. (1988). The Korean American family. In C. H. Mindel, R. W. Habenstein, & R. Wright (Eds.), *Ethnic families in America: Patterns and variations* (3rd ed., pp. 199–229). New York: Elsevier.

Mindel, C. H., Habenstein, R. W., & Wright, R. (1988). *Ethnic families in America: Patterns and variations.* New York: Elsevier.

Minuchin, S. (1974). *Families and family therapy.* Cambridge, MA: Harvard University Press.

Minuchin, S. (1984). *Family kaleidoscope.* Cambridge, MA: Harvard University Press.

Minuchin, S. (1991). The seductions of constructivism. *The Family Networker 15*(5), 47–50.

Nelson, H. L. (1997). *Feminism and families.* New York: Routledge.

Nicholson, L. (1997). The myth of the traditional family. In H. L. Nelson (Ed.), *Feminism and families* (pp. 27–42). New York: Routledge.

Okin, S. M. (1997). Families and feminist theory: Some past and present issues. In H. L. Nelson (Ed.), *Feminism and families* (pp. 13–26). New York: Routledge.

Sanchez-Ayendez, M. (1988). The Puerto Rican American family. In C. H. Mindel, R. W. Habenstein, & R. Wright (Eds.), *Ethnic families in America: Patterns and variations* (3rd ed., pp. 173–198). New York: Elsevier.

Staples, R. (1988). The Black American family. In C. H. Mindel, R. W. Habenstein, & R. Wright (Eds.), *Ethnic families in America: Patterns and variations* (3rd ed., pp. 303–324). New York: Elsevier.

Szapocznik, J., & Hernandez, R. (1988). The Cuban American family. In C. H. Mindel, R. W. Habenstein, & R. Wright (Eds.), *Ethnic families in America: Patterns and variations* (3rd ed., pp. 160–172). New York: Elsevier.

Sue, D. W., & Sue, D. (1990). *Counseling the culturally different: Theory and practice* (2nd ed.). New York: John Wiley.

Tran, T. V. (1988). The Vietnamese American family. In C. H. Mindel, R. W. Habenstein, & R. Wright (Eds.), *Ethnic families in America: Patterns and variations* (3rd ed., pp. 276–302). New York: Elsevier.

U.S. Bureau of Labor Statistics. (1980). *Perspectives on working women: A databook* (Bulletin 2080). Washington, DC: U.S. Department of Labor.

Visher, E. B., & Visher, J. S. (1979). *Stepfamilies: A guide to working with stepparents and stepchildren.* New York: Brunner/Mazel.

Wong, M. G. (1988). The Chinese American family. In C. H. Mindel, R. W. Habenstein, & R. Wright (Eds.), *Ethnic families in America: Patterns and variations* (3rd ed., pp. 230–257). New York: Elsevier.

Chapter 11

Images of Diversity in Career Counseling

I never knew that I could want to be what I wanted.

A female graduate student in response to another female classmate's statement about what, as a child, she wanted to be when she grew up

In this chapter, attention is devoted to the importance of wise and prudent career guidance for young people and the countless number of persons who experience the common and uncertain process of transitioning through a career. In an effort to get assistance, many persons seek counseling. Mentoring, role modeling, self-construct, and alternative ways of assessing abilities and strengths are also explored in this chapter. An identity model is presented to understand different statuses involved in occupational choice. A look at the American workforce between 1992 and 2005 begins our discussion. A case study allows for synthesis of ideas discussed.

CIVILIAN LABOR FORCE OUTLOOK

According to the U.S. Bureau of Labor Statistics (BLS), which develops employment projects for the nation at large, many changes are looming on the horizon for the 21st century. The occupational lists developed in the Storytelling "Student-Constructed Lists of Occupations by Status" suggest that, as is currently the case, gender, race, and education will help paint the future labor picture.

Although noteworthy changes regarding the distribution of women and people of color have occurred in the labor force, more positive changes are needed. For instance, women workers with 4 or more years of college average about the same income as men who have much less education—1 to 3 years of high school (Herr & Niles, 1994).

According to the BLS, which excludes resident members of the armed forces in its calculations, between 1992 and 2005 the rate of growth of the population and the labor force will be slightly slower than in the previous 13 years (1966–79) because of a decline in the birthrate during the 1960s and 1970s. During this time, about 51 million workers will enter the labor force. Although labor force participation rates for women will increase, these rates will be less rapid than they were in the past. As of 1992, women made up 46% of the labor force, whereas men made up 54%. It is estimated that, by the year 2005, women will compose 48% of the labor force. The rate for men is projected to be 52%.

With respect to race and ethnicity, labor force growth of Latinos and Asians will be much faster than that of African Americans and White non-Latinos. Much of this growth will be attributed to immigration, although higher fertility rates among Latinos and certain Asian ethnic groups explain this growth pattern as well. Because White non-Latinos are the majority of the labor force entrants, they will remain the largest group in the workforce despite a decline in share.

The fastest growing occupations during this time period will be related to health or computers, and many of them may not be considered high status according to the list generated in the Storytelling. In fact, the fastest growing occupations will include workers at all levels of educational attainment. Home health aides require no more than a high school diploma, and systems analysts require a bachelor's degree. Although health-related occupations might be among the fastest growing and many do not require a college degree, workers who have the most education have the highest earnings and the lowest unemployment rates. College graduates are not guaranteed employment, but for this group, the unemployment rate in 1992 was 3.2% and

STORYTELLING
Student-Constructed Lists of Occupations by Status

During a recent discussion of gender and work in my Gender Issues in Counseling course, I asked my students to compile lists of high- and low-status occupations. Pay, prestige, status, expertise, power, and rank were factors to be considered in this list formation. The lists were as follows:

HIGH-STATUS OCCUPATIONS	LOW-STATUS OCCUPATIONS
1. Astronaut	1. Service personnel (waitress, maid, store clerk)
2. High-ranking military official	2. Factory worker
3. Chief executive officer (CEO)	3. Sanitation worker (garbage collector)
4. Physician	4. Mother
5. College professor	5. Day care provider
6. Senator	6. Licensed practical or vocational nurse
7. Chairperson of the board	7. Elementary teacher
8. Psychiatrist	8. Truck/Bus driver
9. Lawyer	9. Dishwasher
10. Engineer	10. Poor farmer
11. Scientist	11. Secretary
12. Successful writer/Artist	12. Road crew worker
13. Architect	13. Fast-food worker
14. Celebrity/Model	
15. Athlete	

During the highly charged process of list formation, another category emerged unexpectedly: middle-status occupations. Certain jobs were difficult to classify as either low or high status. Students felt the need to create a middle category:

MIDDLE-STATUS OCCUPATIONS
1. Electrician
2. Plumber
3. Secondary teacher
4. Registered nurse
5. Guidance counselor
6. Mental health counselor

Once the lists had been compiled, I asked my students to study the lists and make some observations. Some quickly identified that the high-status occupations were occupied by persons with a college education. These occupants were often in positions of power and responsibility. Many not only enforced policy but had the authority to make it, as well as to see that it was implemented. Other students observed that the majority of high-status occupants were men. Very few students, however, zeroed in on the fact that a disproportionate number of occupants on the high-status list were European Americans.* An entirely different situation

---

*Students even discussed that these persons tended to be physically attractive, either with respect to beauty, money, and/or power.

existed for occupants of low-status jobs. The majority of persons in these jobs held very little autonomy on the job and often worked in oppressive situations characterized by minimal pay, nonexistent health care benefits, limited flexibility, and unpredictable job security. More often than not, low-status job occupants were women who may or may not have had a post-high school education, people of color, and men who did not have a college degree.*

The middle-status occupations were composed of some persons who had a 4-year college degree but were engaged in work that is traditionally female (e.g., registered nurse, secondary teacher). "Women's work" of caring for others, both the infirm and the young, is devalued in this society although caregiving is essential to society's maintenance. In response to this situation, an intermediate category was created. Although this group may have been comparable to persons in the high-status occupations, vocational training or lack of a college degree disqualified these jobs as high status; an example of this is well-paid persons who are electricians or plumbers. Gender and race emerged as auxiliary characteristics of occupants in either low-, middle-, or high-status jobs and careers.

Tracy

*The importance of these persons having able bodies was noted.

the median dollar earnings were $46,000. For persons with less than a high school diploma, the unemployment rate was 11.4% and earnings were $18,000. Although education pays more, Black and Latino workers have lower average educational attainment than Whites. Latinos are more likely than Blacks and Whites to have less than a high school diploma. In 1992, over 30% of Latinos had less than a high school diploma, compared with approximately 12% for African Americans.

In the fast-growing careers, African Americans and Latinos are underrepresented. African Americans are overrepresented in slow-growing or declining occupational groups (e.g. laborers, farm workers, transport equipment operators) but underrepresented in the fast-growing occupations discussed above, such as computer systems analyst and health professionals, including physical therapists (Herr & Niles, 1994).

According to the BLS, the three fastest growing occupations will be home health aide, human services worker, and personal health aide. Five of the fastest growing occupations require no more than a high school diploma and are in the service occupations. Three of the top five fastest growing occupations requiring a college degree are closely tied to computer technology and include computer engineer, systems analyst, and operations research analyst.

In 1990, the BLS conducted a study of the employment status of college graduates by major. According to Steinberg (1994), 74% of graduates were in the labor force full time, and 11% worked part-time, or fewer than 35 hours per week. Differences in employment were evident, depending on discipline. For instance, 83% of business and management majors were employed full-time one year after graduation, the average salary was $24,700, and the unemployment rate was 5% (see Table 11.1).

Overall, earnings rise with education for a variety of reasons. According to Amirault (1994),

Many highly paid occupations, such as physician and lawyer, are open only to workers with education beyond the undergraduate level. . . . To some

TABLE 11.1
Selected employment data on graduates by fields

	Rate of full-time employment after graduation (%)	Average salary	Unemployment rate (%)
Business/Management	83	$24,700	5
Education	77	19,100	2
Engineering	85	30,900	3
Health Professions	81	31,500	1
History	58	21,300	8
Humanities	59	19,100	6
Mathematics/Computer Sciences	71	27,200	5
Psychology	60	19,200	7
Public Affairs	77	20,800	5
Social Sciences	68	22,200	5

Source: From "The Class of '90: One Year After Graduation," by G. Steinberg, 1994, in U.S. Bureau of Labor Statistics, Three Articles on College Graduates, *p. 10. Washington, DC: U.S. Bureau of Labor Statistics.*

extent, however, advanced degree holders earn more just because they are older, and incomes rise with age as expertise grows and makes workers more valuable to employers. (p. 21)

SOURCES OF DIFFERENCE AND OCCUPATIONAL CHOICE

More than 50 years ago, Hughes (1945) discussed **auxiliary characteristics.** He said these were subconscious notions that people have about which persons occupy certain positions (see also the Storytelling "Ready to Deal"). For instance, when most people think about an astronaut, the image is usually of a European American, able-bodied male and not Mae Jamison, an African American female. When Dr. Jamison is presented as the astronaut she is, there is surprise and, among some, disbelief.

True vocational choice for women and nonwhites is a newly emerging phenomenon and one of insufficient critical mass (Raskin, 1985). Among many European American women, men and women of color, and persons across various racial groups from low socioeconomic backgrounds, ability or aptitude is not the predominant barrier preventing them from pursuing or seriously considering high-status and well-paying careers. Inadequate exposure to people who work in these jobs and with whom students are able to identify contributes to isolation from careers that are deemed unavailable or out of a student's reach. When a European American female graduate student who was reared in a middle-class home says, "I never knew that I could want to be what I wanted," one has to contemplate whether her able-bodied brother would have made the same statement.

STORYTELLING
Ready to Deal

I had just graduated from my doctoral program at North Carolina State University and had accepted a position at the University of Florida. I knew that my 10-year-old Nissan Sentra without air conditioning would not suffice in the year-round humid and hot Florida weather. My quest was to purchase a new car. Before I exposed myself to the salespeople at the numerous dealerships I had selected, I did my homework. I collected computer printouts on the dealer's costs for the cars I wanted to test-drive. I also secured my voucher from the credit union that allowed me to pay the complete amount for the car I chose. I searched for a car on a weekend at the end of the month, as the consumer books recommended. I also dressed casually and had another female companion with me who rode in the back seat to let me know how it felt to be a passenger. I was ready to deal. I had found the car I wanted, and my printout indicated how much flexibility and negotiating power I had with the salesperson. The salesperson did not seem comfortable with my assertiveness, preparedness, and casual attire. It seemed as though my requests to "deal" were being completely ignored. There was no "wiggle-room" to reduce the price because "if I did not want the car, someone else would buy it as is," the salesman told me. I was angry because I had read the consumer magazines, which said I could negotiate if I was well prepared. The type of behavior I encountered occurred not only at one dealership but at several. I finally found a person at a smaller dealership approximately 40 miles outside Gainesville who was ready to deal. He appreciated my hard work and diligence, and we worked out a dollar amount that was mutually respectful.

Mary

Researchers have found a relationship between career aspirations and occupational attainment (Constantine, Erickson, Banks, & Timberlake, 1998). Among many youths of color residing in urban areas, occupational expectations are lower with respect to career attainment. Again, such lowered expectations may be a function of their environments or "exposure to a circumscribed range of jobs" (Constantine et al., 1998, p. 84).

Men, as are women, are expected to enter into sex-stereotyped occupational roles, and thus their presence in occupational roles such as nurse, elementary teacher, or secretary is limited. Moreover, men's masculinity and sexual orientation are sometimes questioned when career choices are in traditionally female occupations. However, more men are choosing to enter female-dominated occupations. Reasons given for such career choices include (a) more freedom of options, including the right to choose less stressful, less aggressive lifestyles, (b) the ability to pursue personal abilities and self-fulfillment not available in many male sex-typed jobs, (c) increased stability and upward mobility, and (d) increased interactions with the opposite sex (Chusmir, 1990, p. 12).

The ability to name for oneself who one is and what one does or does not want in life has implications for career choice. For a person to know that he or she is entitled to the best implies power. This text talks much of **empowerment**, that self-defining process of carefully chiseling out for the self who the self is. Indeed, this process is arduous, emotionally charged, and can be marked by volatility.

IDENTITY AND VOCATIONAL DEVELOPMENT

Marcia (1980) developed a model of identity in adolescence that is applicable to the route to occupational choice. Within this model are four statuses: (a) achieved identity, (b) foreclosed identity, (c) moratorium identity, and (d) diffused identity.

ACHIEVED IDENTITY

The person with an **achieved identity** is able to articulate his occupational choices and his next steps involved in obtaining short- and long-term goals. A realistic understanding of job requirements exist. The person has said yes to commitment to a career while resolving, through struggle, the crisis of indecision and uncertainty (Raskin, 1985). It is important to note that Frederick Douglass once said, "Without struggle, there is no progress."

FORECLOSED IDENTITY

The person with a **foreclosed identity** has essentially made career decisions that are comforting. She has followed a path of least resistance. Occupation choice is familiar, with few unknowns and little exploration, particularly about the negative aspects of the career path. The person in this status is able to articulate the satisfactions available in this occupation. She also has the belief that extrinsic and intrinsic rewards will accrue to her personally (Raskin, 1985). She has made a commitment to a career, but resolution of the crisis and uncertainty surrounding it has not been completed.

MORATORIUM IDENTITY

The individual characterized with a **moratorium identity** has done considerable exploration regarding a career and recognizes the importance of choosing one. Shades of gray regarding the career are rejected, however, because they are seen as confusing and dissonance provoking. Vocational testing is eagerly sought out so that the person can be told by a reliable source what he can do. The person in this status views an error in judgment or a poor occupational choice as irreparable (Raskin, 1985). He may have made a commitment to a career, but it comes without resolving the crises of decision making about his life work.

DIFFUSED IDENTITY

A person with a **diffused identity** views the world unrealistically. She knows very little about a career or the requirements for obtaining it. She rarely articulates long-term goals and has little need even to envision a career path. Immediate gratification is more important than the possibility of achievement or consistency. The person in this status is easily seduced by glamorous occupations. She has made no commitment to a career and certainly has not been aware of a crisis, let alone resolved it.

GENDER AND CAREER DECISION MAKING

The socialization of many women toward family issues often conflicts with career decision making in that a career can be perceived as a liability for a woman. Larson, Butler, Wilson, Medora, and Allgood (1994) said, "Men are socialized primarily to be the family financial provider, a role expressed through career endeavors; consequently, men's family and career obligations run parallel except where secondary nurturant-expressive roles conflict with career efforts" (p. 79).

The messages given to each gender about career choice are dichotomous and ultimately restricting for both men and women. Berger (1985) discussed the implications of career messages on family considerations. Essentially, roles within the family are segregated wherein "men are responsible for linking the family into the world outside the family while women are primarily responsible for understanding and administering to the emotional needs of family members" (p. 322). If men desire to be more expressive within the family (e.g., staying at home with young children while the wife works outside the home), then a conflict ensues. The socialization scripts concerning men as providers and primary breadwinners erupt and are perpetually played out by those who detect a cross-pattern of emotional and career-related behavior.

Far too often, career choice occupies a dominant position in men's identity development at the expense of family relationships (Larson et al., 1994). Conversely, women may postpone career decisions as they anticipate being away from the workforce to raise children. Operating in new roles can be difficult and stressful, but rewards are involved in forging new territory for men and women. Access to choices and information during the career decision-making process is essential. In this way, both genders can be afforded the best options that are unique to each situation.

Toward making good career choices, Jones (1992) identified several strategies. These include learning about personal aptitudes, abilities, work values, personality characteristics, and environmental or physical constraints. It is also suggested that people learn about the worlds of work and education by exploring occupational fields that are appealing and by understanding the U.S. economic system. Acquiring necessary information, generating alternatives, and making and evaluating a choice are also recommendations. In short, a career choice is one of the most substantial decisions of one's life and ought not be entered into arbitrarily. In addition, workplaces and corporations also need to create an atmosphere where work life, family life, and the meaning of success are discussed openly (Covin & Brush, 1991). Not to do so is to encourage a system of work and family life that is unworkable and disappointing for far too many people.

CAREER COUNSELING

Often, **career counseling** is narrowly viewed as just focusing on a person's vocational interests and matching these interests with a job. Career counseling is broader than this, however, and encompasses the personal side of life throughout the life span. Engels, Minor, Sampson, and Splete (1996) said that career counseling deals with such concerns as "self-understanding; broadening one's horizons; work selection . . . and other intrapersonal matters; work site behavior; communication; and . . . lifestyle issues . . . such as . . . integrating life, work, family and social roles, discrimination, stress, sexual harassment, bias, stereotyping, pay inequities, and "tokenism" (p. 134). The career counselor is in a strategic position to provide guidance to students and transitioning adults as they investigate careers and pursue new ones (see the case study "A Career Issue Is a Personal Issue" at the end of this chapter). Some counselors have executed these duties with finesse despite overwhelming paperwork loads, hundreds of students to whom they are responsible, and dwindling campus resources. Some counselors, however, do students a disservice by sending overt or covert messages that, because of race, gender, and/or socioeconomic class, the students are ill-equipped for college or success in a particular field.

Careers are an integral part of people's lives, livelihoods, self-concepts, and statuses. As important as they are to people's lives, career choices are often made with limited information. Scant knowledge about the match between one's personality traits and those of the job, no consultation with persons currently working within the desired or targeted arena, and lack of research about the job describe a typical process of occupational choice.

Career development theory assists counselors in their capacity to provide career guidance to people faced with career choices. The oldest approach to career choice is *trait-factor theory* (Raskin, 1985). A **trait** is any enduring or persisting character or characteristic of a person by which he or she can be distinguished from another; traits are commonly identified with a statistical procedure called *factor analysis* (Jones, 1992). Trait-factor theory maintains that the closer the match between the person's traits and those in the occupation, the better suited and satisfied the person will be.

One criticism of this theory is that it is not developmentally linked and fails to consider the normal fluctuations in cognitions and behaviors over time. Raskin (1985) said, "It lacks a description of the behavior change process, and an explanation of the behavior change that occurs systematically over time" (p. 26). With this theory, the counselor may be highly active, directive, and offer advice; one potential problem is that the client may feel overwhelmed. This occurs primarily because a lot of information is being shared in a relatively short amount of time.

Holland's (1973) personality types are very popular in career assessment. The six types are realistic, investigative, artistic, social, enterprising, and conventional (Jones, 1981). The *realistic* type describes people who work with tools, machines, and objects and tend to avoid social activities. *Investigative* types prefer observing and studying scientific objects and tend to avoid social activities as well. *Artistic* persons have a preference for working freely and creatively, expressing ideas or feelings through dance, drama, writing, or other art fields; these persons tend to avoid highly ordered or repetitive activities. As the name suggests, *social* types prefer helping or teaching people and tend to avoid working with tools or machines. *Enterprising* types prefer selling or persuading other people and tend to avoid activities that require careful observation or study. Finally, *conventional* types prefer activities involving numbers, records, or clerical materials and tend to avoid those that are not well ordered or that demand creative abilities (Jones, 1981). One of the best known instruments designed to assess the six types is the Holland Self-Directed Search.

Other ways of assessing a person's strengths and skills do not require a standardized test, but rather involve the identification of skills, interests, aptitudes, personality characteristics, life goals, and work values (Salters, 1994). Goldman (1990) discussed the benefit of Occ-U-Sort cards. With this method, the person sorts a list of occupations on cards according to desirable or undesirable occupations. The next step involves assigning reasons why occupations have been classified as they have. This process can be clarifying to clients in that they develop an understanding of their reasons for liking or disliking certain occupations.

IDENTITY CONSTRUCTS AND CAREER COUNSELING

Culture interacts with how young people choose careers. For instance, a traditional Asian student may rely on her parents for guidance about the career path she should take. Such a posture may not translate into failure to be autonomous as much as it may be reflective of some Asian values of deference to parents (Herr & Niles, 1994). Likewise, many urban youths may look to indigenous support persons such as family members, role models within the community, and teachers.

Herr and Niles (1994) discussed a variety of ways schools can integrate cultural awareness into a career education program across the developmental pipeline. These include (a) exposure to culturally different role models, (b) development of a sense of cultural pride and respect for others, (c) clarification of self-concept, (d) exploration of work ethics, (e) commitment to the career-planning process as a means of coping effectively with racism and sexism, and (f) dialogue with parents, teachers, and counselors about career options and possibilities. Another idea is interviewing people currently in jobs to which one aspires and asking people about the roads they took to get where they are (Rendon & Robinson, 1994).

IMPLICATIONS FOR COUNSELORS

In 1991, the National Career Development Association, a subdivision of the American Counseling Association, adopted a list of 10 minimum competencies that professionals engaged in career counseling ought to be able to demonstrate: (a) knowledge of career development theory, (b) individual and group counseling skills, (c) individual/group assessment, (d) information/resources, (e) program management and implementation, (f) consultation, (g) special [diverse] populations, (h) supervision, (i) ethical/legal issues, and (j) research/evaluation (National Career Development Association, 1994).

In addition to proficiency in these 10 areas of competency, counselors need to consider a variety of factors that affect students' career aspirations. Included are gender, race, class, and disability. For instance, little is known about career development for persons with disabilities, yet disability alone is insufficient to determine a person's career path (Enright, Conyers, & Szymanski, 1996). Just as career information and career access differ for persons with disabilities in comparison with those without disabilities, differences exist for specific groups of young people. Despite the challenges that exist for youths as they contemplate their career choices, career counselors can be helpful. Constantine et al. (1998) recommended that counselors (a) be cognizant of how environmental stressors such as poverty and violence interact with students' career aspirations and (b) assist students in their ability to cope with these forces. These authors also recommended that family and community members be involved in students' career development processes, involve students in an awareness of barriers to career development, and design interventions that would enhance students' occupational self-efficacy, such as using a library to identify career information.

The type of communication between child and parent regarding career issues and the pursuit of them is important. Young, Paseluikho, and Valach (1997) analyzed videotaped conversations between parents and their children. The researchers concluded that "the recognition of the parent and adolescent having shared or joint goals, as well as individual goals, holds enormous significance for the emotional quality of the parent-adolescent conversation and for the emergent constructions of career" (p. 42). A sense of being on the "same page" is significant for young people as they plan and shape their careers with their parents.

To provide people with assistance as they maneuver through the maze of making critical career decisions, mentoring is extremely important (see the Storytelling "Books, Not Bricks"). Subtle factors work to result in the sorting, grouping, and tracking of minority and female students in stereotyped patterns that prepare them to accept traditional roles and jobs in adult life. In the university environment, this process is evident from the low numbers of professors of color. It is a struggle for many professors to consider seriously women and people of color for jobs, research opportunities, and other important positions. Women with disabilities face even greater challenges as they confront sexist and able-bodied stereotypes (Enright et al., 1996).

STORYTELLING
Books, Not Bricks

A distinguished African American professor who now works at a large research institution relays a story: When he was in high school, he was planning to take brickmasonry, as this was the path most of his buddies were following. He had a caring teacher who encouraged him to pursue science. That teacher-mentor was the catalyst for his career choice, and now he is very successful and a mentor himself to countless students of all races and ethnicities.

Tracy

Mentoring is more than advising about classes. It involves helping students and young professionals become aware of opportunities, such as conferences, job promotions, research, and writing opportunities, and professional organizations. Mentoring requires a genuine interest in the mentee, who is usually younger than the mentor. It involves guidance but also in many cases nurturance and support.

CASE STUDY
A Career Issue Is a Personal Issue

Merv is a 35-year-old physically healthy African American man with a master's degree in business administration. He is the oldest of four children. He and his wife, Fran, are divorcing after 17 years of marriage and are currently living separately. Fran and Merv married shortly after high school because Fran was pregnant. Their only child, son Lauren, is now 17.

Six weeks ago, Merv was promoted on his job as district manager and is pleased. Despite his accomplishments, he thinks his skills are being underused at work. He goes to a private counseling agency for some assistance to discuss his career frustrations and to contemplate his next career moves. His career counselor is Frank Emerez, who is Puerto Rican.

Merv presents with headaches, stomach disturbances, and insomnia. He attributes these conditions to his new position and to intensified travel and "on the road" eating. Merv feels guilty about the divorce (Fran has not worked outside the home except at volunteer and part-time positions), but he has been unhappy for several years in the marriage. Also, divorce is inconsistent with his parents' ideas (they have been married 41 years) and his predominantly Black church community's position concern-

ing divorce. Although not explicitly stated, Merv does not think the community would be supportive of his recent relationship with Kim, a colleague he has been dating. They have similar career interests and aspirations. Kim is 26 and wants Merv to divorce his wife so that she and he can marry and start a family of their own. Kim is European American. Merv thinks Fran does not understand his career interests and has become too dependent on him. They have very little in common except for their son, who will be going to college next year. Even though Fran does not want the divorce to proceed, she will not go to marriage counseling as Merv has asked. Merv has not told Fran of his relationship with Kim. He has been telling Fran that excessive travel and late night appointments have kept him away from home. He also has not told his parents of his decision to divorce.

QUESTIONS

1. How does culture affect Merv's perspective on his career?
2. How might traditional career assessment measures prove to be ineffective for Merv?

3. How does Frank need to hear Merv's presenting career issues in the light of other information about his personal life that has been revealed?

DISCUSSION AND INTEGRATION
The Client, Merv

Although Merv presents with career concerns, his personal transitions as husband, father of an adolescent son, soon to be divorcé, intimate relationship with a woman outside his race, and manager are looming before him. Merv is seriously contemplating leaving his marriage, possibly starting a new marriage with Kim, contending with feelings of disapproval and disappointment from his elders, and confronting feelings of loss and frustration from a frayed relationship. Undoubtedly, Merv's problem orientation, approach to alternatives, and overall decision-making ability are shaped by his multiple identities that exist within a cultural context.

From a practical perspective, Merv needs to be encouraged to consider seriously whether he is ready to leave one marriage and jump immediately into another. Given that Merv married right out of high school, he has not had time to live as an adult on his own and to experience the freedom of being a single man. Merv needs to ask himself what kind of relationship he wants with Kim, other women, and ultimately himself. Again, he has not had the privilege of this type of introspection, and his answers may surprise him. Also, Merv needs to ask how authentically he believes he is living by living a lie. His behavior—sneaking around to be in a relationship with Kim—is in conflict with his spiritual beliefs and his family values. Thus, a connection between his physical complaints need to be made with the stress of his changing relationships with his wife, his child, his family, and his community. Stress reduction activities, such as meditation, physical exercise, and visualization of what he would like his life to look like, might be helpful.

Another practical consideration is how Merv's relationship with Kim might be affecting his success on the job. It is possible that some of Merv's supervisors disapprove of his relationship with Kim because

of its cross-racial context. It is also possible that Merv is experiencing some racial discrimination. Merv's race and its socially constructed meanings need to be considered.

Washington (1987) stated that, when counseling a Black man,

> the ante is greatly raised. . . . There are more walls, blocks, and barriers evident. He struggles not only with the cultural scripts that define manhood but with a true double-edged sword of gender-role constraints plus racism. The latter, racism, being more formidable than the first. (p. 192)

The Career Counselor, Frank

Frank is able to focus on Merv's desires and wants while appreciating his cultural context. It is also important for Frank to assist Merv in unraveling his career aspirations and in identifying a plan toward their completion. This process would need consideration of how Merv's race, gender, and multiple roles interface with his personal notions of what are appropriate action and strategy for him.

It is likely that Frank will use an array of career and personality assessment materials to give Merv greater insight into himself. These include the Strong Interest Inventory, the Holland Self-Directed Search, and perhaps the Myers-Briggs Personality Inventory.

A lifeline would also be a helpful strategy. This qualitative assessment tool (Goldman, 1990) encourages the client to draw a line and place on it pivotal markers in his or her life—for example, first day of school, moves during childhood, divorces, births of siblings, accidents, awards, college, births of children, and deaths of parents. Such an exercise might provide Merv with greater clarity about his career and an array of personal choices, such as when his dissatisfaction in his marriage began and when his psychosomatic complaints arose.

Clear messages about men being providers and breadwinners have affected Merv. These messages most likely feed into his high level of guilt. Arguably, Merv's cultural context needs careful consideration. In African American culture, emphasis is often on the collective, and elders tend to be held in high esteem. Merv's choices could certainly be interpreted by his community as individualistic and "selling out." Merv's education and occupation place him in a high-status, powerful position. Yet, Washington (1987) said that the assumptions about men as powerful, breadwinners, masters of their fate, and privileged describe many White male Americans but is not necessarily the case for certain Black men, who often are benefactors of male privilege but contend, instead, with an oppressive and racist society.

Merv is powerful and successful. His class will protect him from certain issues with which lower-income African American men coexist. Yet, Merv is a Black man whose class does not make him immune from racial discrimination. It is possible that Merv's job performance needs improvement prior to his obtaining the type of position and promotion he ultimately wants. If this is the case, skill building and professional development through continuing education might be important for Merv to contemplate.

An effective way to focus on Merv is by employing narrative techniques. These help clients "story" their lives and see their careers as stories (Emmett & Harkins, 1997). Harkins (Emmett & Harkins, 1997), who is not a counselor, created the term "StoryTech" (ST) to describe a "structured visioning process." His goal was to help people change their lives by rewriting their life stories through the creation of virtual, albeit possible, futures.

Cognitive restructuring would help Merv hear and reflect on the messages he learned from an early age, such as "Real men stay with their families and provide for their children" or "Once Black men get ahead in the world, they date/marry outside their race." These early tapes received from parents, the educational system, the church, and the media at large are reviewed.

Frank is multiculturally competent and aware of his own culture, his biases, and his client's worldview and is clear about interventions that would help Merv. Frank continues, however, to (a) engage in self-examination, (b) increase self-education, (c) learn the truth about racism (that it is limiting to emotional and psychological development), and (d) be conscious of change agents and initiating institutional changes (Washington, 1987).

A support group might also benefit Merv. Gary (1987) reported that, among a group of African American men who brought their interpersonal conflicts to the attention of mental health providers, the major presenting problems were depression, work difficulties, problems relating to others, family difficulties, anxiety, and marital conflict, in that order. Because Merv is concerned about not being a good father or a good son, he can be encouraged to remember that divorce or remarriage will never change who he is in these pivotal roles, which he deeply cherishes. Merv also could be helped to see that he withstood an unsatisfying marriage for several years in order to fulfill his responsibilities as father and husband.

Ultimately, Merv needs to go somewhere, sit down, and be still before he makes a major decision.

SUMMARY

This chapter focused on the ways the identity constructs of race, gender, and class affect the occupational decisions that people make and that are made for them. The importance of mentoring to prepare people for careers was discussed. Common career models were presented. An identity model illuminated different statuses involved in occupational choice. A case study was provided for the purpose of synthesizing chapter material.

REFERENCES

Amirault, T. A. (1994). Job market profile of college graduates in 1992: A focus on earnings and jobs. In U.S. Department of Labor, Bureau of Labor Statistics, *Three articles on college graduates: Outlook to 2005, The class of '90 in 1991, Earnings and jobs of all graduates* (pp. 21–28). Washington, DC: U.S. Bureau of Labor Statistics.

Berger, M. (1985). Men's new family roles: Some implications for therapists. In P. Riker & E. H. Carmen (Eds.), *The gender gap in psychotherapy: Social realities and psychological processes* (pp. 319–332). New York: Plenum Press.

Chusmir, L. H. (1990). Men who make nontraditional career choices. *Journal of Counseling & Development, 69,* 11–16.

Constantine, M. G., Erickson, C. D., Banks, R. W., & Timberlake, T. L. (1998). Challenges to the career development of urban racial ethnic minority youth: Implications for vocational intervention. *Journal of Multicultural Counseling & Development, 26,* 83–95.

Covin, T. J., & Brush, C. C. (1991). An examination of male and female attitudes toward career and family issues. *Sex Roles, 25,* 393–414.

Emmett, J. D., & Harkins, A. M. (1997). StoryTech: Exploring the use of a narrative technique for training career counselors. *Counselor Education and Supervision, 37,* 60–73.

Engels, D. W., Minor, C. W., Sampson, J. P., & Splete, H. H. (1996). Career counseling specialty: History, development, and prospect. *Journal of Counseling & Development, 74,* 134–138.

Enright, M. S., Conyers, L. M., & Szymanski, E. M. (1996). Career and career-related educational concerns of college students with disabilities. *Journal of Counseling & Development, 75,* 103–114.

Gary, L. E. (1987). Predicting interpersonal conflict between men and women: The case of Black men. In M. Kimmel (Ed.), *Changing men: New directions in research on men and masculinity.* Newbury Park, CA: Sage.

Goldman, L. (1990). Qualitative assessment. *Journal of Counseling & Development, 69,* 11–16.

Herr, E. L., & Niles, S. G. (1994). Multicultural career guidance in the schools. In P. Pedersen & J. Carey (Eds.), *Multicultural counseling in schools: A practical handbook* (pp. 177–194). Boston: Allyn & Bacon.

Holland, J. L. (1973). *Making vocational choices: A theory of careers.* Upper Saddle River, NJ: Prentice Hall.

Hughes, E. C. (1945). Dilemmas and contradictions of status. *Journal of Sociology, 50,* 353–357.

Jones, L. K. (1981). *Occ-U-Sort.* Monterey, CA: CTB/Macmillan/McGraw-Hill.

Jones, L. K. (1992). *The encyclopedia of career change and work issues.* Phoenix, AZ: Oryx Press.

Larson, J. H., Butler, M., Wilson, S., Medora, N., & Allgood, S. (1994). The effects of gender on career decision problems in young adults. *Journal of Counseling & Development, 73,* 79–84.

Marcia, J. E. (1980). Identity in adolescence. In J. Adelson (Ed.), *Handbook of adolescent psychology.* New York: John Wiley.

National Career Development Association. (1994). Ethical standards. In D. W. Engles (Ed.), *The professional practice of career counseling and consultation: A resource document* (2nd ed., pp. 26–33). Alexandria, VA: Author.

Raskin, P. (1985). Identity and vocational development. In A. S. Waterman (Ed.), *Identity in adolescence: Process and contents* (New Directions for Child Development, No. 30). San Francisco: Jossey-Bass.

Rendon, K. I., & Robinson, T. (1994). A diverse America: Implications for minority seniors. In W. Hartel, S. Schwartz, S. Blume, & J. Gardner (Eds.), *Ready for the real world: Senior year experience series* (pp. 170–188). Belmont, CA: Wadsworth.

Salters, L. G. (1994). Career planning. In W. Hartel, S. Schwartz, S. Blume, & J. Gardner (Eds.), *Ready for the real world: Senior year experience series* (pp. 31–55). Belmont, CA: Wadsworth.

Steinberg, G. (1994). The class of '90: One year after graduation. In U.S. Department of Labor, Bureau of Labor Statistics, *Three articles on college graduates: Outlook to 2005, The class of '90 in 1991, Earnings and jobs of all graduates* (pp. 10–20). Washington, DC: U.S. Bureau of Labor Statistics.

Washington, C. S. (1987). Counseling Black men. In M. Scher, M. Stevens, G. Good, & G. A. Eichenfield (Eds.), *Handbook of counseling and psychotherapy* (pp. 192–202). Newbury Park, CA: Sage.

Young, R. A., Paseluikho, M. A., & Valach, L. (1997). The role of emotion in the construction of career in parent-adolescent conversations. *Journal of Counseling & Development, 76,* 1, 36–44.

Chapter 12

Images of Cultural Violence and Empowerment

Wolf Song

Take courage;
Do not be frightened;
Follow where you see me riding my white
horse.

A. Grove Day, The Sky Clears: Poetry of the
American Indians

Violence is one of the most pressing problems in today's society. This chapter explores the cultural and social origins of violence. The literature on the interactions among biology, hormone levels, gender, and aggression are reviewed. Select literature on sexual and domestic violence is presented as it affects both women and men. It is understood that both women and men are both victims and perpetrators of violence, yet the greater emphasis is on women and assault. Attention is also devoted to violence among youths. Violence as a social construct intersecting with race, socioeconomic class, and gender are discussed. Although powerlessness and power receive primary focus in Chapter 14, these themes are integrated where appropriate. The ultimate goal of this chapter is to help counselors understand the psychology of the victim/survivor and move her or him toward healing and wholeness. An important element to the therapeutic relationship is that counselors understand the sociopolitical cultural context in which violence is taught, learned, and transmitted in both subtle and blatant ways. A case study is presented to provide the reader with an opportunity to apply information presented throughout the chapter.

STATISTICS ON VIOLENCE

The statistics are sobering, but they speak of an epidemic of violence in U.S. society: Every 18 seconds, a woman is beaten; every 6 minutes, a woman is raped; one in six college women will be the victim of a rape or attempted rape as an undergraduate; half of all rapes are estimated to be date rapes; at least 1,200 battered women's shelters and 600 rape crises centers are in operation across the country; researchers estimate that 25% of the female and 15% of the male population have experienced child sexual abuse; approximately 60,000 women are in prison, 73% for nonviolent drug offenses, and over half of these women inmates were victims of physical abuse and 36% had been sexually abused; African American women's risk of being homicide victims is 1 in 104, compared with 1 in 369 for European American women; and lesbians are more frequent victims of verbal and physical abuse than the general female population. In fact, a 1990–91 study of 561 lesbians found that 29% had been chased, 10% beaten, 11% spat on, 6% sexually assaulted, 35% threatened, and 82% verbally harassed. Alcohol is a factor in 50% of all rapes, 50% of spousal abuse cases, 70% of child sexual abuse cases, and 40% of family court actions; young Black men ages 15 to 24 are 10 times more likely than their White counterparts to be murdered; less than 3% of all Black men are in jail, but they compose 46% of the prison population. Finally, according to some estimates, 92% of teenage prostitutes were sexually molested in childhood, most by someone known and trusted (Blume,

1990; Kromkowski, 1992; Renzetti & Curran, 1992; Women for Racial & Economic Equality, 1991).

BIOLOGY, GENDER, AND AGGRESSION

The statistics and the literature seem to support two universal facts about crime:(a) The bulk of crime, especially violent crime, is committed by the young persons of any culture, and (b) the greater portion of violent crime is committed by the males of any culture.

Another phenomenon of violence is that it reaches its greatest intensity at two opposite extremes: (a) in conditions of close intimacy between people and (b) in impersonal, stranger-to-stranger situations. Researchers have sought to explain these connections by way of biology. For instance, Raine and Dunkin (1990) argued in favor of a genetic basis for antisocial and criminal behavior and cited ample literature to support their position. One problem with their work is a failure to define important terms, such as *antisocial,* or to discuss thoroughly the conception of "genetic basis." They cited research that stated the criminality rate among adoptive children who had criminality among both biological parents and adoptive parents was 40%. This is compared with just a 12% criminality rate when only the biological parents were criminal and less than 7% when only the adoptive parents were criminal. They concluded that the combined effects of genetic and environmental factors is more significant than the effects of these individual factors. The specific type of "criminality" is not referenced, which leads to speculation: Were they referring to murder, larceny, rape, breaking and entering? Also, neither the frequency of the criminal act nor the contextual factors, such as physical and/or sexual abuse in the home of the offender, was mentioned.

Although Raine and Dunkin (1990) asserted there are no genes for criminality, they did maintain that genes exist that "code for proteins and enzymes and that influence psychophysiological and other biological characteristics, depending on environmental context and developmental factors, may or may not give rise to antisocial behavior" (p. 638).

Other prominent researchers and scientists have had similar viewpoints that argued in favor of a connection between biology and aggression. Psychologists Eleanor Maccoby and Carol Nagy Jacklin (1974) concluded from their review of the literature on sex differences that sufficient evidence exists to support a greater tendency for aggression among males. This conclusion was made despite other studies that showed women to be just as aggressive as men in experiments devised to equalize such factors as gender of investigator, gender of hypothetical victims, empathy with hypothetical victims, and guilt feelings (Fausto-Sterling, 1992). In addition to their claim that males are more aggressive, Maccoby and Jacklin reported the following as evidence of sex-related differences in human aggression: (a) Aggression is related to levels of sex hormones, (b) similar sex differences are found in humans and nonhumans, and (c) sex differences are formed early in life, before adult socialization could cause them.

Biologist Anne Fausto-Sterling (1992) extensively examined the literature on sex differences and aggression. In doing so, the popular notion that testosterone is responsible for aggressive and violent behavior in men was strongly refuted. She stated,

> When carefully examined, the biological literature offers little support for the idea that high levels of "male" hormone cause human aggression. Nor does the idea that analogous sex differences in aggression exist in humans and in nonhuman primates hold much water. (p. 148)

In sum, she would have her readers know that there is no substantiated truth to the claim that fetal hormones make boys more active, aggressive, or athletic than girls.

When examining the findings of studies about sex differences in aggression, it is important to attend to the methodological integrity of the studies. Fausto-Sterling (1992) noted that a positive correlation between testosterone level and aggression does not mean that testosterone causes aggression. One basic tenet of statistics is that correlation and causation are very different. In fact, an elevated testosterone level may result from aggressive behavior. Fausto-Sterling argued that the weight of evidence suggests no reliable correlation between level of testosterone, produced by the testes, and acts of aggression. This issue is controversial, as demonstrated by Moir and Jessel's (1991) assertion that "the male brain pattern is tuned for potential aggression . . . In the opposite direction, hormones play an important part in making woman the less aggressive sex" (p. 79). And although history informs us of a time when surgical removal of rapists' genitalia fueled the belief that the violent behavior would be curtailed, Fausto-Sterling (1988, 1992) reported that castration, physical or chemical, does little to lessen aggressive behavior, although it does reduce sexual activity of habitual rapists and child molesters. The testes produce testosterone, which does, in fact, contribute to sexual potency. Yet, *sexual potency* and *aggression* are not synonymous terms. The research does show that stress lowers the testosterone level, which is why women in more highly stressful positions have lower levels of testosterone than women who are not in highly stressful situations. Fausto-Sterling (1992) warned that to conduct research effectively, it is imperative that meanings be clarified and definitions operationalized.

As of late, the established scientific community does not attribute criminality to abnormal chromosomes (see the Storytelling "Y Oh Y"). Instead, it is now known that restricted mental intelligence is associated with criminal behavior, and not biologically linked aggression that is associated with criminality. Clearly, how aggression develops is complex. There are many interacting causes; therefore, one sole cause should not be identified. Factors other than gender play a role, including biological differences in reactivity, social circumstances of the family and the society, and birth order within the family (Fausto-Sterling, 1992).

STORYTELLING
Y Oh Y

A story that arose several years ago illustrates the strength of biological myths surrounding gender. After a man had been arrested for murdering several women, reporters wrongly claimed that the man had an extra Y chromosome. A flurry of articles followed that debated the connection between criminality and the XYY syndrome. Basically, the misguided thinking went something like this: If one Y chromosome causes aggression, imagine what two would do!

Tracy

GENDER ROLES, POWER, AND AGGRESSION

Gender roles are the blueprint for all power relationships because power is the infrastructure of the sex-gender system. **Power** is the process whereby individuals (or groups) gain or maintain the capacity to impose their will on others despite opposition. Invoking or threatening punishment, as well as offering or withholding rewards, is also a part of this dynamic. The United States often measures human worth in terms of power. Manhood and masculinity are frequently assessed by the ability to exert power over others, particularly women and those males perceived as weaker. At an early age, males are taught to expect to use aggression as a resource or benefit toward targeted goals even if unabashed competitiveness is the means by which stated goals are accomplished. As stated in Chapter 7, beauty and sexuality have been women's conventional resources for success and self-worth. Women have been socialized to compete with one another, thereby using their power for success (e.g., the procurement of beauty, securing men).

This current particular definition of power does not embody the creative, empowering, and ennobling aspects of power; thus, from a holistic perspective, it is a limited and restricted viewpoint. The healing and therapeutic dimensions of power, particularly within the counseling relationship, are discussed in Chapter 13.

Differences between sex roles and gender roles, disparities in size and strength, as well as women's lactating capacities, formed the cornerstone of the sex-gender system. As a reminder, in this work, *gender roles* refers to socially constructed concepts, psychological traits, and family, occupational, and political roles; *sex roles* points to behaviors determined by an individual's biological sex, such as menstruation, pregnancy, lactation, erection, and orgasm. And although these terms are often confused, such confusion allows for institutional perpetuation of an unjust system. It appears that, in many if not most societies, men's contributions, responsibilities, and activities are more highly valued than women's.

YOUTHS AND VIOLENCE

Violence has many forms and faces. As stated earlier, persons who tend to be most responsible for violent crime are young males. It appears that African American men 15 to 24 years old residing in predominantly Black urban areas are more likely the victims of crime as well.

According to the U.S. Department of Health and Human Services (1994), between 1987 and 1992 the homicide death rate per 100,000 for 15- to 34-year-old Black males increased from 91.1 to 134.2. The rate for all 15- to 34-year-old males increased from 22.0 to 31.6. Poverty, drug abuse, unemployment, academic failure, feelings of hopelessness, gang involvement, and lack of adequate adult mentoring, involvement, and supervision are among the explanations for these disturbing figures.

Although the above data focus on young Black men, adolescence is a transitional and difficult time for youths across race, gender, and class. For instance, nearly half of all violent juvenile crime occurs between the 6-hour period of 2:00 P.M. and 8:00 P.M. (Adolescent Pregnancy Prevention Coalition of North Carolina [APPCNC], 1998).

These startling figures indicate that youths are extremely vulnerable to perpetrating or being victimized by crime after school. Lack of constructive after-school programs that promote healthy social and academic skills and preventive behaviors increases significantly the likelihood of adolescents becoming involved in crime (APPCNC, 1998). Community and parental involvement are essential in order for youths to learn adaptive behaviors. Granted, these are challenges for youths contending with dangerous environments characterized by gangs, poverty, and high unemployment; however, the ability to resist and to exhibit resiliency has often been bypassed in the literatures. Steward et al. (1998) conducted a study of 208 African America high school freshmen in an urban area. The researchers found that adolescents who reported the most positive psychological adjustment were engaged in demanding activity, diversion, use of family, use of self-reliance, and use of social and spiritual support. It is important to build on the strengths of young people while helping them effectively negotiate the realities facing them. Education, connection to community, humor, and spiritual linkage are vital to this process.

DOMESTIC VIOLENCE

It is astounding that, in the privacy of her home, the likelihood of a woman being assaulted by her partner is greater than that of a police officer being attacked on the job (Renzetti & Curran, 1992). Estimates are that 2 to 6 million women each year are abused by their partners. Kanuha (1994) reported that more than rape, auto accidents, and muggings combined, wife beating results in more injuries that necessitate medical intervention. Although many people may believe that this problem is more common among lower class men, who in feeling economically and occupationally powerless seek to recoup lost power by exerting dominance toward wives or partners, domestic abuse is a national phenomenon that crosses socioeconomic lines (see the Storytelling "Where There's a Will . . . ").

Part of the problem with stereotypes about which populations are battered and who batterers are is related to cultural attitudes about marriage and relationships. According to a survey about everyday life, nearly 28% of married people indicated that slapping a spouse may be necessary or normal (Renzetti & Curran, 1992). It is not uncommon in families where incest and other forms of violence occur that members hold stereotypical views of male and female gender roles, with males being viewed as dominant, powerful, and even physically abusive, and females being viewed as dependent, weak, and obedient (Hoorwitz, 1983).

Clearly, societal forces do not support a woman's choice to exit a violent marriage. Yet, why do women stay in situations that cause them considerable psychological and, in many cases, physical harm? Although from the outside it may appear that a woman is passive in her oppressed state, many women do attempt escape and have done so repeatedly without success (Wilson, Vercella, Brems, Benning, & Renfro, 1992).

Some theories based on psychological, socioeconomic, and cultural factors have been offered to explain why women remain in abusive situations. Perhaps one of the most salient factors in a woman's decision to remain in an abusive relationship is her fear about her safety and her life (Russell & Uhlemann, 1994). From a family systems perspective, some women as children were exposed to violence in their families of origin. Such early socialization may have unconsciously reinforced that their desires and voices were not worthy of expression or acknowledgement (Russell & Uhlemann, 1994). The genesis of violence in many relationships precedes marriage or cohabitation and, in fact, is often experienced initially in high school dating relationships (Gryl, Stith, & Ward, 1991).

Economic reasons also need to be considered as a factor in women's decisions to remain in abusive relationships. Many women are dependent on their husbands or partners for their livelihood and their children as well. A gross imbalance exists in the

STORYTELLING
Where There's a Will . . .

I knew a woman who was once in a battering relationship with her economically successful husband. To escape, she wrote her grocery check $5 over the amount each week and gave the money to a friend to keep for her. After two years of scrimping and saving, she was able to purchase a bus ticket for herself and her child. She left this abusive situation, never to return. She eventually returned to school and completed her college degree, as well as her master's degree.

Tracy

American structural power system, where women are often dependent on men for their economic vitality. Renzetti and Curran (1992) maintained that societies that are rape-free (and arguably batter-free) have a different structural system, in which women are not socially and economically dependent on men; they have control over resources and make decisions alongside men.

Another barrier to exiting a battering situation is the belief in one's psychological and emotional dependence on a man for one's livelihood. Such learned helplessness and distorted sense of self undoubtedly influence a woman's decision to exit a relationship even if it is abusive. Wilson et al. (1992), in a study of 159 women volunteers who had reported to a domestic violence shelter, found a positive relationship between severity of abuse and learned helplessness. The authors indicated this could be explained as follows: First, women who feel less helpless may be less likely to become victims of the same severity of abuse as women who feel more helpless. "Second, increasingly severe abuse may result in increasing levels of helplessness" (p. 65).

Access to resources enables people to impose their wills and desires on other individuals and groups who lack comparable resources. Control over others, which tends to be a male socialization pattern, rests on the power to make decisions. The power to make institutional decisions and to dictate who is deserving or undeserving places the powerholders in a powerful position. A male primary breadwinner who decides how household income will or will not be spent is in a position of power that weighs heavily on those affected by his decisions.

Cultural values provide the primary foundation for gender role socialization. Gender role messages, which often have inflexible religious overtones, affect people's notions of appropriate conduct in relationships. For many women, beliefs about fidelity to, and loyalty in, a relationship reinforce being battered by their husbands or boyfriends. In a 1989 documentary about battered women produced by Lee Grant, an abused woman tells a story of how the pastor's wife responded when queried about the bruise on her arm. Confiding that she had been hit by her husband, the pastor's wife replied, "Oh, he beat you into submission." I wonder how many times this woman had been beaten by her religious husband.

Although European American and middle-class women are more likely to use the services of private physicians or health insurance programs for mental health assistance, the majority of women of color in battering situations are more likely to seek aid through hospital emergency rooms, community health clinics, or social services (Kanuha, 1994). Perceptions among many battered women of color that mental health providers are not welcoming and relevant places for care discourage them from help seeking. Many non-English-speaking women have restricted access to transportation, child care difficulties, and previous racist encounters with mental health providers; thus, help seeking is even more compromised. Bui and Takeuchi (1992), in their study of ethnic minority adolescents' use of mental health facilities, found that poverty status is associated with a higher number of episodes, dropping out of treatment, and shorter periods in treatment.

Despite the women's movement and marked increases in the percentage of women attending college, gross societal inequities based on gender remain. This inequity is manifested, for example, in differential pay between men and women. Following a divorce, the woman's income is much more likely to fall, whereas the man's usually increases (Renzetti & Curran, 1992). Kirp, Yudof, and Franks (1986) stated,

> The present system contains unexpected pitfalls, especially for the poor and for mothers of young children. Indigent divorcées not only get small awards, as would be expected, but are frequently denied any help. Even women who have been homemakers for many years don't usually obtain alimony unless their husbands are well off. Mothers of young children who get divorced after brief marriages fare worst of all. (p. 182)

Certainly, this type of gender injustice is discouraging to women who seek to leave an oppressive home environment. If they have young children, they may be less likely to get any substantial support, emotional or financial. Many women simply feel as if they are in a catch-22 situation: If they stay, they remain battered; but if they leave, they may experience battery of yet a different kind within the very system that alleges protection and impartial justice.

Many people who feel less powerful commonly perceive themselves as lacking the ability to create opportunity or to take responsibility to transform a toxic situation. Unfortunately, a consequence of this perception is not leaving the home and remaining stuck. The potential for empowerment and growth may more likely be realized when a woman is outside an abusive situation that systematically reduces her voice and compromises her development.

SOCIAL AND CULTURAL NOTIONS OF SEXUAL VIOLENCE

More than domestic violence or any other crime, rape is the one crime women fear the most (Renzetti & Curran, 1992). Rape has several definitions. Muehlenhard, Powch, Phelps, and Giusti (1992) concluded that many definitions of rape focus on penile-vaginal intercourse; however, some definitions include anal and oral intercourse and penetration with objects. Other authors have broadened the definitions of rape to include any type of sexual activity that is not consensual. Muehlenhard et al., however, indicated that when penetration is not involved, other terms are used to describe the activity.

The fear that many women have of rape derives not only from the fact that rape is a serious crime but also from its association with other serious offenses, such as robbery and homicide. Moreover, women's fear of rape is related to their perceived risk of being raped. In the United States, 10 women are raped every hour, or 1 every 6 minutes. The fear of being victimized increases enormously after seeing how a relative's or friend's life was irrevocably changed from sexual violence.

Despite its high rate of occurrence, rape has one of the lowest arrest and conviction rates. For instance, in 1988, rape accounted for 6% of violent crimes, yet arrests for rape were less than 2% of total arrests for violent crimes. Only about 1 in 150 suspected rapists is ever convicted (Renzetti & Curran, 1992).

Because of society's devaluation of women, which includes women devaluing other women, the common belief is that rape victims have done something to invite their assaults. This mentality results in women who have been victimized having to prove that what they say happened actually did.

Renzetti and Curran (1992) indicated that many myths about women exist in the culture, such as that women enjoy being taken by force. The mass-produced images of sexual violence against women contribute to this falsehood. Research suggests, however, that sexual images per se do not facilitate aggressive behavior or change attitudes about rape. Distinctions, then, are made between sexual explicitness and ensuing violence against women. For instance, *aggressive pornography* is defined as X-rated images of sexual coercion in which force is used or implied against a woman to obtain certain sexual acts, as in scenes of rape and other forms of sexual assault. Research has found that exposure to this type of pornography may alter the observer's perception of rape and of the rape victim (Donnerstein & Linz, 1987). Where a woman displays a "positive" or pleasurable reaction to sexual violence, the observer tends to be less sensitive to rape, have a greater acceptance of rape myths and interpersonal violence against women, and increase the self-reported possibility of raping (Donnerstein & Linz, 1987, p. 201). Moreover, within a laboratory context, exposure to aggressive pornography increases the acceptability of aggression against women.

Another myth is that when women say no, they really mean yes. This myth is clearly a blatant devaluation of women's voices as it fails to give women authority over their own meanings—that somehow the content of their voices is subject to a higher, legitimating power that happens to be male. Also prevalent is the irrational belief that women falsely accuse men of rape out of shame or revenge and that this supposedly leads to stricter rules of evidence in rape cases that place the burden of proof on the victim.

Although rape is a violation, the reporting of sexual assault cases is largely a function of the interpersonal dynamic. For instance, acquaintance rape, which occurs when the victim knows or is familiar with the assailant, is much less likely to be reported. Nonconsent has been raised in assessing date rape. Whether "no means no" is subject to individual interpretation within a cultural climate that adheres to certain myths, such as that if a man has had previous sexual encounters with a woman, he has a right to her sexually. The existence of a previous sexual relationship between partners does not entitle either party to sex if one party now refuses.

Other common myths about rape include the following: (a) Only young, physically attractive women get raped; (b) women provoke men by teasing them and by the way they walk or dress; (c) a wife cannot be raped by her husband; (d) men cannot be raped; (e) most rapists are sick or mentally ill; (f) most rapes are interracial; and (g) most rapes take place on isolated streets or in dark alleys. Regarding traditional definitions of rape, Muehlenhard et al. (1992) stated that rape can only be labeled as such if there is penile-vaginal intercourse, and the perpetrator must be a stranger who has a weapon. Moreover, the victim, police, prosecutor, and jury all must agree that the incident was actually rape. This definition basically endorses many of the myths of rape stated above and ultimately serves to advantage men over women. Fortunately, other definitions are much broader than this one and state "any form of nonconsensual sexual activity" (Muehlenhard et al., 1992, p. 28).

Many people are surprised to learn that 60% to 80% of rapes are estimated to be date or acquaintance rapes (see the case study "Acts of Faith" at the end of this chapter). Despite the frequency of date rapes, the vast majority of them go unreported; women raped by strangers are 10 times more likely to report the crime than women raped by acquaintances. Research by Koss, Eidyce, and Wisniewski (1987; cf. Renzetti & Curran, 1992) revealed that one in eight female college students reported being victimized during the preceding 12-month period; 84% of those who had been victims of completed rapes knew their assailants; and two thirds were assaulted by dates. What a terrible burden of silence.

In research conducted by Scully (1988), rapists' attitudes about women were revealed. Both admitters and deniers of rape indicated that the women they assaulted had absolutely no value outside the objectified roles they were forced to maintain in the rapes. Some men took a disturbingly common cultural view of women as sexual commodities, which means they are stripped of human status and reduced to malleable objects for a man's gratification. It is not that the rapists failed to understand their actions; many of them knew what they were doing. However, empathy and concern for the victims were lacking. The rapists felt a sense of satisfaction in their belief that their victims felt powerless, humiliated, and degraded. And these feelings are precisely those that rapists want their victims to have. Many men who rape women have stated that if a significant woman in their lives were raped, they would have some anger and perhaps even resort to violence. Clearly, the significant women in these men's lives are objects to be possessed as well.

Can such rapists be distinguished from nonrapists? The psychological profile of rapists is strikingly similar to that of nonrapists. In fact, psychologists are consistently unable to discriminate between rapists and nonrapists through psychological tests because the rapists appear to be "normal." Values, attitudes, and the social structure in which men and women are socialized in the United States may help explain this similarity between men who rape and men who do not.

A component of this social structure involves race. Not surprisingly, race is a variable in the prosecution and outcomes of rape cases. LaFree (1980; cf. Renzetti & Curran, 1992) stated that "the severity of official sanctions imposed on men for the sexual violation of women will depend on the relative power of the suspect, determined in part by the race of each" (pp. 852-853). African Americans accused of victimizing European Americans are treated more harshly within the criminal justice system, especially when a Black man is charged and convicted of raping a White woman. More specifically, Black men are more likely to have their cases filed as felonies, to be sentenced to prison rather than probation, to receive longer prison sentences, and to be incarcerated in a state penitentiary as opposed to a local jail or minimum security facility (Renzetti & Curran, 1992). White men, in contrast, receive more lenient treatment.

Views on the impact of race within the justice system vary, of course. Wilbanks (1994) argued that although racial prejudice and discrimination exist within the criminal justice system, the system itself and as a whole is not racially prejudiced or discriminatory against Blacks.

CHILDHOOD SEXUAL ASSAULT

What is *incest*? Is it limited to the father-daughter relationship? Blume (1990) expanded the definition of incest beyond immediate family members and penetration to

> the imposition of sexually inappropriate acts, or acts with sexual overtones, by—or any use of a minor child to meet the sexual or sexual/emotional needs of—one or more persons who derive authority through ongoing emotional bonding with that child. (p. 4)

This definition, then, includes the neighbor next door, the schoolteacher, a friend of the family, an aunt, as well as the child's biological father or stepfather (see the Storytelling "Let the Healing Begin").

Incest can be and has been discussed within the context of a patriarchal system, in which men (who represent the majority of violators) dominate women through primary control of financial resources. The system also views children and women as subordinate and in many contexts fosters women's dependency on men. The belief that women are objects contributes to men not taking responsibility for their actions, which can lead to blaming women and young girls for being sexually violated. This blaming appears to be what Hoorwitz (1983) did when he placed blame on a wife for her husband's sexual violation of their daughter. Essentially, Hoorwitz stated that the wife abandoned her husband emotionally, which deprived him of essential emotional

STORYTELLING
Let the Healing Begin

On a cold, rainy, Friday evening, 24 young African American women gathered for a church retreat. They anticipated sisterhood and rejuvenation from many of the pressures of work and school. What unfolded was the sharing of stories and the breaking of silence. Of the 24, 8 had had sexual violation in their childhoods—one in three. After a while, the women began to reveal their pain and to talk openly about loss through personal defilement.

Although breaking silence is the beginning of the healing process, it is not the end. A new self has to be reconstructed—one sculpted in the woman's own image. Where love abides, there is hope. Many of the women attending the retreat have received counseling or have been involved in group work to heal. Churches can do this type of work by training ministers, deacons, teachers, and other mature volunteers to listen and to reflect feeling and genuine empathy. If need be, spaces of healing where people come together to support and to be supported need to be created. One thing is essential: The silence must be broken for the healing to begin.

Tracy

support. Thus, the man's incestuous behavior was a result of his anger toward a neglectful wife. The man's stress and feelings of powerlessness can lead him to usurp his power in the home through domination of his wife and child. Hoorwitz's (1983) view is hard to listen to, although it is 17 years old. It blames the wife for the husband's "sexual use" of his daughter. Regardless of the nature of the relationship between a husband and his wife and his feelings of frustration about this relationship or any other life conditions, such as a stressful job or normal existential angst, there is never any acceptable excuse for incest. In this same article, Hoorwitz suggested that incest was a stress-coping strategy used by men. In addition, other methods to cope with stress were also encouraged.

Women, too, function in the role of perpetrator. Women have a large degree of latitude with children in their role as caretakers. A new body of research suggests that women are sexually victimizing children at much higher rates than were earlier suspected (Priest & Smith, 1992). This phenomenon is underreported.

REACTIONS TO BEING VIOLATED

The aftereffects of sexual assault on people's lives can be devastating. Once a person has been victimized, however, the person need not remain a victim. Many people grow to become empowered survivors and even move to being advocates and activists. Because boundaries are not adequately established for people who are assaulted as children to protect themselves, a substantial relationship exists between childhood victimization rates and later incidents in adulthood.

One of the most pernicious outcomes of violence is the terror that many victims of violence feel. Those who fear becoming victims experience a high degree of anxiety and stress that resembles a sense of being out of control. Ratican (1992) indicated that, in comparison with persons who have not been abused, survivors tend to have "higher levels of anxiety, depression, self-destructive and suicidal tendencies, and difficulties with intimate relationships" (p. 33).

Some normal reactions accompany feelings of being violated. They include shock, rage, confusion, fear, self-castigation, resentment, bitterness, denial, and feelings of being spoiled, soiled, dirty, tainted, ruined, or worthless. Chronic depression is also a well-known reaction to childhood sexual abuse. Even in elderly women who were abused as children, the residual effects are evident (Allers, Benjack, & Allers, 1992).

From incestuous relationships, the female victim often has negative views of herself, evidences lack of confidence about her competence in social arenas, suffers from disturbances around sexuality, and has a tendency to meet nonsexual social and emotional needs with sex (Blume, 1990). Essentially, sexual abuse attacks the core sense of self, wherein the survivors believe that, in addition to something bad being done to them, they, too, are bad, worthless, soiled (Ratican, 1992). The intense work of self-construction is done within the context of abuse. Thus, if the abuse occurred in childhood, then the self gets misshapen.

Some survivors have shut down their feelings because feeling is too painful. Depression is common, as are seemingly baseless crying, difficulty getting out of bed, and feelings of hopelessness. Yet, many survivors have lived with such feelings for the majority of their lives, and they have yet to learn that a different as well as better way of being in the world is possible. Anger issues are also common—more specifically, the inability to recognize, own, or express anger, or perhaps even intense hostility toward the entire gender or ethnic/racial group of the perpetrator. In specific situations of violence, counseling is required to help victims regain their sense of equilibrium that was disturbed by being violated. For women, dealing with rage and anger may be not only a new experience but also a scary one. Socialization experiences have taught many women to fear and deny their own anger because it is inconsistent with the accommodating, selfless, and sweet image of femininity. Unfortunately, this disfigured image denies women their own voice and access to emotion, which is crucial to the healing process. Counselors also need to know that, given the stage of recovery, some survivors feel a need to identify with or protect their abusers (Ratican, 1992).

MALE SURVIVORS OF SEXUAL VIOLENCE

For men, being overcome physically or sexually or both is inconsistent with the ideals of masculinity and being a protector. As mentioned earlier, some people actually believe that a man cannot be raped. For the man who is a survivor of childhood sexual assault, the typical socialization processes of restricting emotion, being powerful and aggressive, and not needing help and asking for help (which is an indication of weakness) greatly interfere with help seeking (Good & Mintz, 1990). Men who are survivors of childhood abuse and adulthood rape require psychological assistance to deal effectively with the trauma of having been violated. The counselor should reframe the situation so that the client can understand that he was not in a position to protect himself for reasons he may not see as legitimate (e.g., being a child, being overpowered, being threatened and deciding to survive instead of fight back). Feelings of powerlessness, which are incompatible with what most men are socialized into, is yet another dimension of the counseling event with which the skilled counselor can empathize. Believing that the client, independent of how depressed he may be, is oriented to healing and having the ability to wait with the client for this unfolding process is one of the most effective tools a counselor can have.

EMPOWERING SURVIVORS OF VIOLENCE

Rebuilding after violation is possible. A variety of coping factors are employed after abuse. In a study of 67 adult rape survivors, Frazier and Burnett (1994) found that coping strategies included precautionary measures such as checking the door before opening it, monitoring intake of alcohol, feeling glad to be alive, trying to focus the mind on positive thoughts, and keeping busy. More than half of the women (57%) indicated that some positive change took place as a result of the rape;

some women grew spiritually, others appreciated the quality of their interpersonal relationships, and others engaged in reflective examination of their lives.

An African proverb states that it takes an entire village to raise a child. As a preventive measure to violence, communities need to implement programs that provide a safety net for children wherein they feel connected to others in a meaningful way—and feel that they have viable life choices and are accountable to other people.

Intervention strategies for facilitating the empowerment of people include (a) self-help or consciousness-raising groups, (b) therapist-run groups, and (c) individual psychotherapy. Other ways to increase feelings of empowerment in one's life involve self-defense training and wilderness/survival expeditions.

Sometimes power comes when the survivor confronts the abuser. This should be done only if the survivor is ready. For some, confrontation of the perpetrator may not ever be desired or recommended. Breaking the secrecy, however, is part of the healing. In doing this, myths are shattered. To break the silence, trust is an important dynamic, and understandably many survivors are slow to trust others or are unable to trust at all.

Difficulties with sex in marriage or in intimate relationships is common among survivors of sexual violence, even with spouses and other loved ones. The intimacy of marriage serves to intensify any existing problems a single person may have. It is important to begin dealing with the heaviness and weight of childhood sexual violence prior to marriage.

IMPLICATIONS FOR COUNSELORS

Pinderhughes (1989) said that feelings of the less powerful include less comfort and pleasure, depression, exhaustion, being trapped, helplessness, fear of abandonment, and fear of one's own anger at the powerful. Counselors need to understand that these feelings are normal and part of the healing process. Working with survivors of any type of abuse is bound to touch feelings within the therapist (Ratican, 1992). To be most effective, counselors need to work through their own feelings of anger, sadness, and rage. This type of intense work needs to be done outside the context of providing therapy to a client. Counselors may wish to consider their own personal therapeutic contact or rely on established social and emotional supports.

In schools, guidance counselors can encourage teachers to refer children who might be in vulnerable situations. Sudden and unexplained changes in a child's demeanor (e.g., increased aggressiveness, injury prone, extreme sadness or clinginess or both) and inappropriate sexual play, gestures, and/or language may be warning signs that the child is unable to communicate verbally (F. Cress-Welsing, personal communication, July 9, 1998). Any statements from children about being abused sexually by other children or by adults need to be investigated swiftly and the appropriate school and local authorities (e.g., social services) notified.

Stopping violence involves a multipronged approach. But cultural values and practices need to be examined. For example, addictions are common in the United

States. Alcohol is a factor in 70% of child sexual abuse cases, 50% of all rapes, and 50% of all spousal abuse cases. Although these statistics are in no way glamorous, alcohol and nicotine are glamorized by the advertising industry in both subtle and blatant ways. In many ads, women are depicted as passive and mindless objects with no real power. The phallic is often emphasized for men. As long as women and their bodies are viewed as objects to be conquered and possessed, sex will continue to be seen as something that men get or take from women. Common values in the United States, such as patriarchy, domination, and control, serve to reinforce the prevailing attitudes regarding women and persons perceived to be weaker, such as children and gay men. To believe that such values bear no relationship to violence against women, children, and those perceived as powerless is to fail to understand the enormous impact cultural learning has on human behavior.

CASE STUDY
Acts of Faith

Renee is a 33-year-old Native American Indian woman who is a survivor of a date rape. She is from a working-class family and has two brothers. Her father is a carpenter, and her mother is a nurse's aide. Although Renee is very quiet and shy, she is extremely friendly, very giving of her time and resources (despite her financial limitations), and works very hard to be helpful to others. She is active in her church and spends time working in the soup kitchen and running errands for the sick and shut-in. In fact, it is not unusual for her to maintain long fasts from food for 1 to 2 weeks. Her spiritual devotion is admired by her friends and her church minister. She stays very busy and yet has difficulty completing long-term projects, such as graduate school programs. At times, she moves very slowly and takes more time than normal to complete simple tasks, such as getting ready to go to church and finishing a paper for class. At other times, she has extremely high energy and is able to accomplish multiple tasks by staying up all night for a few days. None of her friends have ever seen her angry. Renee's therapist, Clara Emille, told Renee that she seemed depressed. It had been 10 years since the rape, and Renee basically thought that if she stayed busy enough she would not remember. Recently, she announced that she was leaving her second graduate program prior to completion to begin another program that was more consistent with her life calling.

QUESTIONS

1. What is the connection between Renee's date rape and her current behaviors?
2. Can clinical depression mask itself in hyper-productivity?
3. How does society's gender-cultural values of productivity and women's service to others interfere with an accurate assessment of Renee's issues?
4. Could you counsel Renee's rapist? Why or why not?

DISCUSSION AND INTEGRATION
The Client, Renee

Although Renee does evidence symptoms of retarded psychomotor activity, she also has periods of mania. It appears that Renee may have a bipolar disorder. Renee's service to others in church, selflessness, high productivity (during manic periods), and cheery demeanor can camouflage the well of sadness within.

As much as Renee is committed to God, her long fasts from food may function as a way of not feeling—a means of anesthetizing herself from the horrible pain and memory of being sexually violated.

This violation in the context of her spiritual belief of God as protector exacerbates her feelings of confusion. Renee is experiencing a crisis of faith and most likely questions, If God is protector, savior, and friend, why would God allow an act that is so violating, especially to me, one of God's own? Disruptive to peace are those who give answers that trivialize her pain and reduce God to a powerless and cruel cretin. Moreover, her devout religiosity may be an attempt to seek redemption from feelings of guilt, shame, and disgust regarding what was done to her.

It was most likely very difficult for Renee to report for counseling. Some Native American Indians tend not to disclose personal or family matters to outsiders. In addition, Renee was initially suspicious of her counselor, as many Native American Indians tend to be (Dufrene & Coleman, 1994). Overall, Renee needs to be commended for seeking help with a personal problem that had become unmanageable. Although Renee is filled with feelings of shame for needing counseling, the counseling will provide her with a safe place to heal fully. It takes an incredible amount of energy to reach our for help when one's personal coping strategies are exhausted. Part of the massive depression she is experiencing may stem from the untapped rage she feels that is being turned inward (as manifested through the disordered eating), rather than channeled outside herself. Women tend not to be socialized to experience their anger. Given that it is often construed as contradictory to relationship building, it is likely that Renee's intense anger is frightening, even to herself.

The Counselor, Clara Emille

Well-meaning counselors often want a bag of tricks to help in difficult and confusing situations. What clients need are effective counselors who allow people to tell their stories and to wait with them, in a spirit of faith, until they are able to pass over to higher ground. Sometimes, the best a counselor can do with a client is to be with her or him and to listen when necessary to provide much-needed comfort. It might be helpful for Clara to ask Renee what helps her usher in feelings of serenity and calm.

Life transitions can affect faith, particularly when the person feels abandoned by God. The sensitive counselor is able to hear a crisis of faith in a client and is aware of how to refer the client to qualified spiritual help. Fowler and Keen (1978) developed a 6-stage theoretical model of faith development that "focuses on the making of meaning through the process of understanding self in relation to a higher being" (Watt, 1996, p. 34). It is an important model for counselors to be aware of as they assess the place of faith in their clients' overall development.

Intuitive or projective faith is Stage 1 and is common among young children. For the most part, God is conceived of in magical terms. Stage 2, *mythic or literal faith,* feeling connected to a community, is important where the beliefs are transmitted. Stage 3 is *synthetic or conventional faith.* A sense of identity is lacking as the person is heavily influenced by surroundings. Stage 4 is *individuating or reflexive faith.* Here, the person is more accountable to self in taking responsibility for developing a worldview that is intrinsically derived. Stage 5, *conjunctive faith,* occurs often in midlife. The person is open and receptive to others even at the risk of revisiting previously held beliefs. Stage 6 is *universalizing faith.* Persons in this stage are "severely focused on the goal of a universal community where standards of acceptance and forgiveness are priority" (Watt, 1996, p. 35).

From the nature of the conflict apparent in Renee's story, it appears that she was in Stage 4 of Fowler and Keen's model. Watt (1996) said that people enter this stage when "the conventional perspective of stage 3 begins to collapse due to a lack of congruence between self and expectations of different people" (p. 35). Because of a combination of culture and spirituality, most Native American Indians believe that healers can only be successful if they seek the assistance of spiritual forces (Dufrene & Coleman, 1994). Thus, it is recommended that because Clara is unaware of traditional healing in Native people, she investigate the place of traditional healing in the counseling session to see Renee as a whole person. Dufrene and Coleman (1994) said, "Traditional Native healers or shamans draw on a vast body of symbolism passed down through the centuries. . . . Myths, prayers, songs, chants, sand paintings, and music are used to return the patient symbolically to the source of tribal energy" (p. 146).

Graduate school can be isolating for anyone regardless of race, gender, or background. The counseling event can serve to usher in rhythm and ritual in Renee's life, given the disruption of rape and the isolation of graduate school. It would be helpful if Clara understands the primary place of art, spirituality, and nature in the lives of Native peoples to the healing process, which includes emotional, psychological, and cultural healing. Dufrene and Coleman (1994) indicated that, preferably, counseling be conducted by Native American Indian professionals because such professionals best understand the needs and concerns of this population. They also stated, however, that because of the dearth of such counselors, non-Indian counselors need to be aware of their own biases, values, and beliefs.

To be effective, Clara must recognize that Renee's depression can be representative of healing change but that culture plays an essential role. Garrett and Garrett (1994) wrote, "Native American Indians emphasize a nonverbal communication style. Moderation in speech and avoidance of direct eye contact are nonverbal communicators of respect by the listener, especially for respecting elders or authority figures" (p. 141). Clearly, an adult rape can contribute to depression; however, Renee's speech patterns, eye contact, and overall problem orientation need to be assessed against a cultural backdrop—that she is a Native American Indian. In short, assessing Renee

from a Western lens can result in misassessment, which is what a recommendation to a mental facility would be. Talking to a healer, being part of tribal ceremony, and connecting with loving people from her community would be therapeutic and provide her with nurturance and support. She must work through her feelings of shame.

Among most Native American Indians, noninterference is a way of life in that the natural personality is allowed to unfold according to Indian mores (Attneave, 1982). The person exists as a part of a tribe and group but remains an autonomous individual.

> The source of the individuality is felt to be innate. Parental aspirations do not lend themselves as much to shaping and molding as to freeing the inner self of the child in order that it can become what it is destined to be. (Attneave, 1982, p. 71)

Authors' Note: Counselors need to know that they will not be able to help some client populations effectively because of a lack of expertise and/or because of emotional issues that would interfere with a professional rendering of services. Some counselors would say that although they would and could help Renee, their anger and disgust over the act of rape would preclude their helping the rapist. If this is your assessment of yourself, then you need to be honest about it so that you can practice nonmaleficence, which is to do no harm even to one who has done harm to another. If, however, you are unable to help multiple client populations (e.g., persons who have raped or incested others, persons who have been in adulterous relationships, women who have had abortions), then you are encouraged to seek counseling to explore why so many populations present you with such a moral challenge.

SUMMARY

This chapter examined the cultural and social origins of violence. The literature on the interaction among biology, hormone levels, gender, and aggression was reviewed, as was select literature on incest, rape, and domestic violence. Youths and violence were also briefly discussed. This chapter provided information on reactions to victimization, as well as material on empowerment, which is examined more thoroughly in Chapter 13. To be effective, counselors need to understand the sociopolitical, gender, and cultural contexts in which violence is taught, learned, and reproduced. They also need to know how to facilitate clients' move to wholeness and wellness regardless of the time period in which the violence occurred.

REFERENCES

Adolescent Pregnancy Prevention Coalition of North Carolina (APPCNC). (1998, Winter). Prime time for teen sex and crime. *The Advocate,* pp. 1–2.

Allers, C. T., Benjack, K. J., & Allers, N. T. (1992). Unresolved childhood sexual abuse: Are older adults affected? *Journal of Counseling & Development, 71,* 14–17.

Attneave, C. (1982). American Indians and Alaska Native families: Emigrants in their own homeland. In M. McGoldrick, J. Pearce, & J. Giordano (Eds.), *Ethnicity and family therapy* (pp. 55–83). New York: Guilford Press.

Blume, E. S. (1990). *Secret survivors: Uncovering incest and its aftereffects in women.* New York: John Wiley.

Bui, K. V. T., & Takeuchi, D. T. (1992). Ethnic minority adolescents and the use of community mental health care services. *American Journal of Community Psychology, 20,* 403–417.

Donnerstein, E., & Linz, D. (1987). Mass-media sexual violence and male viewers. In M. S. Kimmell (Ed.), *Changing men: New directions in research on men and masculinity* (pp. 198–216). Newbury Park, CA: Sage.

Dufrene, P. M., & Coleman, V. D. (1994). Art and healing for Native American Indians. *Journal of Multicultural Counseling & Development, 22,* 145–152.

Fausto-Sterling, A. (1992). *Myths of gender: Biological theories about women and men.* New York: Basic Books.

Fowler, J., & Keen, S. (1978). *Life maps: Conversations on the journey of faith.* Waco, TX: Word Books.

Frazier, P. A., & Burnett, J. W. (1994). Immediate coping strategies among rape victims. *Journal of Counseling & Development, 72,* 633–639.

Garrett, J. T., & Garrett, M. W. (1994). The path of good medicine: Understanding and counseling Native American Indians. *Journal of Multicultural Counseling & Development, 22,* 134–144.

Good, G. E., & Mintz, L. B. (1990). Gender role conflict and depression in college men: Evidence for compounded risk. *Journal of Counseling & Development, 69,* 17–21.

Gryl, F. E., Stith, S. M., & Ward, G. W. (1991). Close dating relationships among college students: Differences by use of violence and by gender. *Journal of Social and Personal Relationships, 8,* 243–264.

Hoorwitz, A. N. (1983, November). Guidelines for treating father-daughter incest. *Journal of Contemporary Social Work,* 515–524.

Kirp, D. L., Yudof, M. G., & Franks, M. S. (1986). *Gender justice.* Chicago: University of Chicago Press.

Kanuha, V. (1994). Women of color in battering relationships. In L. Comas-Diaz & B. Greene (Eds.), *Women of color* (pp. 428–454). New York: Guilford Press.

Koss, M., Eidyce, C., & Wisniewski, N. (1987). The scope of rape: Incidence and prevalence of sexual aggression in a sample of higher education students. *Journal of Consulting and Clinical Psychology, 55,* 162–170.

Kromkowski, J. A. (1992). *Race and ethnic relations.* Guilford, CT: Dushkin.

LaFree, F. (1980). The effect of sexual stratification by race on officers' reactions to rape. *American Sociological Review, 45,* 842–854.

Maccoby, E., & Jacklin, C. N. (1974). *The psychology of sex differences.* Stanford, CA: Stanford University Press.

Moir, A., & Jessel, D. (1991). *Brain sex: The real difference between men and women.* New York: Delta.

Muehlenhard, C. L., Powch, I. G., Phelps, J. L., & Giusti, L. M. (1992). Definitions of rape: Scientific and political implications. *Journal of Social Issues, 48,* 23–44.

Pinderhughes, E. (1989). *Understanding race, ethnicity, and power: The key to efficacy in clinical practice.* New York: Free Press.

Priest, R., & Smith, A. (1992). Counseling adult sex offenders: Unique challenges and treatment paradigms. *Journal of Counseling & Development, 71,* 27–32.

Raine, A., & Duncan, J. J. (1990). The genetic and psychophysiological basis of antisocial behavior: Implications for counseling and therapy. *Journal of Counseling & Development, 68,* 637–644.

Ratican, K. L. (1992). Sexual abuse survivors: Identifying symptoms and special treatment considerations. *Journal of Counseling & Development, 71,* 33–38.

Renzetti, C. M., & Curran, D. J. (1992). *Women, men, and society.* Boston: Allyn & Bacon.

Russell, B., & Uhlemann, M. R. (1994). Women surviving an abusive relationship: Grief and the process of change. *Journal of Counseling & Development, 72,* 362–367.

Scully, D. (1988). Convicted rapists perceptions of self and victim: Role taking and emotions. *Gender and Society, 2,* 200–213.

Steward, R. J., Jo, H. I., Murray, D., Fitzgerald, W., Neil, D., Fear, F., & Hill, M. (1998). Psychological adjustment and coping styles of urban African American high school students. *Journal of Multicultural Counseling & Development, 26,* 70–82.

U.S. Department of Health and Human Services. (1994). *Healthy people progress report for: Black Americans.* Washington, DC: Public Health Service.

Watt, S. K. (1996). *Identity and the making of meaning: Psychosocial identity, racial identity, womanist identity, and faith development of African American college women.* Unpublished doctoral dissertation, North Carolina State University at Raleigh.

Wilbanks, W. (1994). The myth of a racist criminal justice system. In R. Monk (Ed.), *Taking sides: Clashing views on controversial issues in race and ethnicity* (pp. 244–248). Guilford, CT: Dushkin.

Wilson, K., Vercella, R., Brems, C., Benning, D., & Renfro, N. (1992). Levels of learned helplessness in abused women. *Women & Therapy, 13,* 53–67.

Women for Racial and Economic Equality. (1991). *191 facts about women.* New York: Author.

Chapter 13

Multicultural Competencies and Skills

How like moths we are when we are caught in the dark, beating our wings against anything that stands between us and the light. Though we strain against barriers, we are the *a tsv s dv*, we are the light or candle that lights the place where we are. Others who follow watch for a signal, a light in the dark, to know they are not alone. We need to take some time to be quiet, to recharge, and it may mean waiting a while in the dark. But whatever our need, if we wait the light will come. And it will illumine us instead of blinding us with its glare.

Joyce Sequichie Hifler, A Cherokee Feast of Days

The path to glory is rough and many gloomy hours obscure it. May the Great Spirit shed light on yours.

Black Hawk

It has been a long path to the development of multicultural competencies in counselor education. In 1982, Sue et al. proposed a definition of **cross-cultural counseling** as "any counseling relationship in which two or more of the participants differ in cultural background, values, and lifestyle" (p. 47). Given this definition, any counseling interaction could be regarded as cross-cultural in that human beings vary with respect to their cultural orientations and their lived experiences as cultural beings. This chapter provides an overview of multicultural competencies and skills. An overview of counselor education diversity training programs is provided. Strategies for becoming a multiculturally competent counselor and guidelines on monitoring dissonance and measuring cross-cultural effectiveness are reviewed. A case study allows for an integration of the material presented.

OVERVIEW OF MULTICULTURAL COMPETENCIES

In 1991, the Association for Multicultural Counseling and Development (AMCD) presented a document to the American Association for Counseling and Development (now American Counseling Association) toward standardization and establishment of specific guidelines for the profession. The goal was to amend and adopt new standards for practice that would encompass a multicultural worldview (Sue, Arredondo, & McDavis, 1992). In 1992, Sue, Arredondo, and McDavis, developed a list of multicultural competencies. In this important document, awareness, knowledge, and skills were described. A few years later, Arredondo et al. (1996) expounded on this list of competencies. Explanatory statements were added to "take the profession further along in the process of institutionalizing counselor training and practices to be multicultural at the core" (p. 56). The three competencies appear in bold. Each competency is followed by italicized statements about attitudes and beliefs, knowledge, and skills. Although Arredondo et al. offered several explanatory statements that provided additional information, these are only briefly summarized below.

COUNSELOR AWARENESS OF OWN CULTURAL VALUES AND BIASES

The first competency is **counselor awareness of own cultural values and biases**. First, with respect to *attitudes and beliefs* (the knowledge aspect follows later), *culturally skilled counselors believe that cultural self-awareness and sensitivity to one's own cultural heritage are essential.* They understand the importance of their own cultural heritage and are able to identify their own cultural groups and associated values and beliefs of these groups. In addition, counselors understand the impact of their cultural groups on them personally.

Second, *culturally skilled counselors are aware of how their own cultural backgrounds and experiences have influenced attitudes, values, and biases about psy-*

chological processes. Explanatory statements include counselors' ability to identify cultural influences on cognitive development, problem solving, and decision making. Counselors are also able to express the beliefs of their particular religions and cultural groups and relate them to dimensions of identity, including disability and sexual orientation.

Third, *culturally skilled counselors are able to recognize the limits of their multicultural competency and expertise.* More specifically, counselors can identify how cultural attitudes, beliefs, and values may interfere with best service delivery to clients.

Fourth, *culturally skilled counselors recognize their sources of discomfort with differences that exist between themselves and clients in terms of race, ethnicity, and culture.* Such differences are acknowledged, ways to handle these differences are understood within the counseling relationship, and they are responsibly implemented.

With respect to *knowledge,* first *culturally skilled counselors have specific knowledge about their racial and cultural heritage and how it personally and professionally affects their definitions of, and biases about, normality/abnormality and the process of counseling.*

Second, *culturally skilled counselors possess knowledge and understanding about how oppression, racism, discrimination, and stereotyping affect them personally and their work.* Counselors are aware of privileges associated with a variety of identities, including race, physical abilities, gender, socioeconomic class, and so on. Moreover, counselors are knowledgeable of the recent research on racism, ways to combat racism, racial identity development, and the relationship of these themes to counselors' professional development.

Third, *culturally skilled counselors possess knowledge about their social impact on others.* More specifically, counselors are aware of the various dimensions of difference and are clear about how nonverbal communication styles differ within and among cultures.

Regarding *skills,* first *culturally skilled counselors seek out educational, consultative, and training experiences to improve their understanding and effectiveness in working with culturally different populations.* Essentially, effective counselors know when they need to refer clients to other helpers and maintain an active list of potential referrals (see the case study "Across the Pacific, Home" at the end of this chapter).

Second, *culturally skilled counselors are constantly seeking to understand themselves as racial and cultural beings and are actively seeking a nonracist identity.*

COUNSELOR AWARENESS OF CLIENT'S WORLDVIEW

The second competency is **counselor awareness of client's worldview.** Again, beginning with *attitudes and beliefs* and then moving on to knowledge and eventually skills, first *culturally skilled counselors are aware of their negative and positive emotional reactions toward other racial and ethnic groups that may prove detrimental to the counseling relationship.* Counselors are honest about their biases relevant to certain racial and ethnic groups.

Second, *culturally skilled counselors are aware of their stereotypes and preconceived notions that they may hold toward other racial and ethnic minority groups.*

Concerning *knowledge*, first, *culturally skilled counselors possess specific knowledge and information about the particular group with which they are working*. Effective counselors know about their clients' cultural values, history, and differences in verbal and nonverbal behaviors.

Second, *culturally skilled counselors understand how race, culture, and ethnicity may affect personality formation, vocational choices, manifestation of psychological disorders, help-seeking behavior, and the appropriateness or inappropriateness of counseling approaches*. Counselors are clear about how societal oppression affects groups and can interpret traditional systems (e.g., regarding personality development) and interrogate how such a system may or may not relate to particular groups.

Third, *culturally skilled counselors understand and have knowledge about sociopolitical influences that impinge on the lives of racial and ethnic minorities*. Counselors are knowledgeable about institutionalized racism, internalized oppression, poverty, and other themes that affect their clients. In addition, they are aware of how the media, written and visual, along with certain policies (e.g., affirmative action setbacks), affect the ways people of color and other groups are perceived in society.

Regarding *skills*, first, *culturally skilled counselors should familiarize themselves with relevant research and the latest findings regarding mental health and mental disorders that affect various racial and ethnic groups*. Counselors are mindful of the research in mental health and career issues that affect different cultural groups and are able to identify a variety of multicultural experiences in which they have been involved.

Second, *culturally skilled counselors become actively involved with persons of color and other groups outside the counseling setting*. Counselors seek to engage in activities that challenge preconceived stereotypes.

CULTURALLY APPROPRIATE INTERVENTION STRATEGIES

The third competency is c**ulturally appropriate intervention strategies.** Beginning with *attitudes and beliefs,* first, *culturally skilled counselors respect clients' religious and spiritual beliefs and values*. In doing so, they are able to identify aspects of spirituality relevant to wellness and healing.

Second, *culturally skilled counselors respect indigenous helping practices and respect help-giving networks among communities of color.* Counselors are also able to integrate their efforts with indigenous helps where appropriate.

Third, *culturally skilled counselors value bilingualism and do not view another language as an impediment to counseling*. Monolingualism is recognized as limiting in itself.

Regarding *knowledge,* first, *culturally skilled counselors have a clear and explicit knowledge and understanding of the generic characteristics of counseling and therapy (culture bound, class bound, and monolingual) and how they may clash with the cultural values of various cultural groups.* Counselors understand the context in which theories and the current counseling knowledge base have arisen.

Second, *culturally skilled counselors are aware of institutional barriers that prevent people of color, women, persons with disabilities, people from low-income groups, and gay/lesbian clients from using mental health services.* By doing so, counselors can also suggest alternatives to traditional systems of helping and communicate with effective others about how to intervene appropriately.

Third, *culturally skilled counselors have knowledge of the potential bias in assessment instruments and use procedures and interpret findings in a way that recognizes the cultural and linguistic characteristics of the clients.* Counselors are able to interpret assessment instruments in the context of a client's culture and are also aware of existing bias in traditional systems of diagnosis, including the *DSM–IV* (*Diagnostic and Statistical Manual of Mental Disorders,* 4th ed.).

Fourth, *culturally skilled counselors have knowledge of family structures, hierarchies, values, and beliefs from various cultural perspectives.* Counselors are aware of various resources within the community that can assist their clients with a host of concerns while recognizing that culture can contribute to clients making decisions that are not culturally consistent with that of the counselor.

Fifth, *culturally skilled counselors should be aware of relevant discriminatory practices at the social and community levels that may be affecting the psychological welfare of the population being served.* This would include knowledge of both state and national policies (e.g., repeals of affirmative action in California).

Regarding *skills*, first, *culturally skilled counselors are able to engage in a variety of verbal and nonverbal helping responses.* They are able to send and receive both verbal and nonverbal messages accurately and appropriately. Counselors are aware of why they use particular communication styles at a given time and are able to modify techniques for a variety of contexts.

Second, *culturally skilled counselors are able to exercise institutional intervention skills on behalf of their clients.* Counselors can help equip clients with coping strategies and effective skills to deal with institutional discrimination.

Third, *culturally skilled counselors are not averse to seeking consultation with traditional healers or religious and spiritual leaders and practitioners in the treatment of culturally different clients when appropriate.* If necessary, counselors are aware of appropriate referrals within indigenous communities.

Fourth, *culturally skilled counselors take responsibility for interacting in the language requested by the client and, if not feasible, make appropriate referrals.* Counselors are able to seek out the services of translators and are familiar with resources that provide appropriate language services to clients.

Fifth, *culturally skilled counselors have training and expertise in the use of traditional assessment and testing instruments.* Counselors understand the cultural context in which traditional assessment tools have developed.

Sixth, *culturally skilled counselors should attend to, as well as work to eliminate, biases, prejudices, and discriminatory contexts in conducting evaluations and providing interventions and should develop sensitivity to the intersections of oppression: sexism, heterosexism, elitism, and racism.* Counselors are able to address the need for change, regarding discrimination, on an organizational level.

Seventh, *culturally skilled counselors take responsibility for educating their clients to the processes of psychological intervention, such as goals, expectations, legal rights, and the counselor's orientation.* Clients are encouraged by their counselors to advocate for themselves through an educational process.*

OVERVIEW OF COUNSELOR EDUCATION DIVERSITY TRAINING

Although the key to implementing and infusing standards for a multicultural society begins with the code of conduct that governs the assessment, intervention, and evaluation practices of counselors, therapists, and teaching faculty, considerable variety exists in counselor education diversity training programs. D'Andrea and Daniels (1991) indicated that cross-cultural counseling is taught in very different ways. Yet, programs that fail to heighten awareness among students about their own biases and prejudices or that provide a partial examination of the topic may risk exposing vulnerable clients to mental health professionals who are ill-prepared to provide quality services.

Pinderhughes (1989) provided definitions of *race, ethnicity,* and *culture* because students are often confused about these terms. Although used interchangeably, counselor education programs need to present to students important distinctions to avoid the improper use of terminology. The benefit of the burgeoning literature in multicultural counselor education programs is that terms are being generated and also clarified (Rollock & Terrell, 1996). D'Andrea and Daniels (1991) stated that considerable controversy surrounds which training models for counselor training are the most appropriate. Dinsmore and England (1996) stated that "no general consensus regarding what set of program characteristics constitutes a standard for multicultural program competence" (p. 59). In their qualitative review of multicultural training programs, D'Andrea and Daniels developed four stages to characterize such training: (a) culturally entrenched, (b) cross-cultural awakening, (c) cultural integrity, and (d) infusion.

At the first stage, multicultural training essentially does not exist. Racial and cultural diversity within this type of department tends to be limited. Thus, material tends to be presented from a *culturally entrenched* perspective. The cultural needs of people of color are rarely considered, and emphasis on other worldviews is virtually nonexistent. D'Andrea and Daniels (1991) did distinguish between counselor education departments that resemble the one just described and departments that are at the second stage, *cross-cultural awakening.* In such departments, faculty are likely to recognize that many counseling theories do not speak to the mental health concerns and needs of many persons from culturally different backgrounds. Interactions with racially and culturally diverse persons professionally and personally are rare. Faculty that are more descriptive of the second stage, characterized as conscientious, behave and think differently from their colleagues in the first stage. At the more advanced third stage, *cultural integrity,* departments understand the importance of cultural, racial, and class issues, which are a core part of the curriculum. At the highest stage, *infusion,* programs integrate the issues of cultural and racial diversity throughout the programs in a way that complements existing material. Students are encouraged to think at higher, more conceptually complex levels.

Gender issues in counselor education also need to be attended to in counselor education and to be treated as central to the counselor training. Moreover, a focus is needed on both men's and women's issues because *gender* refers to both genders. Men's issues tend not to be central to the discussion of gender issues (Hoffman, 1996). Toward implementing gender into the curriculum, the Council for Accreditation of Counseling and Related Educational Programs (CACREP) standards could lead this initiative.

In a follow-up study to D'Andrea and Daniels (1991), Dinsmore and England (1996) sought to broaden the profession's view of multicultural counseling and to delve more deeply into where counselor education training programs stand nationally with respect to multicultural counseling. Overall, these researchers received 60 responses from 90 that were sent to department chairs and program directors of all doctoral- and master-level counselor education program accredited by CACREP. Faculty members totaled 634; 15% were non-White, the African Americans and Hispanics being underrepresented with respect to their proportion in the population. In addition, Whites were disproportionately represented in the ranks where faculty have tenure (full and associate professors). Regarding program offerings, the two most popular designs for multicultural counseling courses were the single course required, with systematic curriculum integration at 32%. The researchers found that, with respect to D'Andrea and Daniels's categories of faculty departments, none were considered to be at the first stage, or culturally entrenched; 12 programs, or 18%, were at the second stage, cross-cultural awareness; the majority, at 67%, were at the third stage, cultural integrity; and 10 programs, or 15%, were at the fourth stage, infusion. According to Dinsmore and England,

> Three regions of the country had counselor education programs at Stage 4 (North Central, Southern, and Western), with the North Central region having the largest percentage (24%) of programs at this stage . . . The majority of the counselor education programs in the North Atlantic (73%), North Central (86%), Southern (86%), and Western (91%) were at the Conscientious Level (Stages 3 or 4) of multicultural counseling program development. (p. 69)

These researchers found that the Rocky Mountain region had 60% of counselor education programs at the cultural encapsulation stage of program development.

A MODEL FOR MULTICULTURAL COUNSELOR TRAINING PROGRAMS

Faculty in counselor education programs have been grappling for some time with how best to teach multiculturalism. Bowman (1996), having reviewed much of the literature, concluded that "multicultural instruction should not be limited to one course but should be infused in all aspects of the training" (p. 16). Focusing on multicultural counseling separately is culturally linked in terms of looking at it linearly and individualistically. As stated above, the multicultural competencies focus on three components: (a) self-awareness, (b) knowledge, and (c) skill. This particular paradigm was initiated by Sue et al. (1982) and expounded on by other theorists. For this reason the model for multicultural counseling training is inclusive of these components. In Bowman's (1996) first component, *learning about the self,* a host of emotions are experienced by the trainee, including confusion, guilt, and tentativeness. For most White students, self-exploration has excluded looking at their racial selves, given that most Whites do not see themselves as White. Often, *American* or *human being* is used as a descriptor (Brown, Parham, & Yonker, 1996).

Some exercises can facilitate introspection. This includes drawing one's culture with crayons and constructing a genogram that outlines family history. Reading McIntosh's (1989) article "White Privilege: Unpacking the Invisible White Knapsack" can be very thought-provoking. The unearned privileges associated with ability, gender, and sexual orientation can also be investigated (see the Storytelling "Maybe Them but Not Me"). Despite integration, U.S. society is very much segregated along racial lines. I (Tracy) am often struck at how often I do not see students of different races walking around together at the university. The second multicultural training component, *learning about others,* can be promoted through experiencing different cultures where one is in the numerical minority. For instance, this could entail going to a Chinese Baptist church or a gay nightclub. Thought-provoking films, which students can be asked to help generate a list of, can be viewed and discussed. The third component is *learning about how one relates to others*. Here, the trainees are encouraged to take what they have learned and apply it. In this regard, laboratory experiences are essential, and competent supervision is vital. According to Bowman (1996), "trainees need opportunities to examine the dynamics of establishing relationships with culturally diverse populations and to question how they apply what they know about self and others to successful cross-cultural interactions" (p. 23). As students are encountering dissonance, they need safe places where they can ask questions and process through information they have not encountered before. Faculty need to support students in their efforts at risk-taking while encouraging all students to be receptive to new, conflicting, and in some cases disturbing ideas from classmates and even professors.

Empirical evidence indicates that cross-cultural counseling courses can have a positive impact on White trainees' racial identity attitudes. Brown et al. (1996) conducted research with 35 (10 men, 25 women) White graduate counselors-in-training enrolled in a 16-week graduate-level multicultural counseling course taught at a mid-

STORYTELLING
Maybe Them but Not Me

One evening during a summer school cross-cultural class in which Mary was my teaching assistant, we were discussing discrimination with our students. Soon, a White woman in her late 30s spoke out adamantly and claimed that as a woman she had not been discriminated against professionally or personally. An awkward silence fell over the room. A few White female students challenged the woman by sharing examples from their own lives about how they had been discriminated against. The woman was unmovable and basically attributed any shortcomings in these women's lives to their lack of effort or motivation. Fascinated by the discussion but also mindful of the increasing frustration and annoyance that many students were experiencing, I asked the student, "How is it that so many women experience discrimination and you have managed to escape it?" The student basically said that she had worked hard and thought her career training had helped her. We went on to another discussion, and the woman, obviously still wrestling with the issues that had been raised in the discussion, blurted out that she had tried for years within her career to be promoted but had not. I suggested that she try harder. She became furious at me (which I anticipated) and said that she had worked very hard. I stood looking at my student and realizing that the denial was breaking up and she was on her way to a breakthrough; her classmates sat in silence. She then began to cry. She realized that she had been dealing with institutional sexism and had attributed it to her own inadequacy.

Monitoring students' dissonance, as well as our own, is a part of effective training in multicultural counseling courses. Checking in with students and asking how they are, acknowledging the hard work we are all doing, and honoring the release of emotion, including sadness and anger, have been helpful.

Tracy and Mary

size midwestern university. The White Racial Identity Attitude Scale (WRIAS) was used to measure changes in racial identity and ultimately to measure cross-cultural training effectiveness. The three components of the class were consistent with the multicultural competencies (a) self-awareness, (b) knowledge about other cultures, and (c) skill development. To encourage self-awareness, a consciousness-raising exercise known as Blue-Eyed, Brown-Eyed was implemented. Essentially, students assigned to the brown-eyed group received preferential treatment. The room contained comfortable chairs, a rug, and food to eat and drink, and music played in the background. Blue-eyed students were not interacted with warmly, had to sit on the floor, were not invited or allowed to eat, and were followed if they left the room. To explore other cultures, guest speakers from different racial and cultural groups were invited. Class resources included texts on multiculturalism, journal articles, and video/audiotapes. To foster skill development, students were asked to submit a three-part final project. In Part 1, they described a cross-cultural helping situation, inclusive of relevant details (who, what, when, where, and how). In Part 2, students critically analyzed the scenario discussed in Part 1. In Part 3, "students were instructed to rewrite the scenario and design a helping intervention that reflected cultural sensitivity and competence" (p. 513). Brown et al. found that Autonomy and Pseudoindependence (see Chapter 4) scores increased. Males evidenced higher Autonomy scores, and women higher Pseudoindependence. Because of the increases in racial identity attitude on the Autonomy and Pseudoindependence subscales, the authors concluded that "the female and male students in the study can be characterized as possessing enhanced abilities to (a) psychologically accept racial differences, (b) appreciate the potential impact of racial attitudes on people of color, (c) exhibit less racist behaviors" (p. 514).

In other research with 128 White counseling graduate students using the WRIAS and the Multicultural Counseling Inventory (MCI), researchers were interested in examining the relationship between White racial identity attitudes and self-reported multicultural competencies. Ottavi, Pope-Davis, and Dings (1994) found that "the WRIAS explained variation in the MCI beyond that accounted for by the demographic, educational, and clinical variables that were found to be significantly correlated" (p. 151). Thus, Ottavi et al. concluded that White racial identity attitudes need to be integrated into the development of multicultural competencies.

The diversity of instruction in multicultural counseling points to the need for a theory about multicultural counseling. Developed by Sue, Ivey, and Pedersen (1996), *multicultural counseling and therapy (MCT)* is a "theory about theories." It provides a paradigm for making meaning of the multiple ways that have been developed to help people. Context is important in this theory, and it does not presuppose that one perspective or way of knowing is superior over another. Instead, each theory represents a particular way of seeing and being in the world.

ASSESSMENT AND DIVERSITY

To guide counselor education departments in their counseling training efforts, Ponterotto, Alexander, and Grieger (1995) developed a multicultural competency checklist. It has six themes: (a) minority representation, (b) curriculum issues, (c) counseling practice and supervision, (d) research considerations, (e) student and faculty competency evaluation, and (f) physical environment. The first four items on the checklist seek to ascertain *diverse representation*—whether 30% of faculty, students, and program support staff are visibly racially/ethnically diverse. Bilingual skills are also important. **Curriculum issues** are covered in five items and reflect course work, pedagogy, and student assessment. An example: Multicultural issues are integrated into all course work. All program faculty can specify how this is done in their courses. Furthermore, syllabi clearly reflect multicultural inclusion. *Counseling practice and supervision* is the third area and contains three questions. The focus here is on students' practicum, supervision quality, and the "Multicultural Affairs Committee," which is recommended as a way to monitor multicultural activities. *Research considerations* has four questions concerned with a multicultural research presence in the program. Statement 14 of the checklist reads, "There is clear faculty research productivity in multicultural issues. This is evidenced by faculty journal publications and conference presentations on multicultural issues." The four items in the *student and faculty competency evaluation* emphasize proficiency in multicultural issues. Statement 19 reads, "Multicultural issues are reflected in comprehensive examinations completed by students." The final two items concern the *physical environment* and whether it reflects diversity in the faculty offices, reception area, and clinic area. The authors of this checklist recognize that very few programs will meet all the competencies in the checklist and suggest that 1-, 3-, and 5-year action plans can be developed to address any gaps.

Many traditional psychoeducational measures used for assessment purposes were not validated with diverse populations in their original sample groups and are based on individual performance or self-report or both. Therefore, the appropriateness and validity of many commonly used psychological and psychoeducational assessment instruments, when used with individuals and diverse populations, may be questionable. The validity and reliability of assessment tools have implications for research. Culturally insensitive research accommodates and further perpetuates inadequate training models and subsequent counseling services. According to Ponterotto and Casas (1991), one criticism of current research on people of color is that important intrapersonal and extrapersonal factors, such as client attitudes, client-counselor racial similarity, communication styles, acculturation, and discrimination and poverty, have virtually been ignored. Furthermore, the research has not considered or studied the tremendous heterogeneity in multicultural populations, which has affected, fostered, and perpetuated ethnic stereotypes and global categorizations. Last, easily accessible subject populations (e.g., White psychology college students from large midwestern universities) that tend not to be representative of the larger community have typically been selected as research populations. This overreliance on research using analogue designs "whereby the subject pools have consisted of pseudo-client (e.g., students) and pseudo-counselors (e.g., graduate students in counseling) instead of 'real' clients and counselors" (Ponterotto & Casas, 1991, p. 78) limits generalizability to actual client and counselor populations. Concern has also been raised over the validity and applied pragmatic utility of the many research findings now appearing in the multicultural literature (Ponterotto & Casas, 1991). Simplistic client/counselor process variables have been overemphasized, and significant cultural, as well as psychosocial, variables that might affect counseling have been disregarded. In other words, important psychosocial variables (e.g., learning styles, communication patterns, racism, oppression, poverty), which may be more difficult to study but are vital to understanding the role of counseling with people of color, have been overlooked. Concomitantly, a high degree of heterogeneity, such as demographic characteristics, class, and attitudes, exists within multicultural populations, yet these intracultural differences tend not to be noted in the research literature.

To demonstrate competence in multicultural assessment, conceptualization of presenting problems, establishment of appropriate interventions, development of client treatment goals, and the formulation of multiculturally sensitive research, psychological service providers and academicians will need to acquire cultural knowledge, information, and skills.

IMPLICATIONS FOR COUNSELORS

The work of unlearning oppressive practices that distance counselors from themselves and their clients is a lifelong and ongoing process. Willingness to be open, to be changed, and to be healed are crucial ingredients in this process of developing not only a nonracist identity but also nonsexist, nonclassist, and nonhomophobic identities. Being honest about the various emotions that are understandably within us as counselors, even during the cross-cultural therapeutic event, is essential. Abernathy (1995) said that "minimal attention has been devoted to addressing the anger that frequently emerges in cross-racial work" (p. 96).

Numerous books, articles, conferences, and associations are in the service of fostering a climate of multiculturalism and equity for all people. The American Counseling Association provides an excellent resource for students, professionals, and practitioners who want to develop themselves and to connect with others who are like-minded and focused on multicultural competence, which is a challenging endeavor. Hartung (1996) noted the difficulty in developing cultural competencies among both faculty and students. He said:

> The task proves difficult because it requires the concerted and committed effort of both faculty and student. The task proves challenging because it calls for examining and confronting one's own perceptions, biases, prejudices, and worldview. The task is multidimensional because it involves heightening personal awareness, expanding cultural knowledge, and honing counseling skills. (p. 7)

Despite these challenges and amid the available resources, nothing appears to be better than having genuine and authentic relationships—not just colleagues, but friends who come to each other's home and talk about their lives as racial, cultural, and gendered beings. This type of sharing and being together allows us truly to talk, understand, and ultimately heal from the scourge of race oppression.

CASE STUDY
Across the Pacific, Home

Moana, age 27, and her family are originally from New Zealand and have lived in Washington for 15 years. Moana's parents are Maori (indigenous people of New Zealand who are of Polynesian descent). Although she has lived in the United States for the majority of her life, Moana and her parents speak Maori in their home and visit their homeland every few years. Moana is working on her master's degree in environmental studies and is interested in working for an environmental agency in Brisbane, Australia, so that she can be closer to her place of birth and to the *tangata whenua* (people of the land), to whom she is very committed. Moana's older brother, Timoti, is a dentist and has two children that Moana is very fond of and with whom she spends a considerable amount of time. Moana reports to the counseling center at her university to discuss her career plans, anticipated move, and stress associated with leaving her family and being so far away. Moana has enjoyed living in Washington, but she misses her extended family and being around other Maori people, of which there is a sizeable population in Australia. Dr. Reid Simms, who has expertise in the psychological stress associated with career transition, is a European American male counselor who has never heard of the Maori people; has rarely been outside the United States except to Canada, Mexico, and Europe; and has restricted interactions with people of color except for some collegial interactions with his colleagues at work.

QUESTIONS

1. Should Dr. Simms, according to the American Association of Counseling ethical guidelines, refer Moana to another counselor?
2. What would Dr. Simms have to do to become more multiculturally competent?
3. What implications do Dr. Simms's current knowledge and skill base have on the quality of counseling services he renders?

DISCUSSION AND INTEGRATION
The Client, Moana

Moana (which means "sea") is Maori and Polynesian. The Maori people tell the story that their ancestors came to Aotearoa/New Zealand (land of the long white cloud) from Hawaiki, somewhere in Polynesia. Another theory maintains that the Maori's ancestors were Chinese, originally from mainland China, who migrated across the Pacific over the centuries—from Taiwan, through the Philippines and Indonesia to West Polynesia, on into the islands of East Polynesia and then New Zealand (Discovery News Brief, 1998). Moana's ancestors arrived in double-hulled canoes about 800 years prior to Captain Cook's visit in 1769. Soon, more British came and the indigenous people were colonized. Countless Maori died from European diseases and land wars, the Maori's land was stolen from them, and promises were broken. The Treaty of Waitangi, signed on February 6, 1840, stated,

Her Majesty the Queen of England confirms and guarantees to the Chiefs and Tribes of New Zealand and to the respective families and individuals thereof the full exclusive and undisturbed possession of their Lands and Estates Forests Fisheries and other properties which they may collectively or individually possess so long as it is their wish and desire to retain the same in their possession. (Orange, 1989, p. 31)

Currently, Maori compose approximately 14% of the population in New Zealand. According to Smith (1997), "the term 'Maori' only became meaningful as a category because of colonisation" (p. 35).

Moana has an understanding of the history of her people and is committed to being more involved in the indigenous movement and advocating for *tino rangatiratanga*, which means "self-determination." She is experiencing stress because of the considerable transitions that moving to Australia will hold for her. Yet, she is excited about the change and new opportunities awaiting her. Her cultural longings are admirable, and she needs to be encouraged for listening to herself and responding to a call that obviously comes from deep within. Because Moana is a New Zealand-born citizen, she has easy entry into the world of work in Australia without needing a visa or other documentation.

The Counselor, Reid Simms

Section A.2 (Respecting Diversity) of the American Counseling Association Code of Ethics and Standards of Practice, Subsection b on Respecting Differences reads:

Counselors will actively attempt to understand the diverse cultural backgrounds of the client with whom they work. This includes, but is not limited to, learning how the counselor's own cultural/ethical/racial identity impacts her/his values and beliefs about the counseling process. (Cottone & Tarvydas, 1998, p. 26)

Given this ethical guideline, it is important that Dr. Simms learn more about Moana's culture. This task may be challenging because Dr. Simms is unfamiliar with Moana's history and geography. However, it does not seem appropriate for Dr. Simms to refer Moana to another counselor simply because he is unaware of her background. Even though Moana's cultural background is crucial to an understanding of who she is and the way she makes sense of her current dilemma, Dr. Simms does know something about the psychological stress associated with her impending move and all that it entails.

Let's look at what Dr. Simms could do in the light of the multicultural competencies that began this chapter. The first competency is **counselor awareness of own cultural values and biases.** Dr. Simms would display multicultural sensitivity if he is aware of his attitudes and beliefs, given the cultural and racial diversity between Moana and himself. Dr. Simms is of English descent and for this reason has spent considerable time researching his own family tree in England. He understands the importance of his own cultural heritage, and is clear about his group's associated values and beliefs, and knows how his parents' Britishness (e.g., formality, individualism) has affected him personally. His history will also tell him that the British, his ancestors, colonized the Maori, Moana's ancestors. Away from therapy, Dr. Simms will need to work through any feelings of guilt or shame he has because of his historical reality. Moreover, if Dr. Simms recognized the limits of his multicultural expertise, this would help him know where his shortcomings are with Moana and how best to overcome them in order not to hamper quality service delivery. Recognizing that his interactions with people from different racial and cultural groups is rather limited and that such lack of exposure may provoke feelings of discomfort within him in this cross-cultural counseling relationship will also help Dr. Simms. Acknowledging the differences is important, as is knowing ways to address them within the counseling relationship. It would not be inappropriate for Dr. Simms to ask Moana questions about her culture or her traditions. It would be irresponsible, however, for Dr. Simms not to do some research on his own or to talk with informed others to reduce his level of inexperience and thus increase his feelings of

competence with Moana. Dr. Simms, independent of his counseling relationship with Moana, also works to understand himself as a racial being and seeks to eradicate a racist ideology from his life. This would entail confronting any of his stereotypes about Pacific Island people or immigrant groups. Part of Dr. Simms's investigation could be to research the effects of colonization on Maori and other indigenous people. For instance, the Treaty of Waitangi is essential knowledge regarding New Zealand and race relations between Maori and Whites (also known as *Pakeha*). Glynn et al. (1997) provided insight into the knowledge of the treaty:

> Despite the promises of the treaty, the history of the relationship between Maori and European people in New Zealand (Pakeha) has not been characterized by partnership and power sharing but rather by political and social domination by the Pakeha majority. This history has progressed through armed struggle, biased legislation and successive educational policies and initiatives that have imposed Pakeha language and knowledge codes at the expense of Maori. (p. 102)

The desire for Moana to return to the South Pacific and be involved in the indigenous movement is indicative of her understanding of her country's history and the injustices that describe what has transpired between Maori and Whites. Toward embracing the second competency, **counselor awareness of client's worldview,** Dr. Simms needs to understand the land takeovers and the genocide—the oppression of Maori people—to best serve Moana's psychological needs. More specifically, an understanding of Moana's culture and ethnicity and their impact on her personhood and career choice is essential. For instance, Maori people value collaborative and collective relationships and are influenced by the sacred connections to their ancestors and to the land.

The third competency is **culturally appropriate intervention strategies.** Moana is largely affected by the traditional spirituality of Maori people and less so by Christian traditions. Dr. Simms is a Christian. As a culturally skilled counselor, he would understand aspects of Moana's spirituality that would be relevant for her overall well-being, such as singing traditional songs (*waita*), honoring the elders, and being on the *Marae* (Maori meeting house). Tate (1998) stated that, among Maori, the making of links is essential and that these links are with *whanau,* or the family. *Whanaungatanga,* or the principles of relationships with family, are eternal. Wehrly (1995) cited other dimensions of Maori culture that are relevant for counseling: *whakamanawa,* which is encouragement and showing compassion; and *mauri,* which is self-esteem and the ability to be in touch with things spiritual. As a culturally skilled counselor, Dr. Simms would be able to consult with traditional healers and, if necessary, make referrals within Moana's indigenous community. Although Dr. Simms does not speak the Maori language, it would be important for him to value bilingualism and be interested in knowing some Maori terms, such as *kia ora,* which is a greeting and welcome.

If Dr. Simms were to administer any type of assessment instrument to Moana to help her clarify career interests and strengths, he would need to understand the potential bias of such instruments, given the cultural context in which they are normed. Despite the fact that Moana has lived in the United States the majority of her life, her cultural context was not part of the norming process.

If Dr. Simms does not consider Moana's cultural heritage, then his interactions with her would be problematic and disrespectful of who she is as a cultural being. Moana and her counselor have some gender, racial, ethnic, and religious differences. These visible differences could have strong implications for the counseling event. Lorde (1978), however, reminded her readers that "it is not differences that immobilize but silence. And there are so many silences to be broken" (p. 44).

Dr. Simms has neither knowledge of Maori people nor much interaction with people of color outside his work. He can be effective with considerable effort on his part. After all, Moana is worth it, and Dr. Simms knows she is.

SUMMARY

This chapter offered an overview of multicultural competencies and skills. An overview of counselor education diversity training programs was also provided, as well as strategies for becoming a multiculturally competent counselor. The importance of monitoring dissonance and measuring cross-cultural effectiveness was discussed through the Storytelling. The case study dealt with the question of referring clients to different counselors when a cross-cultural counseling relationship exists.

REFERENCES

Abernathy, A. D. (1995). Managing racial anger: A critical skill in cultural competence. *Journal of Multicultural Counseling & Development, 23,* 96–102.

Arredondo, P., Toporek, R., Brown, S. P., Jones, J., Locke, D. C., Sanchez, J., & Stadler, H. (1996). Operationalization of the multicultural competencies. *Journal of Multicultural Counseling & Development, 24,* 42–78.

Bowman, V. E. (1996). Counselor self-awareness and ethnic self-knowledge as a critical component of multicultural training. In J. L. DeLucia-Waack (Ed.), *Multicultural counseling competencies: Implications for training and practice* (pp. 7–30). Alexandria, VA: Association for Counselor Education and Supervision.

Brown, S. P., Parham, T. A., & Yonker, R. (1996). Influence of a cross-cultural training course on racial identity attitudes of White women and men: Preliminary perspectives. *Journal of Counseling & Development, 74,* 510–516.

Cottone, R. R., & Tarvydas, V. M. (1998). *Ethical and professional issues in counseling.* Upper Saddle River, NJ: Merrill/Prentice Hall.

D'Andrea, M., & Daniels, J. (1991). Exploring the different levels of multicultural counseling training in counselor education. *Journal of Counseling & Development, 70,* 78–85.

Dinsmore, J. A., & England, J. T. (1996). A study of multicultural counseling training at CACREP-accredited counselor education programs. *Counseling Education and Supervision, 36,* 1, 58–76.

Discovery News Brief. (1998, August 11). *Study: Maori ancestors were Chinese* [On line]. Available: http://www.discovery.com/news/briefs/brief3.html

Glynn, T., Berryman, M., Atvars, K., Harawira, W., Kaiwai, H., Walker, R., & Tari, R. (1997). Research, training, and indigenous rights to self-determination: Challenges arising from a New Zealand bicultural journey. In *International School Psychology XXth Annual Colloquium, Proceedings.*

Hartung, P. J. (1996). Transforming counseling courses: From monocultural to multicultural. *Counseling Education and Supervision, 36,* 1, 6–13.

Hoffman, R. M. (1996). Gender: Issues of power and equity in counselor education programs. *Counselor Education and Supervision, 36,* 104–112.

Lorde, A. (1978). *Sister outside: Essays and speeches.* Freedom, CA: Crossing Press.

McIntosh, P. (1989, July/August). White privilege: Unpacking the invisible White knapsack. *Peace and Freedom.*

Orange, C. (1989). *The story of a treaty.* Wellington, New Zealand: Bridget Williams Books.

Ottavi, T. M., Pope-Davis, D. B., & Dings, J. G. (1994). Relationship between White racial identity attitudes and self-reported multicultural counseling competencies. *Journal of Counseling Psychology, 41,* 149–154.

Pinderhughes, E. (1989). *Understanding race, ethnicity, and power: The key to efficacy in clinical practice.* New York: Free Press.

Ponterotto, J. G., Alexander, C. M., & Grieger, I. (1995). A multicultural competency checklist for counseling training programs. *Journal of Multicultural Counseling & Development, 23,* 11–20.

Ponterotto, J. G., & Casas, J. M. (1991). *Handbook of racial/ethnic minority counseling research.* Springfield, IL: Charles C Thomas.

Rollock, D., & Terrell, M. D. (1996). Multicultural issues in assessment: Toward an inclusive model. In J. L. DeLucia-Waack (Ed.), *Multicultural counseling competencies: Implications for training and practice* (pp. 113–156). Alexandria, VA: Association for Counselor Education and Supervision.

Smith, L. T. (1997). Maori women: Discourses, projects, and *mana wahine.* In S. Middleton & A. Jones (Eds.), *Women and education in Aotearoa* (pp. 33–51). Auckland, New Zealand: Auckland University Press.

Sue, D. W., Arredondo, P., & McDavis, R. J. (1992). Multicultural counseling competencies and standards: A call to the profession. *Journal of Counseling & Development, 70,* 477–483.

Sue, D. W., Bernier, J. E., Daran, A., Feinberg, L., Pedersen, P., Smith, C. T., & Vasquez-Nuttale, G. (1982). Cross-cultural counseling competencies. *Counseling Psychologist, 19,* 45–52.

Sue, D. W., Ivey, A. E., & Pedersen, P. B. (1996). *A theory of multicultural counseling and therapy.* Pacific Grove, CA: Brooks/Cole.

Tate, P. H. (1998, March 29). *Whanaungatanga.* Keynote speech at the meeting of the New Zealand Association of Counselors, New Zealand.

Wehrly, B. (1995). *Pathways to multicultural counseling competence: A developmental journey.* Pacific Grove, CA: Brooks/Cole.

Chapter 14

Empowering Clients

Throw it away. Throw it away. Give your love. Live your life. Each and every day. And keep your hand wide open. Let the sunshine through. 'Cause you can never ever lose a thing if it belongs to you.

Abbey Lincoln, "Throw It Away"*

*   From "Throw It Away," written by A. Lincoln, 1995, New York: Gitanes Jazz Productions. Copyright 1995. Reprinted with permission.

A primary goal of the therapeutic process is to foster self-empowerment for the client and to encourage greater psychological functioning. To facilitate client empowerment, counselors first need to understand their own multiple identities and to confront unresolved issues that could eventually rob them of their personal power and overall efficacy during the therapeutic event (Bernardez, 1987). A primary intention, then, of the therapeutic event is to foster greater self-understanding toward enhanced functioning intrapersonally and interpersonally (Corey, 1991).

Empowerment is viewed as one goal of psychotherapy. Many definitions exist. Pinderhughes (1995) said that "empowerment is defined as achieving reasonable control over one's destiny, learning to cope constructively with debilitating forces in society, and acquiring the competence to initiate change at the individual and systems level" (p. 136). According to McWhirter (1991), empowerment is a process wherein people or groups of people who lack power become cognizant of the power dynamics that operate in their lives (e.g., prejudice, discrimination) and as a result are able to acquire reasonable control in their lives without encroaching on others' rights. An example of empowerment is recognizing how internalized homophobia, manifested through confining behaviors (e.g., avoiding friendships with gay people if one is heterosexual) and self-denigrating thoughts (e.g., feeling that one is sick and crazy if one is gay), impedes progress and the formation of a healthy self-image. Subsequent to expanded awareness, an observable change in thoughts and behavior takes place that leads to more control without infringing on others' rights and that involves the support of empowerment of others. Finally, Dulany (1990) stated that empowerment "is another term for finding one's own voice. In order to speak, we must know what we want to say; in order to be heard, we must dare to speak" (p. 133).

In this chapter, power, individually and interpersonally, are presented as a salient theme in the discussion of empowerment. Factors that render people voiceless and leave them feeling incapacitated regarding their own lives are also a point of focus. The conflict between the traditional male role, empowerment, and seeking therapeutic assistance is also a focal point of discussion throughout this chapter.

DUBIOUS NOTIONS OF POWER AND POWERLESSNESS

Powerlessness is operationalized as the "inability to direct the course of one's life due to societal conditions and power dynamics, lack of skills, or lack of faith that one can change one's life" (McWhirter, 1991, p. 224). Powerlessness results in persons feeling unable to have any meaningful impact on their lives. Feelings associated with this disempowered state were identified by Pinderhughes (1989) as less comfort and pleasure, less gratification, more pain, feelings of inferiority and insecurity, and a strong tendency to depression.

Several conditions contribute to a sense of powerlessness. Loss of a meaningful relationship, dream, or hope or a change in status (including poor physical health, financial strain, or career immobilization) can leave an individual feeling insecure, depressed, and emotionally troubled. Likewise, gains in these areas can be vehicles for transporting power. Often, when our students are asked what makes them feel powerful, many will respond with the following: being listened to, being in a loving relationship, having money in the bank, getting a good education, and having physical health.

Myers et al. (1991) believed that oppression, which is arguably an outgrowth of feelings of powerlessness, occurs when one's power, an internal construct, is externalized or dictated by a force or entity outside the self. They stated that persons who are oppressed adopt a suboptimal conceptual system characterized by the validation of the self as a basis of external legitimation, as opposed to an intrinsic orientation that contributes to a solid sense of self. Within this framework, to conclude that female gender, low socioeconomic status, physical disability, and being a person of color are automatically associated with individual feelings of less power is erroneous. Although these statuses tend to be devalued in U.S. society, such a perspective fails to respect the enormous role of self-determination in shaping personal attitudes. Oppression in the form of racism, sexism, ageism, discrimination against people with disabilities, and homophobia can evoke feelings of powerlessness. This is particularly the case when the institutionalization of policies and practices that confer or deny privilege based on race, gender, class and other identities is wide-scale. These identity constructs, however, need not function as the media for transporting feelings of powerlessness and disempowerment.

A disproportionate share of persons in poverty are people of color: Most jobs are stratified by race, ethnicity, and gender, with women of color at the bottom of the occupational hierarchy and White males at the top; and among Black men, the rates of morbidity, mortality, incarceration, and criminal victimization are higher than among both White men and women and Black women (Gary, 1987, p. 232). Being poor or unemployed, however, does not dictate psychological or moral powerlessness, although these conditions do suggest greater levels of vulnerability before institutions such as police, courts, and schools (Robinson, 1999).

More power is characterized by less tendency to depression, more pleasure, less pain, and feelings of superiority (Pinderhughes, 1989). And although persons who are European American, able-bodied, heterosexual, middle-class, and male are often perceived as the referent point for normalcy, possession of these characteristics does not ensure psychological empowerment (Robinson, 1999). To believe so is to attribute certain psychological and moral characteristics based on identity constructs (e.g., race, gender, class).

POWER AND THE THERAPEUTIC PROCESS

Counselors need to assess for themselves whether they have internalized a societal standard. Does a marginalized, less-empowered status more readily fit a person who is White, male, able-bodied, and middle-class? Historical and contemporary reality are replete with examples where economic and occupational power do not prescribe psychological and moral strength. Likewise, the lack of such demonstrable types of power does not indicate immorality or victimization.

Power and powerlessness are by no means mutually exclusive categories in people's lives. Swanson (1993) maintained that each gender and race has unique feelings of power and powerlessness. Yet, the faulty notion remains that one group's power engenders the other's powerlessness. And although masculinity is often construed with hegemonic power and men's dominance over women, Pleck (1985) contended that men depend on women and perceive women as having power over them in certain arenas. For example, Pleck argued that because of socialization practices in which men are taught to restrict emotionality and women are generally taught to express it (see the case study "A Man Lost and in Need"), women have *expressive power* over men, or the power to express emotion. Another form of power that women have over men is *masculinity validating power,* or men's dependence on women to affirm their masculinity and validate their manhood. A system of this nature reinforces homophobia because it is dependent on rigid adherence to notions of gender and sex-role-appropriate behaviors that operate exclusively in the context of heterosexuality.

Helping professionals who operate from clients' strengths and believe in their clients' abilities to affect positively the quality of their own lives are in a better position to facilitate client empowerment (McWhirter, 1991; Pinderhughes, 1989). Mental health professionals who maintain that clients are victims because of the oppressiveness of the social context and that they have little opportunity to affect power dynamics directly are not instrumental in creating hope and healing. Counselors also need to be careful about mystifying the counseling event, particularly if it accentuates the power differential between client and counselor. Although counselors and therapists possess knowledge of human development and an understanding of how to facilitate client empowerment, the counseling process is by no means a magical one in which the therapist is free of any personal conflicts and the client is solely dependent on the counselor (McWhirter, 1991). Counseling is a reciprocal process wherein the counselor is often very moved and influenced by the client's stories, courage, and acts of resilience. Empowerment in the counseling event ultimately results in the client knowing that she is in a position of authority regarding her life. When future challenges arise, insight is available and can be accessed for better negotiating the situation.

Although power can be abused by fostering client dependence, it can also be used constructively to facilitate growth and insight. Pinderhughes (1989) stated that accepting the reality of one's powerless position can bring a sense of power, an admittedly ironic statement. Reframing the situation to one's advantage (through the help of a skilled counselor) and choosing not to internalize negative behaviors and attitudes are in themselves acts of empowerment. To balance the power differential between client and counselor, empathy is a necessary tool as it represents one of the most important themes in therapy or counseling (Pinderhughes, 1989).

Kaplan (1987) described **empathy** as a function of both advanced cognitive and affective dimensions. She said empathy is "the capacity to take in the experience and the affect of the other without being overwhelmed by it on the one hand or defensively blocking it out on the other hand" (p. 13). She went on to say that the therapist must be able to yield (yielding is a traditionally female quality) to the affect of another person while being able to interpret the meaning of this affect within the cognitive domains. Incidentally, the act of yielding denotes enormous power. In short, the therapist needs to be comfortable with a range of emotions—his and those of another.

Empathy allows the therapist to be touched and affected by what is shared by another. Moreover, empathy allows a respect for differences that exist between counselor and client, as well as an acknowledgment of the similarities. Where appropriate, the counselor advocates on behalf of the client by, for example, making out-of-office interventions. However, empowerment and advocacy differ substantially from rescuing. McWhirter (1991) reminded us as counselors that taking responsibility for doing what another person is capable of doing for the self is disempowering. Ultimately, it prevents the individual from assuming personal responsibility. Counselors need to remember that regardless of the presenting issues that bring a client to counseling, the client needs to know that she is an expert on her life and in collaboration with the therapist is seeking to improve on a situation or to cope more effectively with it. As the client is healing psychologically and emotionally, it is vital that the problem not be seen as located within the client. Narrative therapists often refer to *externalizing conversations,* wherein the goal is to separate a problem from the client. In doing so, the client is not entrapped in self-blame (Monk, Winslade, Crocket, & Epston, 1997). Despite the power imbalance that exists between counselor and client, it is important that the counselor not be perceived as trouble-free. Such a perception can serve to obscure both the counselor and the counseling event.

COUNSELORS, WORLDVIEW, AND CLIENT EMPOWERMENT

Each person is affected by the implicit and explicit messages of **culture,** which refers to elements of values, norms, beliefs, attitudes, and behavior styles (Pinderhughes, 1989). As cultural beings, counselors are no exception. To be most effective, helping professionals need to be aware of their **worldviews,** or how they see the world and interact with it.

To characterize worldview, four dimensions are often used: (a) people/nature relationships, (b) social relationships, (c) activity modality, and (d) time focus. The purpose of these dimensions, outlined in the value-orientation model and described in greater detail in Chapter 2, is not to suggest that one type of worldview is inherently better or worse than another. The crucial point is that there are differences. These differences in worldview, which have their manifestation in the counseling event, are largely molded by culture. For instance, in a culture such as that of the United States, women are more likely to receive a diagnosis of mental disorder, are more often prescribed psychotropic medication, and take more prescription and over-the-counter drugs than men (Crose, Nicholas, Gobble, & Frank, 1992).

Because service delivery is not worldview-free, it is influenced by counselors' personal positions on substantive and controversial issues, such as abortion, politics, gender roles, and race relations. Berger (1985) discussed how some therapists might encounter difficulty, particularly those who have internalized conventional notions of gender role behavior, in supporting men who espouse nontraditional gender roles. Differences in gender roles between counselor and client can be potentially problematic if the counselor is uncomfortable with the nature of the difference or, worse, unaware that discomfort exists. Inevitably, the therapeutic event is limited when therapists leave such issues largely unexamined. Thus, the man who stays at home with his young children while his wife is in the workplace as the primary breadwinner is engaging in nontraditional behaviors that depart from customary notions of appropriate gender role behavior. Although it would be unethical and unprofessional to dissuade this man from staying at home with his children, gender role stereotypes can creep into the counseling event. O'Malley and Richardson (1985) found this to be true in their investigation of sex bias in the counseling event. In this study, both male and female counselors perceived men and women in fairly stereotypical ways. More specifically, mental health professionals believed that a man should have masculine characteristics and not strong feminine ones and that a woman should have feminine traits and not strong masculine ones. Similarly, heterosexual counselors have been conditioned by a homophobic society, and their biases can interfere with their ability to hear and/or respect a gay man's or lesbian's lived experiences (Browning, Reynolds, & Dworkin, 1991).

GENDER, EMPOWERMENT, AND THERAPY

As discussed in Chapter 5, the socialization differences for men and women have been documented widely (Mintz & O'Neil, 1990). Essentially, men tend to be socialized to be assertive, powerful, and independent and to restrict emotion. Women are often socialized to be nurturant and emotional and to direct achievement through affiliation with others, particularly men (Mintz & O'Neil, 1990). Such socialization patterns in early childhood have implications for adulthood intrapersonal and interpersonal relationships (see the case study "A Man Lost and in Need"). Skovholt (1993) said that "learning rigid masculinity—the skill that prepares one to fight and defend—is a major task of childhood and adolescent male socialization" (p. 3).

Regarding the intellectual domain, researchers maintain there are gender differences in development. Again, the male pattern is often presumed to be superior, with men often being regarded as objective or "separate knowers," and women termed subjective or "connected knowers" (Crose et al., 1992). Brown and Gilligan (1992) criticized this perspective:

> To call women connected and men separate seems to us profoundly mis-
> leading; to say that men wanted domination and power while women
> wanted love and relationship seemed to us to ignore the depths of men's
> desires for relationship and the anger women feel about not having power
> in the world. (p. 11)

The role of women in multicultural counseling has not been explored in great depth in the literature. Arredondo, Psalti, and Cella (1993) stated,

> There is a need to attend to women's individual differences within and
> across cultural groups; to the interaction of cultural and gender socializa-
> tion; to forces of sexism, racism, and homophobia and their impact on
> identity, esteem, and empowerment; and to the portrayals of women in the
> multicultural counseling literature. (p. 5)

As stated throughout this text, it is important to look at each client from her respective worldview so that her cultural, gender, religious, and political backgrounds are not ignored but included in the therapy process. Therapists have traditionally taken a unidimensional approach to counseling that negates the female experience in terms of how women use their affect and cognition in connection to their life experiences (Arredondo et al., 1993). Although the majority of people in therapy are girls and women, the prevalence of females in therapy need not be related to a higher degree of mental disturbances among this population. Socialization processes that allow help-seeking behavior to be more familiar among women than it is among men need to be questioned (Crose et al., 1992).

Men have been taught, and subsequently have learned, to restrict emotional expression and to equate seeking help with femininity or the negation of masculinity. This way of conceptualizing manhood is problematic and represents a vicious cycle for men. Good and Mintz (1990) found that men's restrictive emotionality actually seems related to depression and negative attitudes toward seeking professional psychological help. Good, Dell, and Mintz (1989) also found that men's restrictive emotionality decreased men's indicated likelihood of future help seeking and past help-seeking behavior from several sources. In sum, the men who are most emotionally inhibited are at risk of being least likely to get the help they need as they are more likely to have negative attitudes about the helping process. Among African American men, Gary (1987) found an important relationship between depression scores and amount of conflict in male-female relationships. These data strongly suggest that depression has consequences for both intrapersonal and interpersonal functioning.

Gender intersects with other identity constructs; thus, gender similarities do not negate the racial differences, nor do racial similarities negate important gender differences. Chow (1991) discussed the convergence of societal messages about gender and cultural messages on ethnicity for Asian American women: "These women have been socialized to accept their devaluation, restricted roles for women, psychological reinforcement of gender stereotypes, and a subordinate position within Asian communities as in the society at large" (p. 256). Chow's insight may not be true for Asian men, although certain Asian men occupy subordinate positions because of their membership in groups that are devalued. If race and gender are allowed to emerge as the primary status-determining variables, the yokes of gender and racial oppression within similar gender and racial groups becomes dismissed or minimized.

Gender role parings between clients and counselors represent certain power dynamics. When counselor and client are both male, homophobia may prevent the men from forming close alliances with one another as this type of bond may be misconstrued as homosexual. Issues of control and power may also evidence, given the socialization processes of dominance and competition for men in society (Mintz & O'Neil, 1990). The male counselor-female client dyad has until recently been the norm. In this dyad, the man may automatically assume a one-up position or treat the woman as a sex object. The woman may also repress anger because of her fear that it would be viewed as unacceptable (Bernardez, 1987; Devoe, 1990). Certainly, those men who are unwilling to examine their position of privilege become immediately suspect of not being the most effective counselors for women. Furthermore, those men who seek to seduce women and promote dependency are highly inappropriate helpers as well. The female counselor-male client dyad represents the typical caregiving pattern; however, some men may be uncomfortable being in a less powerful position as clients. Women who are tentative about their own personal power may defer to male clients, thus abdicating their professional role. In some contexts, the female therapist may fear the arousal or expression of her own anger and of societally forbidden aggressive impulses toward a male client. Such perceptions threaten important relational bonds with men regardless of the context or power dynamic (Bernardez, 1987).

With growing emphasis on feminist therapy, the female client-female therapist dyad has become most popular. Women who are socialized to devalue themselves and have internalized demeaning messages about womanhood may unconsciously view the female counselor as less capable and competent than a male counselor. Research has found this dyad to be more emotionally intense and to provide for a fuller exploration of childhood experiences (Mintz & O'Neil, 1990). Bernardez (1987) warned that the female therapist needs to avoid both the dread of "female destructiveness" and the belief that all women will be nurturing and have maternal characteristics. Nonetheless, Bernardez reported that female therapists appear to have a greater degree of flexibility than their male colleagues.

FEMINIST THERAPY FOR WOMEN AND MEN

Feminist therapy differs philosophically from traditional psychotherapy in that it seeks to understand the experiences of women within their social contexts while challenging systematic gender inequality. Devoe (1990) stated that "feminist therapy emphasizes the need for social change by improving the lives of women rather than by helping them adjust to traditional roles in society" (p. 33). In feminist therapy, a critique of how a male-dominated and patriarchal society often deems women as other, inferior, and invisible is ongoing. Because psychotherapy is largely influenced by dominant cultural values, the mental health system has participated in the oppression of women by assessing women from a male model. One strength of feminist therapy is that it acknowledges the sexist and unjust society in which women and men live and thus seeks to educate women and men about this while respecting women's anger and men's sadness (Devoe, 1992). Effective counselors need to see how men have been oppressed under the system of patriarchy and sexism as well (Robinson, 1999). Such a perspective has implications for the way clients are viewed and the way clients come to see themselves.

Western psychotherapy is largely influenced by a psychoanalytical framework, European philosophers, and a hierarchical structure based on hegemonic power. More specifically, the therapist, most likely a male, is seen as the expert, and the client, traditionally a woman, is recognized as dependent. Feminist therapy questions this construction and argues that a more collaborative, egalitarian relationship is needed between client and counselor if therapy is to be therapeutic and ultimately empowering. Devoe (1990) spoke about an egalitarian relationship and the importance of an emotional link between the client and her counselor prior to effective therapeutic work occurring. "The counselor must view the client as an equal both in and out of the counseling relationship . . . [T]he personal power between the client and counselor should be equal whenever possible" (p. 35).

More contemporary forms of psychotherapy have challenged the premises of Freudian psychology, such as Adler and Rogers (see Corey, 1991). These theorists, however, have often been silent about the social-political contexts in which women exist—contexts constructed by gender and race relations, which for many women are perceived as oppressive and marginalizing.

Personal power should be equal, whenever possible, between client and therapist (Devoe, 1992). If the therapist's underlying premise is that the woman intuitively knows what is in her best interest, then the therapist accepts a different power position. Undoubtedly, quality professional training and years of relevant experience provide insight into mental health issues, but this learned and external knowledge does not supplant the woman's subjective and constructed knowledge even if she has yet to tap into it. Finally, a feminist perspective allows the counseling process to unfold at the pace that is most comfortable for the client.

Among many women, the enormous strength of gender-based messages results in the internalization of messages that are in direct contradiction to the development of voice and autonomy. For example, a substantial number of women do not understand the value of psychotherapy in general and feminist or womanist therapy in particular. Although participation in movements for social justice tends to increase gender consciousness, Chow (1991) stated that some women of color perceive that uniting with men of color toward racial equality is a higher priority than increasing gender consciousness with White women. From a dialectical perspective, increasing both racial and gender consciousness is crucial because women of color are always, at all times, both female and racial and/or ethnic beings. Comas-Diaz and Greene

(1994) spoke about the intersections of these identities: "Due to the pervasive effects of racism and the concomitant need for people of color to bond together, women of color experience conflicting loyalties in which racial solidarity often transcends gender and sexual orientation solidarity" (pp. 4–5). Consequently, becoming aware of gender issues may be difficult for women of color who contend with both racial and gender discrimination. It is common for women to feel overwhelmed at the dynamics of both layers of oppression. Yet, it is important for women to become aware of multiple identities that need not be experienced as oppressive. While one seeks to unite with people who are oriented toward the amelioration of inequity that transcends divisive gender, racial, and class boundaries, similarities can be a focal point (Chow, 1991). It is also essential for people, independent of the constellation of their identities, to define themselves apart from the context of oppression and discrimination (Robinson, 1999; see also the Storytelling "When Helpers Hurt").

IMPLICATIONS FOR COUNSELORS

It is not possible to empower clients without the counselor being culturally competent. Pinderhughes (1995) outlined the necessary skills and abilities needed to

STORYTELLING
When Helpers Hurt

Clara came into our lives as a gift. She knew Mary first; they were graduate students together. And then I came as a new assistant professor and taught my very first class, Gender Issues in Counseling, with both Mary and Clara. They were stellar students. I learned more than they did. The universe sends great teachers. Clara finished her master's and then a few years later was accepted to the doctoral program. She chose me to be her chair and adviser. What a privilege it is for students to choose you. Clara and I were also friends, spending time at each other's home. We both loved to cook, and Clara was better at it than I. As I went through the tenure process, Clara was there for me and told me that if I did not get tenure I should not "throw my pearls before swine." I slept well after that loving Saturday night phone conversation with her. Knowing her was to stand in the presence of an angel.

Clara had a son who was very troubled. For years, she dealt with his temper, insolence, and dangerous ways. One night, she had him arrested for stealing from her. He was let out of jail the same night he was put in. This son shot Clara as she slept. He killed her. Clara's death was tragic and oppressive. Yet, when I remember Clara, oppression is not an adequate way to define her life. Clara loved so big. She had a stunning and quiet power. She taught me that "it's in every one of us to be free—to be wise." Clara was a free spirit. Her spirit is now free.

Tracy

empower clients: (a) the ability to respect and appreciate the values, beliefs, and practices of all clients; (b) knowledge of specific values and cultural practices of clients; (c) the ability to be comfortable with differences; (d) the ability to change false beliefs; and (e) the ability to think and behave flexibly. The constellation of the client's and counselor's identities has to be considered within the therapeutic context as the identities influence the nature of the presenting problem and its interpretation. Thus, in the empowerment process, cultural competence is a crucial issue. Pinderhughes said,

> Empowerment of diverse populations requires culturally competent practitioners. To intervene effectively, they must be able to avoid using such automatic responses to difference as stereotyping, projection, or distancing. Moreover, they must become aware of internalized responses resulting from their development perspective. (pp. 132, 133)

Given that traditional counseling and psychotherapy are steeped in a Western cultural paradigm, many culturally diverse clients have had less than beneficial experiences with the mental health establishment, which has been insensitive to sociopolitical realities that affect mental and social functioning. Ridley (1989) said,

> Compared to white clients, ethnic minority clients are more likely to receive inaccurate diagnoses; be assigned to junior professionals; receive low-cost, less preferred treatment consisting of minimal contact, medication, or custodial care rather than individual psychotherapy; be disproportionately represented in mental health facilities; show a much higher rate of premature termination; and have more unfavorable impressions regarding treatment. (p. 55)

Although signs of improvement are on the horizon, with many colleges and universities requiring multicultural counseling courses for students in training, the assessment of multicultural and gender competencies continues to be unrealized in many counseling programs (D'Andrea & Daniels, 1991). This is problematic for two reasons: (a) Research documents that some counselors hold stereotypical views of men and women (O'Malley & Richardson, 1985), as well as of people of color (Sue & Sue, 1990); and (b) counselors' unexamined gender, class, and racial biases and prejudices hinder the empowerment of clients (Pinderhughes, 1989).

In some circumstances, having a one-on-one client-counselor relationship is not possible or even desirable. For instance, some women may prefer seeing a female counselor, but their communities may lack available female counselors. Many counselors are inadequately prepared to work with diverse clients who present with particular concerns such as worrying about safety levels or confronting sociopolitical barriers to racism (Washington, 1987). Although the status of being a counselor of color or a woman or both does not ensure that one is able to work effectively with diverse clients, the desire, for example, for a same-race counselor is often a result of identification of "similar emotional and physical experiences with racism, and more of a willingness to confront this external barrier" (Washington, 1987, p. 198).

Finances are yet another factor that may hinder a client-counselor interaction. Costs may be a factor for people who lack insurance or whose insurance does not give them access to a preferred counselor of their choice. Sliding fees can make counseling more accessible to many clients, and although it is not encouraged by the American Counseling Association bylaws, in many communities across race and class, bartering is done within the context of counseling.

CASE STUDY
A Man Lost and in Need

John is a 39-year-old, physically healthy European American male living in North Carolina with his wife, Jill, also age 39. They are working class; both have some college. Jill would like to finish her degree and become a nurse. She works as a nurse's aide at a local hospital. Six months ago, their 12-year-old daughter, Johna, named after her father, died from leukemia. During her daughter's illness, Jill attended a support group for parents with terminally ill children. She also received individual counseling to help her deal with her enormous grief. She continues to do so. Although Jill repeatedly encouraged John to attend counseling and group with her, he refused. He did not want a group of strangers knowing about his personal hell.

Actually, Jill's attendance at group has been a source of conflict between the couple. John complains about Jill talking to people about their private lives, yet Jill notices that John relies on her to help him process his feelings, which has become increasingly more fatiguing for her. Prior to Johna's death, Jill talked at length with her daughter about her love for her and told her how much her daughter had added to her life. Together, they worked on a book and videotapes and recorded some songs together because they enjoyed singing in church together. They drew pictures together of what heaven might look like. John resented his wife talking to Johna as if there was no hope of a cure and refused to act as if death was imminent. He prayed diligently for a cure, did extensive research to find out about his child's illness, and donated his own bone marrow. He and Johna, until she became physically weak, enjoyed bicycle riding and hiking. They also were avid science fiction fans and never missed an episode of "Star Trek."

Three weeks after Johna's funeral, Jill returned to her job as a music instructor. John, an electrician at a power company, chose to return to work 2 days after the funeral. His supervisor told him to take as much time off as he needed. During the 6 months since his daughter's death, John, an occasional drinker, has been consuming more alcohol than is customary. He has insomnia and as a result of his interrupted sleeping patterns at night has been having a difficult time getting out of bed in the mornings. He has lost weight. At times, John withdraws from Jill, still refuses to go to counseling, has stopped going to church, and does not pray anymore. He also refuses to talk to the minister. He has started seeing another woman and is sexually involved with her.

Because of John's declining work performance (e.g., coming in late, making numerous errors), John's supervisor is requiring him to go to counseling if he is to continue in his current position. His counselor is an African American female, Ms. Jensen. She has an master's degree in counselor education and is a licensed professional counselor.

QUESTIONS
1. What types of traditional male role behaviors is John exhibiting?
2. What type of impact is John's male role having on his help-seeking behaviors?
3. Given John's loss, is his depression normal?
4. What types of challenges might Ms. Jensen encounter in counseling with John?
5. Has Jill's gender socialization benefited her in her ability to ask for help during her time of grief?

DISCUSSION AND INTEGRATION
The Client, John

John is a man in need. His only child has died, and he has come to the end of himself. His powerlessness and sadness are evident, as is his need for help.

John appears to be subscribing to a traditional male role. In their research, Thompson and Pleck (1987) found this role to be related to status, toughness, and antifemininity and to be influential on one's thinking about self and interactions with others. Masculine attitudes most likely have predisposed John to feeling negatively about seeking psychological help during his time of loss. His restricted emotionality and perception that he needs to be self-reliant and in control at all times contribute to his belief that he has to deal with his tragic loss independent of others. This attitude makes him vulnerable to depression while serving to perpetuate an unhealthy cycle. Masculinity may have the ability to "ventriloquize the universal" (Wiegman, 1994), but a high tax is associated with it.

Although people have an earnest and existential need to bring meaning to their lives, at times the most valiant inquiries into the far reaches of the soul fail to satisfy. The ability finally to yield to that which hurts and is by all appearances grossly unfair is indicative of power and is the essence of recovery. John's abrupt return to work after burying his daughter suggests that John sought to abort the healing process by returning to life as normal. Change is difficult; however, trying to move ahead as if life could possibly return to the way it was prior to Johna's death is a form of denial. Clearly, working hard and being productive can be useful components of the recovery process, yet to heal properly, ample energy and time are required for transition through the normal depression associated with the loss of a child. John's drinking is indicative of a failed coping strategy. Alcohol can serve as a temporary anesthetic in that it can reduce the intensity of feelings one experiences (incidentally, antidepressants, by their very nature, can have a similar effect). John has a host of emotions he does not want to feel: profound emotional pain over his child's long and painful illness, feelings of failure as his daughter's protector, anger toward a seemingly abandoning and useless God, conflict with his wife over her help-seeking methods, uncertainty about and powerlessness over the future, and a tragic sense of loss and emptiness at not seeing his only child grow, develop, and become a woman.

John has been exposed to socialization messages that he is to be a protector and remain in control. The effective counselor perceives that a significant part of John's pain is connected to his sadness, anger, guilt, and feelings of powerlessness that he was not able to protect his child from the illness that eventually ended her life. His extramarital relationship is one of John experiencing more power in his life. John's sense of control has been interrupted, and for men this often is an intolerable feeling. John has noteworthy strengths. The case study indicates that he did research to become more familiar with his child's illness, he prayed, and he donated bone marrow. In time, John will experience peace as he recognizes that although his efforts did not keep his child from dying, he did all he could. In time, he may see his actions as sufficient. John is in the throes of a crisis of faith. His absence from church, inability to pray, and unwillingness to speak with his minister are partial indications of his internal wrestlings. Although John's anger may not be directly expressed or articulated, John is angry and most likely disappointed in God. For men who subscribe to the traditional masculine role, dealing with existential issues such as death is more difficult. Among women characterized predominantly by the female role, confrontation of existential themes is also more of a challenge than it is for androgynous persons (Stevens, Pfost, & Potts, 1990).

As disruptive as they are to stability and equilibrium, crises can catapult people into higher stages of growth. At work, John has been making multiple mistakes and is overly preoccupied, given his depression, insomnia, and increased drinking. Out of concern for John, the supervisor requires him to seek professional help, which can be a form of saving grace for John. Having to see the counselor will most likely intensify his feelings of powerlessness, but if he can manage to stay with therapy, the help he desperately needs could be provided and received.

If John were African American, his race would matter to the counseling event. Because of socialization, certain groups may find the entire process of counseling to be dissonance-provoking.

The Client, Jill

Prior to her child's death, Jill embraced existential issues both with her child and with herself. Understandably, this was very painful to do, and yet there is considerable strength in being able to accept that which cannot be controlled or understood. Her ability to confront death may suggest she is psychologically androgynous because highly feminine women are more reluctant to embrace such themes (Stevens et al., 1990). Jill was also instrumental in securing the psychological help she needed and evidenced emotional autonomy. She sought help for herself despite John's disapproval (McBride, 1991). Although Good and Mintz (1990) stated that women's socialization patterns may make seeking psychological help less formidable, some women would not have made the same type of choices as Jill. Jill engaged in self-care by realizing that she was facing a difficult time in her life and that she needed help. Jill also respected the process of grieving and remained at home to mourn until she was able to return to work. Although Jill's child died, she can be comforted in the knowledge that healing is not always surviving and that surviving is not always healing. What survives is her memory of her child's love and their love together. While Johna lived, they celebrated life abundantly. Johna knew that both her parents loved her beyond measure. This is the ultimate gift and treasure of life.

To better understand Jill, Ossana, Helms, and Leonard's (1992) womanist identity model, adapted from Cross's 4-stage nigrescence model, is helpful in illuminating this process of self-awareness. The first stage in the womanist identity model is *preencounter,* which maintains that women at this stage accept traditional or stereotypical notions of womanhood. Such notions are often steeped in women's reliance on others for approval and legitimation. Naturally, the locus of control for women in this stage would be external. The second stage, *encounter,* occurs when a woman has an experience wherein she begins to question notions of womanhood and becomes aware of the prevalence of sexism in society. In the third stage, *immersion/emersion,* the woman surrounds herself with other women and literature about and by women. She is critical of the patriarchal context of society and may experience turbulent emotions, such as guilt and anger, toward herself for having been selfless for so long and at society for its history of promoting gender inequity. During the fourth and last stage, *internalization,* the woman defines womanhood on her own terms and is not bound by external definitions or dictates about what it means to be a woman.

It may appear that Jill is in a lower stage of her development, given her traditionally female characteristics: caregiver for her child and husband, and nurse. But looking closely, one can see that Jill sought out needed help to negotiate the most difficult journey of her life. She took time away from her job to heal following her daughter's funeral. She also meets with her pastor regularly for spiritual help and is in a support group with people who truly understand her situation. Such behaviors of courage, vulnerability, and integrity in the face of huge loss, her recognition and coping with of John's emotional demands on her, and getting help despite her husband's protests do not suggest a woman who has not examined her roles of womanhood. Research conducted using the womanist scale by Carter and Parks (1996) on Black and White women found a relationship between womanist identity attitudes and mental health. No relationships were found among African American women, but they were found among European American women. More specifically, White women ($n = 147$) who were not at the highest or internalization stage of womanist identity were more likely to feel depressed, anxious, and scrutinized or under attack. While grieving her child, Jill is healing through the support and love of community.

The Counselor, Ms. Jensen

The counseling event can be powerful. Because power has both constructive and destructive dimensions, it is important to distinguish between power that contributes to personal uplift and power that diminishes one's humanity. *Productive and constructive power* is at the center of a counseling relationship when a counselor creates a holding environment for a client to make passage through a difficult period. *Destructive power* occurs when one has access to resources and dominates another and imposes one's will through threats or the withholding of certain desired rewards despite implicit or explicit opposition from the less powerful.

John is experiencing emotional pain and feelings of powerlessness. Ms. Jensen will benefit John by understanding that he has come to counseling, not of his own volition, but because of an ultimatum from his supervisor. Thus, John's supervisor had power over him. Ms. Jensen would also be wise to realize that, on John's own, he had not availed himself of counseling despite his wife's encouragement. Once in counseling, John may have difficulty disclosing his feelings to a woman, although this dyad represents a traditional caregiving scenario. He may also struggle with the need to be in control. If John is characterized at a low level of racial and cultural identity development, then he may have racial attitudes that are ethnocentric. Thus, he may experience considerable dissonance over the race of Ms. Jensen. It is also likely that John, having come to the end of himself, characterized by his failed coping strategies, is willing to accept help from Ms. Jensen. She might be able to help restore some balance and power in his life by alleviating some of his considerable suffering.

John is experiencing feelings of disempowerment, which has many negative societal labels, such as dumb, crazy, incompetent, and dependent (Pinderhughes, 1995). It is likely that John may resist any counselor; Ms. Jensen would do well not to accept any rejection of the counseling event as a dismissal of her and her professional skills. John's life may have multiple layers that have come unraveled and need restoration: John's personal losses (including his child, his faith, and his identity as a father and husband) are evident by his depression and increased alcohol intake. Although John's course of treatment will require time, John will be unable to heal adequately if he cannot feel his pain. As an advocate, Ms. Jensen may need to assist him in contacting appropriate agencies that can help him control his increased consumption of alcohol.

Swanson (1993) discussed side-by-side intimacy, which is less confrontational for most men than face-to-face. Ms. Jensen may want to encourage John's participation in activities in which John feels he has some power and is in control—**bibliotherapy** (e.g., *Conversations With God* [Walsh, 1996], which chronicles a man's conversations with God about life, faith, loss, and a host of other issues; *When Bad Things Happen to Good People* [Kushner, 1981], which was inspired by a man whose child died because of an illness as well). Running, hiking, and other forms of strenuous exercise would be empowering. In time, John could be encouraged to write a letter to Johna and even a book about his experience, which could be of help to other parents.

SUMMARY

In this chapter, the therapeutic process as a means of fostering self-empowerment for the client toward greater self-reliance and functioning was discussed. The importance of counselors understanding their own identities and confronting unresolved issues that could rob them of their own personal power and inevitably hinder the counseling process was also examined. The conflict between the traditional male role and seeking therapeutic assistance was explored through a case study presentation.

REFERENCES

Arredondo, P., Psalti, A., & Cella, K. (1993). The woman factor in multicultural counseling. *Counseling and Human Development, 25*(8), 1–8.

Berger, M. (1985). Men's new family roles: Some implications for therapists. In P. Ricker & E. H. Carmen (Eds.), *The gender gap in psychotherapy: Social realities and psychological processes* (pp. 319–332). New York: Plenum Press.

Bernardez, T. (1987). Gender-based countertransference of female therapists in the psychotherapy of women. In M. Braud (Ed.), *Women and therapy* (pp. 25–39. New York: Haworth Press.

Brown, L. M., & Gilligan, C. (1992). *Meeting at the crossroads: The landmark book about the turning pints in girls' and women's lives.* New York: Ballantine Books.

Browning, C., Reynolds, A. L., & Dworkin, S. H. (1991). Affirmative psychotherapy for lesbian women. *Counseling Psychologist, 19,* 177–196.

Carter, R. T., & Parks, E. E. (1996). Womanist identity and mental health. *Journal of Counseling & Development, 74,* 484–489.

Chow, E. N.-L. (1991). The development of feminist consciousness among Asian American women. In J. Lorber & S. A. Farrell (Eds.), *The social construction of gender* (pp. 255–268). Newbury Park, CA: Sage.

Comas-Diaz, L., & Greene, B. (1994). Overview: An ethnocultural mosaic. In L. Comas-Diaz & B. Greene (Eds.), *Women of color* (pp. 3–9). New York: Guilford Press.

Corey, G. (1991). *Theory and practice of counseling and psychotherapy.* Pacific Grove, CA: Brooks/Cole.

Crose, R., Nicholas, D. R., Gobble, D. C., & Frank, B. (1992). Gender and wellness: A multidimensional systems model for counseling. *Journal of Counseling & Development, 71,* 149–156.

D'Andrea, M., & Daniels, J. (1991). Exploring the different levels of multicultural counseling training in counselor education. *Journal of Counseling & Development, 68,* 47–49.

Devoe, D. (1990). Feminist and nonsexist counseling: Implications for the male counselor. *Journal of Counseling & Development, 69,* 33–36.

Dulany, P. (1990). On becoming empowered. In J. Spurlock & C. Robinowitz (Eds.), *Women's progress: Promises and problems* (pp. 133–142). New York: Plenum Press.

Gary, L. E. (1987). Predicting interpersonal conflict between men and women: The case of Black men. In M. S. Kimmel (Ed.), *Changing men: New directions in research on men and masculinity* (pp. 232–243). Newbury Park, CA: Sage.

Good, G. E., & Mintz, L. B. (1990). Gender role conflict and depression in college men: Evidence for compounded risk. *Journal of Counseling & Development, 69,* 17–21.

Good, G. E., Dell, D. M., & Mintz, L. B. (1989). Male role and gender role conflict: Relations to help seeking in men. *Journal of Counseling Psychology, 36,* 295–300.

Kaplan, A. G. (1987). Reflections on gender and psychotherapy. In M. Braud (Ed.), *Women and therapy* (pp. 11–23). New York: Haworth Press.

Kushner, H. (1981). *When bad things happen to good people.* New York: Avon.

McBride, M. (1990). Autonomy and the struggle for female identity: Implications for counseling women. *Journal of Counseling & Development, 69,* 22–26.

McWhirter, E. H. (1991). Empowerment in counseling. *Journal of Counseling & Development, 69,* 222–227.

Mintz, L. B., & O'Neil, J. M. (1990). Gender roles, sex, and the process of psychotherapy: Many questions and few answers. *Journal of Counseling & Development, 68,* 381–387.

Monk, G. D., Winslade, J., Crocket, K., & Epston, D. (1997). *Narrative therapy in practice: The archaeology of hope.* San Francisco: Jossey-Bass.

Myers, L. J., Speight, S. L., Highlen, P. S., Cox, C. I., Reynolds, A. L., Adams, E. M., & Hanley, P. (1991). Identity development and worldview: Toward an optimal conceptualization. *Journal of Counseling & Development, 70,* 54–63.

O'Malley, K. M., & Richardson, S. (1985). Sex bias in counseling: Have things changed? *Journal of Counseling & Development, 63,* 294–299.

Ossana, S. M., Helms, J. E., & Leonard, M. M. (1992). Do "womanist" identity attitudes influence college women's self-esteem and perceptions of environmental bias? *Journal of Counseling & Development, 70,* 402–408.

Pinderhughes, E. (1989). *Understanding race, ethnicity, and power: The key to efficacy in clinical practice.* New York: Free Press.

Pinderhughes, E. (1995). Empowering diverse populations: Family practice in the 21st century. *Families in Society: The Journal of Contemporary Human Services,* CEU Article No. 50, 131–140.

Pleck, J. H. (1985). Men's power with women, other men, and society: A men's movement analysis. In P. Ricker & E. H. Carmen (Eds.), *The gender gap in psychotherapy: Social realities and psychological processes* (pp. 79–89). New York: Plenum Press.

Ridley, C. R. (1989). Racism in counseling as an aversive behavioral process. In P. B. Pedersen, J. G., Draguns, W. J. Lonner, & J. E. Trimble (Eds.), *Counseling across cultures* (pp. 55–78). Honolulu: University of Hawaii Press.

Robinson, T. L. (1999). The intersections of dominant discourses across race, gender, and other identities. *Journal of Counseling & Development, 77,* 73–79.

Skovholt, T. M. (1993). Counseling and psychotherapy interventions with men. *Counseling and Human Development, 25,* 1–16.

Stevens, M. J., Pfost, K. S., & Potts, M. K. (1990). Sex role orientation and the willingness to confront existential issues. *Journal of Counseling & Development, 68,* 47–49.

Sue, D. W., & Sue, D. (1990). *Counseling the culturally different: Theory and practice.* New York: John Wiley.

Swanson, J. L. (1993). Sexism strikes men. *American Counselor: Counseling and Development, 68,* 21–25.

Thompson, E. H. & Pleck, J. H. (1987). The structure of male role norms. In M. S. Kimmel (Ed.), *Changing men: New directions in research on men and masculinity* (pp. 25–36). Newbury Park, CA: Sage.

Walsh, N. D. (1996). *Conversations with God: An uncommon dialogue.* New York: Putnam.

Washington, C. S. (1987). Counseling Black men. In M. Scher, M. Stevens, G. Good, & G. Eichenfield (Eds.), *Handbook of counseling and psychotherapy* (pp. 192–202). Newbury Park, CA: Sage.

Wiegman, R. (1994). Feminism and its mal(e)contents. *Masculinities, 2,* 1–7.

Chapter 15

Different Counseling Approaches to Understanding Diversity

Mis raices las cargo siempre conmigo enrolladas me sirven de almohada. (I carry my roots with me all the time rolled up. I use them as my pillow.)

Francisco Alarcon, poem in The Hispanic Condition: Reflections on Culture and Identity in America

This final chapter explores different approaches to counseling in a diverse and multicultural world. Emphasized are transcultural and universal approaches, which involve an acknowledgment of, and appreciation for, the multiple identities embodied within each person.

New and effective ways of envisioning the world are paramount for counseling practitioners in a new century. Counselors who can behold a new vision are needed, as are models that critique cultural patterns that encourage imbalance and disharmony, encourage egalitarianism between client and counselor, and foster a respect for spirituality as central to healing. This ultimately means crossing borders that so easily divide, such as race, gender, culture, and sexual orientation, and gaining insight into the cultural socialization processes that shape personal attitudes, beliefs, behaviors, and perceptions. Once a person moves beyond an intellectual understanding of another and begins to experience the reality of diverse people as a personal encounter, a border crossing has commenced.

Within the past two decades, cross-cultural and multicultural perspectives have emerged both in the literature and in research methodologies (Atkinson & Hackett, 1988; Cross, 1971, 1991; Helms, 1984, 1989, 1990; Ponterotto, 1988; Sue & Sue, 1990). Identity models and identity theories have also been developed (Atkinson, Morten, & Sue, 1989; Cass, 1979; Cross, 1971, 1991; Downing & Roush, 1985; Helms, 1990; Parham & Helms, 1981) that have helped bridge the gap between traditional psychological theories and current mental health issues related to gender, race, culture, ethnicity, and sexual orientation. Although current psychological theoretical orientations have variable effectiveness with a broad array of clients, many are not optimal for clients representative of diverse populations. A psychological resistance model is featured, and several case studies are offered as a way of integrating this concept into various counseling scenarios.

HEALTHY PSYCHOLOGICAL RESISTANCE

Ample literature espouses the need for healthy psychological resistance as a strategy for countering oppression and cultivating empowerment. *Oppression* represents an act that prevents a person from being fully human or alive (Freire, 1988). It is a dehumanizing process that involves acts of "violence" that range from psychological to physical injury being inflicted on a person. A person who is psychologically dependent on others to define who he is, is likely to perceive himself as an object or person who lacks power to determine his destiny personally. Once a person's thinking is externally determined by others, past and/or present, his behavior is more susceptible to external manipulation. Such a person is vulnerable to accepting an inferior societal status.

The global burden of racism, sexism, ethnocentrism, homophobia, and classism speaks of a need for the development of empowering resistance paradigms. Constant energy is expended to live optimally within a society that is discriminatory, demeaning, and depleting (Brookins & Robinson, 1996; Robinson & Howard-Hamilton,

1994; Robinson & Ward, 1991). Psychological resistance is universal and transcends race, gender, age, class, and culture independent of the constellation of one's identities. The resistance modality adapted from Robinson and Ward (1991) distinguishes between resistance that is survival oriented and oppressive and resistance that is optimal, empowering, and liberating. *Optimal resistance* is oriented toward empowerment and is characterized by a person's ability to avoid internalizing negative societal messages that can foster unhealthy self-images and self-depreciatory behaviors.

Healthy forms of resistance are directly tied to an accurate knowledge of one's historical, racial, and cultural connections (Robinson & Ward, 1991). Reflected in this mode of resistance are the seven principles of the *Nguzo Saba*. According to Karenga (1980), the Nguzo Saba represents a basic value system that is African in origin and that enables people to establish "direction" and "meaning" in their lives. The seven basic values that constitute the Nguzo Saba system are *Umoja* (unity), *Kujichagalia* (self-determination), *Ujima* (collective work and responsibility), *Ujaama* (cooperative economics), *Nia* (purpose), *Kuumba* (creativity), and *Imani* (faith). These seven primary values, combined with elements of the resistance modality model (Robinson & Ward, 1991), can serve as a paradigm for enhancing personal growth across race, culture, and gender (see Tables 15.1 and 15.2). The case studies depicted below seek to demonstrate the versatility and adaptability of this model.

TABLE 15.1
Psychological resistance modalities

Survival/Oppression	Liberation/Empowerment
Disconnectedness from knowledge of self; separateness from communities of support	**Umoja** – unity with others that transcends age, gender, class
External locus of control; self is defined by others in a way that devalues women and people of color	**Kujichagalia** – self-determination/definition; rejection of oppressive attempts to demean self
Excessive individualism, overly self-reliant and selflessness	**Ujima** – collective work and responsibility
Inability to ask for help; materialistic behavior	**Ujaama** – cooperative economics; sharing of fiscal and human resources
Meaninglessness; self-worth based on material goods and the external; immediate gratification to escape life's harsh realities	**Nia** – purpose and mission
Replication of existing and dysfunctional models; maintenance of status quo; lack of insight or perspective on prevailing problems	**Kuumba** – creativity; creating new paradigms that empower the self and the collective
Emphasis on the here and now; not looking forward and not looking back; looking at appearances	**Imani** – faith; emphasis on an intergenerational perspective; spirituality

Source: From "Rites of Passage as Resistance to Oppression," by C. B. Brookins and T. L. Robinson, 1996, Western Journal of Black Studies. *Adapted with permission.*

TABLE 15.2
Psychological resistance strategies

Suboptimal	Optimal
Subconsciously internalizing demeaning and external definitions of self	Know and affirm self
Isolating self from others (unauthentic relationships)	Establish and maintain cooperative relationships with others
Emphasizing material possessions	Dialogue with others about living
Discounting one's responsibility to help others fulfill their goals	Provide support to self, family, and others (peer support networks)
Believing that one does not have the skills or knowledge to fulfill one's dreams or goals	Establish independent businesses
Using quick fixes to cope with difficult living conditions (drugs, school failure, excessive eating, unplanned pregnancies, violence)	Confront and repudiate oppressive circumstances through constructed knowledge
Denying one's racial and ethnic connections; denying the role of sexism in people's lives	Work with others to promote their empowerment
Exhibiting excessive autonomy	Nurture spiritual center (meditate, cultivate solitude, commune with nature)
Being chronically stressed, pressed, and depressed	Know that everything is all right, despite appearances
Maintaining life-negating thinking patterns ("Things are not going to get any better"; "I'm all alone")	Maintain life-affirming thinking patterns ("Everything is working for my good"; "I am never alone")

Source: From "Rites of Passage as Resistance to Oppression," by C. B. Brookins and T. L. Robinson, 1996, Western Journal of Black Studies. *Adapted with permission.*

Unhealthy or suboptimal resistance represents dysfunctional and short-term adaptations to an oppressive environment, an environment that facilitates chronic feelings of powerlessness within the person and the community. Self-determination is not a primary operating factor because the person's self-image is largely shaped and defined by external and economic forces that have oppressive roots.

UMOJA

The first principle, *Umoja*, refers to unity, solidarity, and harmony that transcends many societal differences that are far too often divisive, such as race, religion, age, and gender. Suboptimal resistance is characterized by disconnectedness from self-knowledge, as well as alienation from communities of support. During the process of learning to adopt a healthy resistance framework, a period of inner dissonance is likely while survival orientations are gradually abandoned and replaced by liberation-oriented thinking. Communicating this natural developmental process to the client may help ease some of the irregular rhythm associated with this growing process (see the case study "*Umoja*").

CASE STUDY
Umoja

An example of optimal resistance is 26-year-old Clara, an African American graduate student in engineering at a large state university. Clara is one of a few women of color in her department and college. On a regular basis, she contends with racist and sexist statements from colleagues and faculty. One of Clara's colleagues recently asked whether she was self-conscious about having received a minority research grant. She responded politely but firmly that she was very proud of having received her grant, that it funded her studies more than adequately, and that it was a confirmation to her that she was an excellent researcher and an apt grant writer. Clara also belongs to a Buddhist meditation group, is a Big Sister to an African American teenage girl who lives in a low-income housing project, and is a member of a book club that meets monthly and is composed of women and men of diverse racial backgrounds. Her support systems outside the university, as well as her open communication with her adviser and other committee members, provide her with a sense of connection and access to internal and external opportunities. Although she recognizes that graduate school is at times very stressful, she is self-knowing, spiritually centered, and committed to her primary goal: getting her Ph.D.

A suboptimal portrait of Clara would depict a young woman who led an imbalanced existence characterized by isolation from a supportive personal or academic community. Resistance oriented toward survival involves disconnection from others, and in Clara's case it could be a result of an irrational belief that socioeconomic class, racial, and educational differences are far greater than any similarities, such as commitment to peace and racial equity. Enormous psychological and physical stress from academic timelines, competition with other graduate students, fear of not completing one's studies successfully, and unrelenting general stress of graduate school would monopolize Clara's life.

KUJICHAGALIA

The second principle is *Kujichagalia,* which means self-determination. In terms of resistance oriented toward survival, the self is largely defined by external influences, including the media (see the case study "*Kujichagalia*"). The media have a long history of depicting men as unidimensional, selfish, and sex-dominated. Such depictions contribute to inaccurate depictions and lead to stereotypes.

Persons who are self-determined define themselves through a subjective knowledge base. Possessing knowledge of the oppressive dynamics that exist within society, persons are empowered to confront and resist oppressive messages through defining self in alternative ways.

CASE STUDY
Kujichagalia

A resistor is 14-year-old Benson, a Native American male whose school experiences are alienating. His people's history is not accurately reflected in the curriculum, and his teachers often assume that he lacks ambition because of his quiet, unassuming manner. Although school feels very silencing, Benson's tribe, family, and community are a source of strength. His spiritual connections to his Native American heritage enable him to determine for himself who he is and how he will live his life. Benson recognizes that he needs to remain in school despite the difficulty and anger he sometimes feels. He has access to his own constructed knowledge and has found it necessary to keep two sets of notes while in class—the teacher's notes that Christopher Columbus sailed the ocean blue in 1492, and his own story about the presence of native peoples in the Americas (North and South) long before Columbus ever came and "discovered" America.

Suboptimal resistance for Benson would resemble alcohol addiction, school failure, and allowing his self definition to be a reflection of others.

UJIMA

The third principle is *Ujima,* which represents collective work and responsibility. Suboptimally, the person is excessively individualistic and overly self-reliant (see the case study "*Ujima*"). This profile describes the U.S. culture regarding the commonly held values of individualism and independence. Many people, including counselor education students and their faculty members, have difficulty with the idea of seeking therapy even when it may be sorely needed. It is needed just for an opportunity to focus on the self and grow emotionally, which everyone has space for. Needing help is stigmatized because it is likened to being weak and inadequate, as opposed to being whole.

CASE STUDY
Ujima

Arthur is a 26-year-old Mexican American teacher. He recently has been diagnosed with multiple sclerosis. Although he is in a lot of pain and suffers from depression, he refuses to share his diagnosis with his family or community, who are eager to help. Arthur has become rather distant and difficult to communicate with. He wants to deal with his problem on his own and in his own way.

If Arthur were more of an optimal resistor, he would understand the importance of community and respect the circle of life, of giving to others and receiving from them. There is an ability to ask for and to give help. Burdens and successes are shared mutually with others.

UJAAMA

Ujaama, the fourth principle, refers to cooperative economics. Emphasis is on the sharing of resources through the convergence of the "I" and the "we." Suboptimal resistance reflects an attitude of "I got mine, you get yours." This paradigm involves extreme selfishness and individualistic behavior (see the case study "*Ujaama*").

CASE STUDY
Ujaama

An example of suboptimal resistance is Rachel, a 50-year-old single Jewish American office manager. Rachel's family of origin was nearly at the poverty line. Through hard work and perseverance, she earned bachelor's and M.B.A. degrees and received several job promotions over the years . She believes in the American dream, in meritocracy and a just world ideology, and that if you work hard, then you will be rewarded with material things. People who do not have are those who simply do not work hard enough. After 26 years with her employer, Rachel has been released because of downsizing. She comes to counseling for help with a series of losses: her job loss and the loss of a 25-year relationship with her husband, Ted. Ted complained that Rachel's priority was her work and not their relationship.

Within an optimal resistance framework, Rachel would understand the benefit of sharing resources (financial and human) with others, knowing that without meaningful human connections, she is experiencing a lesser life. Within the counseling event, Rachel would be encouraged to explore the fear of poverty that surrounds her work ethic and the notion that bad things happen only to lazy people. To be effective with Rachel, it is important to understand her childhood experiences with poverty and her Jewish culture.

NIA

Nia is the fifth principle and represents purpose that benefits not just the self but the collective body as well. Resistance oriented toward empowerment emphasizes meaningful work and purposeful relationships for life to be as fulfilling as it can be (see the case study "*Nia*").

CASE STUDY
Nia

Malone, a 67-year-old European American retiree, widower, and cancer patient is an optimal resistor. He enjoys his extended family composed of friends, children, and grandchildren. He is involved in community and volunteer work, dates regularly, and is engaged in lifelong learning. Although he is receiving chemotherapy, he feels optimistic about his healing, meditates, takes herbs, exercises, and is a member of a support group.

Survival-oriented resistance seeks to meet immediate needs and is characterized by a pervading sense of meaninglessness. In desiring escape from drudgery, poor choices or "quick fixes" such as alcohol addiction, obesity, and unplanned pregnancy can and do result. Unhealthy resistance for Malone would be to view life without purpose and meaning. Alone, ill, and with no place to go during the day, Malone has experienced a deterioration of mental and physical health because of his depressed state of mind and being. Because he is out of contact with other healthy resistors from whom he can learn and teach, he is oppressed and merely surviving.

KUUMBA

Kuumba is the sixth principle and represents creativity. Suboptimal resistance is maintaining the status quo and replicating existing models, although they may be irrelevant (see the case study "*Kuumba*").

CASE STUDY
Kuumba

Nineteen-year-old Candace is a sophomore in college. She subconsciously believes in traditional notions of gender socialization: "Always let the boys win," "don't be too smart," "if you say no to sex, then the guy will leave." Candace also equates her body size with her self-worth and thus invests inordinate attention on physical appearance. Her academic performance is above average; however, she is in college primarily to get a husband. She presents to the college counseling center after contracting herpes from her ex-boyfriend, who now has a new girlfriend.

In learning to be an optimal resistor, Candace would begin to realize that maintaining the status quo (being selfless, not asking herself what she wants, and being excessively dependent on others [particularly boys for approval], are examples of externalizing her personal power). In time, she would begin to understand that the men worthy of her time and attention are open to her ideals and are not interested in trying to make her over. She would become educated on gender socialization issues, and through therapy, assertiveness training, bibliotherapy, and a support group, she would unlearn many of the damaging messages that encouraged her not to take care of herself in the first place. She would grow to be honest with herself and romantic partners about her incurable but manageable sexually transmitted disease.

Suboptimally, Candace would continue to want to be with her ex-boyfriend, although he is not similarly interested, hurry into another relationship for the sake of having a boyfriend, continue to be unreflective about her responsibility to herself, and behave as if happiness is external to herself.

IMANI

The last principle is *Imani,* or faith. Optimal resistance involves an ability to be patient and to believe that good is happening independent of external appearances (see the case study "*Imani*").

CASE STUDY
Imani

Although Malone, a resistor discussed above, has been diagnosed with cancer, he embodies the principle of *Imani* by believing that his healing is under-

way despite the pain, decreased energy, and loss of hair. He trusts that God is doing a mightier work in his life despite the appearance of things.

Suboptimal resistance is being fixated on the present circumstances. It is characterized by mindlessness of connections with others, the unborn and the deceased, and the entire universe as a whole. It is believing that things are not working or improving because they do not look as if they are. This form of resistance is limited to the present and to what can be discerned through the physical senses.

NARRATIVE THERAPY

Narrative therapy that emanates from a postmodern paradigm has emerged primarily from the work of Michael White and David Epston. Primary sources of inspiration for them were Gregory Bateson and Michael Foucault. With narrative therapy, counselors seek to deconstruct a problem. In other words, the counselor is interested in knowing how the problem originated and its impact on people's self perceptions. Other facets of narrative therapy are mapping influences and externalizing conversations. Take, for example, a woman, Susan, whose alcohol addiction has contributed to her losing her job and to strain within her marriage. An externalizing conversation would separate the alcohol addiction from the woman, rather than focus on how this addiction is internal. The latter could lead to self-reproach. Mapping the influences of the problem refers to the counselor and the client better understanding what effect the drinking has had on her and her family (Monk, Winslade, Crocket, & Epston, 1997). An alternative story allows the client to stand in the presence of change, independent of how small he or she appears, and to celebrate movement and growth. Often, with seemingly intractable problems, clients feel that nothing is changing; however, narrative therapy looks at change no matter how microscopic. In doing so, the client is more able to see a different development in relation to the story that is problem-focused.

In narrative therapy, discourses, not the people, are seen as problematic. Discourses, according to Winslade, Monk, and Drewery (1997), "position individuals in power relations with one another" (p. 229). They are a set of ideas and structuring statements that underlie and give meaning to social practices (Monk et al., 1997). Heterosexist discourses, for example, allege that being heterosexual is superior to being gay, lesbian, or bisexual. Discourses, then, serve to objectify people, which leads to subject positions without voice or agency (J. Winslade, personal communication, April 1998).

ALTERNATIVE HEALING STRATEGIES

The number of helping professionals is insufficient to address adequately the psychological and emotional ills afflicting people. For this reason, church and community groups, in consultation with mental health professionals, can offer sensitive paraprofessional training to mature leaders that focuses on the development of listening skills. Individuals, couples, and/or groups who are experiencing transition and need support can benefit greatly from this low-cost, highly effective service. Training can also review when to refer to or engage in collaborative efforts, particularly when an individual presents with problems that appear to be out of the helper's league. As people recover from various wounds of psychological and emotional affliction, supportive communities composed of family and friends are needed.

hooks (1993) said that if places of healing do not exist, then they must be created wherein "sharing with one another ways to process pain and grief, Black women challenge old myths that would have us repress emotional feeling in order to appear 'strong.' This is important because bottled-in-grief can erupt into illness" (p. 104). In healing, balance and harmony are restored (Shore, 1995).

"Home psychoanalysis" (hooks, 1993), or informal spaces where people feel free to share their stories and receive nonjudgmental support, need not minimize the importance of receiving professional help when warranted. Loving and authentic spaces need to be created so that people may heal and move forward, catch their breaths, regain and create new rhythms, and reclaim their voices. Granted, therapists and counselors provide valuable service to people in need, but other havens can and do promote healing.

EFFECTIVE LAY-LED HEALING

The following incomplete list may be helpful:

- Book and film circles are where people gather, not just to talk about the books and films they are reading and seeing, but to think reflectively about the connections between the written texts and the motion picture on their lives and the lives of others.

- Dance/movement to culture-specific music (e.g., African drumming, Native American Indian drumming, Latin salsa, Irish folk songs) can be done individually or with others.
- Affirmations, written on a daily basis, provide ritual and rhythm to life while promoting positive thinking.
- Kitchen table talk is an informal gathering of friends around the kitchen table to eat and to talk about whatever is on people's hearts and minds.
- Massage is a loving way to affirm oneself, relax, and experience soothing human touch.
- Latin dancing is high touch, and the music is soulful and stirring.
- "Howling at the moon" sessions (J. Weeber, personal communication, March 1996) occur when men and women gather each month during the time of the full moon to celebrate the faithfulness and continuity of nature and the universe, commune with each other, and restore ritual to life (see the Storytelling "The Healing Circle").

Other approaches can be very instrumental to the healing process. These include physical exercise, prayer, meditation, yoga, journaling, aromatherapy, and baththerapy. In cases of extreme and debilitating depression, however, drug therapy or antidepressants under the careful supervision of a medical doctor and therapist have been and can be useful for many until higher levels of functioning are present.

CREATIVE ARTS

Creative arts can be very helpful to the therapeutic event. According to Gladding (1997), "creative arts refers to any art form, including visual representations (paintings, drawings, sculpture), poetry, drama, and music, that helps individuals become more aware of themselves or others" (p. 354). The National Coalition of Art Therapies Association (NCATA) is an interdisciplinary organization that supports all art therapies. Drawings, photography, cartooning, drama, cinema, games,

STORYTELLING
The Healing Circle

It was a weekend gathering in Cherokee—a celebration of autumn. We gathered to become more centered and aware of ourselves and our connections with nature, the four directions, and one another. We were smudged with the clearing sage herb, we drummed, we sat in silence, we shared our stories, we found heart-shaped rocks and told their stories, we lay by the river and listened to the water flow gently on. The beauty of the full moon, the trees, and the birds' songs was restorative and allowed a quieting hush to fall over our souls. What a wonderful way for people to heal in the absence of a known ailment.

Tracy

poetry/metaphor, bibliotherapy, working with sand, writing, and music and move-ment all fall under the umbrella of creative therapies.

An example of a game that can foster understanding of self and others is included in McGrath and Axelson (1993). They suggest that people list the types of games they played as children and still continue to play. The game is described: idea of game, "good" guy player, and "bad" guy player. Questions that could be asked include "Did you develop certain kinds of understandings about life or culture—yours or others'—from these games?" and "Whom did you want to be when you played the game?"

WELLNESS

To encourage healing, whether using creative therapies or more traditional ones, a holistic and multidimensional approach is essential where mind and body are seen as one. Crose, Nicholas, Gobble, and Frank (1992) indicated several components to such a model: (a) physical health and wellness that incorporates exercise, eating behaviors, and body image; (b) emotional health and wellness encompassing coping style and attitudes toward self-disclosure; (c) intellectual health and wellness involving mental status, flexibility, and educational learning history; (d) social health and well-ness composed of social network, relational style, and attitudes toward relationships with others; (e) occupational health and wellness containing work history, vocational goals, and attitudes toward work and leisure; and (f) spiritual health and wellness that embrace overall life satisfaction, meaning in life, and beliefs about death.

The use of metaphor can also be very therapeutic with clients who may have a difficult time articulating the depth of their emotion. A client who has a conflicted relationship with her mother could be asked, "What color is the relationship you have with your mother?" "What shape is it?" "Is it an ocean, river, or gutter?" "What does it like to eat?" and "Who are its friends?" Such questions enable the client to externalize the pain/conflict toward talking about it.

IMPLICATIONS FOR COUNSELORS

Is it truly possible to conceptualize counseling from a different lens? Speight, Myers, Cox, and Highlen (1991) offered a new definition of multicultural counseling that is steeped within the context of optimal theory. In this new definition, individual unique-ness, human universality, and cultural specificity are all recognized and seen as inter-related. According to Speight et al.,

> With this redefinition multicultural counseling courses would be organized
> around themes that seem to cut across various racial, ethnic and cultural
> groups. Rather than having each identified group as a class topic, theoreti-

cal issues relevant to all groups would be addressed, including identity development, oppression, worldview, ethics, and spirituality. (pp. 32, 33)

Many people living in a stressful and highly impersonal society experience feelings of loneliness and meaninglessness. This is particularly true if immediate family and established friendships exist elsewhere. Feeling detached, even within a marriage or a coupled relationship, is also a common experience of both men and women. Relationship difficulty is certainly not exclusive to single persons.

Essential counseling tools are part of a new paradigm for understanding diversity. One such tool is **relabeling** (Pinderhughes, 1989). Via relabeling, the counselor has an opportunity to focus on the client's strengths and to work toward helping the client see coping strategies as legitimate in a climate where these may have previously been mislabeled. For example, from the resistance paradigm presented above, 15-year-old Matt, a Japanese American male high school student, would be regarded as assertive and tenacious, with strong leadership potential, instead of as aggressive and disruptive when he respectfully challenges his teachers in class or politely asks for explanations regarding policies and procedures. As a means of rechanneling energy, a guidance counselor could encourage Matt to occupy leadership roles at his school. In this way, Matt's assertiveness would be better understood.

Reframing is also an important counseling tool. Here, the counselor helps the client see his or her situation with more hope. Heather, 45, is now a widow. She commented sadly when looking at a family photograph taken with her husband that there were two of them. Now, she is all alone. A counselor reframe would be that, in time, when another photograph is taken, someone else may be with her.

It is also essential that counselors understand the importance of the creative process as a part of the healing taking place. Shore (1995) said that "when clients become artists they have tools for activating their own compost and fertilizing their inner lives" (p. 93). It is essential that clients realize they can author their own lives and tell the stories they would like to have reflect their own journeys.

SUMMARY

The counselor who is culturally encapsulated (Wrenn, 1962) is limited in helping clients with developing racial awareness. Prior to assisting others, all counselors are encouraged to spend time and effort toward gaining the necessary awareness of themselves and others as beings with multiple identities. Although training culturally skilled counselors is the responsibility of all training programs, it is essential that counselors graduate from those programs with more than a piecemeal understanding of how to work with diverse clients. A comprehensive theoretical scheme or model from which to operate is desired. The primary aim of this chapter was to explore various alternative and less well known approaches that could be used in conjunction with traditional approaches to empower counselors to work more effectively with all their clients.

REFERENCES

Atkinson, D. R., & Hackett, G. (1988). *Counseling non-ethnic American minorities.* Springfield, IL: Charles C Thomas.

Atkinson, D. R., Morten, G., & Sue, D. W. (1989). *Counseling American minorities: A cross-cultural perspective.* Dubuque, IA: William C. Brown.

Brookins, C. B., & Robinson, T. L. (1996). Rites of passage as resistance to oppression. *Western Journal of Black Studies.*

Cass, V. C. (1979). Homosexual identity formation: A theoretical model. *Journal of Homosexuality, 15,* 13–23.

Crose, R., Nicholas, D. R., Gobble, D. C., & Frank, B. (1992). Gender and wellness: A multidimensional systems model for counseling. *Journal of Counseling & Development, 71,* 149–156.

Cross, W. E. (1971). The Negro-to-Black conversion experience: Toward a psychology of Black liberation. *Black World, 20,* 13–27.

Cross, W. E. (1991). *Shades of Black: Diversity in African American identity.* Philadelphia: Temple University Press.

Downing, N. E., & Roush, K. L. (1985). From passive acceptance to active commitment: A model of feminist identity development for women. *Counseling Psychologist, 13,* 695–709.

Freire, P. (1988). *Pedagogy of the oppressed.* New York: Continuum.

Gladding, S. (1997). *Community and agency counseling.* Upper Saddle River, NJ: Merrill/Prentice Hall.

Helms, J. (1984). Toward a theoretical explanation of the effects of race on counseling: A Black and White model. *Counseling Psychologist, 12,* 153–165.

Helms, J. (1989). Considering some methodological issues in racial identity counseling research. *Counseling Psychologist, 17,* 227–252.

Helms, J. (1990). *Black and White racial identity: Theory, research, and practice.* New York: Greenwood Press.

hooks, b. (1993). *Sisters of the yam: Black women and self-recovery.* Boston: South End Press.

Karenga, M. (1980). *Kawaida theory.* Los Angeles: Kawaida.

McGrath, P., & Axelson, J. A. (1993). *Accessing awareness and developing knowledge: Foundations for skill in a multicultural society.* Pacific Grove, CA: Brooks/Cole.

Monk, G. D., Winslade, J., Crocket, K., & Epston, D. (1997). *Narrative therapy in practice: The archaeology of hope.* San Francisco: Jossey-Bass.

Parham, T., & Helms, J. E. (1981). The influence of Black students' racial identity attitudes on preference for counselor's race. *Journal of Counseling Psychology, 28,* 143–147.

Pinderhughes, E. (1989). *Understanding race, ethnicity, and power: The key to efficacy in clinical practice.* New York: Free Press.

Ponterotto, J. G. (1988). Racial/ethnic minority research in the *Journal of Counseling Psychology*: A content analysis and methodological critique. *Journal of Counseling Psychology, 4,* 410–418.

Robinson, T. L., & Howard-Hamilton, M. (1994). An Afrocentric paradigm: Foundation for a healthy self-image and healthy interpersonal relationships. *Journal of Mental Health Counseling, 16,* 327–339.

Robinson, T. L., & Ward, J. V. (1991). A belief in self far greater than anyone's disbelief: Cultivating resistance among African American adolescents. *Women & Therapy, 11,* 87–103.

Shore, L. I. (1995). *Tending inner gardens: The healing art of feminist therapy.* New York: Harrington Park Press.

Speight, S. L., Myers, L. J., Cox, C. I., & Highlen, P. S. (1991). A redefinition of multicultural counseling. *Journal of Counseling & Development, 70,* 29–36.

Sue, D. W., & Sue, D. (1990). *Counseling the culturally different: Theory and practice* (2nd ed.). New York: John Wiley.

Winslade, J., Monk, G., & Drewery, W. (1997). Sharpening the critical edge: A social constructionist approach in counselor education. In T. Sexton & B. Griffin (Eds.), *Constructivist thinking in counseling practice, research, and training* (pp. 228–245). New York: Columbia University Teacher's College.

Wrenn, C. G. (1962). The encapsulated counselor. *Harvard Education Review, 32,* 444–449.

Epilogue

Uncover the rare jewels
nestled within your being
they have been there waiting
wanting you to see
the power you have
in your own life
to love and to be free
to know the holiest gift
of all time—
simplicity

Tracy Robinson, "Windrush" 1990

Our work was born from a desire to gaze respectively at the multiplicity of identities that compose each client who presents at counseling, her or his heart burdened with a gnawing and unresolved issue. Our message is intended also for us as counselor educators. By teaching, we are commissioned to safeguard and nurture each student who occupies a seat in our classrooms. They depend on us to challenge, enlighten, and help them unlearn the scripts that promote imbalance and disharmony so that they go forth and do good. We depend on them to do the same for us. Both of us are both emphatic about how teaching is a privilege, an honor, and a calling. We are grateful to our students for expanding our minds with their subjective and contextualized knowledge bases.

As African American women in academia, we coexist in environments where we are in the numerical minority. This becomes apparent at faculty meetings, commencements, and other gatherings in higher education where our racial and gendered presences are not the norm. Because we are healthy psychological resistors, we have learned the importance of deflecting demeaning messages on the basis of our own intuitive knowledge. As women of color conducting empowerment-based research on women, men, and people of color, we are convinced that it chose us before we chose it.

Throughout this text, our goal has been to call attention to the convergence of race, gender, and culture in people's lives. In so doing, we have discussed age, sexual orientation, physical ability and disability, physical attractiveness, religion, and class. Given our ambitious task, we are the first to recognize the flaws in our conceptual scheme. For these omissions, we trust that as we continue to grow and learn, we will attend to these gaps responsibly and speedily.

Our overarching hope is that this work will foster truthful dialogue. Although racism was the first issue with which we recall embracing in our lives as African Americans, sexism looms heavily. To quote from the movie *Dolores Claiborne,* in which actress Kathy Bates starred, "It is a depressingly masculine world." And such a world is challenging for both the men and women in it.

We honor our collective and individual identities and hope that our work is both a celebration of the moment and a praisesong of all that is yet to be.

NAME INDEX

SUBJECT INDEX

culturally appropriate intervention strategies by, 274–276, 284–285
cultural self-awareness of, 272–273, 284
cultural values implications for, 46–47
diversity training for, 276–277
diversity understanding implications for, 20, 318–319
empathy of, 112
empowerment implications for, 298–300
family status implications for, 220–225
gender role conflict implications for, 111–113, 115–116
Latino family therapy, 223–224
middle-class training bias for, 172–177
multicultural training model for, 278–280
Native American Indian families and, 224–225
physical attributes implications for, 160
racial identity implications for, 87–89
school diversity implications for, 198–200
sexual identity formation issues and, 131–132, 133, 134, 135
socioeconomic class implications for, 181–182
statused identities implications for, 68
violence implications for, 263–264
worldview issues for, 293–294
Creativity value, Nguzo Saba, 46, 309, 314
Criminal justice system, racial prejudice in, 259–260
Criticism, gender role and, 112
Cross-cultural awakening in multicultural training programs, 276
Cross-cultural awareness continuum model, 197–198
Cross-cultural counseling, 7
Cross-Cultural Counseling Inventory (CCCI), 199
Cross-cultural friendships, 87
Cuban Americans, 38, 39
Cultural Adaptation Pain Scale (CAPS), 83
Cultural awareness in cross-cultural awareness model, 198
Cultural capital, 177–179
Cultural deficiency counseling model, 6
Cultural diversity versus multiculturalism, 6, 196
Cultural encapsulation, 11, 198
  case study about, 20–21

counselor education programs and, 277
of counselors, 319–320
middle-class counseling bias and, 173
Cultural identity model in family therapy, 219, 220
Culturally appropriate intervention strategies, 274–276, 284–285
Culturally diverse/different counseling model, 6
Culturally entrenched multicultural training programs, 276
Cultural violence. See Violence
Culture(s), 26–53. See also Worldview(s)
  activity value orientation of, 29, 30
  career choice and, 240
  case study about, 47–48
  cross-cultural awareness model and, 198
  definition of, 276
  dimensions of, 28–30
  diverse identities in, 10–12
  family therapy and, 225
  human nature value orientation of, 29
  implications for counselors of, 46–47
  man-nature value orientation of, 29–30
  relational value orientation of, 29, 30
  self-conceptualizations and, 31–46
  socioeconomic class and, 177–179
  storytelling about, 29, 31, 38, 41, 44, 46
  time value orientation of, 29, 30
  values and, 30–31
Curanderos, Latino, 40
Curriculum differentiation, 191
Curriculum ghettos, 194, 202
Curriculum issues in multicultural counselor training, 280

Dance/movement to culture-specific music, healing and, 317
Date rape, 258, 259
  case study about, 264–266
Death beliefs, wellness and, 318
Defensive stage in racial consciousness development model, 85
DeGeneres, Ellen, 137
Democracy, diversity in, 7
Denial of conflicts state in Latino/Latina sexual identity formation, 138
Depression
  disability and, 161
  in feminine persons, 154
  in gays/lesbians, 136
  gender role conflict and, 110, 114–115
  racial identity exploration and, 91

Destructive power, therapy and, 303
Diagnostic and Statistical Manual of Mental Disorders, 4th ed., client culture and, 275
Diffuse boundaries in structural family therapy theory, 218
Diffused identity, vocational choice and, 237–238
Dignidad, Latino, 39
Dihydrotestosterone, 100
Disability(ies), 157–159. See also Physical attractiveness/ability/disability
  case study about, 161–163
  class and, 180
  discrimination against people with, 291
  diverse identities in, 16–17
  as primary status trait, 17
  social attitudes toward, 158–159
  stereotypes regarding, 66
  storytelling about, 159, 160
Discourses, narrative therapy and, 316
Discrete self, 32–34
Discrimination awareness at social/community levels, 275
Disintegration stage in White racial identity model, 84
Dissonance stage
  in OTAID model, 86, 88
  in R/CID model, 81–82
Diverse identities, 2–25. See also Status, visible identifiers of
  "A, B, C" dimensions of, 9, 15
  case studies about, 9–10, 20–22
  cross-cultural awareness model and, 198
  culture and, 10–12
  disability and, 16–17
  ethnicity and, 13–14
  gender and, 14–15
  images of, 10–20
  implications for counselors, 20
  multicultural counseling development for, 5–7
  overview of, 7–9
  race and, 12–13
  sexuality and, 15–16
  socioeconomic class and, 17–19
  spirituality and, 19–20
  storytelling about, 5
Diversity in schools. See Schools
Diversity understanding in counseling, 306–321
  alternative therapy strategies for, 316–318
  case studies about, 311, 312, 313, 314, 315
  creative arts as therapy for, 317–318
  implications for counselors, 318–319
  lay-led healing and, 316–317
  narrative therapy model and, 315–316